T0330430

The Rise of the
Marginal Utility School
1870-1889

The Rise of the

Marginal Utility School

1870-1889

by

R. S. Howey

Columbia University Press

A Morningside Book

COLUMBIA UNIVERSITY PRESS MORNINGSIDE EDITION
COLUMBIA UNIVERSITY PRESS
NEW YORK   OXFORD
Originally published by the University of Kansas Press
© Copyright 1960 by the University of Kansas Press
Reprinted by arrangement with the University of Kansas Press

Preface by George J. Stigler and Introduction to the
Morningside Edition copyright © 1989 by Columbia University Press

LIBRARY OF CONGRESS CATALOGING-IN-PUBLICATION DATA
Howey, Richard S., 1902–
The rise of the marginal utility school, 1870–1889
R.S. Howey.
p.   cm.
"A Morningside book."
Reprint. Originally published: Lawrence : University of Kansas Press, 1960.
Includes bibliographical references.
ISBN 0-231-07152-3 (cl.) ISBN 9-231-07153-1 (pbk.)
1. Marginal utility—History—19th century.
2. Economics—History—19th century.   I. Title.
HB203.H6   1989
330.15'7'09034—dc20   89-22066
CIP

PRINTED IN THE U.S.A.
Casebound editions of Columbia University Press books are Smyth-sewn and
printed on permanent and durable acid-free paper.

For
MARION

CONTENTS

PREFACE

After 1890, the academic subject of economics differed markedly from the same subject in the years before 1870. During these twenty years, economics underwent as crucial a transformation as had taken place in any earlier period. The insertion into economic analysis of the idea of marginal utility in the intervening twenty years accounts for part of the difference. Prior to 1871, no economist made any substantial and recognized use of marginal utility, while for a long time after 1889 most economists felt constrained either to use marginal utility or to disapprove its employment. Consequently, we cannot understand well the modernization of economics that took place between 1871 and 1889 unless we appreciate the part that the rise of the Marginal Utility School played. In short, a history of the rise of the Marginal Utility School has a general value in that it illumines one feature of the development of modern economics.

The limitation of the study to this twenty-year period makes it possible to cover most phases of the rise of the Marginal Utility School, even some of the trivial or supplementary aspects. A thoroughgoing study of marginal utility in the period from 1871 to 1889 complements the earlier partial histories by taking into account an important division of the history of the idea previously neglected. It ought to provide a sounder footing for other investigations, particularly of the history of the subsequent elaboration of the idea of marginal utility and its eventual partial replacement.

Besides introducing much new material, this study of the rise of the Marginal Utility School hopes to temper many minor and a few major interpretations developed in other historical accounts. The chief correction consists in excluding the presumption that acceptance of the idea of marginal utility came quickly. It did not. The idea penetrated the thinking of economists most slowly, and had to win its victories, one by one, over inertia and, less frequently, over active opposition. Histories of economic thought often leave the impression that no sooner did Jevons, Menger, and Walras publish, than their views informed the world and that, accordingly, after 1871-74, the thinking of economists had a different flavor. The break in thought, however, did not take place in that fashion. The Marginal Utility School emerged at the end of these twenty years, but throughout this period, and for a long time thereafter, the idea of marginal utility stood alongside the older views as a new but minor variant of economic thought.

This study may be divided, for convenience, into parts. The first part (chapters I-V) furnishes an introduction, in that it goes back into the years before 1871 to seek some light from the earlier history of Jevons, Menger, and Walras, whose work at the outset of the eighteen-seventies signaled the beginning of the rise of the Marginal Utility School. The second part (chapters VI-VII) limits itself to a comparison of the role of utility in the monumental books by Jevons, Menger, and Walras. After having disposed of the origin and the contents of these epochal books, we then observe the slow spread, and occasional rediscovery, of the ideas they contain (chapters VIII-XXV). The final chapter and the appendix give a concluding and detailed study of the manner in which histories of economic thought heralded the rise of the Marginal Utility School.

PREFACE TO THE MORNINGSIDE EDITION

Professor Howey wrote a doctoral dissertation that is receiving, and deserves the rare honor of receiving, a reprinting three decades after its first appearance. No one before or after has written so comprehensive and careful an account of the evolution of the marginal utility theory from its formulation by Jevons, Menger and Walras to 1890. Howey's meticulous scholarship traces the treatment of the theory by these economists and their contemporaries in rich detail.

His account needs little amendment by later scholarship. He is not always exact on the more technical details of the theory: for example, complementarity is only touched upon; and Wicksteed's method of measuring marginal utility (pp. 131–32) is correct for additive utility functions. Such minor points aside, his account remains remarkably reliable.

The marginal utility was celebrated on its approximate centennial, and readers who wish also to learn of later developments and other perspectives on the period will find useful the symposium in *The Marginal Revolution in Economics* (*History of Political Economy*, Fall 1972). They will also want to consult the English translation of Gossen's marvellous *The Laws of Human Relations* (MIT Press, 1983). For the formative period 1871–90, however, Howey remains the standard source.

George J. Stigler
Center for the Study of the
Economy and the State
University of Chicago

INTRODUCTION TO THE MORNINGSIDE EDITION

THE ORIGINS OF MARGINALISM

I

John A. Hobson coined the word "marginalism" in his *Work and Wealth* (1914) when he needed an expression to cover the acceptance by economists of both marginal utility and marginal productivity.[1] The first coinage occurred when he wrote of "the wide acceptance which 'marginalism' has won in academic circles." The acceptance, of course, had been of the idea, not of the word. By context, Hobson gave the word a disparaging tinge, since he found the concept faulty and its policy conclusions unwelcome. He repeated the word "marginalism" seven times in his *Work and Wealth*. In 1909 Hobson had referred to economists who used marginal analysis as "marginalists."[2]

The word "marginalism" was infrequently used in the twenty-five years after Hobson's innovation. None of the reviewers of Hobson's *Work and Wealth* identified the word "marginalism" as a neologism. Almost alone, Hobson helped to keep the word in circulation by inserting a chapter, "Marginalism in Neo-Classical Economics," in his *Free Thought in the Social Sciences* (1926). Two years later, the thorough index of the fourth edition of the *Handwörterbuch der Staatswissenschaften* contained only one reference, a reference to Hobson, under the subject heading of "Marginalismus." The words "marginalism" and "marginalist" seldom appeared in the *Encyclopaedia of the Social Sciences* (1930–35).[3]

The widespread employment of marginal cost, marginal revenue, marginal rate of substitution, and marginal propensity to consume in economic analysis during the 1930's provoked Richard A. Lester to complain in 1946 that the "minutiae of marginalism" were consuming one-half to one-third of the leading American textbooks.[4] This complaint by Lester marks the reintroduction of the word "marginalism"

1. Pp. 174-75, and 331.
2. John A. Hobson, *The Industrial System* (New York, 1909), p. 114.
3. 1:166, 175, 176; and 10:609.
4. Richard A. Lester, "Shortcoming of Marginal Analysis for Wage-Employment Problems," *American Economic Review* 36 (1946): 63.

into economics, once again as a disparaging term. The next year, Lester gave further prominence to the word "marginalism" by inserting it in the title of an article.[5] Fritz Machlup, who prepared the longest reply to the antimarginalists, assented to the acceptance of the word by adopting it in the first part of his reply.[6]

The marginalism controversy that Lester had begun in 1946 died out by 1961. It left the word "marginalism," however, flavored by the discussions of that controversy. For example, the meaning of "marginalism" is restricted to considerations of the helpfulness of marginal cost or marginal productivity in economic analysis in the subject index of the American Economic Association's *Index to Economic Articles* (formerly *Index of Economic Journals*), which listed no articles under "marginalism" from 1925 to 1945, listed largely articles on the Lester controversy from 1946 to 1961, and listed nothing under "marginalism" from 1962 to 1966. At least two authors have characterized "marginalism" as the essence of non-Marxist economics.[7]

The newness of the word "marginalism" is evident from the dictionaries. The word first entered a general dictionary in English in 1966 when *Webster's Third* defined "marginalism" as "economic analysis that stresses use of marginal qualities in the determination of equilibrium." Portuguese dictionaries are the only ones in another language that define "marginalism" in terms of more than one of its "qualities."

A recognizable and continuous history of marginalism began with the advent of the "quality" now called "marginal utility." There already are several studies[8] of the beginnings of marginal utility, and hence of this aspect of the origins of marginalism. According to the conventional accounts, marginal utility, in a form later acceptable to economists, was first successfully and independently created during the twelve years from 1862 to 1874 by William Stanley Jevons, Carl Menger, and Léon

5. Richard A. Lester, "Marginalism, Minimum Wages, and Labor Markets," *American Economic Review* 37 (1947): 135-48.
6. Fritz Machlup, "Marginal Analysis and Empirical Research," *American Economic Review* 36 (1946): 518-54.
7. The following are the longer histories of marginal utility: George J. Stigler, "The Development of Utility Theory," *Journal of Political Economy* 58 (1950); R. S. Howey, *The Rise of the Marginal Utility School, 1870-1889* (Lawrence, Kans., 1960); and Emil Kauder, *The History of Marginal Utility Theory* (Princeton, 1965). A great sourcebook of the history of marginal utility is William Jaffé, *Correspondence of Léon Walras and Related Papers* (Amsterdam, 1965), in three large, packed volumes. Fuller information on many of the subjects treated below can be located in these works by consulting their subject headings and indexes.
8. Leo Köppel, *Grenznutzentheorie und Marxismus* (Leipzig, 1930); Hermann Lehmann, *Grenznutzentheorie* (East Berlin, 1968).

Walras. It is generally agreed that the most fruitful of these years was 1871, the year when both Jevons and Menger published their books on the subject.

Marginal productivity, the second "quality" which Hobson's term "marginalism" covered, also had many antecedents. It was not fully discovered and identified, however, until after 1890 and hence did not receive systematic consideration until after marginal utility had been accepted by a number of potentially influential economists.

This acceptance was crucial. This first marginal "quality" was not quickly welcomed as a part of economic theory. Acceptance required a conscious effort by Jevons, Menger, and Walras to win supporters, an effort that met with considerable indifference and some opposition. Perhaps the time was ripe for eventual success. After 1870 the universities, the only locale where marginalism has ever flourished, not only grew rapidly but also accepted economics as a subject for study.

II

William Stanley Jevons (1835–1882) was the *only* writer to publish accounts of a general marginal utility theory in the 1860's. Jevons, twenty-four years old and a student at University College, having just returned to London following five years of work in Australia, wrote in his diary on February 19, 1860, that he had arrived at "a true comprehension of *Value*."[9] Later that year he wrote to his brother: "One of the most important axioms is, that as the quantity of any commodity . . . which a man has to consume, increases, so the utility or benefit derived from the last portion used decreases in degree." "I have no idea," he added, "of letting these things lie by till somebody else has the advantage of them, and shall therefore try to publish them next spring."[10]

Jevons' first public statement, however, was delayed until October 7, 1862, when he was barely twenty-seven. On that date, in Cambridge, the Secretary read, to Section F of the British Association for the Advancement of Science, Jevons' "Notice of a General Mathematical Theory of Political Economy." No one besides the Secretary is known to have heard the paper read. The next year an abstract was printed in the *Report of the Thirty-Second Meeting of the British Association for the Advance-*

9. J. A. LaNauze, "The Conception of Jevons' Utility Theory," *Economica*, n. s. 20 (1953): 357.

10. Harriet A. Jevons, ed., *Letters and Journal of W. Stanley Jevons* (London, 1886), pp. 151-52.

ment of Science (1863). No one is known to have mentioned this printed abstract in the next ten years.

Obviously, whatever circumstance started Jevons toward marginalism had to have influenced him before, or during, the first months of his twenty-fourth year. Earlier he had felt the impulse to accomplish. "I have an idea," he wrote to his sister when he was twenty-two, "which I do not object to mention to you, that my insight into the foundations and nature of the knowledge of man is deeper than that of most men or writers. In fact, I think it is my mission to apply myself to such subjects, and it is my intention to do so." [11] In the same letter he told of his discovery that political economy was "a sort of vague mathematics which calculates the causes and effects of man's industry." He took seriously his inclination to make use of mathematics, for he wrote, while still in Australia, looking forward to returning to England and having in mind his mission and the nature of political economy, "I wish especially to become a good mathematician, without which nothing, I am convinced, can be thoroughly done." [12]

Jevons had also acquired an equally essential inclination to connect utility with economic analysis. It is likely that his interest in utility came partly from Jeremy Bentham's writings, with which he could have become familiar while attending University College after returning to England. Bentham's influence on Jevons appeared first in the published abstract of Jevons' paper where, though he did not refer to Bentham, he used Bentham's phraseology, for example, Bentham's phrase "springs of action." His mother had provided an earlier source of his inclination toward utility when she read to him, at the age of nine, Richard Whately's *Easy Lessons on Money Matters for Young People* (1833). Jevons himself said, when he was older, that he had learned his "first ideas of political economy" from this book. [13] Whately, according to his biographer, regarded his *Easy Lessons* "as of more real importance than his larger works." [14] Jevons' recollection of the purport of Whately's dictum, "It is not . . . labour that makes things valuable, but their being valuable that makes them worth labouring for," [15] or of Whately's vivid illustration of

11. Ibid., p. 101.
12. Ibid., p. 119.
13. W. Stanley Jevons, *Political Economy* (New York, 1878), p. 5.
14. E. Jane Whately, *Life and Correspondence of Richard Whately, D.D.* (London, 1866), 1:377.
15. [Richard Whately], *Easy Lessons on Money Matters for the Use of Young People* (London, 1833), p. 33.

his statement, may have survived the intervening fifteen years and helped guide Jevons in the first months of 1860.

Of his own abilities Jevons wrote, "Give me a few facts or materials, and I can work them up into a smoothly-arranged and finished fabric of theory, or can turn them out in a shape which is something new."[16] Jevons had recognized a few of his "facts or materials" before he arrived in London. He soon found more. Besides studying philosophy, he enrolled in Augustus De Morgan's class in calculus, and in the class in political economy given by Jacob Waley, a star pupil himself of De Morgan's mathematics. In Waley's class he found the opportunity to consider the details of John Stuart Mill's *Principles of Political Economy* and, of course, from De Morgan he secured welcome instruction in the differential calculus. Early in 1860, Jevons worked all of his "facts or materials" into a "finished fabric of theory" that he realized was "something new."

III

Unlike Jevons, Carl Menger (1840–1921) left no correspondence or diaries that could disclose the sources of the new ideas contained in the *Grundsätze der Volkswirtschaftslehre* (1871), his first, and last, published contribution to marginalism. Although nothing is known that would directly invalidate the surmise that the *Grundsätze* resulted from ideas generated much earlier, a statement in the *Grundsätze* made it seem likely that the book was largely developed shortly before 1869 when Menger needed a *Habilitationsschrift* to qualify for a lectureship at the University of Vienna. In the statement in question Menger said that the field treated was "in no small degree . . . the product of recent development in German political economy."[17] This "recent development" was a discussion on value among German scholars that continued into 1869,[18] and to which Menger apparently intended to add the last word.

The German scholars gave Menger a subject for his *Habilitationsschrift* when they confronted him with the rudiments of an unsatisfactory non-labor theory of value. To improve this theory Menger added the key idea of marginalism, expressing it by saying that value equaled "the importance of the least important of the satisfactions assured by the whole available quantity and achieved with any equal portion."[19] No

16. Harriet A. Jevons, *Letters and Journal of W. Stanley Jevons*, p. 96.
17. Carl Menger, *Principles of Economics* (Glencoe, Ill., 1950), p. 49.
18. Ibid., p. 306.
19. Ibid., p. 139.

similar idea can be found in the writings of any German scholar that Menger had read earlier. In a way, the key idea is a mathematical one, and both Jevons and Walras acknowledged the relation between the calculus and their formulations of marginal utility. Menger, on the other hand, never publicly associated his version with the calculus. For this reason, as well as for the reason that his expressed views on methodology appeared hostile to the use of mathematics in economics, it has been presumed that mathematics played no part in the development of Menger's ideas on economics before 1871. J. A. Schumpeter attempted to explain the mathematics of Menger by saying that "the Austrian utility theorists, by operating the concept of marginal utility, actually discovered the calculus."[20]

However, there is evidence that Menger's formulation of marginal utility may not have been the simple rediscovery of the calculus that Schumpeter implied. It would not be, if, as seems to be the case, Menger was familiar with the calculus before 1869. The likelihood of his familiarity is established by a letter he wrote to Sigismund Feilbogen, who published a translation of it in 1911 in the *Journal des Economistes*.[21] "La philosophie et la mathématique," Menger wrote, "ont compté de tout temps parmi mes études préférées." Menger's first letter to Walras contained additional evidence of his familiarity with mathematics. Walras first learned of Menger in a letter of June 22, 1883, from Aulnis de Bourouill who had just (twelve years after its publication) discovered Menger's *Grundsätze* and who described it as "un livre de *théorie pure* avec des idées de mathématiques (comparaison de quantités distinctes) et arrivant par là à la doctrine sur le taux d'échange."[22] Walras hastened to open correspondence with Menger. Menger's reply contained a discussion of mathematical economics which it seems unlikely that he would have written had he not had an interest in and knowledge of mathematics.[23] In the reply Menger listed ten mathematical works on political economy which he had in his library and offered to lend to Walras. A library of this kind and size would hardly be owned at this time, even by a bibliophile such as Menger, if he had only faint connections with mathematics. Further, one of the ten books was by Cournot. In his letter to Feilbogen, Menger had said that the writings of Cournot "devaient exercer sur mon esprit une influence particulière."

20. Joseph A. Schumpeter, *History of Economic Analysis* (New York, 1954), p. 18.
21. *Journal des Economistes*, 6ᵉ série, 31 (1911): 56-57.
22. Jaffé, *Correspondence of Léon Walras*, 1:766.
23. Ibid., 1:768-69.

It is lamentable, especially in connection with a consideration of Carl Menger's mathematics, that nothing is known of the relations between him and his slightly younger brother, Anton. Anton Menger began pursuing mathematics as a hobby in 1867, and between 1891 and 1894 published a number of memoirs on the reform of the calculus under the assumed name of Dr. Julius Bergbohm. Carl Menger may have felt, between 1867 and 1871, the influence of his brother's strong interest.

IV

The first political economist to have direct cognizance of the marginal analysis of Léon Walras (1834–1910) was Joseph Garnier, editor of the well-established *Journal des Economistes*. Walras, then thirty-eight years old, had in 1873 sent Garnier sixty pages of proof from his forthcoming *Eléments d'économie politique pure*,[24] asking him, as editor, to consider them for publication.

Two months later, in a second attempt to draw attention to his book, which was still being printed, Walras read a summary paper, "Principe d'une théorie mathématique de léchange" before the Académie des Sciences morales et politques. Of this first appearance in public of his major ideas he wrote to a friend: "J'ai fait dans ma science une importante découverte. C'est celle que j'ai communiquée à l'institut aux vacances. La communication entière a été froidement reçue."[25]

After some hesitation, the Académie published Walras's paper in its *Séances et travaux* for January 1874, the first appearance in print of his contribution to marginalism. Walras realized that few would ever see his paper if it did not appear elsewhere. Accordingly, he repeated his request to Garnier to publish part of his manuscript in the *Journal des Economistes*. After a delay Garnier refused on the ground that "cela ne serait pas apprécié par les 0,99 de notre public."[26] Garnier, who often befriended Walras, tempered his refusal with the promise of other assistance, "en votre qualité de fils de A. Walras, de professeur d'économie politque, d'abonné, d'homme d'esprit, quoiqu'un peu rageur."[27] Walras accepted at once, gratefully.[28] Garnier, as part of his promised assistance, reprinted Walras's paper from the *Séances et travaux* in the April 1874 issue of the *Journal des Economistes*. From this reprinting Jevons first noticed the similarity of Walras's views to his own.

24. Ibid., 1:318-19.
25. Ibid., 1:354.
26. Ibid., 1:350.
27. Ibid.
28. Ibid., 1:351-52.

Walras had sought from mid-1873 on, to enlist the support of A. A. Cournot, to whom he felt a debt, inviting him to the lecture Walras gave before the Académie, discussing with him their differences of viewpoint, asking for intervention with the publisher Hachette, and requesting his help in writing an article on mathematical political economy.[29] Cournot, who died in 1877, was willing and interested, but he could help little, not only because he was busy with his own publications and family matters but also because he had lost the effective use of his eyes shortly after he had published his *Recherches sur les principes mathématiques de la théorie des richesses* (1838), with the consequence that he had given up all mathematics for the preceding thirty years.[30]

Walras's interest in political economy, according to his own account, had been first aroused in 1848 by overhearing his father, Auguste Walras, reading from one of his own manuscripts on political economy. "J'ai appris ainsi, à quatorze ans," Léon Walras reminisced, "que la terre et son service avaient une valeur intrinsèque rovenant de leur utilité combinée avec la limitation de leur quantité."[31] This suggestion of a reasonable connection between value and utility may have helped lead Walras to marginalism. It was, however, almost ten years later that Léon Walras first began to think of himself as a political economist. The turn came in the summer of 1858 when, after being forgiven by his father for having wasted four years and 7,000 francs in an unsuccessful attempt to become a mining engineer, Léon Walras began his professional career by promising to carry on his father's unfinished work in political economy.[32] Twenty-five years later, in writing to his mother of his own intellectual history, he said, "C'est un peu comme un tableau à l'huile dont mon père m'aurait fourni l'esquisse au crayon."[33]

What did "l'esquisse au crayon" contain? It contained an emphais on utility and its relation to scarcity, resulting in the concept of *rareté*, which took the form of a ratio and was far from marginalism. It also contained Auguste Walras's unexplained encouragement of the use of mathematics in political economy. The sketch left much either to be filled in or corrected.

Léon Walras struggled vainly from 1858 through 1870 to earn a

29. Ibid., 1:326, 330-32, 366-67, 375, 421-22.
30. Ibid., 1:331-32.
31. Léon Walras, "Un initiateur en économic politique: A. A. Walras," *Revue du Mois* 6 (1908): 181.
32. Jaffé, *Correspondence of Léon Walras*, 1:2.
33. Ibid., 1:761.

living and to obtain a foothold in political economy. In those twelve years in Paris, he failed to add the vital connection between mathematics and utility to the sketch, although he tried twice, first in 1860 and again in 1869–70.[34]

Walras's career might have continued in this way had he not received an unexpected appointment as a professor at Lausanne. This appointment brought him release from old obligations and offered new opportunities. Undoubtedly it altered the course of the marginal revolution. He arrived in Lausanne on December 11, 1870, in part because of his parents' payment of 3,000 francs, or more, to hire a substitute for his army service. In these fresh surroundings he renewed at once his effort to combine political economy with mathematics. "Le dimanche matin," he wrote to his wife shortly after he had arrived in Lausanne, "je suis allé voir un autre de mes collègues M. Gay, professeur de mathématiques à l'Académie, avec lequel j'ai travaillé quelques problèmes d'économie politique."[35]

When did Walras first capture the elusive, essential idea of marginal utility? William Jaffé, who has read *all* the correspondence and related papers, published and unpublished, said that there was "not the slightest inkling of a theory of maximization of utility either in L.W.'s pre-Lausanne papers or in the various outlines and prospectives of his work up to October 19, 1872."[36] The "inkling" on that date was Walras's remark in a letter to a colleague that he was going over his forthcoming publication with Antoine Paul Piccard, professor of mechanics at Lausanne, "en vue de la correction des formules algébriques."[37] Earlier, Piccard had given an expository note to Walras which, Jaffé said, "played more than a casual role in bringing mathematical light to L.W."[38] If Piccard brought the "mathematical light" to Walras, then Walras's *Eléments* came close to being published with no marginal utility in it, since Walras already had a manuscript and had begun to seek a publisher. Over a month earlier, in a letter to the publisher Guillaumin, he had said that his work on pure economics "est aujourd 'hui presque entièrement terminé," and that it was in a form "tout-à-fait nouvelle," meaning that he had used the mathematical method.[39]

34. Ibid., 1:216–21.
35. Ibid., 1:264.
36. Ibid., 1:309.
37. Ibid., 1:307.
38. Ibid., 1:308.
39. Ibid., 1:298.

V

The preceding sections are intended to show that marginalism was developed between 1862 and 1873 by newcomers to political economy. The newcomers, Jevons, Menger, and Walras, having the outlook of young men, felt free from allegiance to prevailing and encumbering views on political economy. Each also had a marked sense of mission. Through different circumstances each had come to magnify the part that wants or utility play in an understanding of economics. Marginal utility emerged when these three men, from different countries, coupled their ideas of wants or utility with a basic concept of the differential calculus.

The further history of the development of marginalism, from 1873 through most of the 1880's, was the history of a search for acceptance and support of marginal utility. Marginalism, as a recognized part of economics, did not originate until supporters were found and acceptance achieved. Jevons, Menger, and especially Walras were the principal figures in this struggle for recognition. The fact that they were newcomers deprived them for a long time of allies.

Jevons and Walras soon discovered each other, but it was almost ten years later when Walras and Menger first corresponded. It was quickly pointed out to them that there had been predecessors. The main predecessor was Hermann Heinrich Gossen, whose discovery Jevons announced by letter to Walras in 1878.[40] Walras and Jevons agreed without delay that Gossen had preceded them. They did not agree on the other predecessors. Johann Heinrich von Thünen was called to Walras's attention by George Friedrich Knapp in 1874,[41] and to Jevons' attention by Robert Adamson in 1876.[42] Walras found little to interest him in Thünen, saying finally in a letter to Jevons, "je doute malgré tout qu'il y ait grand'chose à y prendre."[43] Jevons never commented on Walras's evaluation; but he only mentioned Thünen's name in the 1879 edition of his *Theory,* where he gave almost seven pages to Gossen.[44] Charles Letort advanced the name of Jules Dupuit in his review of Walras's *Eléments* in 1874.[45] As in the case of Thünen, but for different reasons, Walras did not accept Dupuit as a predecessor. Walras gave Jevons in

40. Ibid., 1:581.
41. Ibid., 1:401.
42. Ibid., 1:508.
43. Ibid., 1:532.
44. Pp. xxxv-xlii, xliv.
45. Jaffé, *Correspondence of Léon Walras,* 1:458.

1874 a judgment on "le mémoire de M. Dupuit" saying that "Dupuit y a effectivement abordé le problème de l'expression mathématique de l'utilité; mais il ne l'a nullement résolu."[46] Jevons later wrote to Walras, "It is impossible not to allow that Dupuit had a very profound comprehension of the subject and anticipated us as regards the fundamental ideas of utility."[47] Walras replied at once that he was not of Jevons' "avis sur le mérite des Mémoires de M. Dupuit."[48]

Carl Menger seemingly won followers with little exertion. The amount of his exertion, however, may be underestimated, since more is known about his results than his activities. Apparently he first captured the allegiance of his two principal supporters, Eugen Böhm-Bawerk and Friedrich von Wieser, on the merits of his *Grundsätze* alone. The start of the Austrian School, however, was delayed, for Wieser published nothing on marginalism until 1884, and Böhm-Bawerk did not start until 1886. No details of Menger's part in these publications are known.

Jevons realized that he had to seek out means to spread his views. Accordingly, he published, in 1866, a longer version of his original paper in a place more certain to be noticed, the *Journal of the Royal Statistical Society*. Later he prepared and was able to have published by Macmillan a book-length elaboration, his *Theory of Political Economy* (1871). In 1875 Jevons wrote to Walras, whom he had come to regard as an ally, "I have no doubt whatever about the ultimate success of our efforts, but it will take some fighting."[49] In the second edition of his *Theory* (1879), Jevons provided marginalism with its first history and its first bibliography, both of which gave status to the subject and furthered understanding. But Jevons was busy with other things, lacked a taste for pushing, and, unfortunately, died in 1882. He never learned that Menger had similar views.

Walras was the most energetic of the three in systematically and continually seeking recognition and support. A good part of the three large volumes of William Jaffé's superbly arranged *Correspondence of Léon Walras and Related Papers* recounts the ups and downs of Walras's unremitting efforts from 1873 to 1909 to ensure acceptance of the new economics.

Walras thought that he knew what had to be done. He had a plan for scientific revolution that went beyond the announcement of the

46. Ibid., 1:456.
47. Ibid., 1:533.
48. Ibid., 1:535.
49. Ibid., 1:474-75.

revolutionary discovery. "Ce n'est pas tout que de faire des découvertes," Walras wrote to his mother in 1883, "il faut savoir se faire une position qui vous permettra de les faire connaître."[50] He had sufficient revolutionary fervor to spend his own capital to help finance the marginal revolution. Walras estimated, in 1901, that he had spent, from his inherited capital, 50,000 francs (equal to ten times his highest annual salary) to spread his doctrines.[51]

From the beginning, Walras fancied that French political economists would ignore his work. Walras's fancy spurred on the internationalization of the struggle to introduce marginal utility into political economy. This internationalization was one factor contributing to the eventual success of the struggle, and hence to the origin of marginalism.

The plan for internationalization first appeared when Walras told Joseph Garnier in 1873 that if the French persisted in dismissing him as "un rêveur," he would appeal "au jugement public de l'étranger."[52] He actually began systematically to seek foreign supporters on March 12, 1874, at which time he addressed similar letters to "un ami en Angleterre et un en Allemagne," both fellow members in the cooperative movement, and to a professor at Geneva who was familiar with Italy.[53] In these three letters he asked for a select list of professors and editors to whom he could send an offprint of his article in the *Journal des Economistes* with the hope of subsequently entering "en relation avec celles qui seraient disposeés à approfondir mes idées pour les discuter."[54] Walras apologized in one of these letters for appearing "quelque peu altéré de publicité," saying that since his work was "très scientifique et peu populaire," he had to look far to find even a small group of readers.[55] He explained further that readers were especially necessary to him, since his publisher would print the second part of his forthcoming volume only after the first part was certain to sell enough copies to pay for itself, an agreement which delayed the printing of the second part of Walras's *Eléments* until 1877.[56] He estimated that his *Eléments* would have a chance to succeed if thirty persons in France, England, Germany, and Italy could be found "en état de le lire, de le juger et de le faire avaler au public."[57]

50. Ibid., 1:761.
51. Ibid., 3:187.
52. Ibid., 1:344.
53. Ibid., 1:359-61.
54. Ibid., 1:360.
55. Ibid.
56. Ibid., 1:361.
57. Ibid.

Walras's first three letters turned up two Italian, seven German, and sixteen English prospects; but only one Italian and two English correspondents responded to Walras's overtures. The Italian was Alberto Errera, who opened Italy to marginalism. Jevons was the first Englishman to reply, saying that he had already read Walras's article in the *Journal des Economistes.* "It is satisfactory to me to find that my theory of exchange," he wrote on May 12, 1874, "which, when published in England, was either neglected or criticized, is practically confirmed by your researches."[58] This union of purpose between Walras and Jevons strengthened the forces creating marginalism. Of the coincidence of their discoveries Walras wrote to another correspondent that he hoped that "la singularité de cette rencontre piquera votre curiosité et vous amènera à vouloir prendre une connaissance approfondie de l'ouvrage de M. Jevons et du mien."[59] The other Englishman to anwer was Professor T. E. Cliffe Leslie, who pointed out that Jevons had a similar theory with which neither he nor John Stuart Mill agreed.[60]

Walras repeated that same procedure for entering into correspondence with interested economists when the first part of his *Eléments* (1874) appeared, sending copies "à presque tous les professeurs d'économie politique de l'Europe."[61] On this occasion, Jevons provided Walras with the names of six economists who might respond;[62] only one, G. H. Darwin, became a correspondent. Walras mailed the second part of the *Elément* (1877) with no more effect. In fact, his campaign for readers must have resulted in far fewer than he had anticipated; after all his effort, by 1881 he could count only three "élèves dignes de ce nom": Aulnis de Bourouill, von Winterfeld, and del Pezzo.[63]

After 1881, prospects brightened. In almost every year between 1881 and 1890, additional writers recognized and supported the idea of marginal utility. In 1882, Herbert Somerton Foxwell, who became Walras's principal English consultant following Jevons' death, sent Walras a list of twelve English prospects."[64] From the list Walras was able to open a correspondence with Alfred Marshall and F. Y. Edgeworth which, in some ways, was encouraging. In 1883, Aulnis de Bourouill brought Menger and Walras together, with the consequence that the marginal revolution now added another national dimension. In his first letter to

58. Ibid., 1:393.
59. Ibid., 1:420.
60. Ibid., 1:395.
61. Ibid., 1:424.
62. Ibid., 1:427.
63. Ibid., 1:681.
64. Ibid., 1:738-39.

Walras, Menger said that he had been aware of Walras's writings for some time, but it is not clear that he had appreciated the extent of the similarity of his viewpoint with that of Walras.[65] Perhaps the appreciation was absent because Menger did not think the similarity present. On the other hand, Walrus emphasized their similarity when he wrote to Menger, "Nous nous sommes évidemment posé le même problème, Monsieur; et nous avons évidemment entrepris de le résoudre par la même méthode."[66]

The year after Menger was introduced to Walras, Friedrich von Wieser published his *Über den Ursprung und die Hauptgesetze des wirtschaftlichen Werthes* (1884). It was a book based on Menger's views, the first indication that there would be an Austrian School, and the book in which the word *Grenznutzen* was first used. It had a narrow circulation. Walras did not know it in 1886[67] and did not obtain a copy until 1887.[68] Charles Gide's proposal to Walras in 1885 to found a new French journal "ouverte aux idées critiques" indicated some warming of the French coolness that Walras had felt so long.[69] In 1886, Eugen Böhm-Bawerk's "Grundzüge der Theorie des wirtschaftlichen Güterwerts" appeared in the *Jahrbücher für Nationalökonomie und Statistik,* a primary forum for German professional opinion on economics. Walras wrote Böhm-Bawerk at once of "un premier et rapide examen m'en ayant fait connaître toute l'importance."[70] In this same year Walras wrote the second history of marginalism, which he put in the preface to his *Théorie de la monnaie* (1886). Late in 1887, Walrus found a Russian mathematical economist, Ladislaus von Bortkiewicz, who became a valued correspondent and a reliable defender.[71]

Walras had first heard from Philip Henry Wicksteed in 1884 when Wicksteed wrote, "I am now reading your 'Eléments' with extreme interest."[72] Four years went by before Walras heard from him again. Foxwell, who continued to advise Walras on English economists, recommended Wicksteed in 1886 as "a very able man, an enthusiastic follower of Jevons" and in 1888 as an "admirable writer" who "is bringing out an Introduction to Mr. Jevons' Theory of P.E."[73] Wicksteed sent

65. Ibid., 1:768-69.
66. Ibid., 1:771.
67. Ibid., 2:152.
68. Ibid., 2:187.
69. Ibid., 2:42.
70. Ibid., 2:152.
71. Ibid., 2:229-37.
72. Ibid., 2:12.
73. Ibid., 2:160-61, 259.

Walras a copy of his *Alphabet of Economic Science* (1888), and Walras responded that he had read the volume with "un vif plaisir."[74] The next year, "un vif plaisir" was also the exact phrase with which he described his feelings after examining the copy of *Principii di economia pura* (1889) which Maffeo Pantaleoni had sent him.[75] The hold that marginalism had in Austria in 1889 was shown by the appearance in that year of three other books using marginal analysis: Rudolph Auspitz's and Richard Lieben's *Untersuchungen über die Theorie des Preises*, Eugen Böhm-Bawerk's *Kapital und Kapitalzins, Zweite Abteilung, Positive Theorie des Kapitales*, and Friedrich von Wieser's *Natürliche Werth*.

VI

In the years 1862 to 1887, diverse names were given to the new way in which utility was being treated. Jevons coined the expressions "final degree of utility," "final utility," and "terminal utility" in the search for a satisfactory term. Menger used "importance of the least important of the satisfactions" to denote the same idea. Walras tried three forms, "intensive utility," "*rareté*," and "the intensity of the last want satisfied" to cover an identical concept. By 1887 it seemed likely that "final utility" might win out as the standard term, at least in English. Even the term *Grenznutzen* which Friedrich Wieser had introduced in his *Ursprung* (1884) was translated as "final utility."

Late in 1888 a word appeared that in time replaced "final utility" in English and that will probably also replace all terms previously used in other languages. It was the word "marginal," first introduced by Philip H. Wicksteed in his *Alphabet*, where it occurred on an average of twice on each page, a massive occurrence for a first use. Adoption followed slowly. For example, the word "marginal" is not found in Edgeworth's review of the *Alphabet* in 1889.[76] Nor is it found in Edgeworth's Presidential Address before Section F of the British Association later that year, even though he referred to Wicksteed's *Alphabet* and mentioned "final utility" and "final disutility" many times.[77]

It has been easy to surmise that Wicksteed adopted the word from Wieser. Wieser had first translated "final utility" into *Grenznutzen* in 1884, hardly a literal translation. There is no evidence, however, in the *Alphabet* or elsewhere, that Wicksteed had been influenced in his intro-

74. Ibid., 2:307.
75. Ibid., 2:331.
76. *The Academy* 35 (1889): 71.
77. *Report of the Fifty-Ninth Meeting of the British Association for the Advancement of Science* (London, 1890).

duction of the word "marginal" either by Wieser's *Ursprung* or by any of the infrequent uses by other writers of the word *Grenznutzen.* It may be added that "marginal utility" is a nonliteral translation. It is an unlikely one as well, particularly since the expression "final utility" had been used increasingly for seventeen years as an equivalent. The *Annals of the American Academy of Political and Social Science* for 1890 contained two translations of articles by Böhm-Bawerk in which the word *Grenznutzen* was rendered, as would be expected, on every occasion into "final utility."[78] The word *Grenze* was also found in Menger's *Grundsätze,* but it should be, and was in the English edition, translated as "limit" and not as "margin."

Edgeworth, in his article "Margin (in economics)" for Palgrave's *Dictionary of Political Economy* (1896), said that Wicksteed "first used the phrase 'marginal' instead of 'final utility.' " Another reliable reporter, James Bonar, said in 1889 that " 'marginal utility' is a happy phrase used by P. H. Wicksteed."[79] Neither Edgeworth nor Bonar suggested any connection with Wieser. Strangely, Wicksteed never mentioned "marginal utility" in the article "Final Degree of Utility" that he wrote for Palgrave's *Dictionary.* A statement at the end of Wicksteed's article said, "Jevons's 'Final Degree of Utility' is the *Grenznutzen* of the Austrian School."

The second book to include the word "marginal" was Alfred Marshall's *Principles of Economics* (1890). Marshall used the word less frequently than Wicksteed, averaging one use to every fifteen pages. It might be thought that Marshall learned the word "marginal" from Wicksteed. Yet no one has said that such was the case. In the first edition of the *Principles* Marshall gave a personal explanation of the origin of the term. "The term 'marginal' increment I borrowed from von Thunen," he wrote, "and it is now commonly used by German economists. When Jevons' *Theory* appeared, I adopted his word 'final,' but I have been gradually convinced 'marginal' is the better."[80] Marshall's explanation was inexact in some ways. Thünen did not use the term " 'marginal' increment"; neither, for that matter, did Marshall outside the passage just cited. Thünen used the noun *Grenze* only once, and then in the sense of the "limit" beyond which the employer would hire no laborers.[81]

78. 1:244-71, 361-84.
79. *Quarterly Journal of Economics* 3 (1889):344.
80. Alfred Marshall, *Principles of Economics* (London, 1890), p. x.
81. Johann Heinrich von Thünen, *Der isolirte Staat,* Zweiter Theil, Erste Abtheilung (Rostock, 1850), p. 178.

Marshall felt that his explanation was amiss and consequently changed the footnote in the second edition to read thus:

The term "marginal" increment is in harmony with von Thünen's methods of thought and was suggested to me by him, though he does not actually use it. It has been for some time commonly used by Austrian economists on the initiative of Prof. Wieser, and it has been adopted by Mr. Wicksteed. When Jevons' Theory appeared, I adopted his word "final"; but I have been gradually convinced that "marginal" is the better. [In the first edition this footnote implied wrongly that the phrase, as well as the idea of, "marginal increment" could be traced to von Thünen.][82]

This was scarcely an improvement. What did he mean by "adopted"? Marshall also introduced twice in the index of the second edition the sentence "Wieser first used the term Marginal Utility." Later editions dropped this misleading sentence.

The new word "marginal" did appear, perhaps for the first time, as the English translation of the German word *Grenze* when Böhm-Bawerk's *Positive Theorie des Kapitales* (1889) was turned into English by William Smart in 1891. It was also so rendered by Christian A. Malloch's translation of Wieser's *Natürliche Werth* (1889) in 1893. But Smart, and his student Malloch, must have learned the word "marginal" from Marshall's *Principles* rather than from their German-English dictionaries.

The word "marginal" was applied by Wicksteed to ten different nouns and by Marshall to thirteen different nouns. The only noun modified by "marginal" that Wicksteed and Marshall had in common was "utility." The other nouns of Wicksteed were desire, desiredness, effect, effectiveness, usefulness, value, value-in-use, want, and worth. The other nouns of Marshall were capital, cost of production, demand price, disutility of labor, dose, efficiency of a factor of production, effort, expenses, increment, produce, return, supply price, and utility of money.

It is probable that the word "marginal" was introduced, not as a translation of *Grenze*, but as a handier substitute for "final." "Marginal" was more flexible, since it permitted, among other things, the use of such phrases as "at the margin" or "on the margin." Both Wicksteed and Marshall made use of this advantage. Wicksteed employed the noun "margin" twenty-four times, Marshall half that many. This was appealing because it brought marginal analysis in line with a type of analysis, long met with in English political economy, which consisted in centering attention on the circumstances at the "margin of cultivation."

82. Marshall, *Principles*, 2d ed., p. xiv.

"Margin" was thought to be widely used, in this sense, when Wicksteed and Marshall wrote. "The expression 'margin of cultivation' has become," Simon N. Patten said in 1889, "through long usage, a classical expression for one of the most fundamental ideas of economics."[83]

The expression "margin of cultivation" had been introduced by Thomas Chalmers in his *On Political Economy in Connection with the Moral State and Moral Prospects of Society* (1832). Following the example of "Sir Edward West and Mr. Malthus," he began his discussion with a consideration of "the extreme limit of cultivation."[84] Chalmers repeated this expression once and then switched, without explanation, to "the extreme margin of cultivation," an alternative expression which he only used twice.[85] He also used the expression "last and farthest margin."[86] After those three uses of the word "margin" he reverted to his original term "limit," using it frequently, often writing "extreme limit," "certain limit," "natural limit," "least possible limit," or "existing limit." A German translation of "the limit" is *die Grenze*.

Chalmers alone probably could not have introduced the word "margin" into the vocabulary of political economy. The introduction became effective when it received, in addition, the approval of John Stuart Mill. In his *Principles of Political Economy* (1848), Mill included Dr. Chalmers among "authors of the highest name and of great merit," a position not usually given to him.[87] Mill said that Chalmers had the merit of expressing his opinions "in a language of his own, which often uncovers aspects of the truth that the received phraseologies only tend to hide."[88] "It is well said by Dr. Chalmers," Mill wrote, "that many of the most important lessons in political economy are to be learned at the extreme margin of cultivation."[89] Mill mentioned the "margin" a number of other times, attributing the word to Chalmers. The translation of the word "margin" into German is interesting. Adolph Soetbeer turned "at the extreme margin" into "auf dem äussersten Rande" in his German translation (1852) of Mill's *Principles*,[90] and he translated Mill's expression "extreme limit" as "die äusserste Grenze."[91] Thus the word "margin" (and hence

---

83. *Quarterly Journal of Economics* 3 (1889): 356.
84. P. 2.
85. Pp. 21 and 45.
86. P. 32.
87. 1:82-83.
88. 1:94.
89. 2:234.
90. 2:149.
91. 2:206.

the word "marginalism") links, as it properly should, the work of Jevons, Menger, and Walras with that of West, Malthus, and Mill. In this sense, marginalism appears as the confluence of two streams of analysis.

VII

The incorporation of marginal analysis in the general treatises of economics marked the final or acceptance stage in the origin of marginalism. For the sake of conciseness, only American textbooks are considered here.

Richard T. Ely's *Outlines of Economics* (1893), the American textbook most widely selected by professors of economics during the next forty years for use in their classes, had been prepared as a revision of his *Introduction to Political Economy* (1889), which had hardly contained a trace of marginalism. The *Outlines* included a little more marginalism. It introduced Jevons, Menger, and Walras in a short history of economics and commented on the Austrian School, then becoming known in the United States. In its index it listed "Marginal Utility," but in the text, only a sketch of the idea of marginal utility was found, and no mention of the word itself.

The first edition of Ely's *Outlines* served from 1893 to 1907. In these fifteen years marginal analysis entered the competing textbooks of A. T. Hadley (1896), C. J. Bullock (1897), H. J. Davenport (1897), E. T. Devine (1898), F. W. Blackmar (1900), F. A. Fetter (1904), H. R. Seager (1904), and E. R. A. Seligman (1905). For the most part the textbooks discussed only marginal utility, although marginal productivity was also a topic in those of Hadley and Seligman.

The appearance of Ely's revised *Outlines* (1908) reflected a change in marginalism. After its editors had added marginal productivity as part of the explanation of the return to labor and capital, no other textbook excluded it. Ely's *Outlines* went through four later editions, 1916, 1923, 1930, and 1937, keeping approximately the same content of marginalism.

Other leading American textbooks of the period from 1908 to 1936, all of which gave essentially the same coverage as did Ely's textbook, were those of Alvin Johnson (1909). F. W. Taussig (1911), Irving Fisher (1911), F. M. Taylor (1911), J. R. Turner (1919), Henry Clay (1919), T. N. Carver (1919), O. F. Boucke (1925), Lionel Edie (1926), L. A. Rufener (1927), F. B. Garver and A. H. Hansen (1928), P. F. Gemmill (1930), F. R. Fairchild (1930), Broadus Mitchell (1932), and F. S. Deibler

(1936). This was a twenty-eight-year plateau. Both marginal utility and marginal productivity had been accepted. There was no other use of marginal analysis in these textbooks.

In the 1930's new uses for the marginal concept were introduced in the journals and the specialized literature. Marginal utility lost favor, and the marginal rate of substitution took its place, partly as an immediate result of J. R. Hicks and R. G. D. Allen's "A Reconsideration of the Theory of Value" (1934).[92] Marginal cost and marginal revenue, twin guides to maximization that had for long appeared in isolated instances, came in for extended use in Edward Chamberlin's *The Theory of Monopolistic Competition* (1933) and in Joan Robinson's *Economics of Imperfect Competition* (1933). John Maynard Keynes began the unusual use of marginal terms as constants in *The General Theory of Empoyment, Interest and Money* (1936).

These changes reached the textbooks between 1937 and 1947. Two texts, one by A. L. Meyers, the second by A. M. McIsaac and J. G. Smith, both published in 1937, first showed plainly the acceptance of the ideas of Edward Chamberlin and Joan Robinson. Lorie Tarshis' textbook in 1947 gave the Keynesian marginal terms a prominent place.

A textbook which represented the new character of American textbooks after 1947 was P. A. Samuelson's *Economics* (1948), a book which came to dominate the growing market. It was still flourishing at the time of its revision in 1970. This revision covers essentially the same marginalistic subjects as the first edition, but devotes more than twice as much space to them. The amount and character of marginalism in other current textbooks is much the same as in Samuelson's textbooks.

Marginalism in American textbooks has had three acceptance plateaus: the first, 1893–1907; the second, 1908–1936; an interval of change, 1937–1947; and the third, 1948–   ?

92. *Economica*, n. s. 1 (1934): 52-76, 195-219.

Chapter I

THE FORMATION OF JEVONS' OPINIONS ON MARGINAL UTILITY

I

The concept of the *utility* or *satisfaction* that an article gives its consumer first found a key place in the study of economics between the years 1871 and 1889. Its introduction marked a radical change in the viewpoint of economists. Although earlier economists had not wholly ignored utility, they had not used it effectively because generally they had not regarded it from a convenient point of view. Previously they had considered it mainly, in its most cumbersome and obvious form, as the *total* utility a person obtains from a given consumption. The adoption of the "marginal" standpoint, the standpoint which centers attention on *changes* in the total utility corresponding to *changes* in the amount of consumption, opened the way to its effective employment. Thereafter, when economists took a rigorous, overall view of their subject they studied the economizing (maximizing) of utility, while before they had investigated the economizing (minimizing) of cost.

The new "marginal" viewpoint usually is thought to have begun with the contemporaneous and major publications of William Stanley Jevons, Carl Menger, and Léon Walras.[1] An investigation of how these influential books came to be written may conveniently start with the first of these writers. For William Stanley Jevons discovered the significance of marginal utility on February 19, 1860, over ten years before he published his principal book on the subject. J. A. La Nauze established this date from the unpublished diary that remained in the hands of Jevons' son.[2] In an entry dated February 3rd to 5th Jevons had written that he "was almost entirely engaged in commencing a work on Pol. Econ. . . . Value to be established on the basis of labour . . . ," thus admitting that he was following in the van of the English Classical School. Two weeks later, February 19, 1860, he wrote, "At home all day and working chiefly at Economy, arriving as I suppose at a true comprehension of *Value* regarding which I have lately very much blundered." La Nauze reasoned that Jevons meant by his having "very much blundered" his earlier subscription to the labor theory of

1

value, and by the "true comprehension of *Value*" the utility theory of value.

Jevons himself confirmed the approximate date of his discovery in the following long excerpt from a letter written to his brother Herbert, June 1, 1860:

During the last session I have worked a good deal at political economy; in the last few months I have fortunately struck out what I have no doubt is *the true Theory of Economy,* so thorough-going and consistent, that I cannot now read other books on the subject without indignation. . . . I obtain from the mathematical principles all the chief laws at which political economists have previously arrived, only arranged in a series of definitions, axioms, and theories almost as rigorous and connected as if they were so many geometrical problems. One of the most important axioms is, that as the quantity of any commodity, for instance, plain food, which a man has to consume, increases, so the utility or benefit derived from the last portion used decreases in degree. The decrease of enjoyment between the beginning and the end of a meal may be taken as an example. And I assume that on the average, the *ratio of utility* is some continuous mathematical function of the quantity of commodity. This law of utility has, in fact, always been assumed by political economists under the more complex form and name of the Law of Supply and Demand. But once fairly stated in its simple form, it opens up the whole of the subject. . . . I have no idea of letting these things lie by till somebody else has the advantage of them, and shall therefore try to publish them next spring.[3]

This is the first statement of the central tenet of the Marginal Utility School. It is complete and accurate. It establishes, without doubt, that Jevons had worked out the main principles of the school long before Menger or Walras gave the problem any attention.

What led this twenty-four-year-old student at the University of London to introduce the idea of marginal utility into his own version of economics? This chapter selects no single source of his innovation, but lists instead a series of unconnected circumstances that, in varying and slight degrees, improved the likelihood of the outcome.

II

Although he never implied that any of them led him to his use of utility, Jevons did generously credit a number of writers for aid in formulating his ideas.[4] One of these was Nassau William Senior, the first Drummond Professor of Political Economy (1825-30) at Oxford. Senior's successors in the Drummond Professorship, Richard

Whately (1830-32) and William Foster Lloyd (1832-36), might also have influenced Jevons, although he did not mention them. To them could be added the first Whately Professor at Trinity College, Dublin, Mountifort Longfield (1833-38). All of these now receive credit as precursors of the Marginal Utility School, and we might easily suspect that Jevons had felt their influence.[5] They wrote either slightly before or soon after his birth; their ideas on utility awaited his discovery when he returned from Australia in 1859 to set himself seriously at work on the subject of economics.

Jevons never acknowledged that he had profited directly from the work on utility of any of the Drummond and Whately Professors. He did mention Senior in connection with utility, but he gave us no reason to believe that he knew of Senior's work on marginal utility before he himself made his own independent discovery in 1860. Jevons did, however, have a boyhood encounter with the opinions of Richard Whately that could have prepared his mind for the acceptance of utility as his key tool years later. For Jevons began his education in economics, according to his wife's account, when his mother read to him Archbishop Whately's *Easy Lessons on Money Matters*.[6] He himself wrote near the end of his life that in "early boyhood I learned my first ideas of political economy from a copy of these lessons. . . . "[7] If he really paid attention to this early instruction, and if the influence shaped his later views, we might, with some reason, attribute part of the responsibility for his acceptance of the marginal utility theory of value to the Archbishop, since Whately, as the following paragraph shows, repudiated the labor theory of value and accepted a loose utility version.

When anything that is desirable is to be had by labour, and is not to be had *without* labour, of course we find men labouring to obtain it; and things that are of very great value, will usually be found to have cost very great labour. This has led some persons to suppose that it is the labour which has been bestowed on any thing that *gives* it value. But this is quite a mistake. It is not the labour which any thing has cost that *causes* it to sell for a high price; but on the contrary, it is its selling for a high price that causes men to labour in procuring it. For instance, fishermen go out to sea, and toil hard in the wet and cold to fish, because they can get a good price for them; but if a fisherman should work hard all night, and catch but one small fish, while another had, perhaps, caught a thousand, by falling in with a shoal, the first would not be able to sell his one fish for the same price as the other man's thousand. It has now and then happened that a salmon or a sturgeon has leaped into a boat by chance; but though this has cost no labour, it

3

is not for that reason the less valuable. And if a man, in eating an oyster, should chance to meet with a fine pearl, it would not sell for less than if he had been diving for it all day.

It is not, therefore, labour that makes things valuable, but their being valuable that makes them worth labouring for.[8]

How fateful that Jevons had this passage from Whately read to him at the impressionable age of nine! And how remarkable that he still recalled the occasion thirty-five years later!

We need perhaps to explain how Jevons could have missed the writings on utility of the Oxford and Dublin professors. The primary excuse for Jevons' oversight is that professors in the England of his time had a much different, and lower, status, both with regard to economics and with regard to English university education, than they do now.[9] Students rarely attended the few professorial lectures given, nor did many other persons. Reportedly only one listener remained to the end of Senior's first lecture at Oxford.[10] Until the time when Jevons began to write, the Drummond Professors never, in fact, resided at Oxford. The obscure position of these professors hid their work from Jevons' notice.

Where did professors at Oxford and Dublin obtain their bias toward utility, a bias so highly developed that one of them gave an almost perfect exposition of the role that marginal utility played in value theory? Most probably this early band of utility economists had their unanimity of view because they followed the lead of either Senior or Whately. It was a group dominated by a person rather than an idea. Senior has a reputation vastly superior to Whately in the field of economics, perhaps deservedly, yet there is much evidence that Whately may have shaped Senior's views rather than vice versa. It would seem the natural relation, for Senior first met Whately when he hired him as his tutor in 1811. Also Senior probably owed his election as professor to Whately and consequently kept his benefactor's views in mind in his lectures. Nor can we doubt that Whately, rather than Senior, was the principal interconnecting link in this early group of utility economists. Whately certainly played a part in the election of Lloyd, the star utility economist of them all. In Dublin he lost no time in founding the professorship bearing his name, keeping personal control of the appointments.

Neither Whately nor Senior wrote much on the subject of value. Senior first discussed value, and then most briefly and without reference to utility, in an anonymous review he prepared of two

4

articles on agriculture.[11] He next considered the same subject in 1826 in a definition of the term "value" contributed to the appendix to Whately's *Elements of Logic*.[12] Here he disapproved of Ricardo's connection of value with cost, but he gave no clue that the correct connection is with utility. He returned for the last time to the subject of value in his professorial lectures in the year 1826-27, a series which did not appear in print, however, until ten years later. "Of the three conditions of value, utility, transferableness, and limitation in supply," Senior wrote, "the last is by far the most important."[13] This hardly rings like the statement of a utility economist. Senior, of course, did go on to give a statement of the principle of diminishing utility, but he gave it in connection with his explanation of why "our desires do not aim so much at quantity as at diversity."[14] Whately never wrote anything on the connection of utility with the theory of value other than the paragraph quoted above. But it certainly matched the totality of Senior's writings on the subject, and it appeared in print before Senior had published more than a word on the same subject.

How could either Whately or Senior convert all the other early Drummond or Whately Professors to a utility theory of value in view of the strongly entrenched position of the labor theory of value? The conversion most likely occurred because none of these professorial writers on the theory, even including Senior (at least in 1825), knew enough about Ricardian economics to make the acceptance of some other system a difficult matter. The first English academic economists differed widely from present-day economists in the extent and depth of their preparation. For the most part, the study of economics played little part in their lives. They won the elections to their professorships on grounds other than their knowledge of the economic literature of the time, they delivered their lectures, published a sample of them, continuing their main work in the meantime in law (Senior, Longfield) or in the Church (Whately, Lloyd), and generally published little if anything on economics after the end of their professorial tenure.

No one can find any evidence from their writings that any of these early English professors of political economy had ever read Ricardo's *Principles* carefully, if at all. They held original ideas more because they did not know the content of Ricardo's theory of value than because they realized its defects and sought to remedy them. All they needed was a slight shove in the right direction, such as Whately or Senior could and did give, and they stayed on the course away from the shoals of the labor theory of value. No wonder that the members of the English Classical School ignored them, for they scarcely knew enough about the subject to warrant an attack.

Since they stirred no controversy at the time, since no subsequent writers mentioned their ideas, Jevons came across no traces of their work in London in the winter of 1859-60 when he worked on the theory of value.

III

T. W. Hutchinson advanced the view that a consideration of the problems of railroads or other businesses with large overhead costs had provided the impetus common in many countries that led economists to marginal economics during the last part of the nineteenth century.[15] If the Drummond and Whately Professors did not shape Jevons, perhaps the railroads did. His birth date, September 12, 1835, and birthplace, Liverpool, England, certainly put Jevons' whole early life in close contact with the building of the original English railroads. Jevons had an early interest in the subject, to be sure, for he had written for the Australian newspapers on railroads.[16] His article, however, shows no realization of the relation of marginal costs to the successful operation of a railroad and, of course, has nothing to do with marginal utility. Nothing else in Jevons' work bears out a direct link between the railroads and his use of marginal analysis, particularly marginal utility analysis.

J. R. Hicks made an indirect bridge between the railroad problem and Jevons' marginal analysis by way of Dionysius Lardner's *Railway Economy*.[17] Hicks suggested that, through reading Lardner, Jevons had felt the influence of Cournot and thus had received the idea of marginal analysis for application to utility from that authentic source itself. Perhaps so, but with as much, or more, justification, we could say that Jevons had come under the influence of Dupuit when he read Lardner. For Lardner expressly based his analysis of railway expenses on "a series of papers on the distribution of the expensés of a railway in the 'Annales des Ponts et Chaussées' and other periodicals."[18] Lardner specifically mentioned Pierre Adolphe Jullien, whose principal article on transportation cost appears in the same volume that contains Dupuit's now famous article "De la mesure de l'utilité des travaux publics."[19] Not only did Dupuit publish in the identical volume to which Lardner turned for

6

support, but the article he published there concerns the problem of optimum rates, a subject in which Lardner had an interest, and it uses demand curves in its analysis, a procedure Lardner also employed. How could Lardner have avoided seeing Dupuit's writings on the economics of transportation? Of course, little or nothing of the express message of Dupuit came through Lardner in a clearly recognizable form, as little or none of Cournot came through.

IV

Jevons had found his interest in economics less than two years before he discovered the importance of utility. At the age of twenty-two, while still in Australia, he wrote to his sister that "thoroughly to understand the principles of society appears to me now the most cogent business."[20] Before this time (1858) he had what everyone might have supposed was an enduring and keen interest in the physical sciences. He never explained his change from the physical to the social sciences beyond saying that there "are plenty of people engaged with physical science, and practical science and arts may be left to look after themselves."[21]

After he once announced this new interest in economics he adhered to it steadfastly. A year later he wrote his sister that although the physical sciences provide "almost an infinite field for work . . . more is really to be done in the scientific investigation of man."[22] At the same time he contemplated staying by the method of the physical sciences at least to the extent of applying mathematics to his study of society. "Most of my theories," he said, "proceed upon a kind of mathematical basis, but I exceedingly regret being unable to follow them out beyond general arguments."[23]

As a consequence of his new inclination he set about the study of both economics and calculus when he returned from Australia and began work at University College, London, in the autumn of 1859. It was the systematic study of economics at this time that provided him with the immediate incentive for the discovery of marginal utility. At the time Jevons attended, Jacob Waley held the professorship of Political Economy at University College and consequently in some way may have incited Jevons' utility discovery. But his influence must have been indirect and certainly unintended. Waley's main interest lay in the law, where he had a notable career, and he gave only a small fraction of his time to economics. His main tasks as a professor consisted in delivering a course of lectures and in set-

7

ting an examination. When Jevons attended, Waley lectured each Tuesday, commencing November 13, 1859, from 5:20 to 6:20 in the evening, giving about twenty lectures during the year.[24] Jevons could not have heard many of them in the three months between the time when he began to listen to Waley and the date on which he finally saw the connection of utility with the problems of economics. The topics that Waley listed for his lectures follow closely the order of the chapters in J. S. Mill's *Principles* and did not offer Jevons any direct help in his use of utility.[25]

Jevons' work on utility may well have accounted for his poor showing in the spring examination in political economy. Very probably he spent too many hours on his own novel ideas and too little effort on the reading in Mill that Waley prescribed, to do as well as he believed he should. He thought that he ought to have won first place. Instead he tied for third.[26] Jevons blamed Waley and attributed his own relative failure to "a difference of opinion, which is perfectly allowable, having prejudiced the professor against my answers."[27] Without other evidence we may well take this student's charge against the professor lightly. We can be sure that Waley's supposed prejudice could not have arisen from a total ignorance of mathematics, since he himself had taken a first place in mathematics when he graduated B. A. at London University in 1839.[28] Further, the examination that he set in 1860 contained few, if any, questions that could have given Jevons an opportunity to use his own new views of utility, or of the relation of mathematics to economics. It did have many questions that offered him a chance to use an extensive knowledge of Mill.[29] Waley also showed his lack of prejudice against Jevons some six months later when he co-operated in awarding the Ricardo Scholarship to the latter. But whether or not Jevons did less well than he had anticipated because of a neglect of Mill or because of any antipathy he could have aroused in Professor Waley, the course of lectures given by Waley and the preparation for the examination provided the incentive for his concentrated attention to economics, and hence to marginal utility, at this time.

V

Emil Kauder associated the differences in the explanation of value with the religious backgrounds of the early economists.[30] He found that the Protestants leaned toward a labor theory and the Catholics toward a utility theory. Kauder admitted that his thesis did not apply in the same way to economists of the nineteenth century, when economists "in general no longer thought in accordance with their religious backgrounds."[31]

Nonetheless, religion played a part in Jevons' use of utility, though not of the sort Kauder specified. Not that Jevons ever displayed any interest either in the content or forms of religion. But his parents did, and their early upbringing of him exerted an influence. Both of his parents belonged to the Unitarian Church and doubtless met each other through their common interest in Unitarianism. An account of his mother's life says that she "married Thomas Jevons, the Unitarian."[32] At the time of the marriage she was the thirty-year-old daughter of a leading citizen of Liverpool, William Roscoe (bankrupt, but still prominent culturally), while Thomas Jevons belonged to a family of small manufacturers that had moved recently from near Birmingham and that never had enjoyed much success. The marriage between Thomas Jevons and Mary Anne Roscoe had, as its most notable issue, the son whom the mother named William Stanley after her brother, and for whom she wrote celebrating the occasion of his birth a sonnet with the opening lines:

> Bright beam of joy, amidst the gloom,
> My lovely babe! My latest born![33]

In most ways W. S. Jevons resembled his mother's side of the family rather than his father's. His mother had spent her first thirty years in close association with her father and, although she died before William Stanley reached adolescence, she evidently had managed to transfer to him many of the remarkable characteristics of her family. Later, when Jevons attended University College, he lived with a maternal uncle who gave him a further acquaintance with the Roscoe family.

Unitarianism carried with it a special set of attitudes toward authority and proof, some parts of which Jevons must have learned from his parents. He certainly showed a willingness to defend unorthodox positions, in value theory as well as in other kinds of theory and, although this impulsion toward nonconformity doubtless had many sources, the nonconformist religion of his parents must have given it essential encouragement. Unitarianism also contained a rationalistic, analytical view of man and nature, a desire to resolve situations into their elemental and component parts. Jevons applied this approach to economics, for marginal utility theory consists of the

9

resolution of consumption into many distinct parts and in an analysis of the relations among them.

Unitarianism also had several direct influences on Jevons. It barred him, so long as he dissented, from Oxford or Cambridge. Accordingly he went to University College, London, and came under all the influences there present. And the Unitarian Church provided Jevons' most active and notable disciple, Philip Wicksteed. Wicksteed might have known of Jevons under any circumstances, but the fact that Jevons dissented must have helped recommend Jevons' *Theory* to Wicksteed. Without the connection between Wicksteed and Jevons, the development of utility theory would have followed a wholly different course in England.

VI

Undoubtedly Jeremy Bentham's writings did more than any other identifiable circumstance to swing Jevons toward the use of utility. Jevons acknowledged this reliance on Bentham in the preface to the second edition (1879) of the *Theory,* where he said that Bentham's ideas "are adopted as the starting point of the theory given in this work. . . ."[34] In the first edition of the same book, the second chapter had had a completely Benthamic twist and had begun with the statement that "we must undoubtedly accept what Bentham has laid down upon this subject."[35] But most important of all, Jevons' first short account of his utility theory (read publicly in 1862 and initially published in 1863, a good eight years before the first edition of the *Theory*) had had the influence of Bentham marked plainly in at least half of its fourteen paragraphs. The second paragraph says, in part, that "a true theory of economy can only be attained by going back to the springs of human action—the *feelings of pleasure and pain*. . . ."[36] What could ring more clearly of Bentham than a reference to "the springs of human action"? From this early statement we learn that Bentham was not one of the several authors uncovered by Jevons between the time he first wrote on utility theory and the beginning of the seventies when he offered it in a developed form, and used later to give support to his discovery.[37]

When and how did Jevons make the first acquaintance with Bentham's work to the extent that he could use it in his economic analysis? Bentham, of course, had been available for long. He had belonged to the preceding generations and had died three years before Jevons' birth. John Bowring completed the collection of his

10

many scattered writings into the *Works* in 1843, while Jevons still lived as a boy in Liverpool. University College, which he attended both before and after he went to Australia, could have often reminded Jevons of Bentham, who may have had a hand in the creation of the college itself.[38] The library at University College received his books and papers between 1832 and 1853,[39] and the Anatomical Museum displayed his effigy, skeleton, clothes, and walking stick.[40] But Jevons probably never looked closely at Bentham until he returned from Australia, especially since his earlier interests had not followed Bentham's lines. When Jevons returned to London he took up the study of philosophy as well as that of economics. He must have given a good many hours to this subject, for he tied for first place in the college examination on philosophy with one of the best students at that time.[41] His preparation for this examination seems a likely occasion for him to have familiarized himself with the ideas of Bentham.

How much could Jevons profitably have borrowed from Bentham in developing his utility theory of value? Only, in truth, the general idea of a pleasure and pain calculus. Two major considerations bar any direct use of Bentham by Jevons, outside the somewhat irrelevant discussion of the dimensions of pleasure and pain. First, Bentham never dwelt on the pleasures that the daily use of ordinary goods gives people. Marginal utility looks entirely at pleasures of this kind of consumption. In the second place, Bentham hid whatever glimpse of marginal utility he had so well in the bulk of his writings that few people today can uncover it. We must not think, in short, that Jevons only had to look within Bentham's *Works* to discover the idea of utility he needed to round out his mathematical view of the economic process. Bentham had disagreed with Adam Smith's solution of the diamond-and-water paradox in a passage that we can now interpret as containing the essence of the idea of marginal utility. But it remained an extremely minor part of Bentham's economics, and his economics had been a very small section of his total literary output.[42]

VII

"The writer . . . ," Jevons says in the first edition of his *Theory*, "who appears to me to have most clearly appreciated the nature and importance of the law of utility, is Mr. Richard Jennings. . . . "[43] Jennings had first published his opinions on marginal utility in

11

1855,[44] and reaffirmed them in a second book the next year.[45] Jevons mentioned only Jennings' first book, the *Natural Elements of Political Economy,* and certainly never knew the author personally even though both had London addresses. The date at which he first read Jennings' book makes a difference in the nature of his obligation. Did he first see the *Natural Elements* when he lived in Australia? Or did he read it after he returned to England but before he evolved his own similar theory early in 1860? Or did he find it between the time he gave his views their early published form and the time he set about writing the *Theory* during the winter of 1870-71? The last supposition has the most evidence to support it.

To be sure, Jevons could have examined Jennings' book in Australia. A substantial London firm had published it and might have sold it through bookshops in Sydney. But Jevons paid it no attention if he did first read it in those years, for we know enough of his views in his Australian period to conclude that they did not take on any color from Jennings. Especially do we know that even after he returned to England Jevons held a labor theory of value, a view Jennings explicitly warned against.[46] We do not have equally strong evidence that Jevons did not obtain the clue to the proper use of utility from the *Natural Elements* in February, 1860. In that event, Jevons would owe a large debt to Jennings. He could have been led to the *Natural Elements* by a recently published book of John Elliot Cairnes, where he would have found references to Jennings that ought to have aroused his curiosity.[47] But there is considerable evidence that he never knew of Jennings at this time. In the first place, he never alluded to Jennings under these dates in his *Letters & Journal* or in his two early publications on the subject. Nor did he say anything in any of his later writings about his discovery of Jennings in this period. Further, although his views on economics are in accord generally with Jennings', they do not show, in their early statements, any similarity of form of expression that would hint that he had studied Jennings carefully. We can tell by inspection of Jevons' two early pieces on utility that he had read Bentham, but we can gather from them no clue that he had seen Jennings. His *Theory,* on the other hand, mentions, lauds, and quotes Jennings. In many parts it bears a close resemblance to the *Natural Elements* in form and example. Consequently it seems most likely that he discovered Jennings after he took his degree from London University and went to Owens College in Manchester, where he taught economics among other things.

Although Jevons quoted passages only from the *Natural Elements* he could have used Jennings' second book, *Social Delusions concerning Wealth and Want,* with equal effect, for it deals with the same subject matter in much the same way. Both books have in them numerous ideas with which Jevons would have found himself in complete agreement. In the first place, Jennings, although he never employed a mathematical notation himself, advised the use of mathematics in the social sciences, a circumstance that should have appealed to Jevons if it did not influence him. Jennings had possibly read something of early mathematical economics, or at least looked at it, for he used on the title-page of his first book a quotation from William Whewell's papers on the subject.[48] Later he expressed in these words the possible benefits from the application of mathematics to social phenomena: "If it shall ever be found possible to bring to the investigation of these co-ordinate branches of philosophy [psychology and economics] the aid of pure mathematical science, in what degree their language will become more settled, their observations and experiments better directed, and the remote consequences of passing phenomena more faithfully deduced, will be most justly apprehended by those who are most conversant with the history of natural philosophy."[49] Jevons realized that Jennings had appreciated the use of mathematics and quoted another relevant passage on this subject.[50]

Jennings took a clear and strong position when he renounced the labor theory of value. He called it "the great fundamental fallacy, that *all value is derived from human labour;* a fallacy which, although expressed in an abstract proposition and in limited terms, poisons, in its ulterior consequences, the whole administration of our political economy."[51] He quoted Richard Whately in support of his opinion and tied himself in that way to that possible fountainhead of utility theory among the Drummond Professors.[52] Jevons covered over two pages of his *Theory* with one of Jennings' expositions of marginal utility.[53] Jennings gave another example of his effective use of the idea of marginal utility in the following quotation:

. . . no Value can be attached to a limited amount of such objects as exist in unlimited quantities, for the obvious reason that if such an amount were to be withheld, others of equal magnitude could be substituted for it, and this until all the wants of human nature should be

13

satiated. We further observed, that when a moderate quantity of a Commodity has reached the senses of the consumer, each successive addition
of the Commodity produces sensations progressively less and less satisfactory, and *vice versâ*; hence we concluded that, in proportion as
objects are less abundant, any limited quantity must be held more
valuable, and in proportion as they are more abundant, it must be held
less valuable, the Value of every Commodity being dissipated as it increases in quantity, like a circle in the water, till "by broad spreading it
disperse to nought." [54]

This is really a better statement of the idea of diminishing marginal
utility and its relation to the value of goods than the one that Jevons
quoted, and it shows how clearly and perfectly Jennings understood
the relationship. Jevons also cited Jennings on the subject of the increasing marginal disutility of labor.[55] Jevons had expressed this
idea in his earliest statement of the subject, but he saw fit when he
later reworked it in the *Theory* to use Jennings' statement of the
principle.

Much more expressly than Jevons, Jennings tried to wed
economics to the developing subject of psychology. He expressed his
opinion of the generality of psychological or subjective economics in
this elegant sentence: "Matter comes in contact with human organs
externally, as in consumption, or laborious efforts are originated in-
ternally, as in production and distribution; from these causes there
arise sensations, which are more or less satisfactory, or the reverse;
these sensations, when remembered together with the objects, or together with the actions in which they originated, give rise to complex conceptions, in which the objects and the actions are regarded
as more or less valuable: thus, briefly described, is constituted the
chain of causation which leads inwards from matter to the seat of our
ideas."[56] "Why, then," he asked later, "do not our masters in this
branch of political philosophy systematically advert to the principles
of human nature, and apply for assistance, in the midst of their perplexities, to those laws and conditions, a knowledge of which has
won distinction . . . in the annals of mental philosophy?"[57] Jennings
drew to this end on the psychological literature of this time. He
quoted Thomas Brown's *Lectures in the Philosophy of the Human
Mind* (1820) and James Mill's *The Analysis of the Phenomena of
the Human Mind* (1829).[58] This may seem like a modest use of
psychological literature. We must remember, however, that the
histories of psychology mention only one other notable English

14

writer in the first half of the nineteenth century, John Stuart Mill, of whom, of course, Jennings knew.[59]

Chapter II

JEVONS' FIRST PUBLICATIONS ON UTILITY

I

During the summer of 1860, Jevons again paid some attention to economics, especially to the subject of capital.[1] And in the spring of 1861 he worked on his *Statistical Atlas,* which attempted to throw light on "commercial storms."[2] But from this time on until after he received his M. A. in June, 1862, he was mainly absorbed in the studies for his degree. In September of 1862, over two years after he had announced his views on utility to his brother, he returned to theoretical economics. At that time he sent two papers on economics to the meeting of the British Association for the Advancement of Science in Cambridge. He did not read them himself, presumably because of his long-standing nervousness in front of an audience. Of his paper entitled "Notice of a General Mathematical Theory of Economy," a paper which contains his first publication on the subject of utility, he wrote his brother: "Although I know pretty well the paper is perhaps worth all the others that will be read there put together, I cannot pretend to say how it will be received—whether it will be read at all, or whether it won't be considered nonsense. . . . I am very curious, indeed, to know what effect my theory will have both upon my friends and the world in general. I shall watch it like an artilleryman watches the flight of a shell or shot, to see whether its effects equal his intentions."[3]

The effect did not equal his intentions. The secretary reported to Jevons that he had read both papers and that the second one, "On the Study of Periodic Commercial Fluctuations," was approved.[4] The outcome dampened Jevons' spirits. He wrote on the last day of 1862 that the year had seen " . . . my theory of economy offered to a learned society (?) and received without a word of interest or belief. It has convinced me that success in my line of endeavour is even a slower achievement than I thought. This year has taken much youthfulness out of me."[5]

We can only conjecture who attended this meeting in Cambridge. The following were quite likely among those present on the occasion: Edwin Chadwick, president of Section F and possibly Bentham's most enthusiastic disciple; Henry Dunning Macleod, one

16

of the section's secretaries who himself read a paper; Edmund Macrory, the other secretary and the one who read Jevons' papers; Henry Fawcett; W. T. Thornton; Herman Merivale; and David Chadwick, all of whom presented papers. We can also name three writers who, since they were in Cambridge at this time, might have heard Jevons' papers read but probably did not. The first of these is Alfred Marshall, who had arrived in Cambridge in 1862 to begin his second year of study.[6] The second is William Whewell, a resident of Cambridge, and a vice-president of the British Association, who ought to have felt attracted by the title of the one of Jevons' papers on the application of mathematics to economics, for he had himself written on this then novel subject years before. The third is Fleeming Jenkin, who eight years later stimulated Jevons to write his principal book, who attended the meetings of the Association, but who doubtless spent his time at other sections.

What an odd circumstance that, among those who could have easily listened to Jevons' paper that introduced marginal utility, and who ought to have had the disposition to do so, but who almost certainly did not hear it read, we find Alfred Marshall, whose friends later advanced his claims as an independent discoverer of marginal utility theory; William Whewell, the first Englishman to associate mathematics and economics; and Fleeming Jenkin, who subsequently used graphical devices in the solution of economic problems in a way that alarmed Jevons and caused him to hasten the publication of the *Theory* to establish his priority!

II

The next year the published report of the meetings in Cambridge put the ideas of Jevons on marginal utility into print for the first time under the title "Notice of a General Mathematical Theory of Political Economy."[7] The "Notice" contains one page of small type divided into fourteen numbered paragraphs. Into this short space Jevons packed all the essentials of his system. He presented his argument simply without any mathematical notation or graphical device. The first paragraph advocates reducing the main problems of economics to a rigorous mathematical form. Paragraphs two to seven begin by offering pain and pleasure as springs of conduct but admit that other motives must be recognized, and end with the statement of the idea of diminishing marginal utility. Paragraph eight identifies pain with labor. The ninth paragraph contradicts an assumption of the labor theory of value. The center of this "Notice" lies in paragraph ten that defines the conditions of the equilibrium of exchange between two persons who bring two goods to market. In the next paragraph Jevons extends his model from two individuals and two commodities to several individuals and many commodities. Few people know that Jevons insisted, at the start of his work on economic theory, on what economists now call the "general equilibrium." Paragraph twelve connects production with the problem of exchange. Jevons considers capital and interest in the next to the last paragraph and ends with a paragraph in which he promises to amplify the model still further in the future.

Three years later he published a longer version of this paper in the *Journal of the Statistical Society of London*, with the title, "Brief Account of a General Mathematical Theory of Political Economy."[8] This journal was sent to the Society's three to four hundred members, certainly the largest audience of people likely to appreciate specialized arguments on utility theory in England. The "Brief Account" is over three times as long as the earlier "Notice."

In the first seven sections, the "Brief Account" follows closely the outline given in the "Notice." Although he says that the "easy comprehension" of the "quantitative laws [of economics] has been prevented by a neglect of those powerful methods of expression which have been applied to most other sciences with so much success,"[9] he himself made no use of mathematical notation or of anything except the simplest mathematical ideas. He introduced a new paragraph concerning the manner in which we "always treat feelings as being capable of *more or less . . .*" and on how "an estimation of the comparative amounts of feeling is performed in the act of choice or volition."[10] He amplified, too, the idea of *intension* and *duration* of pleasure. He ended his discussion of the anticipation of utility with the remark that "the effects of *foresight* merely complicate without altering the other parts of the theory."[11] Yet he urged in the "Brief Account" in a sentence he had omitted from the "Notice" "that we must carefully distinguish *actual utility* in present use from *estimated future utility. . . .*"

Jevons made the most significant changes in the section which introduces the idea of diminishing marginal utility. He probably rewrote this particular section before offering it in 1866, since he introduced different terminology to express his ideas. Especially is this true of the expression by which he conveyed the idea of marginal

18

utility. In his first reference to the idea in the letter to his brother in the middle of 1860 he had referred to the degree of "the utility or benefit derived from the last portion used . . . " and probably also had intended the same conception when he wrote of the "*ratio of utility*."[12] In the "Notice" of 1863 Jevons began by speaking of the "*ratio of utility* on the last increment . . . " and asked that it be called "the *final ratio of utility*."[13] Here in 1863 for the first time Jevons used the word "final" in connection with utility. In the paper in 1866 he first referred to "the utility of the last supply of an object . . .," and then said, "We must recede to infinitesimals, and what we shall call the *coefficient of utility,* is the ratio between the last increment or indefinitely small supply of the object, and the increment of pleasure which it occasions, both, of course, estimated in their appropriate units."[14] This is a new term, the "*coefficient of utility,*" of which the earlier paper had no trace. The term "final ratio of utility" recurs later in the same paper with no definition. Jevons possibly changed the first "final ratio" to "coefficient" but did not change the second.

The longer account also has in it added emphasis and a few additions. Jevons gave an emphasis to the importance of the law of diminishing utility that his earlier publication lacked. He called it in 1866 "the most important law of the whole theory."[15] He included the case of indivisible goods, whereas earlier he had stuck to the case of perfectly divisible goods, and he commented on the economic significance of the failure of his system of equations in the case of indivisibility.[16] He also included a paragraph that points out that we will not find the conditions of his model, which are those of "*theoretic perfection and complication,*" in the real world where we will have to be content with "*approximate and empirical laws.*"[17] He made an application of utility by working out in more detail the idea of the gain in utility that results from trade.

In the "Brief Account" Jevons elaborated the connection of exchange with the production of goods themselves. He realized that when he introduced the production of goods he added sets of unknowns and an equal number of sets of equations. Jevons—to repeat at more length what was briefly mentioned earlier—stated the essential ideas of the *general* equilibrium before Walras had ever published on the subject. Here is his statement of the idea in 1866:

The principle of exchange thus deduced in the case of two persons and two commodities, applies to any number of persons and commodi-

19

ties. It, therefore, applies not only to the general inland trade of a country, but to the trade between aggregates of men or nations—international trade.

The number of equations is very rapidly increased according to the simple law of combinations.

.   .   .   .

Combining the theory of exchanges with that of labour and production, the quantity which each person produces will be dependent upon the result of the exchanges; for this may greatly modify the conditions of utility.

A new set of unknown quantities are thus introduced; but it will be found that just as many new equations to determine them may be established. Each such equation is between the utility of the last increment of produce and the increment of labour necessary to produce it.[18]

Walras nevertheless deserves all of the credit he gets, for he developed in detail the broader, more complicated kind of model. Jevons only stated his plan at this point and apparently forgot it afterwards.

III

In the five years following 1866 no book on economics referred to either of Jevons' early publications on utility. Apparently the only mention either of them received at the time was a short review of the "Brief Account" in the *Journal des économistes* by Maurice Block, who later gave marginal utility its first extensive consideration in a history of economic thought and whom writers sometimes class as a member of the Marginal Utility School.[19] Block paid principal attention to Jevons' advocacy of the use of mathematics in economics. Had Walras, who was a reader of this periodical, attended to what Block said, he might have become acquainted with Jevons' utility theories some five years earlier than he did.

Jevons gave the idea of utility little attention after the middle of 1866 until he began to write *The Theory of Political Economy* in the winter of 1870-71.[20] Even his address as president of Section F showed no interest in the abstract theoretical branches of economics.[21] No one could predict from it that Jevons would publish the next year one of the outstanding books of the century on economic theory.

Sometime after he delivered this address he took up the writing of *The Theory of Political Economy*. His wife recounted this shift, but gave no explanation of it: "For the last three or four years Mr.

Jevons' thoughts had been mainly occupied with logic, but during this winter he returned with renewed interest to political economy, and devoted himself entirely to the writing of *The Theory of Political Economy*. The work was of such absorbing interest to him that he made rapid progress with it, to the detriment of his health, as it afterwards proved."[22] H. Stanley Jevons, the son of William Stanley Jevons, first announced a clue to the circumstance that led Jevons to return suddenly to the writing of the *Theory* in the winter of 1870-71. His announcement, which appears in the preface he prepared for the fourth edition of the *Theory* in 1911, runs as follows:

According to one of my father's MS. notes, which I have been lucky enough to discover, the publication of the *Theory of Political Economy* might have been delayed considerably later than 1871 had it not been for the appearance in 1868 and 1870 of articles by Professor Fleeming Jenkin . . . which are distinctly mathematical in method and contain a number of very ingenious geometrical diagrams illustrating the laws of supply and demand. My father in this note mentions that Professor Jenkin had opened a correspondence with him on the subject of the mathematical treatment of economics and the use of curves, and that this was followed by the publication of the latter's "Graphic Representation of the Laws of Supply and Demand," and concludes: "Partly in consequence of this I was led to write and publish the *Theory* in 1871."[23]

J. M. Keynes obtained a copy of this note to which H. Stanley Jevons refers and included it in an article on William Stanley Jevons. Keynes wrote:

This note (as nearly as I can decipher it—written, as usual, on the back of an old envelope) runs as follows:—

"In regard to this & certain other essays of Professor Fleeming Jenkin, it seems desirable that I should make the following explanation, to prevent misapprehension. My theory was originally read at the Brit. Assoc. in 1862, & printed in the Stat Journal in 1867 (*sic*). In March 1868 Prof Jenkin wrote an article for the Br. Quarterly Review (*sic*) in which he restated (?) . . . the law of supply and demand in math language. He courteously sent a copy to me and requested my opinion thereon; in replying I sent a copy of the paper mentioned above, & a correspondence ensued concerning the correctness of the theory, in the course of which curves were used in illustration by both parties.

In 1870 appeared Prof. Jenkins "Graphic Illustration (*sic*)" in which no reference is made to my previous (?).

Partly in consequence of this I was led to write & publish the Theory in 1871.

In 1872 Prof. Fleeming Jenkin published in the Proceedings of the Roy Soc Edin (?)."[24]

Unfortunately none of this correspondence between Jenkin and Jevons is known to survive. We can, of course, look at the three articles by Jenkin which Jevons mentioned. They constitute Jenkin's entire list of publications on the subject of economics. They reveal that Jevons feared only that Jenkin's use of mathematics would rob his own prospective publication of priority. At least he should not have feared that he would lose his priority in the use of utility, for Jenkin would have nothing to do with that part of Jevons' arguments.

The first article that Jenkin wrote on a subject in economics concerned trade unions. He had become interested in them because of a strike in a plant where he served as an apprentice. In his article, Jenkin included one section on the relation of political economy to trade unions.[25] In it Jenkin does not use anything like the idea of utility, but does use a mathematical notation. Jenkin never related utility to value. In fact, he stated a cost-of-production theory of value when he says that the price of goods "which can be multiplied at will is rightly supposed to depend ultimately on the cost of production."[26]

Two years later Jenkin wrote again on the same subject but increased considerably his emphasis on the demand and supply analysis, this time giving it a graphic representation.[27] In this article he gave to English economics for the first time a full paraphernalia of demand-and-supply curves. It does not, however, include a treatment of any aspect of the subject of utility, except insofar as the reader may presume that the utility of the good to the purchasers underlies the position of the demand curve.

Fleeming Jenkin did not accept the importance of the idea of utility in economic analysis even in the third and last piece of writing on economics, an article written after he had corresponded with Jevons and after he had seen Jevons' *Theory*. Following a clear account of the idea of consumer's surplus and producer's surplus in connection with the problem of the incidence of taxation, Jenkin states his objection to the use of utility curves rather than demand curves as follows: "Professor Jevons has used curves to integrate what he terms the utility gained by exchange in a manner analogous to the above; but utility, as he defines it, admits of no practical measurement, and he bases his curve, not on the varying estimates of value set by different individuals each on what he has or what he wants, but on the varying utility to each individual of each increment of goods."[28]

Once started, Jevons composed *The Theory of Political Economy* rapidly. It was published in October, 1871.

Chapter III

MENGER'S PREPARATION FOR THE PUBLICATION
OF THE *GRUNDSÄTZE*

I

As we have seen, Jevons published a good deal before his major book on economics appeared at the beginning of the eighteen-seventies. Walras, likewise, had a long publishing history prior to the appearance of his most important book. Some of these writings help explain the course of the development of their views on marginal utility and its relation to economics. We have no available earlier writings by Menger to consider in the same manner. In his bibliography, the *Grundsätze* heads the list of Menger's publications.

In addition, both Jevons and Walras left a reasonably complete record of their lives both before, and after, the publications of the books that established their reputations. Jevons wrote journals and saved copies of his letters. Léon Walras, likewise, kept his letters and notes. For Menger we have no similar primary source, and as a consequence, we know few of the outward circumstances of Carl Menger's early life.[1] Only a shadow of the course of his ideas before 1871 remains.

We only know that an Austrian civil servant, nearing the end of his twenties, after receiving in 1867 a *Dr. Jur.* degree from Cracow for work done mostly at Vienna and Prague, and after acquiring at home some inclination towards the study of social sciences (at least his two brothers turned in that direction), sought to teach at the University of Vienna and, as a first step thereto, prepared as a *Habilitationsschrift,* his *Grundsätze der Volkswirtschaftslehre.*

According to his son, his notes show that he turned to a study of economics and its literature in the autumn of 1867, that he was unsatisfied with both the practical and theoretical significance of the cost theory of value, and that he developed his own views on subjective value late in 1867 and in the spring of 1868.[2] Wieser said that Menger told him that he had been drawn to the development of his ideas while a journalist covering market conditions for the *Wiener Zeitung.*[3] At this time he reportedly noted that the prices of goods did not seem to be determined in the manner that his study

24

of economics would have led him to believe. As a consequence he came to believe that utility rather than cost controlled the price of a good.

II

Menger's ideas doubtless crystallized during the time of his employment with the *Wiener Zeitung*. But other forces moved him in the direction of a new theory of value, aside from his observation of markets. Earlier he had developed studious interests that had turned toward economics. In pursuing his studies he had run across a controversy then going on over the subject of value among German economists. It was quite as much this controversy as anything else that caused him to formulate his own ideas. Menger said as much in the statement that "the reform of the most important principles here attempted is therefore built upon a foundation laid by previous work that was produced almost entirely by the industry of German scholars."[4]

Menger must certainly have had reference to the following writers whom he lists as being concerned with the central theme of the *Grundsätze*: Eberhard Friedlander; A. E. F. Schäffle; Hermann Roesler; Otto Michaelis; Arnold Lindwurm; Karl Knies; and Johann von Komorzynski.[5] A glance shows that the usual lists of the predecessors in the development of marginal utility do not contain these names.

What did Menger owe to these seven articles by German authors on the subject of value? In the first place, we may say that Menger did not borrow from any one of them any idea that comes close to the idea of *marginal utility*. Menger could not possibly borrow this idea from them, because not one of these articles contains as much as a hint of marginal utility. And since Menger's main contribution concerns this idea, these writers clearly do not influence Menger's principal contribution. But they did influence him in other ways. Indeed Menger would probably never have written the *Grundsätze* had not these seven articles first appeared in Germany. This widespread German discussion of the nature of value spurred Menger on to write his book. The freedom from subservience to the labor theory of value that these German authors enjoyed permitted Menger to explore, without any feeling of guilt, the byways of the analysis of needs and to construct the Austrian version of the marginal utility theory of value. Thus Menger composed his *Grundsätze* with a sense

25

of the continuity of national thought, while, in contrast, Jevons designed his *Theory* to break with the main current of English thought on value. Walras' position, on this score, lay between Menger's and Jevons', since French economists have a more eclectic and less positive position.

Menger's references to his indebtedness to the German writers on value in the generation before 1871 mean only that he regarded his own work as a capstone to the series of seven articles that he evidently had read carefully. He aimed to say the last word on the subject. The detailed references to the works of the different writers, which Menger gave in the *Grundsätze,* show that he had only the slightest particular indebtedness to any of them.[6] He criticized more often than praised whenever he singled out specific parts of the seven articles for attention. In general, Menger, in his references to the seven writers, did not flatter them in the way that Jevons, or even Walras, flattered his predecessors.

Menger also mentioned in the *Grundsätze* a list of writers known for their use of utility in the estimation of value: Bastiat, Condillac, Galiani, Lauderdale, Senior, and Turgot.[7] In addition he referred to Genovesi, J. B. Say, and Auguste Walras, all of whom others later associated with the predecessors of the utility school, although Menger himself did not so identify them. None of those in either group played a major role in the history of marginal utility, for none of these writers connect the idea of diminishing marginal utility with the problem of value.

III

Forty years after the publication of the *Grundsätze* Menger threw some supplementary light on the writers who had influenced his thought before 1871, in a letter he wrote to explain his position at Vienna.[8] In this letter, Menger recalled his father's large library and attributed to it a familiarity with good books at an age when other boys occupied themselves with stamp collections and adventure stories. Among the authors who wrote on economics and whom Menger remembered he had read early in life are a number—such as J. B. Say, Lauderdale, and Condillac—whom other writers subsequently characterized as predecessors of the Marginal Utility School. As to these writers, the letter adds nothing to what the references to them in the *Grunsätze* already imply.

But the name of A. A. Cournot in Menger's letter does startle us.

Of course Cournot did not use utility itself in his analysis, but he did use derivatives freely, and the first derivative of a function gives the essence of the idea of *marginal* utility. The incorporation of Cournot's name is startling because F. A. von Hayek, who, from his long and many connections with the Austrian School, should know quite well the Viennese view of the matter, states that "particularly significant is his [Menger's] apparent ignorance, at the time when he wrote the *Grundsätze,* of the work of Cournot, to whom all the other founders of modern economics, Walras, Marshall, and very possibly Jevons, seem to have been directly or indirectly indebted."[9] Apparently no one has ever called Menger's statement of his knowledge of Cournot into question. Of course Menger did not say expressly to which of Cournot's many and different books he acknowledged indebtedness. We infer, however, from his steadfast interest in economics and from his subsequent discussion in the letter, that Menger must refer to the *Recherches sur les principes mathématiques de la théorie des richesses* of Cournot.[10] At least the letter makes it clear that Menger in 1911 did not think that he had ignored the "work of Cournot," as Hayek states that he had.[11]

27

Chapter IV

LÉON WALRAS' OBLIGATION TO HIS FATHER

I

Léon Walras acclaimed his father to be the principal source from which he drew his ideas on utility and value. "C'était la théorie de feu mon père et mon maître," Walras said, "que la rareté est la cause de la valeur d'échange."[1]

Auguste Walras, the father of Léon, died of sorrow, according to the doctor who attended him.[2] Perhaps the father communicated to the son some of the disposition that led to his own unhappiness, for Léon Walras had a band of discontent in his own nature similar in extent and character to that of his father. Auguste Walras had attended the École Normale Superieure in the same class with A. A. Cournot. Unlike Cournot, however, he did not receive any training in mathematics, for he followed a course in philosophy and humanities. After he left the École Normale in 1822 he spent his lifetime in the French school system either as a teacher or administrator in a lower secondary school (collège) or as a superintendent of schools (inspecteur d'académie).

Auguste Walras never felt satisfied with his work. He had trouble with his superiors and he moved from one place to another: to Valence, Saint-Étienne, Évreux, Lille, Caen, Douai, and finally to Pau. Perhaps he was dissatisfied because he never obtained any academic status that required him to teach economics. France offered few such opportunities during his life, for only the Collège de France and the Conservatoire National des Arts et Métiers had professorships in economics. When Jean Baptiste Say, who held both of these chairs, died in 1832, Auguste Walras offered himself as a candidate. He failed, of course, to obtain either chair; instead, Adolphe Blanqui became professor at the Conservatoire and P. L. E. Rossi at the Collège de France.[3] The father, like the son, did not find a use for his talents in economics in France. Both represented unpopular views, and had very specialized talents for which France offered an extremely limited market. Insofar as Auguste Walras deserved the title of economist, he merited it for activities outside his academic duties, for his personal studies, his writings, his public lectures, and for the influence on his son.

28

II

The subject of economics had, for Auguste Walras, an early and lasting fascination. According to his own account, his interest in the concept of "property" first led him to examine economics in the hope that the economists could throw more light on that subject than the jurists.[4] He commenced his study of "property" after his first unsatisfactory brush with teaching, when he returned to Paris with the decision to follow the study of the law. Finding no more help from the economists than from the jurists, he began to formulate his own views of economics sometime in the eighteen-twenties, perhaps around 1826. His formulation centered in a study of the theory of value. After he arranged his ideas in the form of a book, he had the difficulty of an unknown and young author in finding a publisher. He published part of the MS in a periodical[5] before he found the necessary assistance to bring it out as a book with the title, *De la nature de la richesse et de l'origine de la valeur.*[6] It contains little besides a study of value and is perhaps the first long book ever published on that subject.

In Auguste Walras' search for the cause of value, he found no satisfaction in the labor theory of the English Classical School and as little in the utility theory of writers such as J. B. Say. He clearly attempted to reject both labor and utility as a cause of value. Like Jevons, Menger, and his own son, Auguste Walras saw the flaws in the existing theories and tried to remove them with a new theory. On the positive side, Auguste Walras traced the cause of the value of a good to a phenomenon which he termed *rareté*. He concerned himself with this idea of *rareté* as the cause of value many times during the remainder of his life: he published three articles on the subject;[7] he wrote another book on the same lines in 1849, his *Théorie de la richesse sociale ou résumé des principes fondamentaux de l'économie politique;*[8] he taught several free public courses in economics at Évreux, Paris, and Pau, in which he doubtless touched on value.[9]

III

It is well known that Léon Walras adopted this word *rareté* from his father and used it in the sense of marginal utility. But it is equally clear that the father did not have the son's interpretation in mind. At several points it seems as though the course of his argu-

29

ment would lead him to the idea of marginal utility. Yet it never did. For instance, in his discussion of the free goods, air and sunlight, he wrote, "Quel est le prix d'un mètre cube d'air? . . . Que me donnera-t-on en échange d'un rayon de soleil?"[10] Here he looked directly at the cubic meter of air and at the single ray of sunshine. Why did he not discover the idea of marginal utility at this very moment? He had replaced his consideration of the total quantity of air with the consideration of a single cubic meter and a regard for all of sunlight with the regard for a single ray. Auguste Walras must have realized that the key to value lies in disregarding the whole and concentrating on the part. He thus seems inches away from a marginal utility theory of value. He needed only to say that another single cubic meter of air has no value because it provides no utility, while the previous meters of air do, and to make a similar statement for sunshine. But he did not make these statements. Instead, he concluded with the true but ineffectual explanation that since Providence had supplied us with all we can use no one needs to buy any. He failed to see what so many before him likewise had failed to see.

Certain differences in the purpose and character of his analysis made it easy for Auguste Walras to avoid the later conclusions of the Marginal Utility School, conclusions which seem so obvious today. For one thing, Auguste Walras sought, in the main, only the *cause* of value. He wished largely to find some criterion by which to decide whether a good does or does not form a part of the wealth of the country. Notice carefully the title of his first book: *De la nature et de l'origine de la valeur*. Mark also the title of his last book: *Théorie de la richesse sociale*. He never had any interest in investigating the relative values of the different goods that constitute the wealth of the country. He had no interest in price as an allocating device. The pioneers of the Marginal Utility School had the advantage that each of them sought the principle that apportions the economy's resources to the production of different goods and then divides these goods among the various consumers. Auguste Walras needed to know only a principle through which he could select things to be included in his definition of property. For such a limited purpose *rareté* served well; he did not require so elaborate a concept as marginal utility.

A second circumstance that made it impossible for Auguste Walras to conceive of the idea of marginal utility was the fact that he never considered the problem of an individual's consumption of different quantities of a single commodity.[11] The consumer in Auguste Walras' analysis consumes different goods, which different goods give him different levels of satisfaction, but he never varies the amount of consumption of a particular good. A good, in short, of a particular kind has, in Auguste Walras' analysis, an *intensité* of utility to the individual. Utility varies in quantity only in its extension, which meant, to Walras, in the number of individuals who enjoy the good. Clearly, throughout Auguste Walras' analysis, the consumer has only the choice of consuming or not consuming and never has the opportunity to consume more or less of a good. For example, Walras pointed out many goods that particular consumers do not desire. Consumers in good health do not desire medicine. Only a soldier or hunter wants a gun. Women have no use for razors and men no need for bracelets and earrings. Walras never considered the question of the diminishing marginal utility of medicine, guns, razors, or bracelets, largely because he thought of each individual using a fixed required amount, a dose of medicine, a gun, a razor, or a bracelet.

The ratio of the quantity of the good available to the number of prospective consumers (each of whom uses a single unit of the good) gives, in Auguste Walras' writings, the *rareté* of the good. *Rareté,* as a number, means the fraction of the population that can have its wants for this particular good satisfied. It does not mean "marginal utility" as we now understand this term. Auguste Walras stated his definition of *rareté* as follows: "Or qu'est-ce qui détermine la rareté et la valeur qui en est la suite? C'est premièrement le nombre ou la quantité des biens limités, et, en second lieu, le nombre des hommes qui en ont besoin, autrement dit la somme des besoins qui en sollicitent la jouissance. La rareté n'est que le rapport entre ces deux nombres."[12] At one place in his writing he appears to come close to the essentials of marginal utility when he likens *rareté* to speed.[13] But Auguste Walras did not intend to imply the idea of speed at a point. He thought of speed as average speed over the entire distance, and he likewise thought of *rareté* as the average number of consumers per unit of the good.

IV

Although Auguste Walras did not have a notion of marginal utility of the kind that later came into such prominence in economics, he did leave to his son an impressive list of views on economics which, since his son regarded them seriously, helped to turn him in the direction of marginal utility analysis. As we have noticed, Auguste Walras introduced his son to a radical viewpoint in economics, the viewpoint that neither the utility theory of value nor the labor theory of value can stand close investigation and that, therefore, a new theory should replace them. Auguste Walras called the new theory that replaced the older theory, *rareté*. The father also approved the use of mathematics in economics even though he did not put his view into practice, a view equally or more radical than the opinion that labor or utility did not suffice to explain value. Léon Walras adopted the new name for the theory that his father suggested, but fortunately he altered the theory to which it applied. He further adopted the view on the relation of mathematics and economics that his father suggested, but, unlike his father, he put this view into practice.

Chapter V

LÉON WALRAS, 1858 - 1873

I

Léon Walras did not make the changes in his father's system of thought that introduced the complete idea of marginal utility until seven years after his father's death in 1866. He began writing, however, on the subject of economics in 1860. His books and articles written between 1860 and 1873 help in the understanding of his reliance on his father's economic views. They show, in this way, the nature of his early conception of utility.

Léon Walras recorded his first encounter with economics and the theory of value, an encounter in which, at the age of fourteen, he listened to his father read part of a manuscript to a neighbor. Of this occasion Léon Walras wrote: "Je me glissais auprès d'eux, et, assis dans un coin, j'écoutais avidement cette lecture. J'ai appris ainsi, à quatorze ans, que le terre et son service avaient une valeur intrinsèque provenant de leur utilité combinée avec la limitation de leur quantité. . . ."[1] Léon Walras wrote this account over a half a century after the event. As a reminiscence it may hold only a part of the truth. But with this limitation it does offer an explanation of the beginning of Léon Walras' allegiance to his father's value theory.

II

After Léon Walras finished his education in 1858 he returned to Paris from a visit to his parents at Pau, evidently with parental forgiveness for wasting his last years in the pretence of studying mining engineering while he actually spent his time dabbling in literature. His father advised him to turn from literature to the social sciences. While he was looking for a subject to write on, he received a letter from his father containing a strong criticism of Proudhon's views, a topic they had evidently discussed before.[2] Léon Walras adopted the refutation of Proudhon as the subject for his first book. His father had not only in a sense suggested the critical study but had also continued to contribute much to the development of the idea through the letters that he sent to his son during this period. Auguste Walras should really share with the son the responsibility of authorship.

33

Before the publication of this book, Léon Walras wrote a long book review that made use of his father's devices, including his father's explanation of value.[3] Near the beginning of the review he said that "on peut énoncer que la valeur d'échange et la propriété naissent ensemble de la rareté ou de la limitation en quantité des utilités."[4] This sentence, which gives Léon Walras' first pronouncement on the theory of value, shows how early and how completely he accepted his father's outlook on the subject. But here, as with his father, he needed only to decide whether a good has or has not value so that he could tell whether or not to classify it as property.

In his first book, *L'Économie politique et la justice*, Léon Walras followed his father's theory of value to the letter.[5] In his first discussion of value in this book he wrote that it "a donc son origine dans la limitation en quantité des utilités qui les fait rares."[6] Léon Walras added nothing to his father's value theory at this time beyond an attempt to relate the idea of *rareté* to the notion of supply and demand, perhaps in an effort to reconcile his father's opinions with the influential ones of Joseph Garnier.[7] He agreed with his father that neither of the two current rival theories of value contains the truth, yet this opinion did not rouse in him quite the antagonism it did in his father. The same faults of analysis that had restrained his father also held him back. He never had an occasion to investigate the circumstances that determine the relative amounts of value that goods have. At this date in his writing and thinking he did not even examine the nature of the pricing system incidentally. He had a social or philosophical interest in value rather than an economic interest. Consequently, he never considered the relation to an individual's satisfaction of the consumption of different amounts of a commodity. Unless he considered the satisfaction from a good as a function of the amount of the good consumed, he had no chance to encounter the key idea of marginal utility.

III

Walras' next book was the *Théorie critique de l'impôt précédée de souvenirs du congrès de Lausanne*.[8] Léon Walras made no use of any variety of value theory in connection with taxation, but nonetheless he introduced his father's views on value gratuitously and out of context: "Dans le traité *De la nature de la Richesse et de l'origine de la Valeur*, mon père établissait, en 1831, que le fait de la valeur d'échange a sa cause non dans le fait du travail, comme l'avaient dit A. Smith et Ricardo, ni dans le fait de l'utilité, comme le disait J.-B. Say, mais dans le fait de la limitation dans la quantité des choses utiles. Cette théorie est la vraie, et elle est la seule d'où l'on puisse inférer que la valeur d'échange a sa mesure dans la rareté ou dans le rapport de la demande à l'offre, c'est-à-dire de la somme des besoins à la somme des provisions."[9]

Just at this time, Auguste Walras sent his son a long letter on the subject of value that may have played a part in helping the son break out of the deadlock on value that his father's set of conceptions entailed.[10] In it the father showed misgivings about some of the ideas he had held on consumption, and they may have later influenced the son. He considered a difficulty in expressing his idea of *rareté* in mathematical terms that had not previously bothered him. Before, he had thought of *rareté* as the ratio of the number of prospective consumers in the market to the number of units of the good, on the assumption that each consumer would desire only one unit of the good. This idea of consumption effectively prevents the use of a utility function. In this letter Auguste Walras took a slight step away from the position by introducing into his consideration the circumstance that some individuals may consume more of a given good than others, and that therefore in representing *rareté* by a fraction, the numerator can no longer consist of the number of consumers. He stated this point very specifically in the following words:

. . . . Un homme qui boit un litre de vin par jour équivaut à deux hommes qui n'en boivent qu'un demi-litre. Il represente également quatre hommes qui n'en boiraient qu'un quart de litre. Une femme qui use six paires de souliers par an équivaut à trois femmes qui n'en useraient que deux paires. Un homme qui est constamment malade, et qui a, chaque jour, besoin du medecin, équivaut à 365 personnes qui ne l'appellent qu'une fois l'an. Voilà ce qui nous empêche de déterminer *l'unité de besoin* pour toutes les espèces de biens ou de denrées qui se consomment dans la société, et telle est, si je ne me trompe, l'obstacle qui s'oppose à ce que les mathématiques s'emparent de l'économie politique, comme elles l'ont fait de la méchanique, de la physique de l'acoustique et de l'optique. Voilà du moins ce qui rendra plus lente et plus difficile l'application des mathématiques à la théorie de la richesse sociale.[11]

Notice that Auguste Walras did not take the further and necessary step to explain that the successive half-litre bottles of wine consumed by the individual who drank two litres each day have unequal importance to him, just as each of the six pairs of shoes must have a different significance to the woman who wore six pairs a year. He never eyed the unequal importance of successive units of consumption, as did his son, and Jevons, and Menger ten years later. He may have stopped where he did because he did not think that the individual could freely choose to consume either much or little wine, or to have many or few shoes. Instead, Auguste Walras may have thought that the individual could afford either much or little wine, or few or many shoes. Or Auguste Walras may have felt that some force within or without the nature of the individual requires that he regulate his consumption in a particular way. In any case, unless the consumer can choose freely, he cannot experience or, at the very least, cannot make use of, any concept of marginal utility.

IV

From the time of the publication of the *Théorie critique de l'impôt* until he wrote his *Recherches de l'idéal social* in 1868 Léon Walras seldom mentioned the theory of value. Most of the topics that he chose to write on during this seven-year period concerned practical matters. He did review Cournot's *Principe de la théorie des richesses* for *L'Independent de la Moselle* in 1863.[12] It gave him an opportunity to express himself both on utility and on mathematical economics of which he did not make use. In his *Recherches de l'idéal social,* which consists of a series of public lectures that he gave in 1867 and 1868 and which he published first in *Le Travail,* he returned to his father's ideas on utility again, to speak this time with emotion since his father had died in 1866.[13] But he added nothing to what he had said about his father's ideas earlier.

V

What writers on economics, besides his father, influenced Walras' views on utility during this early period? In the first part of the *Éléments* (1874) Walras credited Genovesi, Senior, Condillac, and J. B. Say with the use of utility in their analysis of value.[14] In the second part (1877) he brought attention to Jules Dupuit's connection with the discovery of utility before anyone else had publicly noticed Dupuit as a predecessor.[15] This attention of Walras to Dupuit in 1877 does not mean that Walras learned from Dupuit before 1873. Certainly Walras never intended that it should. Walras' reference did not flatter Dupuit, for he said that Dupuit's ideas on

36

utility are no better than Say's. He had said as much, or more, to Jevons in private correspondence during the year.[16] His most specific charge is that Dupuit never differentiated between the utility curve and the demand curve. This criticism is justified, but the insistence on the rigorous distinction between the two curves imposes too harsh a requirement on a writer who treated the subject of utility as early as 1844. It is somewhat of a puzzle why Walras continued throughout his life to ignore Dupuit's claims as a predecessor of the Marginal Utility School, especially in the face of Jevons' candid acceptance of Dupuit as a predecessor of the first rank.[17] At best he evidently made an error of judgment. At worst his neglect may perhaps be blamed on Walras' unconscious jealousy of Dupuit, a jealousy dating back to the early sixties in Paris when Walras had small success in gaining a foothold in French economics while Dupuit enjoyed much esteem as the result of so little apparent effort —a jealousy which did not diminish with the passage of time. Walras showed a continual concern with the problem of priority and with the nature of the contribution he had made to the progress of economics, and whereas he willingly admitted that Gossen had exploited earlier the idea of marginal utility in a volume unknown to anybody, he felt unwilling to concede anything to Dupuit's works, which all economists in France knew. Clearly Léon Walras had read some of the writings of Dupuit on marginal utility before 1877. Possibly he had read them before 1874. He could have profited immensely from them in the formulation of his ideas on marginal utility. Obviously, too, he could have ignored before 1877 the good sense that they contain as he continued to ignore it ever afterward.

VI

The next few years were hard ones for Léon Walras, and he had no time for value theory until after his appointment to the University of Lausanne in 1870. The first clear intimation of the new turn that his ideas had taken after he had reached Lausanne came in the paper that he read to *l'Académie des sciences morales et politiques* at the meetings of August 16 and 23, 1873.[18]

Evidently Walras prepared his paper for the *Académie* by extracting from the manuscript that later became his book. He left out of the paper, for example, all the arguments in the *Éléments* that depend on the use of a general functional notation. He relied on geometry alone for exposition. Jevons, it may be remembered, had depended in his first paper wholly on a verbal analysis, not even using graphs. Walras simplified his exposition by using only his most elementary case in the paper, the case of the two individuals who exchanged two goods. He analyzed it by means of demand curves which he in turn derived from the utility curves of his exchangers.

He omitted from the *Éléments* only one small but significant section that he had incorporated in the paper. In the 1873 paper he had a longer section on the problem of the measurability of utility than he allowed to remain in the manuscript for the corresponding 1874 part of the *Éléments*. This change is significant in that it must reflect his uncertainty in the face of this grave problem. In a way it foreshadowed the attitude he was to take for the remainder of his life toward the question of measurability: the attitude of saying as little as possible about it. In the *Éléments* he said that the difficulty is not insurmountable, for all we have to do is to assume that utility is measurable.[19] In the earlier paper he had to an extent elaborated slightly this rather flimsy justification of his procedures. For one thing, he included a sentence which said that this was the procedure followed in physics in the measurement "des éléments comme les masses."[20] Later he sensed correctly that if he was to "assume" measurability, the less said about the justification, the better.

Chapter VI

ASPECTS OF MARGINAL UTILITY THEORY AS SET FORTH IN JEVONS' *THEORY*, MENGER'S *GRUNDSÄTZE*, AND WALRAS' *ÉLÉMENTS*

I

The three important books that launched the Marginal Utility School came out at the beginning of the eighteen-seventies. William Stanley Jevons' *Theory of Political Economy* and Carl Menger's *Grundsätze der Volkswirtschaftslehre* both appeared in 1871. The first part of Léon Walras' *Éléments d'économie politique pure* followed in 1874 and the second part in 1877. We have already examined the circumstances that led these authors to write these books that started utility theory on its way. As a next step in discussing the rise of the Marginal Utility School, we will compare certain aspects of these three quite independent books.

The three books offered a body of discussion of utility theory far higher in quality and much greater in scope than that contained in the many earlier fragmentary discussions. It provided the sound base upon which the Marginal Utility School rose. In this chapter we will consider in turn the founders' terminological differences, treatment of the utility of the factors of production, view of supposed utility secured by exchange, subdivisions of total utility, problems arising from divisibility, and finally conclusions on the problem of measurement. The next chapter will contain a view of the handling of other problems that arose: interpersonal comparisons, the form of the utility function, marginal utility of income, maximization, the labor theory of value, and the relation to demand curves.

II

Not one of these pioneer members of the Marginal Utility School used the term "marginal utility." The term did not, as explained elsewhere, enter the German language until 1884, the English until 1888, and the French until later.[1] Jevons died before the phrase was coined. Menger lived long after the term "marginal utility" came into common use but never used it himself. Walras stuck to his own peculiar and original synonym for "marginal utility" and never adopted the new term. It did not come into wide use among other economists until the eighteen-nineties.

Both Jevons and Walras at least employed the term "utility" with the meaning now usual in economics, but Menger did not even do that. He insisted that utility, as we now define the word, plays no part in the determination of the value of a good. Menger was a member of the Marginal Utility School who not only never used the word "marginal" but also never used the term "utility" as other people do. For the most part Menger avoided the word "utility." When he did use it he pointed out its inappropriateness for the consideration of value.[2] We may well wonder how Menger could have used "utility" in such a way that it had little to do with value. It is likely that the chief difference in Menger's use of the term lay in his refusal to associate variations in the quantity of utility with variations in the quantity of the good, although he never specifically said so. Menger evidently regarded utility as a quality in much the same way that he would have regarded death as a quality not subject to degrees. Therefore, he firmly opposed associating value, which has gradations, with utility, which comes in a lump.[3]

Menger used "importance of satisfactions" instead of "marginal utility." Satisfaction itself was like utility in that it never varied in amount. But the importance of the satisfaction did.[4] He limited himself to a discussion of the importance of satisfactions that fill concrete needs, by which he meant needs filled by some part of the total quantity of the good. This was the way in which he spoke of the idea of marginal utility. These procedural and verbal differences are apparent in his first general statement of what later becomes known as the law of diminishing marginal utility: " . . . the satisfaction of any one specific need has, up to a certain degree of completeness, relatively the highest importance, and that further satisfaction has a progressively smaller importance, until eventually a stage is reached at which a more complete satisfaction of that particular need is a matter of indifference."[5] Notice the total absence in this quotation of any reference to goods.

Jevons, on the other hand, organized his exposition in terms of the very goods that Menger never specified. At the beginning of his discussion of utility he said that "it is convenient to transfer our attention as soon as possible to the physical objects or actions which are the source to us of pleasures or pains."[6] As a result, Jevons attributed the power to satisfy wants to a good and called this power "utility."[7] He had, consequently, the following description of diminishing marginal utility outwardly dissimilar to the one Menger gave: "The variation of the function expressing the final degree of utility is the all-important point in all economical problems. We may state, as a general law, that *it varies with the quantity of commodity, and ultimately decreases as that quantity increases.*"[8]

Walras had the same approach as Jevons. He merely mentioned the circumstance that the individual derived satisfaction from filling wants. He concentrated attention on the goods that have the power to satisfy wants and that, accordingly, have utility. For this reason, his first expression of the law of diminishing marginal utility reads somewhat like Jevons' but not like Menger's: " . . . I postulate that intensive utilities always diminish from that of the first unit or fraction of a unit consumed to that of the last unit or fraction of a unit consumed."[9]

At first Walras characterized the phenomenon now called "marginal utility" by the expression "intensive utility." He had borrowed the term from his father, who had used it to describe the "plus ou moins grande urgence" of the wants that the consumer feels.[10] After he introduced this term Walras repeated it ten times within a few pages. Then he suddenly began to use *"rareté"* instead, a term that he likewise had borrowed from his father and the term for marginal utility most closely associated with the writings of Léon Walras. He defined *rareté* as "the intensity of the last want satisfied by any given *quantity consumed* of a commodity. . . . "[11] From this passage on, Léon Walras used either the expression *"rareté"* or his definitional phrase "intensity of the last want satisfied" to denote marginal utility.

Walras evidently changed his terms in the midst of his composition, partly to underline the influence of the last unit of consumption in the consumer's behavior. He presumably wished, by the use of the term "intensity of the last want satisfied," to reveal an order of consumption that his graphs and functions did not show. It was not a good reason to make the change.[12] Jevons had followed exactly the same dubious procedure in the *Theory*. He first defined marginal utility without regard to any specific order of consumption on the part of the consumer and then changed to a term he hoped would convey an idea of the importance of the final or terminal unit of any

41

good which the consumer uses. He spoke at first of "intensity of utility," or of "degree of utility," but substituted "final degree of utility" or "terminal utility" when he wished to stress the order of consumption.[13] Menger did not emphasize any time pattern of consumption.

III

All three of the pioneer writers on utility recognized that the factors of production yield utility only in that they produce goods to satisfy consumers' wants. Menger singled out this relationship for the most elaborate study. He divided artificially all goods into different orders in which the value of a higher-order good depends explicitly upon the values of the goods of first order (those immediately suited to consumption). Menger referred to the "direct" and "indirect" satisfaction of human needs from goods of the first and higher orders respectively.[14] In this way Menger has a sort of general equilibrium model. It is an imperfect one, however, for it stresses a cause-and-effect relationship that makes it the exact opposite of a market in which there is simultaneous determination. For this reason Walras had a view of the economic process superior to the one that Menger offered. In his most complete system, Walras had the values of all products and all factors completely interconnected.[15]

Jevons had a name for the utility from a factor of production, "mediate" utility[16] (in contrast with "immediate" utility from a consumption good), but in general he gave the least satisfactory treatment of the relation of the price of factors to the marginal utility of the consumption goods that they produce. He began, as both Menger and Walras did, with an analysis of the determination of the value of consumers' goods. They, however, later tied production to the consideration of consumption. Jevons may have had some similar procedure vaguely in mind, but he never completely accomplished it. Jevons fell more under the sway of the traditional framework of exposition, for, immediately after completing his section on exchange, he spent three chapters on the customary subjects of labor, rent, and capital, which, with a chapter of concluding remarks, completed his book.

IV

Jevons, Menger, and Walras noted that the usefulness of many goods frequently comes from the fact that these goods command

42

other goods in exchange, rather than from the direct satisfaction that the goods return their owners. Walras made the least use of this distinction, although he once stated the idea clearly in the following sentence: "Once all things that can be appropriated . . . have been appropriated, they stand in a certain relationship to each other, a relationship which stems from the fact that each scarce thing, in addition to its own specific utility, acquires a special property, namely, that of being exchangeable against any other scarce thing in such and such a determinate ratio."[17] In the remainder of his analysis he made explicit use only of what he called "specific utility," the utility directly derived from the good itself, although he never again mentioned this term.

Jevons remarked that people value goods, not only because they satisfy needs when consumed, but also because the individual may exchange them for other desirable goods.[18] Jevons fastened the name "acquired utility" to things that have the power of procuring us direct utility through exchange.[19] He tried, unsuccessfully, to make further use of this concept of acquired utility. He said that the "intensity of the need that we have for *more*" of a commodity measures its value, and then added: "But the power of exchanging one commodity for another greatly extends the range of this utility. We are no longer limited to considering the degree of utility of a commodity as regards the wants of its immediate possessor; for it may have a higher usefulness to some other person, and can be transferred to that person in exchange for some commodity of superior utility to the purchaser. The general result of exchange is, that all commodities sink, as it were, to the same level of utility in respect of the last portions consumed."[20]

Menger used the adverbs "directly" and "indirectly" to modify the activity of the individual in obtaining satisfaction, depending on whether the person obtains the enjoyment by the consumption of the commodity itself, or by means of exchange. Menger separated value into "use value" and "exchange value," depending on whether it refers to goods which derive their "value by being employed *directly* in the first case and *indirectly* in the second."[21] He showed that while goods may have use value only or exchange value only, usually they have both, in which case the greater of the two determines the importance of the satisfaction and consequently the economic value of the good.

Surely this implication, by all three of these writers, that *ex-*

43

change value enters as a factor determining exchange value is a basic error. No one of them managed to incorporate the idea in any rigorous way into his argument and, presumably, for the plain reason that it is impossible to make the incorporation. It clearly played no part in the graphs of Jevons and Walras. The use of indirect utility would put a kink in every utility curve at the value at which the utility of the money received for the good was greater than further units of the good itself. To the extent that the marginal utility of income remains constant, the marginal utility curve of the individual for a specified article would flatten. Only for free goods would the marginal utility curve ever touch the quantity axis if the utility curve includes the satisfaction possible through the exchange of the good. Further, every alteration in the exchange value of the good would shift the position of this kink in the curve. Clearly, curves of this kind cannot help to determine exchange value, since they themselves depend upon exchange value.

Related to this idea of indirect utility is the fact that exchangers typically offer in exchange all or none of the good they have in their possession. Producers offer all of their product for sale. Users typically offer none of the product for sale. The pioneers noted this circumstance, remarked the difference of it from the so-called models or generalized examples they had used to illustrate exchange, and frequently tried to explain the difference. Menger did no more than mention the circumstance that some individuals offer for exchange the whole stock of goods they own and others offer none.[22] He could follow this loose procedure in part because he never employed a mathematical model to illustrate the economic process such as Jevons and Walras used. Consequently he could not perceive so clearly the results of offering all or none on the validity of his logic. But even in the case of Menger's arithmetical models the circumstance that the exchangers give all or none should have required some explanation. In Walras' and Jevons' expositions any defect of this kind showed more clearly, and required comment. Jevons referred to the case as a "failure" of the equations of exchange.[23] Walras also realized that, since a good has no *rareté* to an individual who uses none of the good, his system of equations would fail in Jevons' sense. Walras supplied in place of the blank a hypothetical *rareté* of the good which he put in parenthesis to signify that it represents "the intensity of the last want which *is* or which *might have been* satisfied."[24]

44

V

Since Jevons and Walras used mathematical models in the exposition of their ideas on utility, they found it convenient to assume the continuous divisibility of quantities. They both realized that all, or most, of the quantities that concern economic life did not divide in this way, and that, for this reason, their models did not fit reality. To forestall criticism on these grounds both Jevons and Walras altered their basic models in order to make room for indivisibilities in the quantities of good consumed. Menger, since he used arithmetic tables that are discontinuous by nature, had no call to amend his analysis to encompass obviously indivisible goods. On the contrary, he paraded his discontinuities and emphasized them.[25] Menger even imparted this characteristic of his work to his immediate successors in Vienna, who never used continuous functions, and who consequently had their work encumbered in a way that writers elsewhere avoided.

Jevons began with increments of finite size but soon thereafter stated that the law of diminishing utility "may be considered to hold true theoretically, however small the increments are made. . . ."[26] He knew that indivisibilities did not fit into his most general model where they would be another cause of "failure" of his equations of exchange. He knew, too, that examples of discontinuities occur in domestic trade with "every sale of a house, factory, or other building. . . ."[27] Consequently he constructed special models to deal with inequalities. His first one was a model for the exchange of two indivisible goods in which the equations of exchange reduce to two inequalities. These show that each of the two exchangers prefers the good of the other person. He went on to more elaborate cases, concluding with the example of bottles of ink.[28] For this case he drew a graphical solution that showed that the buyer must determine whether each successive bottle gives more utility than the utility the money would return if spent elsewhere.

Discontinuities did not trouble Walras in the first edition of the *Éléments* as they had Jevons, but at several places he clearly showed his awareness of the problem. Walras first called attention to discontinuous variables in his discussion of individual demand curves. He drew a "step curve" to illustrate a discontinuous individual demand curve. He offered the same resolution of the difficulty that Jevons had brought forward, when he mentioned that these discontinuities disappear, or apparently disappear, when the demand of a large number of individuals replaces the demand for a single individual.[29] This justification really ought to have offered him little consolation, since, in the main, his models rest on utility functions, not subject to aggregation, rather than on empirical demand functions. Later, Walras had another suggestion for handling discontinuous utility functions. He suggested the substitution of continuous functions for discontinuous ones, presumably as approximations.[30] Walras gave here the best solution of the problem of indivisibilities. No mathematical model does more than approximate ever so roughly the conditions of the world. A frank realization of the fundamental discrepancy between a mathematical model and the supposed nature of reality will give better results than the imposition of a strain on the model itself through the introduction of elements that interfere with the model's flexibility.

VI

The systematic presentations of Jevons, Menger, and Walras imply the measurability of pleasures, wants, needs, or utilities. Each of these authors realized in some degree the necessity for facing the contradiction that, although his discussion assumed the measurability of such things, no one ever had measured this kind of quantity. Each one sensed, correctly, that his procedures consequently required a defense against future critics. As it turned out, no part of marginal utility analysis was more steadily attacked through the years. The question of the measurement of subjective quantities is still a lively one in economic theory.

The problem worried Menger least. His effort to justify his procedure consisted in a single footnote in which he stated that he did not intend the numbers that he had assigned to represent successive degrees of importance "to express numerically the *absolute* but merely the *relative* magnitudes of importance of the satisfactions in question."[31] He elaborated by saying that "when I designate the importance of two satisfactions with 40 and 20 for example, I am merely saying that the first of the two satisfactions has twice the importance of the second to the economizing individual concerned." Menger was unaware that he had introduced the essence of measurability (in the cardinal sense) when he spoke of one satisfaction being twice another. He evidently believed that he had removed the basic objection to a use of subjective quantities when he denied the importance of any particular zero point or of any unique unit of measurement. He did, of course, himself choose both a zero point and a certain unit of measurement in his principal example of the application of measurement to satisfaction. He selected as a satisfaction of zero value the satisfaction from a good that would add nothing to the total of satisfactions. His greatest satisfaction would have an arbitrary importance value of ten, a number assigned to a unit of the commodity "on which our lives depend. . . . "[32] In between these two extremes ranged nine other stages of satisfaction.

Walras likewise anticipated the objection that he treated immeasurable things as measurable. In the following paragraph Walras cut the Gordian knot by saying that he had "assumed" measurability:

> The above analysis is incomplete; and it seems impossible, at first glance, to pursue it further, because intensive utility, considered absolutely, is so elusive, since it has no direct or measurable relationship to space or time, as do extensive utility and the quantity of a commodity possessed. Still, this difficulty is not insurmountable. We need only assume that such a direct and measurable relationship does exist, and we shall find ourselves in a position to give an exact, mathematical account of the respective influences on prices of extensive utility, intensive utility and the initial stock possessed.
>
> I shall, therefore, assume the existence of a standard measure of intensity of wants or intensive utility, which is applicable not only to similar units of the same kind of wealth but also to different units of various kinds of wealth.[33]

Walras' bland assumption of a cardinal measurement that he never justifies is not a resolution of the problem. He admitted, after his fiat on measurability, that his utility functions "are not determinable" and that only the demand function which depends on the utility functions "remains empirical."[34] However, he would have no part in the measurement of utility by means of the pecuniary sacrifice of the consumer (as shown by a demand curve), and he pointed out in this regard all the inadequacies of the analysis of Dupuit.[35]

To relieve the honest doubts of those who might think the study of economics impossible because of an inability to measure utility, Jevons first offered the hope that, although measurement at the time was impossible, it might well be measured in the future. Jevons opened with the generalization that "nothing is less warrantable in science than an uninquiring and unhoping spirit."[36] He pointed out that measurement had come slowly in studies other than economics. "Previous to the time of Pascal," he asked, "who would have thought

47

of measuring *doubt* and *belief?*"[37] He added electricity and heat as illustrations of fields of study in which measurement came only after students had investigated them for some time.

Jevons insisted that "there can be no doubt whatever that pleasure, pain, labour, utility, value, wealth, money, capital, &c. are all notions admitting of quantity . . .," and, therefore, presumably measurable.[38] He mentioned Bentham's suggestion that pleasures and pains be measured in order to test legislation. Jevons admitted that he did not know where Bentham's "numerical data are to be found."[39] He did, however, know where to find the numerical data of economics. In economics, Jevons said that the "numerical data are more abundant and precise than those possessed by any other science, but that we have not yet known how to employ them."[40] As examples of the raw data of economics he mentioned "private account books, great ledgers of merchants and bankers and public offices, the share lists, price lists, bank returns, monetary intelligence, Custom-house and other Government returns," and "thousands of folio volumes of statistical, parliamentary, or other publications. . . ."[41]

Why then did Jevons not construct utility curves from these abundant data? He offered two excuses or explanations. First, he mentioned "want of method," and second he alleged a want of "completeness."[42] His second excuse contradicted his earlier estimate of the abundance and precision of the raw data in economics, as well as his statement that the "very abundance of our data is perplexing."[43] In fact, Jevons seemed to think of the want of completeness of the basic statistics as the more important of the two circumstances, for he said that he knows "not when we shall have a perfect system of statistics, but the want of it is the only insuperable obstacle in the way of making Political Economy an exact science."[44]

Jevons only hinted, in his introductory chapter, at the method he would employ to measure utility if he had "perfect statistics." His only hint lies in his statement that "we can no more know or measure gravity in its own nature than we can measure a feeling, but just as we measure gravity by its effects in the motion of a pendulum, so we may estimate the equality or inequality of feelings by the varying decisions of the human mind. The will is our pendulum, and its oscillations are minutely registered in all the price lists of the markets."[45] As Jevons revealed later, this statement means that he would use demand functions as approximations of utility functions,

48

with price as a rough measure of marginal utility. Walras might have objected in principle to this procedure, as he objected to the same method when Dupuit "confused" demand curves and utility curves, but he might have waived some of his objections after a closer look at the specific details of Jevons' method that remove, in part, the objections that Walras felt to Dupuit. At least, Walras never made the same objections to Jevons' association of marginal utility and demand that he had made to Dupuit's similar, but less refined, procedure.

Jevons returned to the problem of measurement again in a later section called "Of the Measurement of Feeling and Motives."[46] In this second section on measurement, so different in spirit from his earlier observations, he began with the discouraging statement that "we have no means of defining and measuring quantities of feeling, like we can measure a mile, or a right angle, or any other physical quantity."[47] Jevons forgot that he held forth high hope for measurement, at least indirect measurement, only a few pages before, for he now said that "numerical expression of quantities of feeling seems to be out of the question."[48] He came close to limiting himself to an ordinal view of utility when he stated that "if we can compare the quantities directly, we do not need the units . . .," that he did not claim "for the mind any accurate power of measuring and adding and subtracting feelings . . .," that we "seldom or never affirm that one pleasure is a multiple of another in quantity . . .," and that his theory "seldom involves the comparison of quantities of feeling differing much in amount."[49] However, he did not push this simpler view of measurement.

Jevons slipped back to his cardinal conception of the measurement of individual feelings as soon as he began, in the next chapter, to consider pleasure and pain. "Two days of the same degree of happiness are to be twice as much desired as one day," he said in a statement that certainly implied the cardinal measurement of the duration if not the intensity of pleasure.[50] In a figure he showed the diminishing intensity of the pleasure from equal intervals of time, another sure sign that cardinal utility had come back into his considerations.[51] When Jevons came to the chapter on utility he wrote, somewhat ambiguously, that utility "must be considered as measured by, or even as actually identical with, the addition made to a person's happiness."[52]

Jevons explicitly sketched his plan to use demand curves as approximations of utility curves only after he already had used the utility functions in his determination of exchange rates. The utility functions that served him in the analysis of exchange presume cardinal utility. The assumption of the cardinal measurement of utility does not stand out because Jevons used a general functional notation and illustrated his conclusions with graphs of utility curves that retain only the principal characteristics he attributed to his generalized functions. He evidently missed, in having to proceed at this level of generalization, some of the concreteness he had found in the physical sciences where the investigator determines the shape and parameters of the functions he uses.

As a consequence, Jevons returned for a third time to the idea of measurement.[53] This time he was optimistic. From the statistics of demand he hoped to determine "at least approximately, the variation of the final degree of utility—the all-important element in Economy." He realized that he must assume utility of money income as constant for the demand curve to approximate a utility curve. He did not expect the result to be any "simple compact law like that of gravity." But in the end he thought that "their determination will render Economy a science as exact as many of the purely physical sciences . . .," even though the functions of the "main elements of expenditure" remain impossible to obtain since economists cannot assume the marginal utility of income constant in considering necessities. Contrary to his expectations, economics in the years after Jevons did not follow the path he foresaw, the path of the physical sciences, of determining the form of the utility functions (or any economic functions, for that matter) and making use of these specific functions in subsequent analysis.

Chapter VII

FURTHER ASPECTS OF MARGINAL UTILITY THEORY AS SET FORTH IN JEVONS' *THEORY*, MENGER'S *GRUNDSÄTZE*, AND WALRAS' *ÉLÉMENTS*

I

None of the principal arguments of Jevons, Menger, and Walras depend on the assumption of an ability to compare the utilities of different individuals. In the main, these three economists never imply interpersonal comparability. Although each supposes the cardinal measurement of utility, the units chosen for any one individual have no specified relation to the units of any other individual.

Only Jevons, however, emphasized the impossibility of interpersonal comparisons. Menger and Walras, although they never made interpersonal comparisons any more than Jevons did, never stated a general objection to the practice. In the following passage, Jevons gave the classic statement of the objection to such comparisons, in a form agreed to, more or less generally, by all economists down to the present: "The reader will find, again, that there is never, in a single instance, an attempt made to compare the amount of feeling in one mind with that in another. I see no means by which such comparison can ever be accomplished. The susceptibility of one mind may, for what we know, be a thousand times greater than that of another. But, provided that the susceptibility was different in a like ratio in all directions, we should never be able to discover the profoundest difference. Every mind is thus inscrutable to every other mind, and no common denominator of feeling is possible."[1]

Nevertheless, Jevons did not avoid wholly (nor did his successors) the quite natural casual interpersonal comparisons of the kind that people generally make. He said, for example, that the utility of an additional penny to a family earning fifty pounds a year exceeds the utility to a family having an income of a thousand pounds a year. How could he have made such a comparison if he followed strictly his own ban on interpersonal comparison? Similarly, both Menger and Walras at times leaned toward rough interpersonal comparisons. Menger assumed that he knew enough about what went on in the

51

human mind to say that "the use value of one and the same good is usually very different for two different individuals. . . ."[2] Walras has been charged with the assumption of interpersonal comparability in his attempted proof that free competition maximizes the utilities of an economy.[3]

Jevons also deviated from the assumption of interpersonal incomparability when he resorted to totals or averages of different individuals' utilities. Clearly the idea of average or total utility for a group supposes some degree of interpersonal comparison. Jevons was unable to avoid the attraction of the average, especially when it helped him out of the difficulty of indivisibilities and even though it contained the seed of comparison. Jevons approached this use of the average by stating that economics usually treated an aggregate of individuals.[4] He cannot, of course, treat an aggregate sensibly without making a comparison between the individual parts of the aggregate. His first aggregates did no harm, for they were of demand curves. Finally, however, Jevons resorted to the concept of a "trading body," which permitted him to aggregate utility functions despite the fact that he had declared against interpersonal comparisons.[5] The term "trading body" denoted any body either of buyers or sellers, from an individual to the "inhabitants of a continent." He referred to consumption in connection with a "trading body," but at the place where he discussed a "trading body" in general terms he made no reference to the utility of goods. When he came to use the idea in his determination of the rates of exchange, however, Jevons suddenly gave his "trading body" a utility function.[6] Thereafter, the "trading body" behaved exactly as a person, and Jevons referred to it as such.[7] He presented his general statement of the equilibrium of exchange in terms of the utility functions of "trading bodies."[8] Later, without recourse to his idea of a "trading body," he drew a utility curve of wool to Australia.[9] No doubt Jevons unwittingly assumed interpersonal comparability in these cases.

Menger avoided this use of averages or totals probably because he had, in general, a less strictly quantitative outlook and because he felt no need to avoid the use of indivisibilities by this route. Menger commented on the idea of average use value only once and that time unfavorably.[10] Walras did not average the utilities of different individuals in the first edition of the *Éléments*, although he introduced averages of this kind in the second edition, following, perhaps, Jevons' bad example.[11]

52

II

Neither Jevons nor Menger nor Walras discussed explicitly the form of the utility function that he used. Yet from the number of things they stated incidentally we can piece together a good idea of the kind of functions that they must have had in mind. The three pioneers of marginal utility theory agreed on the general characteristics of these functions as they agreed in so many other ways.

All three of the writers used a function in which the marginal utility of a certain good to an individual depends on the quantity of that good, and on the quantity of that good alone. Thus they ruled out the strict observance of the inter-commodity relationships surrounding complementary and substitute goods.[12] Nor did they include in their functions such possible variables as the income of the consumer, the distribution of the income of the population, the quantities of the good consumed by other persons, the prices of the goods themselves, or any rates of change in these or other variables in the system.

Jevons, Menger, and Walras emphasized, and most properly, the fact that the marginal utility decreases when the quantity of the good increases (diminishing marginal utility), as the most significant characteristic of their marginal utility functions. Menger thought of this characteristic as reflecting common experience, but he noted that scholars had not paid much attention to it. Jevons stressed both the naturalness and the importance of diminishing marginal utility. Although Walras spoke of "postulating" the quality of diminishing marginal utility in his utility function, he probably did so on the same assumption of common experience that Jevons and Menger made. None of them gave any exception to this fundamental relationship. Jevons expressly said that there are no exceptions.[13] No one of the writers attached significance to changes in the rate at which marginal utility declined (the convexity or concavity of their utility curves). All of Jevons' curves were concave from above. Both Menger's tabular representations and the curves in the first edition of Walras' *Éléments* were linear.[14] In the 1877 part of the *Éléments* Walras quoted Dupuit, who had described the utility curve as concave from above, but he did not comment on Dupuit's assumption.[15]

Jevons, Menger, and Walras never used dynamic functions. Jevons said that "only as a purely statical problem . . . I can venture to treat the action of exchange."[16] He avoided the problem of dynamics because "it would surely be absurd to attempt the more difficult question when the more easy one is yet so imperfectly within our power."[17] Walras never mentioned in the first edition of the *Éléments* the fact that he used a static analysis only, although he inserted a sentence to this effect in later editions.[18] Menger used the idea of "time" occasionally, but largely in connection with the nature of production. He had one section in which he considered the "*capacity* of human needs *to grow*," and in which he concluded that this capacity did not interfere with his analysis.[19] In general, however, his analysis is static.

None of these writers at the beginning of the eighteen-seventies paid strict attention to the general circumstances of consumption in their examples of diminishing utility. They implied, however, that the goods which their functions represent consist of physically *homogeneous* commodities that the consumers intend to consume *in addition* to the other (unspecified) goods that they utilize in the consumption process during the period in question. In his first example of diminishing marginal utility Jevons asked that we consider "the whole quantity of food which a person consumes on an average during twenty-four hours to be divided into ten equal parts."[20] He must have meant some abstract quantity of food, for he could not physically divide a day's food into equal and similar parts, with qualities which the consumer would recognize and value. Later Jevons stipulated for his theory of exchange a commodity "perfectly uniform or homogeneous in quality . . ." in order that it have a single price in a market.[21] Jevons evidently assumed, too, that the consumer has exactly the same quantities of clothing, shelter, and all incidental goods whether he consumes one unit of food or ten. He never pointed out, however, that the level of consumption of other goods must be the principal circumstance that determines the shape of the consumer's utility function for food.

Menger's table supposed the same situation, although Menger took even less pains to explain his variable than had Jevons. A reader must construe the first column in Menger's principal illustration to represent the additions of total satisfaction from eleven equal portions of some homogeneous food, on the assumption that the amounts of the other goods the person consumes do not influence his satisfactions. Walras' statement that first introduces his utility function implies likewise a homogeneous commodity added to units of consumption, with the quantities of all other goods not influencing the outcome in any way.

The utility functions that Jevons, Menger, and Walras used all relate to the utility that an *individual* receives from the goods that he consumes, and these functions lead *him* to buy and sell quantities of the goods in his *own* interest. Consumption, in other words, presumes the physical use of the good by the individual to whom the function relates. The individual drinks water, eats food in general, beef or mutton in particular, smokes tobacco, burns beechwood, etc., and for these purposes he buys quantities of these goods. None of the writers on utility at this time, and only a few later, mentioned the circumstance that the purchaser of consumers' goods buys the bulk of his purchases for the *other* members of a household. Therefore, to explain consumption, either in 1871 or at present, the utility functions should relate to the household. At least the person who actually makes the purchases must know the nature of the utility functions of the other members of the household as well as his own.[22]

III

Jevons, Menger, and Walras shared the assumption that the satisfactions from different goods have some common abstract quality that the individual can sum for a total that has meaning to him. This vital assumption came naturally to these economists of the eighteen-seventies, but earlier and later writers denied that the individual could compare the satisfactions from diverse goods. The assumption of comparability underlies the relationship now usually known as the marginal utility of income, or money income, or simply of money.

Menger's verbal type of exposition contained no explicit reference to this idea, but it also contained no expressed ideas that would conflict with a concept of the marginal utility of income. Menger would doubtless have agreed that, as the amount of money that an individual has to spend increases, the total satisfaction that he obtains increases, but that the satisfaction added by concrete units of income diminishes from unit to unit. Walras, too, stated the dependence of total utility on the income of the consumer, but he did not use the idea in subsequent analysis.[23]

In contrast, Jevons not only had a good idea of the notion of the marginal utility of income but also made a considerable use of it. Jevons had the advantage of a familiarity with Daniel Bernoulli's application of the marginal utility of income to gambling, as well as

Laplace's distinction between *fortune physique* and *fortune morale*.[24] Jevons defined the idea of the marginal utility of income in these words: "It will be seen that we now conceive, in an accurate manner, the utility of money, or of the supply of commodity which forms a person's livelihood. Its final degree of utility is measured by that of any of the other commodities which he consumes."[25] This is undoubtedly the first express statement of the marginal utility of money or income in its modern form. Here Jevons reveals why marginal utility of income must decrease as income increases: since the marginal utilities of the goods bought decrease, so must the marginal utility of income. He did not take into account the possibility that the individual may change the character of his consumption as well as the amount when his income increases.

Jevons granted that the marginal utility of income may remain approximately constant over a short range of income. In consequence he introduced his readers to the type of partial-equilibrium economic analysis in which the marginal utility of money remains constant. He pointed out that he can use this kind of analysis only when the money an individual spends "does not make him appreciably poorer," as in the case of salt, but that he cannot when purchases "appreciably affect the possessions of the purchaser . . ." as in the case of meat.[26] He drew a graph that assumed a constant marginal utility of income over a range of income sufficient to buy six bottles of ink, in order to show how the individual would decide the optimum number of bottles of ink to purchase.[27] This was the first demand curve ever drawn that makes explicit the assumption of the constancy of marginal utility of income. Later, many other writers employed the same device. Jevons made his greatest use of the marginal utility of income when he reversed this process and interpreted a demand curve of an individual as a utility curve, on the assumption that the marginal utility of money remains constant.

IV

Jevons, Menger, and Walras made a central and important use of their utility functions in connection with the problem of exchange, or value. In this way, they differed from such earlier writers on utility as Bernoulli, Senior, and Dupuit who had written utility functions of much the same kind but who never had used them for the expression of an equilibrium in exchange. This concerted use of their utility functions marks the most important advance in utility analysis and the beginning of the Marginal Utility School. It connects, in a most essential way, the process of maximization of utility with the economic problem. Menger stated a version of the notion of maximization towards the commencement of his discussion of economy when he promised to show how the consumers "direct the quantities of goods (consumption goods and means of production) at their disposal to the most effective satisfaction of their needs."[28] Jevons also said that economics concerns the process of maximization of utility. "To satisfy our wants to the utmost with the least effort . . ., in other words, to maximize comfort and pleasure, is the problem of Economy."[29] Walras' "Theorem of Maximum Utility" expresses the proposition that the "object in trading is to gratify the greatest possible sum total of wants. . . ."[30] This is the new tone that the Marginal Utility School introduced into economics. It sounds obvious now but it was not obvious at the time. Not that any earlier economists would have denied that human beings generally move in the direction that their self-interest leads them. The idea of the pursuit of self-interest, and its sanction as a worthy goal, had acceptance among economists long before 1871. So did the idea of the importance of consumption. But the idea that maximization of such a concept as utility plays a weighty part in determining such economic quantities as value, output, and input had not yet dawned on many people. The earlier economists thought that people pursued their self-interest in a world where the determination of the important parameters of conduct such as value and the quantity of goods produced proceed from sterner or different outside causes (such as pain cost). Had Jevons, Menger, and Walras continued to restrict their analysis as the earlier economists did, they would have found little use for the utility functions. There had to be an important use for utility in economics before there could be a Marginal Utility School.

But neither Jevons, Menger, nor Walras, for all their discussion of maximization, proceeded directly to obtain the maximizing conditions in the way that formal mathematical procedures would suggest. Menger, of course, did not employ any mathematical analysis and accordingly would not use the methods of maximization common to mathematics. Both Jevons and Walras used mathematical notations and procedures. We might have expected that they would have approached the problem of maximization directly by pointing to the quantities to be maximized, then stating the conditions to

57

which the maximization was subject (budget conditions), and next developing at least the necessary conditions (if not the sufficient) for a maximum. The necessary conditions would then have taken the familiar form of a set of ratios between the marginal utilities of the consumer and the prices of the goods. But instead, all three writers began their analysis, not with the total utility function of the consumer, of which all three certainly knew the importance, but with the marginal utility functions which they could use immediately to express the conditions of the maximum. They all show more concern with the existence, as a fact in experience, of marginal utility than with its related quantity, the total utility of the individual. To that end they described the idea of marginal utility at length. This is not to be thought of as a loss. We may doubt that anything like the idea of marginal utility could have arisen from an exposition of a few pages of succinct necessary conditions for a maximum. The school they founded became known, because of this somewhat indirect emphasis, as the Marginal Utility School rather than as the Maximum Utility School.

V

All three of the pioneers explicitly repudiated the labor theory of value. This repudiation shaped one of the common bonds among them. At the time they wrote, the labor theory of value had more prestige, and more followers, than any rival theory of value. Consequently, the three writers shared a certain danger in their opposition to an esteemed part of the intellectual equipment of the economists of the world. Each of them clearly stated his repudiation of the labor theory of value. Walras wrote that "the theory which traces the origin of value to labour is a theory that is devoid of meaning rather than too narrow, an assertion that is gratuitous rather than inacceptable."[31] Words of this kind clearly ruffle those who have already committed themselves to an acceptance of the doctrine. Menger castigated the labor theory of value more harshly than did Walras. "Among the most egregious of the fundamental errors that have had the most far-reaching consequences in the previous development of our science," Menger wrote, "is the argument that goods attain value for us because goods were employed in their production that had value to us."[32] Jevons ran the greatest risk of the three in the rejection of the labor theory of value, since this particular theory in its most developed form had England as a homeland. Consequently, Jevons attended more closely to the labor theory of value than either Walras or Menger. He even made some effort to reconcile his utility theory of value with the prevailing views in England when, at the end of his chapter on exchange, he wrote that "labour affects supply, and supply affects the degree of utility, which governs value, or the ratio of exchange."[33] However conciliatory his exposition, he nonetheless stated his disapproval of the labor theory of value in the following terms: "The fact is, that *labour once spent has no influence on the future value of any article*: it is gone and lost for ever. In commerce, by-gones are for ever by-gones; and we are always starting clear at each moment, judging the values of things with a view to future utility. Industry is essentially prospective, not retrospective; and seldom does the result of any undertaking exactly coincide with the first intention of its founders."[34]

VI

Menger had a looser idea of a demand function than either Jevons or Walras. While he realized that the quantity sold in a market depends on the price asked for the good,[35] he gave demand functions only a few verbal references. He never illustrated them, as he might have, with a table of the kind that he used in his discussion of the theory of price. Nor did Menger connect them directly with the satisfactions that the individuals receive from the goods they buy. Walras, on the other hand, began his analysis with given demand curves and obtained his equilibrium market conditions before he ever said a word about utility. Later he introduced utility to establish the foundations on which his demand functions rest.[36] Jevons regarded demand curves from another viewpoint. He investigated them mainly in the hope of discovering some way to obtain data for the construction of an individual's utility curves.

It should be observed that while the demand curves of Jevons appear to the eye to be exactly the same (with axes reversed) as those of Walras, they nevertheless are drawn on quite different assumptions. Walras' demand curves also differ from the partial equilibrium demand curves now in use in economics. For example, Walras' first demand function has two variables, not because of the *ceteris paribus* assumptions of present-day demand curves, but because the market he considers holds definite quantities of only two goods and because the traders express the price of one good in terms of the units of the other good. Even Walras' collective demand curves retain an element of this difference. Jevons' curves are more in the spirit of the demand curves that later became popular. He assumed that the individual surrenders such a minor part of the good that he brings to market, that the exchange does not alter the marginal utility of his own good, or in other words, that the individual's marginal utility of money remains constant. Walras never used this hypothesis and upbraided Dupuit for undertaking an analysis which does. Jevons, of course, realized that he could not draw a demand curve of this kind for any commodity that took a large part of the individual's income.

Chapter VIII

REVIEWS OF JEVONS' *THEORY*

I

Although the English failed to notice the early publications of Menger and Walras, as they might have if they had had any technical economic journals, they did herald the publication of Jevons' *Theory*. Four major reviews appeared, supplemented by a half-dozen short, unsigned notices in journals and newspapers. Let us consider, first, the short notices in journals, then the newspaper reviews, and finally the long major reviews in periodicals.

II

The *Athenaeum* ran a perfunctory review that never mentions "utility" and that concludes with the apology that it gives "an inadequate notice of an admirable work."[1] A longer notice in the *British Quarterly Review* applauds both the use of mathematics and the use of utility in economic analysis.[2] We find the short notice that reveals the closest reading of Jevons' *Theory* in the *Westminister Review*.[3] It outlines Jevons' views understandably and apparently approves of his use both of mathematics and utility.

III

English newspaper reviewers gave Jevons' *Theory* quite long and, on the whole, favorable reviews.[4] The *Manchester Daily Examiner and Times* covered half a page with its article, "Jevons on the Theory of Political Economy."[5] The reviewer said that it will "exercise far greater influence on the future study of the science than the author seems to imagine. . . ." A good deal of the review consists in a selection of quotations from Jevons' *Theory*, of which most refer to utility. "Probably the exact nature and conditions of utility have never been so successfully defined," the reviewer said, "and the admirable manner in which Mr. Jevons illustrates his subtle distinctions cannot be too much commended."

The review article, "Professor Jevons on the Theory of Political Economy," in the *Manchester Guardian* also fills over half a page.[6] The reviewer, apparently familiar with the current state of economic thought, welcomed Jevons' *Theory* as a "bold and muscular attack upon authority. . . ." He gave due attention to marginal utility which he recognized as, in Jevons' view, "the distinctive and determining element in the science of political economy." "If once accepted," the reviewer continued, "it is one of those large and luminous deductions, which not only serve in the solution of specific problems, but shed a general light over the whole field of investigation." The reviewer recognized that Jevons is brought into direct collision with his predecessors, Adam Smith, Ricardo, and Mill, but he did not wholly accept Jevons' position and tried to do what he could to reconcile the old and the new views.

The review in the *Glasgow Daily Herald* is not so uniformly favorable as the two reviews in the Manchester newspapers (possibly because of Jevons' many connections in Manchester), but it does provide a close and critical examination of Jevons' use of utility.[7] It objects to the fact that Jevons followed Bentham in the assumption that a person can sum up utilities, or subtract them from each other. To make this assumption, the reviewer held that Jevons must assume, first, that pleasures "differ from each other only in intensity . . ." and that in the second place "it would be requisite to have some unit of pleasure generally agreed upon by which they might be measured and reckoned." The reviewer admitted neither of these assumptions. He refused to admit that the "pleasure of a good dinner . . ." differs from the "pleasure of making a scientific discovery . . ." only in the sense of "less or more," and he pointed out that even Jevons could not conceive the possibility of a unit. The reviewer also objected that a good deal of Jevons' new terminology has as many ambiguities as the terms it replaced. He brought up the objection, made frequently later, that we know the ratio of the final degrees of utilities only from the exchange ratios and cannot, therefore, use them to explain these same ratios; or, in other words, that we cannot know the utility functions independently of the equations of exchange.

IV

One of the four major reviews of the first edition of Jevons' *Theory* has no signature.[8] The others came from well-known writers. John Elliot Cairnes wrote the review of Jevons' *Theory* for the influential *Fortnightly Review*.[9] Alfred Marshall began his career with a review of Jevons' *Theory* in the *Academy*.[10] In the United

States, Simon Newcomb prepared a long review for the *North American Review*.[11] The reviews, in general, differ in tone. Both Newcomb and Cairnes gave general praise to Jevons' *Theory;* Marshall limited his commendation severely; the reviewer in the *Saturday Review* criticized without praising. In every case the reviewer disagreed with Jevons' use of utility but not always for the same reason.

Marshall recognized that the book's "main purpose is to substitute for Mill's Theory of Value the doctrine that 'value depends entirely upon utility.' " In opposition Marshall strove to reconcile a theory of value based on labor with Jevons' value theory based on utility. The first sentence that Marshall ever published reveals the tone he reserved throughout his life for those who reject too casually the teachings of the great economists of the past, particularly the great English economists. Marshall's first published sentence says: "This book claims to 'call in question not a few of the favorite doctrines of economists'." This sentence (and the remainder of the review) implies that Jevons did not substantiate his claim. Marshall began his denial of this claim with the following quotation from Jevons: "Though 'labour is often found to determine value,' yet it does so 'only in an indirect manner by varying the degree of the utility of the commodity through an increase in the supply.' " Marshall then added that "it is almost startling to find that the author regards the Ricardian theory as maintaining labour to be the origin of value in a sense inconsistent with this last position." The difference between the two theories startled Jevons: Jevons' presumption that a difference exists annoyed Marshall.

Again Marshall showed his often mentioned spirit of reconciliation when he stated: "Although the difference between the two sets of theories is of great importance, it is mainly a difference in form." Marshall argued that Jevons' theory of utility was correct if Jevons realized that he simply rewrote Ricardo and Mill in another form. Marshall also denied Jevons any credit for originating the idea of marginal utility when he wrote that "it is a familiar truth that the total utility of any commodity is not proportional to 'its final degree of utility'. . . ." Marshall did not tell who held this *familiar* truth.

In the comment on the above review that Marshall left in manuscript form, he repeated the idea that Jevons intended to make his notions appear unnecessarily original: ". . . he [Jevons] seemed perversely to twist his own doctrines so as to make them appear more inconsistent with Mill's and Ricardo's than they really were. . . . My youthful loyalty to . . . [Ricardo] . . .boiled over when I read Jevons' *Theory*. . . . I have a vivid memory of the angry phrases which would force themselves into my draft, only to be cut out and then reappear in another form a little later on, and then to be cut out again."[12] Actually, Marshall never did cut out all the "angry phrases."

V

In a limited way, Cairnes, in his review of Jevons' *Theory* joined, Marshall in toning down Jevons' claims to originality. "That theory," Cairnes wrote, "is not absolutely new; at least it seems to me that I perceive in it a conception of the law of value at bottom the same with that propounded by Bastiat in his 'Harmonies Economiques'." Cairnes, unlike Marshall, had other adverse criticisms. One of these was his complaint that Jevons had no valid measure of the final degree of utility except the exchange value of the good. Cairnes wrote: "So that what we come to is this—exchange-value depends upon utility, and utility is measured and can only be known by exchange value. . . . I own it seems to me to come so close to an identical proposition, that I am unable to distinguish it from that species of announcement. I fail to perceive in what way it throws light on any problem of economic science. . . . If the 'terminal utility' can only be known by the exchange-value, how are we helped to a knowledge of the latter by being referred to the former?" This criticism is the same as the one that the reviewer in the *Glasgow Daily Herald* had introduced earlier.

Cairnes floundered in his attempt to show that Jevons could not measure pleasure or satisfaction directly. In part, he seemed to base his charge on the peculiar belief that pleasure or satisfaction has no connection with Jevons' concept of utility. ". . . I think it would be generally agreed," Cairnes wrote, "that the pleasure derived from wearing a shirt or coat—given the constitution of the man and the climate—is not sensibly different now from what it was a century ago." But since all articles made of cloth had fallen in price during the last century, Cairnes contended that Jevons could not determine their value by the pleasure or satisfaction they occasion. A plain lack of understanding of marginal utility shows here; the increased production of cloth would lower the marginal utility sufficiently to permit a lower price to prevail even though man's utility functions had not changed.

Cairnes really did understand the idea of diminishing marginal utility, and the argument above must stand as a temporary lapse. In fact, he used the variation in marginal utility as a part of a second argument against utility in which he stated that the " 'terminal utility' of a pound of tea will be greater to a washerwoman than to a fine lady . . ." presumably because the fine lady has more tea than the washerwoman. Cairnes concluded from this interpersonal comparison that some readers "might be disposed to infer that, according to Mr. Jevons's theory, the washerwoman ought to pay more for her tea." This last desperate argument by Cairnes has no merit, and it shows a lack on the part of Cairnes both of any willingness to understand Jevons and of a knowledge of the applications of the marginal utility theory.

VI

The anonymous review of Jevons' *Theory* in the *Saturday Review*, which Jevons thought more worthy of attention than any of the other reviews, contains no praise whatsoever. It deserves attention, however, as Jevons said it did, because it reveals some knowledge of economics on the part of the reviewer, as well as a reasonably close reading of the book, and because it attempts to meet Jevons on his central issues. At the outset, it deprives Jevons of any originality in the same way that both Marshall and Cairnes did, by stating that "we have been struck by his general agreement with the writers to whose authority he declines. . . ."

The reviewer expressed his views on the relationship of the measurability of utility to the use of utility in economic analysis in the following paragraph:

But what is the measure of utility? To this we can discover no answer in Mr. Jevons's book. . . . Undoubtedly we can tell that one pleasure is greater or less than another; but that does not help us. To apply the mathematical methods, pleasure must be in some way capable of mathematical expression; we must be able to say, for example, that the pleasure of eating a beefsteak is to the pleasure of drinking a glass of beer as 5 to 4. The words convey no particular meaning to us; and Mr. Jevons, instead of helping us, seems to shirk the question. We must remind him that, to fit a subject for mathematical inquiry, it is not sufficient to represent some of the quantities concerned by letters. If we say that G represents the confidence of liberals in Mr. Gladstone, and D the confidence of conservatives in Mr. Disraeli, and x and y the numbers of those parties; and infer that Mr. Gladstone's tenure of office depends upon some equation involving dG/dx and dD/dy we have merely wrapped up a plain statement in a mysterious collection of letters.

This argument is not easy to answer and probably gave Jevons pause.

As a final criticism, the reviewer in the *Saturday Review* compared Jevons' problem of exchange with Mill's international trade example. He said that they are the same except that, with Jevons, the total amount of the good cannot be increased or decreased, and that each exchanger has a strict monopoly. "His problem," he proceeded, "is therefore equivalent to this; suppose that the British Museum had all the existing remains of Greek sculpture, and the Louvre all the existing remains of Roman sculpture; at what rate would they exchange collections, no other purchasers being in existence? The problem is so far removed from reality that it may be scarcely worth considering. . . ." The reviewer tried to show that the equations would not work even if they did not represent a fictitious case removed from reality. If the exchange rate stands at 5 corn for 1 beef, A. would exchange until he has enough beef, but it is unlikely that the exchange would satisfy B. Then B. can offer 2 beef for 5 corn. But A. might not take any more no matter what B. offers. The reviewer added that "neither do we see why the rate which would content both of them should ever be hit upon. In short, all we can say is that they will exchange beef and corn till one or both of them choose to leave off; but when that will be depends partly on the desire of A. and B. for beef and corn, and partly on their acuteness in higgling." Perhaps this quotation only implies that the path to the equilibrium in the actual determination of the final ratio differs from the end exchange ratio. If so, this interpretation takes the equations as a too literal interpretation of the process of the determination of the final exchange rate. The equations only mirror the final result.

At the end the reviewer draws his indictments together in the following summary: "In fact, to sum up our view of Mr. Jevons's conclusions, we should say that he wishes to determine the rate of exchange by the utility to the dealers, without introducing the ordinary play of supply and demand; he therefore imagines a case where supply and demand do not operate; he finds, as might be expected, that the only answer is, that the result depends in some way on personal peculiarities which evade examination; and he wraps up this mysterious conclusion in symbols which are mere verbiage, as they contain functions which neither are nor can be determined."

VII

Simon Newcomb's review in the *North American Review* contains more praise for Jevons' economics than do all the other three long reviews put together. Of the four writers, only Newcomb approved Jevons' application of mathematics to economics. "Holding that this mode of expression is now what political economy stands most in need of," Newcomb summarized, "we welcome every attempt to introduce it, and commend the work as showing that there, certainly are truths of this science which admit of exact mathematical expression and reasoning." As did the other reviewers, Newcomb recognized that the central part of the work rests on utility and he held that to be a significant fact, for, he said, the "basis of the work is a theory of utility which may well supersede the old distinction of value in use and value in exchange."

Like all reviewers Newcomb had criticisms. Perhaps his principal criticism was that, although Jevons' theory of utility is "entirely correct in its results, so far as it can be applied to the actual circumstances of trade . . .," it is of "very limited application." Newcomb thought that the circumstance that dealers hold most of the stocks of goods limits the usefulness of Jevons' theory, since these stocks have no direct utility to the dealers. Jevons himself had called attention to this case. But whereas Jevons had regarded this case as of minor importance, Newcomb held it to be of major significance. Newcomb asked whether it is not "rather unsatisfactory to found a science upon a set of equations which shall hold true or fail according as the producer of a commodity does or does not keep an infinitesimal amount of it for his own use." Newcomb also found it difficult to consider the utility of a stock of goods, not to the merchant but to the manufacturer who would use them in the production of further goods. "But how," Newcomb asked, "shall we learn the utility . . . of horse shoes to a farrier, or of railways to an engineer?" Actually Newcomb proposed, in a somewhat incidental manner, his own solution for this difficulty. He stated that, when we apply the equations to any concrete case, "we apprehend that the utility of the commodity to the seller or producer will disappear from the equations altogether, and the relation will appear as one between the conditions of production on the one side, and the utility of the commodity to the purchaser on the other."

Newcomb's association with the physical sciences doubtless led him to desire to form the actual utility functions from the data of price and quantity, as Jevons thought that he could form them, and to try to use these equations in the solution of real problems concerning the equations of exchange. He did not feel content to restrain the mathematical notation to functions whose form he could only partly specify. In the following quotation he showed this natural eagerness to obtain practical, worth-while results:

Utility thus depending on the supply, it is possible to express the relation between the two by an algebraic equation, if we have the necessary data for forming this equation. There are the quantities of each kind of goods sold, and the price at which the sales are effected under various circumstances. From such data the equation is to be formed by induction.

. . . .

An interesting application of the law would be to find the quantity of each article which an individual with given wants and a given income would purchase. The necessary data being given the manner in which each dollar of his income would be spent, always supposing him to spend with perfect intelligence, would be a matter of mathematical deduction.

His dissatisfaction with the final results of Jevons is seen in the following quotation: "The fact is, that our author has laid a foundation for us, but has not built upon it himself, nor shown us how to do so. His theory of utility is very valuable as enabling us to understand what we see in the commercial world, but it does not furnish sufficient means of investigating it." Newcomb's connection with the physical sciences also explains his rejection of Jevons' idea of founding a calculus of pleasure and pain. Newcomb said that he could not conceive the idea of the calculus of pleasure and pain "to have any sound philosophical basis." Actually, Newcomb only objected to the concentration of attention on the pleasure and pain rather than on the actions of the man resulting from the pleasure and pain. "We may make the acts of man undertaken with a view of gaining pleasure and avoiding pain the subject of a calculus," Newcomb admitted, "but this can hardly be considered as measuring pleasure and pain themselves."

VIII

T. E. C. Leslie wrote the only signed review of the second edition of Jevons' *Theory*.[13] Two unsigned shorter reviews, after explaining the contents, praise the book uncritically.[14] Leslie, as one would expect from his well-known interests, confined his attention largely to Jevons' scope and method, subjects on which he disagreed with Jevons but on which he made some apparent effort to do Jevons justice. His ire, however, rose occasionally as when he suggested that he had no objection to mathematics being used in the exposition of Ricardian economics, since it would please him to see Ricardian economics "obscured in every treatise in which it is put forward by a liberal use of the calculus." Or, as when in his argument that we ought not to use mathematics, he asked whether though the "*Times* might be printed in shorthand, and much ink and paper thereby saved, . . ." it would "conduce to the enlightenment of the public to make that economy." Leslie agreed with a statement of diminishing marginal utility, but appeared to think it ruled out in some way by the circumstance that the price of a good "is affected by so many other conditions that it bears no constant mathematical ratio to the amount of supply." Leslie restated this same idea later when he wrote that value depends "also on other conditions which defy all mathematical powers of calculation." Leslie concluded his comments on utility with a hope that historians would give utility a thorough study. "The order which the evolution of human wants follows is," Leslie wrote, "one of the enquiries that await a rising historical and inductive school of economists. . . ."

Chapter IX

JEVONS ON UTILITY IN THE PERIOD 1871-1882

I

Jevons' ill health prevented him from attending to his studies for a good part of the year that followed the publication of the first edition of the *Theory* in October, 1871. He first considered again the subject of utility in a letter to J. L. Shadwell of October 17, 1872.[1] Shadwell had urged him to retain Adam Smith's measure of value in terms of labor, since there was no way to measure happiness. Jevons countered with the argument that many things lend themselves only to indirect measurement through their effects. He agreed that he might use the "average pain which a common labourer undergoes during, say, a quarter of an hour's work after he has been ten hours at work . . ." to "measure the utility to him of his last increments of wages. . . ."[2] But he argued that he could also use "the ordinary or average good occasioned to a man by an ounce of bread *after ¾ lb. of bread have already been eaten* . . . as a unit of pleasure, remembering of course that the pleasure derived from any commodity is not proportional to that commodity."[3]

Jevons, in this letter, also repeated his earlier hope that he could obtain numerical values for his formulae when commercial statistics became perfect, since prices "express the relative esteem for commodities, and enable us to compare the pleasure produced by the final increments of the commodities."[4] "Had we complete tables of prices compared with quantities consumed," Jevons said, "we could determine the numerical laws of variation of utility."[5] Jevons admitted that he "was not sufficiently careful to point out the process by which we might (with perfect statistics) turn all the formulae into numerical expressions. . . ."[6] He concluded rather lamely with the statement that he had only intended to take "the first step, which was to get the formulae correctly . . ." and added in the same sentence the rather unrelated though important statement that "the main point of difference from Adam Smith was the distinguishing of the *degree of utility from the total amount of utility.*"

For the next year Jevons spent most of his time completing his *Principles of Science,* which appeared February 2, 1874. It contains a long section on the subject of measurement ending with a reference

70

to measurement in the social sciences. "Economic statistics," wrote Jevons, having in mind, perhaps, the determination of the content in his utility functions that he had mentioned in his *Theory* in 1871, and again in his letter to Shadwell the next year, "comprehending the quantities of commodities produced, existing, exchanged, and consumed, constitute another most extensive body of science."[7] However he gave no more or better explanation of how he hoped to obtain the constants in any utility function than he had earlier.

II

Jevons learned about Walras' work on utility sometime in late April or early May of 1874. Léon Walras' article, "Principe d'une théorie mathématique de l'échange," appeared in the April issue of the *Journal des économistes*. Walras sent Jevons an offprint on May 1, without realizing at the time that Jevons had written on a similar subject. At this time Walras knew Jevons "seulement comme auteur de travaux estimés sur la question de la variation des prix et de la dépréciation de la monnaie."[8] A few days after Walras sent his first letter to Jevons, Johan d'Aulnis de Bourouill, a Dutch student of economics, wrote Walras pointing out the similar character of the work that Jevons had done on utility.[9]

Jevons wrote on May 12, 1874, to Walras that, before the offprint that Walras had sent arrived, he already had noticed in the *Journal des économistes* his "very remarkable theory."[10] He advised Walras that his own "theory of exchange, which, when published in England, was either neglected or criticised, is practically confirmed by your researches."[11] He pointed out, in detail, his own claim to priority in the matter, and noted that Walras' "theory substantially coincides with and confirms mine, although the symbols are differently chosen, and there are incidental variations."[12] Jevons asked at the end of the letter, and as delicately as he could, the extent of Walras' acquaintance with his own writings.

Walras replied in a long letter on May 23, 1874.[13] He explained that he had only recently been informed of Jevons' work on utility by d'Aulnis de Bourouill. He agreed that the coincidence between his and Jevons' papers on the points that Jevons had indicated "est éclatante," but he also picked out certain differences which he thought significant. Walras pointed out that he could not see that Jevons had derived his equations from a consideration of maximum satisfaction, or that Jevons had used them to obtain demand functions with which to establish subsequently the equilibrium conditions. In both particulars Walras correctly sensed a difference in detail, but the difference raised no contradiction between the two views.

He did not pursue a consideration of the differences any further but turned to setting out the details of the origin of his own ideas so as to leave no doubt that he had borrowed nothing from Jevons. He suggested that, although the theory had not met with a ready acceptance in France or England, several Italian economists had given it their support. He ended with the offer to submit both Jevons' and his letters to the *Journal des économistes* for publication. Jevons replied on May 30, 1874, thanking him for the proofs of the *Éléments* which Walras had sent him, and asking for additional time before forming an opinion as to whether they differed on any essential points.[14] He admitted Walras' entire independence in his researches. He thanked Walras for offering to acknowledge his priority on certain points through the publication of their correspondence, and ended with the offer to do what he could to make Walras' theories known to England. The letter of Jevons and the reply by Walras appeared in the *Journal des économistes* for June, 1874.[15]

During the summer of 1874 Jevons also corresponded with d'Aulnis de Bourouill, who had become interested in the new economics. Jevons wrote to him of his disappointment over the fact that his *Theory* had not met with a better reception in England but did mention that "a certain number of younger mathematicians and economists . . . have entered into the subject . . .," particularly George Darwin.[16] He expressed pleasure that d'Aulnis de Bourouill contemplated writing a book along the lines of Jevons' and Walras' work, and hoped that a French or English edition would follow the Dutch. In an earlier letter, d'Aulnis de Bourouill had written that he hoped to treat the subject of the "variation of the curves of utility," a subject in which Jevons had expressed interest. On the subject of indivisible commodities Jevons said that he had little to offer beyond what he gave in the *Theory*, but that he regarded his indeterminate solution as unsatisfactory. Early in the autumn he again wrote to d'Aulnis de Bourouill that he had "reflected much upon the point which you mentioned, namely, the exchange of indivisibles . . .," but he could not find any way of improving what he had already said.[17] In this last letter Jevons expressed the belief that, instead of trying at the moment to work out "the theory with fulness and correctness . . . we need still more at present to make known its simple principles. . . ."[18] In this same vein he wrote that Walras' book "is in no way adapted to make the principles of the theory more popularly known. . . ."[19]

III

In November of 1874, Jevons published his first observations on utility since the appearance of his *Theory*. It was a paper he had read to the Manchester Statistical Society on "The Progress of the Mathematical Theory of Political Economy."[20] In it he gave a most elementary, nonmathematical exposition of the marginal utility theory of value, in the course of which he paid Léon Walras the first attention paid him in the English language. He certainly followed the suggestion he had made in his last letter to d'Aulnis de Bourouill of attempting to expound the subject in simple terms rather than trying to elaborate or to extend utility theory.

After his appearance before the Manchester Statistical Society Jevons did not spend much time on the subject for several years. During this time he corresponded with d'Aulnis de Bourouill about his recently published dissertation that dealt with utility theory,[21] with G. H. Darwin concerning his defense of Jevons against Cairnes,[22] and with Foxwell on Marshall's relation to Jevons' theory.[23] He wrote Walras expressing the opinion that now, at last, the theory of marginal utility had begun to make some progress. Jevons stated his hope in the following paragraph: "I think that a considerable change of opinion is taking place in England. Various correspondents express their acquiescence, and some of the professors are beginning to bring the theory before their students. When I was in Cambridge two months ago I found that the subject was much better understood there than I had supposed, and I have little doubt about its gaining ground gradually. . . ."[24] He moved to London in 1876 and at University College read an introductory lecture on "The Future of Political Economy" that hardly mentioned utility.[25] Jevons discovered Dupuit in 1877 and wrote Walras "that Dupuit had a very profound comprehension of the subject, and anticipated us as regards the fundamental ideas of utility."[26] In March, 1877, he published a primer called *Political Economy,* which had in it a very little about utility.

Once the primer was out of the way he began to think of a second edition of the *Theory* and commenced to assemble a bibliography that he wished to append thereto on the subject of the mathematical treatment of political economy. In the course of his bibliographical search, he discovered the work of H. H. Gossen. He first told of this discovery in a letter to his brother on August 21, 1878, in the following words:

> Within the last few days I have had rather a disagreeable incident in the discovery, by Adamson of Owens College, of an unknown German book, by a man called Gossen, containing a theory of political economy apparently much like mine. There are, in fact, a whole series of books, hitherto quite unknown, even on the Continent, in which the principal ideas of my theory have been foreshadowed. I am, therefore, in the unfortunate position that the greater number of people think the theory nonsense, and do not understand it, and the rest discover that it is not new. I am getting on but slowly with the new edition, and altogether am rather at a standstill.[27]

It took him some time to recover from the shock that Gossen had worked out the use of utility in much the same way that he and Walras had. He wrote Foxwell about Gossen at the beginning of September, 1878, and drew what consolation he could from the thought that the "theory in question has in fact been independently discovered three or four times over, and must be true."[28] Shortly thereafter he sent notification of his discovery to Léon Walras.[29]

In the spring of 1879, Jevons completed the second edition of the *Theory of Political Economy*. He added a long new preface in which he apologized to mathematicians for the mode of his presentation, but lamely declared himself unwilling to change his ways.[30] He also included an account of the bibliographical discoveries that he had made since 1871, notably the discovery of Walras, Dupuit, and Gossen. This preface presents an early picture of the development of the idea of marginal utility.

Jevons made a few additions to the second edition of the *Theory* besides his preface and the bibliographic appendices. He introduced four new sections on the subject of the "dimensions of economic quantities,"[31] and he had new expository sections on the theory of value.[32] He also introduced two new sections intended to supply additions to his utility theory. The first addition that Jevons made extends his theory to take into account cases in which the good has a negative or zero marginal utility, working out in detail the manner in which the difference in these signs affects his equations of exchange.[33] He also added a new analysis of joint production in which he came to the conclusion that cost of production never rules for these jointly produced goods, and that the utility theory of value consequently holds in all cases.[34]

In the last year of his life, especially after he had given up his teaching duties and settled down to a literary career, Jevons had often in his mind the preparation of his large treatise on economics, and managed to find time, now and then, to work on parts of it. He left the uncompleted manuscript among his literary remains. It was later published with the title, *The Principles of Economics: A Fragment of a Treatise on the Industrial Mechanism of Society and other Papers*.[35] This posthumous work, which contains Jevons' only extended treatment of general economics after his publication of the *Theory* in 1871, does not have a single word on the subject of marginal utility. It does often speak of utility. In fact it has several chapters on the subject. Strangely enough, however, none of these sound as if they came from a member of the Marginal Utility School. Nor does the list of chapters that Jevons included, but on which he prepared no manuscript, offer any more hope that he would have introduced any further consideration on utility had time permitted him to complete his work. He evidently thought that he had finished with the subject.

Chapter X

ALFRED MARSHALL

I

After his review of Jevons' *Theory* in 1872, Alfred Marshall next wrote on a subject in which he might have expressed his views on utility when he published an article, "On Mr. Mill's Theory of Value," in 1876.[1] However, Marshall did not use the term "utility" at any point in this article, although he mentioned Jevons twice.[2] We may suppose that he omitted any reference to utility because of the circumstance that he intended the article primarily as a defense of Mill's theory of value against Cairnes' criticisms, a defense that obviously needed no reference to utility. But nonetheless, the noteworthy fact stands out that five years after the publication of Jevons' *Theory*, Alfred Marshall, who had reviewed this book and who certainly had understood its main purport, wrote on the subject of value in wholehearted support of Mill and without an apparent qualm at his total omission of any reference to utility.

II

Alfred Marshall first published an economic analysis that made use of marginal utility in 1879. In that year two books showed some influence of Jevons: *The Economics of Industry*,[3] written in collaboration with his wife; and *The Pure Theory of Domestic Values*, privately printed.[4]

In *The Pure Theory of Domestic Values*, Marshall began his investigation of value with the introduction of demand and supply curves and only afterwards came around to the use of the idea of utility. It is the demand schedule that carries most of the burden of his explanation of consumer's rent. Marshall discussed consumer's rent initially in terms of *satisfaction* rather than of utility, and he measured in his example the satisfaction of an additional ton of coal by the price of the coal. "Now that which a person would be just willing to pay for any satisfaction rather than go without it," Marshall writes, "is . . . the 'economic measure' of the satisfaction to him."[5] In those simple straightforward days of the eighteen-seventies, the measurement problem was no bugbear to Marshall. To obtain the whole of the "economic measure" of the individual's consumer's rent in the coal example he added the differences between the prices the individual would pay for each successive ton rather than go without and the price he does pay, and concluded that the "whole consumers' rent[6] which he derives . . . is . . . £22½."[7]

It was after having gone almost the whole way in his analysis that Marshall finally introduced Jevons and utility into his discussion by means of the parenthetical statement that "we may put the same thing in another way."[8] This is exactly what Marshall did. He simply restated his earlier argument except that he replaced the word *satisfaction* with the word *utility,* and while doing so mentioned Jevons' name twice. In short, Marshall interpreted the demand curve of an individual as the individual's utility curve for the good. The same numbers read from the axes of the individual's demand curve serve to interpret the quantities of the same individual's utility curve.

Marshall apparently concluded that only the fact "we cannot estimate the quantity which he would purchase at a given price . . ."[9] prevented the construction of the utility schedule for any individual. This difficulty seems like a small one, but it evidently was the excuse that led Marshall to jump from an examination of the individual's demand curve to a collective demand curve. Marshall said that "the statistics of trade will generally enable us to draw the Demand curve of the commodity for the whole market . . ." and "by this means we are enabled to find the economic measure of the value in use of the commodity to the several members of the community."[10] At the same time he admitted the new difficulty that his composite value-in-use curve measures human satisfaction only roughly, because the measure involves the assumption that "a pleasure that is worth a shilling to one man . . . [equals the] . . . pleasure that is worth a shilling to any other man."[11] Marshall knew that this assumption contains an untruth, for "a satisfaction which a rich man values at a shilling is slight in comparison with one for which a poor man will be willing to pay a shilling."[12] Marshall added another limitation on the use of the demand curve to determine consumers' rent of a group, since the demand curve can be known accurately only in the immediate vicinity of the existing market price. Consequently the market demand curve can be used only to estimate changes in the total utility and not the amount of the total itself. Neither of these limitations, however, deterred Marshall from continuing to use the concept of consumers' rent. In fact, the last part of this paper consists primarily in an investigation of the effect of various taxes on consumers' rent, so defined and so limited, ending with his well-known case in which the "Government" can increase the "common weal" by taxing increasing cost industries and subsidizing decreasing cost industries.[13]

III

Marshall's statement on marginal utility in *The Economics of Industry* is understandably briefer than in *The Pure Theory of Domestic Values*, because the latter was designed to be read by professional economists while the former was prepared for the quite unprofessional use of extension classes. But essentially the use of marginal utility is the same in both books. As before, Marshall uses price to measure utility; only his example is different: he uses flannel instead of coal. "To use Mr. Jevons' happy phrase," Marshall said, "the *Final Utility* of a yard of flannel to him [the customer] is measured by one shilling."[14] Nor did he hesitate to say that the "Final Utility [of sixpence] is greater in the case of the poorer man than in that of the richer," and thus to demonstrate his ability to make interpersonal comparisons.[15] Evidently the phrase "final utility" pleased Marshall at this time; he called it a "happy phrase." Later, he turned against it, for undefined reasons, and substituted the phrase "marginal utility."

Actually, as a reading of *The Economics of Industry* will show, Marshall did not incorporate the idea of marginal utility into his theory of value by 1879. He used the idea of utility in connection with value, to be sure; but his use remained secondary or incidental; marginal utility partly explained demand, and demand partly determined value. In his preface he promised to "construct on the lines laid down in Mill's *Political Economy* a theory of Value, Wages and Profits, which shall include the chief results of the work of the present generation of Economists."[16] Jevons appeared as one of the very few of the "present generation," and the book shows much more closely the lines of Mill. The position that Marshall assigned Jevons is clear from his evaluation of Jevons' contention that utility rather than cost of production determines value. Marshall gave support to neither Ricardo nor Jevons but attempted characteristically to reconcile the two:

It is then incorrect to say, as Ricardo did, that Cost of production alone determines value: but it is no less incorrect to make utility alone,

78

as others have done, the basis of value. It is certainly true that utility is a condition of value always; and that in cases in which the supply of the commodity is fixed, utility determines price. It is true that the price of every commodity must be the measure of its Final utility; that is of its value in use to those who are only just induced to purchase it. But it is not true that this Final utility determines value: for it changes itself, according to the Law of Demand, with every change in the amount of the commodity that is offered for sale. This amount, and therefore the Final utility of the commodity, depend upon the relation between the circumstances of supply and those of demand.[17]

The part of *The Economics of Industry* on value came to dissatisfy even Marshall, who, probably partly on this account, finally suppressed the book after the publication of his *Principles*.[18] Marshall often expressed a poor opinion of *The Economics of Industry*. In a letter written in 1907 he said that "[I] found myself committed to writing a cheap popular book, which was necessarily superficial, and which I loathed."[19] After Marshall suppressed *The Economics of Industry*, not everyone shared his views. Edgeworth thought well of it and reported that Jevons had praised it highly to him.[20] And F. W. Taussig said that "it showed the marks of an acute, independent, forward-making mind . . ." and that as "a piece of exposition, it has qualities not surpassed, not always maintained, in the later writings; and it remains good to read and to ponder on."[21]

IV

Marshall next mentioned marginal utility when he reviewed F. Y. Edgeworth's *Mathematical Psychics* for the *Academy* in the middle of 1881.[22] This book of Edgeworth's pleased Marshall as much as Jevons' *Theory* had annoyed him in 1872. "This book shows clear signs of genius," Marshall wrote as the opening sentence, "and is a promise of great things to come." Marshall never attempted to substantiate his initial sentence of praise; on the contrary, he used most of the remainder of his space in mildly adverse criticism of methods or minor points. He realized that Edgeworth's principal result paralleled Jevons, and stated so flatly. Marshall attributed to Edgeworth "a new interpretation," an application to "new uses," and the deduction of a "list of cases in which the terms of contract are unstable or indeterminate." But these attributions cannot explain the acceptance by Marshall of Edgeworth's *Mathematical Psychics* when he so plainly stood opposed to Jevons' *Theory*. The increased familiarity that the ten intervening years brought to the

79

idea of the use of utility in economic analysis bears more weight unconsciously in shaping Marshall's turn of viewpoint.

Two of Marshall's many publications between his review of Edgeworth's *Mathematical Psychics* and the publication of the first edition of his *Principles* might well have contained some trace of Jevons' use of marginal utility. Only one of the two, however, *The Present Position of Economics,* a printed version of the inaugural lecture he delivered at the University of Cambridge on February 24, 1885, when he took over the chair in economics, referred to Jevons or gave even a hint of the influence of marginal utility on economics. The other, a short letter from Marshall to the *Quarterly Journal of Economics,* having the title "On the Theory of Value," mentions neither Jevons nor utility and argues principally on the validity of his own concept of the "expenses of production" in connection with the theory of value.[23] In his inaugural review of the present position of economics, Marshall called attention to Jevons three times, but he did not specifically connect Jevons with utility.[24] In fact Marshall reviewed the position of economics in 1885 without ever using the word utility at all. Marshall never approached closer to the idea of utility than when, for instance, he said that the organon of economists must have "reference to an analysis of the positive motives of desire for different goods . . ."[25] or when he said that "the same sum of money measures a greater pleasure for the poor than for the rich. . . ."[26]

Clearly Marshall in 1885 entertained no notion that the advent of the triumvirate at the commencement of the seventies had revolutionized economics. He must have begun seriously to elaborate the idea of utility and to connect it more securely to his organon for economic analysis in the years from 1885 to 1890, the years when he first held his professorship at the University of Cambridge, with Jevons recently dead, and with the task of constructing his *Principles* at hand. In the years from 1871 up to the time he went to Cambridge in 1885 the idea of marginal utility played an inconsequential role in his work or thinking on economic problems. Only in the *Principles* published in 1890 did marginal utility come forth as an important and integral part of his economic analysis.

V

In view of all the evidence that Marshall paid slight heed to marginal utility until after 1889, why do historians of thought sometimes list Marshall among the people who independently discovered the idea? Pantaleoni published the first assertion that Marshall had taught the theory of marginal utility at Cambridge before he had read Jevons' *Theory*.[27] He did not say where he had obtained this information, but he may have inferred it from the correspondence of Herbert Somerton Foxwell and Jevons which had been published in 1886.

Foxwell was the only one of Marshall's students during the years 1869 to 1871 to comment on Marshall's lectures during that period. No doubt his comments on this subject to Jevons contributed to the belief that Marshall independently originated the idea of marginal utility, although he never openly acclaimed Marshall an originator of marginal utility theory. However, late in 1874 or early in 1875, Foxwell may have written something in this vein directly to Jevons, with whom he had an acquaintance, for, in a letter of February 7, 1875, Jevons replied to Foxwell expressing gratitude for having told him of the "ideas current in philosophical subjects in Cambridge . . ." and added that "I was not aware that Marshall had so long entertained notions of a quantitative theory of political economy, and think it a pity that he has so long delayed publishing something on the subject."[28] This sentence, of course, says nothing of "utility," but Jevons implied in the next sentence that it might concern utility when he said that "what I contend is that my notion of utility is the correct one, and the only sound way of laying the foundation for a mathematical theory."[29]

Nearly five years later Foxwell evidently brought up the matter again, for Jevons replied as follows on November 14, 1879, in more detail than previously and with a hint of irritation:

> As regards Marshall's originality, I never called it in question in the slightest degree, having neither the wish nor the grounds. On the other hand, you seem to forget that the essential points of my theory were fully indicated as far back as 1862, at the Cambridge Meeting of the British Association. I have no reason to suppose that Marshall saw any printed report of my first brief paper; but of course, on the other hand, in my book of 1871 (*Theory of Political Economy*) I could not possibly have borrowed anything from Marshall. But these questions are really of little or no importance now that we have found such earlier books as those of Gossen, Cournot, Dupuit, etc.[30]

Foxwell mentioned that Jevons' *Theory* and "the teaching of Professor Marshall, who had previously revived and extended the teaching of Cournot . . ." had exerted an exceptional influence on eco-

81

nomic theory in England.[31] But a revival and extension of Cournot would not require at all the use of marginal utility.

VI

Another source of the view that Marshall had used marginal utility in his analysis before he read Jevons' *Theory* was no doubt the biography of Marshall written by John Maynard Keynes. Keynes himself relied somewhat on his fellow Cantabrigian Foxwell, still alive and active at the time Keynes wrote. In the biography Keynes never actually said outright that Marshall used the idea of marginal utility in any way before 1871, but he managed none the less to leave that impression. Talcott Parsons, for example, said that "Keynes tells us that Marshall was an independent discoverer of the principle of marginal utility," and in support of his assertion, cited page 23 of the *Memorials of Alfred Marshall*.[32] A reading of this page reveals that Keynes only implied that Marshall had discovered the principle of marginal utility independently. The paragraph that contains the strongest implication of Marshall's originality comes on the two preceding pages, where Keynes said:

By 1871 his progress along these lines was considerably advanced. He was expounding the new ideas to pupils and the foundations of his diagrammatic economics had been truly laid. In that year there appeared, as the result of independent work, Jevons' *Theory of Political Economy*. The publication of this book must have been an occasion of some disappointment and annoyance to Marshall. It took the cream of novelty off the new ideas which Marshall was slowly working up, without giving them—in Marshall's judgment—adequate or accurate treatment. Nevertheless it undoubtedly gave Jevons priority of publication as regards the group of ideas connected with "marginal" (or, as Jevons called it, "final") utility. Marshall's references to the question of priority are extremely reserved. He is careful to leave Jevons' claim undisputed, while pointing out, indirectly, but quite clearly and definitely, that his own work owed little or nothing to Jevons.[33]

Literally no part of this paragraph says that Marshall worked with marginal utility before he read Jevons' *Theory*. The expression "these lines" of the first sentence and the expression "the new ideas" of the second sentence probably refer to Marshall's use of diagrams. The statement that the publication of Jevons' *Theory* took the "cream of novelty" off the "new ideas which Marshall was slowly working up" could refer to many things besides utility. In the last part of the paragraph, the part that mentions utility, Keynes made

82

Marshall claim independence but did not himself evaluate **Marshall's** claim.

Keynes once more discussed the relation between Marshall and Jevons in his article "William Stanley Jevons" which he read before the Royal Statistical Society in 1936.[34] Keynes wrote that Jevons' *Theory* "was not as uniquely original in 1871 as it would have been in 1862 . . .," for the assumed reason that "there were several economists, notably Walras and Marshall, who by 1871, were scribbling equations with x's and y's, big Deltas and little d's."[35] Nonetheless Keynes gave Jevons credit for the "first treatise to present in a finished form the theory of value based on subjective valuations."[36] Keynes called Marshall's review of Jevons' *Theory* "tepid and grudging," and Marshall's references in the *Principles* to Jevons "somewhat grudging."[37] Keynes concluded his examination of the relation of Marshall and Jevons, without pronouncing for or against Marshall's claim for independence, in the following sentences: "Indeed, it was preposterous to suggest that Jevons could have derived anything from Marshall. But for more than another decade [after 1879] . . . 'what Marshall gave in his lectures in 1869' was to be an inhibition and a taboo on the publications of others. In later years Marshall was, perhaps, a little uneasy whether a certain fundamental lack of sympathy had led him to do injustice to Jevons."[38]

In the discussion that followed the reading of Keynes' paper on Jevons, several members of the Royal Statistical Society turned their attention to the topic of the relation between Jevons and Marshall. H. S. Jevons, the son of W. S. Jevons, said that "Mr. Keynes has dealt most fairly with the question of the indebtedness of Marshall to my father, and vice versa,"[39] but he also pointed out an observation of Keynes that he could not "altogether endorse."[40] He objected to Keynes' statement that his father and Marshall had the same approach. His father, the son said, had belonged to the "psychological economic school" which came down from Bentham through Senior, while Marshall had inherited his viewpoint from J. S. Mill, a member of a "perfectly distinct school of thought."

VII

Marshall himself gave support to the view that he had originated the idea of marginal utility theory. He openly implied in print that such was the case, although he never did more than imply. Even in his review of Jevons' *Theory*, Marshall led his readers to believe that he had known about marginal utility all along when he introduced the subject of marginal utility by calling it a "familiar truth."[41] In the first edition of the *Principles* he said that he had borrowed the term "marginal" from von Thünen, then adopted Jevons' "final" but "had been gradually convinced that marginal is the better."[42] For several reasons this account in the *Principles* is hard to believe. In the first place, von Thünen never used the German equivalent of "marginal." Someone must have called Marshall's attention to his error, for in the second edition he corrected it and offered the following unsatisfactory explanation that the "term 'marginal' increment is in harmony with von Thünen's methods of thought and was suggested to me by him, though he does not actually use it," adding apologetically that "in the first Edition this footnote implied wrongly that the phrase, as well as the idea of, Marginal Increment, could be traced to von Thünen."[43] This contention of Marshall's in the first edition of the *Principles* also is not congruent with the fact that Marshall called "final utility" a "*happy phrase*" in his *Economics of Industry* in 1879, which meant at least that for some time he must have persisted without regret in his adoption of Jevons' expression. Marshall's memory does not show to good advantage on this controversial point, as on many others.

The second edition of the *Principles* contains another statement by Marshall that might be interpreted as a claim that he had used marginal utility in his analysis before. In speaking of consumer's rent, the topic in connection with which he first used the idea of marginal utility, Marshall said that the "notion of Consumers' Rent was suggested to the present writer by a study of the mathematical aspects of demand and utility under the influence of Cournot, von Thünen and Bentham."[44] This quotation remains in the third edition (1895) of the *Principles*. Marshall removed it from the fourth edition (1898). If this is a claim, Marshall leaned solely on the recollection of what took place over twenty years before, unsupported by evidence. No writer ought to presume to claim priority in the origin of ideas simply on the basis of what he recalls that he thought at a much earlier period.

All the above claims could be dismissed as unintended were it not for the fact that Marshall once stated in correspondence in unequivocal terms that he taught the doctrine of marginal utility in 1869. This he did in a letter, written in 1883, to Léon Walras:

". . . I cannot be said to have accepted the Jevons doctrine of 'final utility'. For I had taught it publicly in lectures at Cambridge before his book appeared. I had indeed used another name, viz.: 'terminal-value-in-use'. But, following the lead of Cournot, I had anticipated all the central points of Jevons' book and had in many respects gone beyond him. I was in no hurry to publish, because I wished to work out my doctrines on their practical side."[45] Here, Marshall flatly stated in private correspondence what he never set out in print. How much trust can we put in Marshall's memory, especially his memory of having used the word "terminal" or "terminal-value-in-use" instead of "final degree of utility"? For Jevons used the word "terminal" expressly in this connection in the *Theory* as an alternative to "the final degree" in the following expression: "I may suggest that this distinct feeling of value is probably identical with the final degree of utility. While Adam Smith's often quoted *value in use* is the total utility of a commodity to us, the *value in exchange* is defined by the *terminal utility,* the remaining desire which we or others have for possessing more."[46] While Marshall himself never used the expression "terminal value-in-use" or "terminal utility" at any time in any of his writing, in his review of Jevons' *Theory* in 1872, he employed the expression "final degree of utility" enclosed in quotation marks.[47] In *The Pure Theory of Domestic Values* and in *The Economics of Industry,* he reduced this expression to "final utility," as he did also in the first edition of the *Principles,* where he used it along with "marginal utility."[48]

In his correspondence with other persons Marshall often took up the subject of his relation with Jevons, but he was never so forthright in his contention as he had been with Walras. For instance, in 1900, Marshall wrote to J. B. Clark that he "got 'marginal' from von Thünen's *Grenze*" and that he had read that work "probably in 1869 or 70. . . ."[49] Marshall may correctly recall the time, more than thirty years earlier, when he read a particular book, but he cannot correctly attribute his use of "marginal" to Thünen's *Grenze,* for the reasons already given.[50] He seems to have forgotten his earlier correction of this misstatement. In another letter to Clark in 1908, Marshall said that "my main position as to the theory of value and distribution was practically completed in the years 1867 to 1870 . . . and that, when Jevons' book appeared, I knew at once how far I agreed with him and how far I did not."[51] Marshall did not specify the word "utility" in either of these letters, yet he doubtless intended to imply that he shared in the discovery of the idea of marginal utility.

A year or so after the letter to Clark, Marshall addressed an interesting version of the same account to L. C. Colson: "Before 1871 when Jevons' very important *Theory of Political Economy* appeared, I had worked out the whole skeleton of my present system in mathematics though not in English. My mathematical Note XXI concentrated my notions; but the greater part of the earlier notes and especially Notes XIV—XX were evolved in substance about the same time."[52] Notes XIV-XXI in the *Principles* concern slightly different matters in different editions, but nowhere do they concern utility. These "Notes" would supply the skeleton framework for a demand-and-supply analysis such as Marshall gave in his *Pure Theory of Domestic Values* but have nothing to do with an analysis of utility. Marshall's "Notes" that touch on the subject of utility precede the ones he specifically called to the notice of Colson.

Marshall wrote, in much the same tone and for the same purpose, to E. R. A. Seligman in the years between 1896 and 1900. Here again utility entered only by implication in association with related topics. In denying the relation between his work and that of Fleeming Jenkin, Marshall said to Seligman on April 6, 1896, that "it is a matter of no moment but as a fact my obligations are solely to Cournot; not to Fleeming Jenkin or Dupuit. I had given the main substance of my doctrines in lectures a year or two before he read his paper at Edinburgh; while I read very shortly after that a paper at Cambridge in which I showed the curves in my present chapter on monopolies."[53] Here Marshall gives the same reference to early lectures that he mentioned previously, but he does not specifically mention utility. The published chapter of the "paper at Cambridge" has no mention in it of utility and holds to a simple demand-and-supply analysis of price by means of mathematics, particularly by graphs.[54] Marshall could have learned most from Jenkin's two earlier papers. None of Jenkin's work, however, uses utility in any form.[55] Marshall had sufficient early familiarity with Jenkin's writings on economics to refer to them in his review of the first edition of Jevons' *Theory* in 1872.[56]

Marshall repeated his statement about the early lectures in another letter to Seligman on April 23, 1900, when, in speaking of his *Pure Theory of Foreign Trade* and his *Pure Theory of Domestic Values,* he said that the "substance of them was given in great part—

in lectures very early; before the publication of Jevon's [*sic*] theory."[57] Again another letter to Seligman the same year contains the suggestion that he had used marginal utility before 1871, although here, as before, Marshall carefully avoided any direct reference either to priority or to utility. Probably Seligman had written Marshall to ask him to review a book. At any rate Marshall brought the matter up in connection with reviewing. On the subject he said: "But it has always been against my rule to write reviews. I have only written one in my life: that was of Jevon's [*sic*] *Theory* when it first appeared, and then I wrote only because there was no one else who had been working systematically on the subject of that book in England."[58] Perhaps at this time it is helpful to note that Marshall wrote nothing at all prior to 1871; and that he touched on utility only three times in all his writing up to 1890: in the reviews of Jevons' *Theory*, in his *Economics of Industry*, and in his *Pure Theory of Domestic Values*. On none of these occasions did he use utility in any way that would lead a reader to think that he even held the idea highly, let alone that he had a paternal interest in it. It is clear, too, that no one has ever said that he had heard Marshall lecture on marginal utility or any topic resembling it during the years before 1871. It is also evident that Marshall never published any statement of his belief in his own originality, although he felt no qualms in hinting at it in print, and in correspondence he did go so far as to state it baldly.

VIII

His relation to the discovery of the use of marginal utility was considered in the articles written around 1942 in celebration of the centennial of Marshall's birth. Joseph A. Schumpeter expressed the only doubt that anyone has expressed on Marshall's claim to originality, and he qualified his doubt so completely that few could object to it. Schumpeter said of Marshall's *Principles* that "its originality does not stand out as, on the merits of the case, it should because for us it is just one member of a family which had grown up or was growing up at that time. Moreover, the other members of that family were no doubt independent of Marshall, whereas his habits of work and his methods of publication make it impossible for the historian of economic thought to be equally positive about his version."[59] Schumpeter accepted the version that Marshall first read Mill and Ricardo, felt "shocked at the haziness and carelessness that both authors, but especially Mill, displayed with respect to cogency of proof and determination of results," and used his mathematical training to put the works of both authors into mathematical notation. This is an old story, often repeated, for which there is no evidence. It is certain that Marshall's equations in his "Mathematical Appendix," the only equations he ever published in any number, do not relate to Mill or Ricardo. This statement implies that a person with a training in mathematics such as Marshall's should be able to sit down with a copy of Ricardo's or Mill's *Principles,* reduce them to differential equations, and come out with important findings on marginal utility. This way of speaking probably overestimates both Marshall's mathematical facility and his economic insight, in 1866-71, as well as the power of people generally to bring the subjects of mathematics and economics together. Only William Whewell, either before or after, published an attempt to do what Marshall is said to have accomplished. And Whewell's equations show no evidence of a realization of the need to introduce utility.[60]

In another article which appeared in the year of the centenary of the birth of Marshall, G. F. Shove maintained that a good many early writers, particularly Thünen, Cournot, John Stuart Mill, and Ricardo influenced Marshall markedly in the years 1867-70 but that Marshall owed nothing to any writers after 1870. This thesis explains any similarity between Marshall's *Principles* and the works of later writers, on the ground that Marshall's training in mathematics led him to change the older writings to make them complete, consistent, and general, and that these changes anticipated the work of the later writers. Shove placed Marshall in the history of economic thought as a direct descendant of Ricardo through Mill and omitted Jevons entirely or placed him in a subordinate position at one side. The following three quotations illustrate how completely Shove replaced Jevons by Marshall in the history of economic thought:

In its country of origin Alfred Marshall's *Principles* stands with Adam Smith's *Wealth of Nations* and Ricardo's *Principles* as one of the three great watersheds in the development of economic ideas: with the usual qualifications, we may divide the history of English political economy into three distinct epochs—the Classical, the Ricardian and the Marshallian or reformed-Ricardian.[61]

Thus the three streams of economic theory which took their rise in the seventies tended to flow in separate channels—the Austrian school, the Lausanne school and the English or Marshallian—instead of merging into a single flood, though there were, of course, more or less important percolations from one to the other.[62]

Thus outside England and Austria, where the native systems established almost undisputed sway, Marshall's *Principles* and the writings of Walras acted side by side to stimulate and mould the renaissance of theoretical economics in Europe.[63]

Here Marshall stands not beside Jevons but far above him.

Since Shove had this attitude toward Marshall, he took especial pains to contradict the view of Marshall as a conciliatory spirit who took the cost analysis of the earlier economists and reconciled it with the utility analysis of Jevons, Menger, and Walras. Marshall's "analytical backbone," Shove wrote, "is not, as many have supposed, a conflation of Ricardian notions with those of the 'marginal utility' school."[64] Shove insisted that Marshallian economics "is of the true Ricardian stock, neither a cross-bred nor a sport."[65] Shove did not originate this opinion. He took it from Marshall himself, who was naturally forced to it by the conviction that his views on utility preceded those of Jevons, Menger, or Walras. He first expressed this conviction in a letter to John Bates Clark in 1908 (first published in the *Memorials of Alfred Marshall* in 1925) in which he said: "One thing alone in American criticism irritates me, though it be not unkindly meant. It is the suggestion that I try to 'compromise between' or 'reconcile' divergent schools of thought. Such work seems to me trumpery."[66] Marshall was wrong in thinking that the view of him as a "conciliatory spirit" had an American origin. It really originated in England, spread widely, and persists today. Credit for its origin goes to L. L. Price, whom Marshall mentioned in the *Principles* as having read "all the proofs."[67] Price wrote a long review of the first edition of the *Principles* that in the following passage laid the foundation for the idea that Marshall's fame rests mainly on his resolution of the divergent views of Ricardo and Jevons:

As the case then stood [before Marshall], it was difficult for the student . . . to believe that in the picture as drawn by Ricardo, and in that executed afterwards by Jevons, he had unfinished sketches before him, which could be combined into one grand whole. . . . Why should there be such a sudden breach in the continuity of thought, such a complete reversal of an earlier tradition?

To these perplexing questions Professor Marshall's work affords an answer. There is no such breach, and no such reversal. The newer work can be combined with the old, and the result is a grander conception, without any infringement of the first principles of artistic drawing; for the unity of the design is unimpaired. It is even rendered more prominent by the process.[68]

L. L. Price incorporated a brief version of his opinion of Marshall's relation to Jevons and Ricardo in his *A Short History of Political Economy in England,* published in 1891, the first appearance of Marshall's *Principles* in any history of economic thought.[69]

Most, but not all, later histories of economic thought followed the lead of L. L. Price if they included any consideration of Marshall's relations to the Ricardo-Mill school and to Jevons. Luigi Cossa said in 1893 that Marshall "adopts from Jevons the theory of a final degree of utility . . . and then straightway . . . points out that this notion of marginal utility both explains and also completes the current account of the cost of production. . . ."[70] Lewis Haney referred to H. J. Davenport's "chapter headed 'The Attempt at Reconciliation; Marshall' " and added that although "this is a fairly good characterization . . . 'Marshall's synthesis' might have been better."[71] Alexander Gray, in 1931, wrote that Alfred Marshall "as a first approach, is perhaps best viewed as representing an endeavour to give Austrian ideas their due place . . . and thus to effect a synthesis of the Austrian ideas and the older Political Economy."[72] And in 1940 Edmund Whittaker said that "just as he drew on the ideas of Jevons, so Marshall incorporated in his theories the doctrines of Mill on the side of production."[73]

G. F. Shove's article on Marshall in 1942 evidently accomplished what the publication of Marshall's letters had failed to bring about, for, since that date, several histories have denied that Marshall composed a blend of Jevons and Ricardo and in fact have appeared somewhat inconsistently to characterize Marshall as both a true descendant of the Classical School and at the same time an early originator of the marginal utility doctrine. Eric Roll's *History of Economic Thought,* first published in 1938 and revised in 1942, holds an equally equivocal position. Roll put Marshall on an equal footing with Jevons and Menger as a pioneer of marginal utility theory. "It is known that by 1871," Roll wrote, "the year in which Jevons's *Theory* and Menger's *Grundsätze* were published, Marshall had already developed a similar approach."[74] Roll stated that Marshall broke with the English tradition less than the Austrian and the pure mathematical economists, and he waved away the appearance of eclecticism in Marshall as an illusion caused by "the very elaborate quality of his system."[75]

A recent textbook on the history of economic thought by John Fred Bell said that it "may be contended that Marshall's ideas on demand and utility were arrived at quite independently of Jevons or the Austrians, since his work on economics dates from 1867-1868, before either Jevons' or Menger's writings appeared."[76] Bell quoted Shove on Marshall's originality, pointed out that Alfred Marshall's economics "should not then be regarded as a mechanical synthesis, as it has been for many years," and later added that Marshall "undertook to rewrite and rehabilitate the economics of Smith, Malthus, Ricardo, and Mill." Another recent history of economic thought follows a variant of the pattern set by Shove. "By 1871," Philip Charles Newman wrote in his long chapter on Alfred Marshall, "he had already been working out his ideas within the framework of diagrammatic economics, when Jevons came out with his *Theory of Political Economy.*"[77] Newman thought that Marshall "made it very clear, however, that, although Jevons had had priority of publication, his own work had been done completely independently."[78] Newman accepted too the view that Marshall did not reconcile Jevons or the Austrians with the Classical School, and supported his acceptance by the statement "that this was not so was evident both from the fused, integrated character of his book, and from the many novel ideas which are not to be found in any of the theories of his predecessors."[79] "What Marshall did do," Newman concluded, "was to show how the various parts of the classical theory . . . can be expressed in terms of supply and demand."[80] Here again the historian forces Marshall to play a peculiar role. This new view of Marshall, however, has not yet penetrated the recent non-English histories of economic thought, which continue to portray Marshall as an eclectic.[81]

So stands the confused position of Marshall with respect to his use of marginal utility in economics. Marshall's own peculiar attitude toward his role in the history of economic thought did nothing to clarify his position, to say the very least. The difficulty is compounded by the strength of the friendship of many writers for Marshall, which led them to take liberties with evidence that they would not take with someone they knew less well or held in less esteem. Yet Marshall's reputation is too substantial to require his being credited with anticipating Jevons. In the history of marginal utility alone Marshall enjoys a firm place even without mention of the problem of innovation. For one thing, Marshall's *Principles* contributed as much as did any one other book to embed the idea of marginal utility in the general body of economic thought.

Chapter XI

F. Y. EDGEWORTH

I

Of the few writers besides Marshall who treated the subject, Francis Ysidro Edgeworth made as good use of the idea of marginal utility in the period up to 1890 as did any other writer in England, but he used it more in connection with topics generally associated with the subjects of philosophy and psychology than with topics included in economics. Consequently histories of economic thought seldom connect his name with the development of marginal utility. Nor did the reviews of his three-volume *Papers Relating to Political Economy*,[1] or his obituary notices.[2]

Edgeworth came to Oxford in 1867 after four years at Trinity College, Dublin, and received his B. A. degree in 1873. At this time, the beginning of the "modern period" in economics, and for many years afterwards he showed no concern with economics. In fact, Edgeworth evidently thought that his immediate interest lay in the legal profession, for after 1873 he went from Oxford to London, where, among other things, and with "straitened means," he gave enough attention to the study of law for the Inner Temple to call him to the bar in 1877. However, the study of law did not furnish his only interest, or an abiding one, for he never practiced; and during the period between 1873 and 1877, when he read law, he also busied himself with his first love, philosophy, and wrote his first publication thereon.[3] It was a one-page note concerning "Mr. Matthew Arnold on Bishop Butler's Doctrine of Self-Love" that appeared in *Mind,* the admirable journal of philosophy and psychology, of which the first issue had come out earlier the same year.[4] A later article in this same journal by Alfred Barratt, which criticized parts of Henry Sidgwick's *The Methods of Ethics,* provided the immediate incentive for Edgeworth to prepare the first of the three short books he wrote during his life.[5]

This book, the *New and Old Methods of Ethics, or "Physical Ethics" and "Methods of Ethics,"* deals wholly with the dispute between Sidgwick and Barratt.[6] Perhaps Alfred Barratt's attendance at Balliol College, Oxford, in the years just before Edgeworth entered that college helped to draw Edgeworth's attention to this particular discussion of ethics. After setting out the principal differences between these two authors, Edgeworth considered mainly the part of the discussion of hedonism that turns around the subject of the measurement of pleasures and pains. "Setting out from Bentham's formula 'the greatest happiness of the greatest number'," the reviewer in *Mind* said of the second section of *New and Old Methods of Ethics*, "(which although unsatisfactory is said to contain implicitly the idea of an exact Utilitarianism) and fully equipped with the latest conceptions of psychophysics as defined by Fechner, Wundt, &c., and with those formulae of the calculus of variations which are applicable to the problem, the writer reaches a number of conclusions respecting the best possible (that is the most felicific) distribution of the external means of happiness."[7]

It is evident that Edgeworth's book consequently contains an attack on what many people think of as the *economic problem*. Hedonism always includes this kind of economic problem. Yet the results of a hedonistic analysis usually, and in the case of Edgeworth particularly, do not coincide with the results from an economic analysis. At least Edgeworth did not reproduce many of the conclusions that Jevons, Menger, and Walras had obtained on the identical problem. One reason is that he did not direct his analysis to an interpretation of the phenomena of price and exchange. Thus, his results imply no such relation between exchange or prices and "felicity" as did the conclusions of Jevons, Menger, and Walras. Although Edgeworth restricted his analysis to non-price situations, he expanded it in another direction by admitting interpersonal comparisons of utility to an extent that Jevons, Menger, and Walras had avoided.

Edgeworth's major conclusions follow more from his admission of the interpersonal comparisons than from any other part of his argument. His conclusions include: "(1) In the case of races or societies so nearly related in the order of evolution as the Aryan, equality of distribution is the law. . . . (2) Population ought to be limited . . . (3) the quality of the . . . [people] . . . should be as high as possible . . . [but] . . . indefinite improvement of quality is no longer to be wished . . . [if it] . . . is only possible by means of a diminution of population. . . ."[8]

The relation between "hedonism" and "marginal utility economics" shows itself clearly with Edgeworth. Edgeworth started with the same problem as Jevons did, but he did not end at the same

94

place in his first attempt. Henry Sidgwick had had all the tools that Edgeworth and Jevons used and held a professorship of economics, but he did not wind up at the same place either. Even Bentham did not really wring from the elements of analysis he had present in his system anything like marginal economics. Economists had to read Bentham, digest him, and then turn him into economics. Economists must add something to and take something away from hedonism, as ordinarily construed, before it becomes marginal utility economics. Jevons and Gossen could make the transformation; Sidgwick never could; and Edgeworth did not in 1877.

II

In the eighteen-seventies, and to a degree even earlier, three separate strands of thought contained an examination of the individual's reaction to his satisfaction: *marginal utility* in economics; *hedonism* in philosophy; and *psychophysics* in the new field of psychology. All three probably stemmed from some common underlying set of conditions. But on the surface they were distinct movements in thought. Writers who used one of the three sets of ideas seldom knew anything about the other two. Edgeworth is a person who began by dabbling in two of the movements. In his first book he cited Bentham, Sidgwick, and Barratt in hedonistic philosophy; and Weber and Fechner in psychophysics. In the beginning, he did not show any recognition of marginal utility economics.

Usually histories of economic thought mention *hedonism* but ignore *psychophysics* entirely. Only L. H. Haney gives a brief note to it.[9] The article by George J. Stigler on "The Development of Utility Theory. I" contains the longest historical discussion of the relation of marginal utility to psychophysics: two pages.[10] Only Edgeworth of the early writers on marginal utility gave much attention to it, and then mostly before he turned definitely to economics.

Psychophysics had begun with Ernst Heinrich Weber's work at Leipzig in 1831, although the term "psychophysics" did not come into use until much later. Weber's experiments hold a prominent place in the history of quantitative psychology.[11] Economists notice Weber only because his experiments concerned sensations which resemble utility, although not the same, and because he framed a law about sensations which has a similarity to the law of diminishing marginal utility, especially in the express form stated earlier by Bernoulli.

95

Weber experimented with the ability of a man to perceive differences between weights. In an early experiment he gave a person one object that weighed thirty-two ounces and a second that weighed only slightly less, and then asked, "Which weighs more?" On receiving the reply that the person could not discriminate, Weber decreased the weight of the second object until the subject could tell which weighed more. In that way Weber ascertained the "just perceptible difference." One of his subjects could distinguish, by lifting, between weights of 32 and 30.5 ounces. Thus 1.5 ounces constituted the "just perceptible difference" for this individual when the object weighed in the neighborhood of two pounds.

We can see that the problem of Weber has a resemblance, though not a close one, to the problem of marginal utility. The resemblance rests on the circumstances that both concern the reaction of the individual to external circumstances, and that both deal with differences in totals. The feeling of weight, however, differs from the feeling of utility anticipated from the consumption of goods.

Weber next examined the change in the "just perceptible difference" in weights that occurs as a result of an alteration in the weights themselves. Would the same individual who could only distinguish another weight as less than 32 ounces if it weighs at least 1.5 ounces less, need a 1.5 ounce difference if the first object weighed not 32 ounces but 4 ounces? Weber's further experiments confirmed the common-sense view that the individual did not. His experiment showed that a given weight-lifter would need a difference in weight of roughly .2 of an ounce when the first object weighs only 4 ounces. On the scant basis of very few experiments Weber generalized that the "just perceptible difference" has a proportional relationship to the amount of the weight.[12] Weber extended his generalization with similar results to judgments of differences in the total length of a line, and in the recognition of variations in tones. Subsequently psychologists called this generalization "Weber's Law."

Weber's Law bears a relation to the law of diminishing marginal utility, but only a relation of analogy. As the number of ounces of the object increases, each ounce of the object has less influence on the ability of the individual to judge relative weights: a diminishing marginal effectiveness of ability to judge differences follows from consecutively added units of weight. An individual can distinguish between 10 and 11 ounces, but he cannot distinguish between 100 and 101 ounces; for the 101st ounce influences the individual's sense

96

of weight much less strongly than does the 11th ounce. In a discussion of utility, an additional dollar added to income makes a noticeable difference when the individual has only $10 but would be unnoticed when he has $100; for the 101st dollar influences the person's total satisfaction much less strongly than does the 11th dollar. Here, however, the similarity ends.

For obvious reasons no economist mentioned Weber's experiments in the years immediately following their initial publication in 1834. His work, however, bore fruit in psychology when Gustav Theodor Fechner set out on a path similar to the one that Weber had followed, discovered that Weber already had covered some of the same ground, and then pushed on to new results. He first conceived the idea of measuring mental activity or sensations in 1850, briefly mentioned his new ideas in 1851, published a preliminary report in 1858 followed by an important application in 1859, and issued his principal work on the subject, his *Elemente der Psychophysik*, in 1860.[13] Thus Fechner did not publish his results that launched the study of psychophysics in earnest until after H. H. Gossen and Richard Jennings had published their books on utility in the eighteen-fifties.

Fechner's contribution was the use of the "just perceptible differences" of Weber to measure sensitivity. He considered each state of sensitivity to be measured by the number of the "just perceptible differences" that bring it about. The 1.5 ounces that might constitute the "just perceptible difference" between the sensation of weight of an object that weighs 32 ounces and one lighter, has one unit of weight sensation. The 1.43 ounces that we must take from an object that weighs 30.5 ounces in order that it appear still lighter stands as the second unit of weight sensation. Proceeding by parts through the whole of the weight to some level near zero, Fechner obtained the total number of units of weight sensation of the whole to the individual. This idea of defining a unit of weight sensation as a "just perceptible difference" had little effect on utility theory.[14]

Here, then, in 1860, we find the beginning of psychophysics, a subject which occupies a place in psychology comparable in many ways to the place held in economics by marginal utility. Both psychophysics and marginal utility economics stressed the relation between the individual and external stimuli. Both the new psychology and the new economics made use of mathematics. Both reached the conclusion that the responses of the individual decrease in some way as the amount of stimulus increases. Both Fechner and Jevons realized that Bernoulli had written out this relationship over a century earlier.[15]

Psychophysics and marginal utility economics also differ in many respects. They differ basically in the nature of the responses to the stimuli. Marginal utility economics considers the *satisfaction* that the individual anticipates from consumption. Economists assume that a meaningful total results from the addition of the anticipated satisfaction of different goods. Psychophysics limits its view to *sensations* associated with weight, distances, tones, and the like. Any sum of these diverse sensations lacks meaning. Psychophysics stops with the individual; no further conclusions result from the explanation of the individual's responses to the stimuli. On the contrary, economics makes use of the individual's marginal utility only as a starting point for a sketch of the operation of the whole economic system. Psychophysics concerned itself with measurement from the start, while marginal utility economics shunned the problem of measurement for a considerable period. Psychophysics, too, rested its conclusions on laboratory experiments; marginal utility economics, on its appeals to common experience. Perhaps because psychophysics did make use of the laboratory it expressed its conclusions from the first in the form of specific functions, while marginal utility economics continued to contain only functions with a minimum of express content.

Psychophysics with all its similarities and differences had a head start on marginal utility economics, for, as set down above, it had attention drawn to it in 1860 by the appearance of Fechner's *Elemente der Psychophysik,* a good ten years before the customary date of the beginning of the Marginal Utility School. During the sixties and the first part of the seventies it received widespread comment, criticism, and extension on the Continent at the hands mainly of German writers, but it arrived in England only in the middle part of the eighteen-seventies.

Psychophysics first came to the notice of the English through the writing of James Sully, a friend of F. Y. Edgeworth.[16] It is reasonable to suppose that Edgeworth took part of his interest from Sully. In fact, he said at the beginning of his first book that "I have to thank my friend Mr. James Sully, author of 'Sensation and Intuition', 'Pessimism', &c., for having revised and corrected the fol-

98

lowing pages during their passage through the press, and for many suggestions."[17]

In his autobiography James Sully spoke of Edgeworth on a few occasions but not always by name.[18] Sully attributed to the Savile Club his meeting with "F. Y. Edgeworth, whose many-sidedness of mind refuses to be contained even under two categories."[19] Edgeworth evidently had suggested that Sully move to the quiet of Hampstead to find relief from the noise of the city, a discomfort to which Sully was especially sensitive.[20] In the paragraphs below Sully tells something about his life in Hampstead insofar as it concerns Edgeworth, whom he refers to as "my bachelor chum," and Jevons:

It was he [my bachelor chum] who attracted me to Hampstead, quite as much, I think, by the prospect of having him as a neighbor as by his praises of the salubrity of the Northern Heights. I responded to his brotherly overtures by selecting for my home a cottage only a few steps from his abode. We met almost daily, now for a short after-breakfast walk, now for a longer tramp, in which Stanley Jevons might join, and now on a skating expedition to Hendon or Elstree. Later on, the bicycle came upon the scene, aiming a blow at our unhurried peregrinations on foot. I used to join him now and then, though knowing that I was a sort of cog to his impatient wheels. In another bodily exercise I was quite unable to join him—the early morning dip in the bathing pond. Valiant as I was in attacking, on a hot summer day, ice-cold water in Switzerland or Norway, I could not in cold blood face the early-morning plunge in winter.

Our lines of study overlapped somewhat, and this, together with the multiplicity of his interests, made conversation fluent. His mind seemed to be ever simmering with new problems, and upon meeting him on the edge of the Heath, he would at once put me a poser of the form, "If you had so much money to invest, and the conditions were so and so, would you be ready to risk it?" I was amused at his supposing that I might be troubled by a superfluity of wealth, but did my best to answer his query. It was delightful to know, when starting for my morning view of Harrow-on-the-Hill, that I should find him somewhere near the White Stone Pond. I recognized his cloaked figure at some distance moving very slowly with bent back, and loved to startle him out of his fit of abstraction, to see him spring upwards with something of a bird's movement of flight, and to hear his cheery outburst, "Hallo, Sully!"

Although my junior, he seemed, as the older inhabitant, to take special care of me. This was due in part to the sweet courtesy of his nature, for he came from the isle of hospitality. Among those delicious memories to which I can return again and again was a week spent with him in his ancestral home, a summer week made the more fragrant by his delicate attentions. Propinquity no longer makes it easy for me to get possession of his genial and sustaining comradeship. Nevertheless, I

99

cherish the dream that, if ever I reach the Elysian Fields, I shall be welcomed once more by that sudden upward spring and that thrilling "Hallo!"[21]

III

Even in 1879 when he published "The Hedonical Calculus" Edgeworth showed no contact with economics.[22] He was still in the land of hedonism and psychophysics. Nonetheless, this article makes a sufficient use of notions resembling marginal utility for us to consider him as a belated, independent discoverer of the principle of diminishing marginal utility. In his means-and-end problem, which was the same one that he had had in the *New and Old Methods of Ethics,* he used as the "first postulate" of his analysis a broad form of the law of diminishing marginal utility. He stated his postulate as follows: "The rate of increase of pleasure decreases as its means increase. The postulate asserts that the second differential of pleasure with regard to means is continually negative. It does not assert that the first differential is continually positive."[23] He supported his "first postulate" both by recourse to experiences and to authorities. The authorities that he cited do not include a single writer of the Marginal Utility School. Edgeworth gave as authorities: "Buffon in his *Moral Arithmetic,* Laplace in his *Essay on Probabilities,* William Thompson in his *Inquiry into the Distribution of Wealth,* and Mr. Sidgwick in the *Methods of Ethics . . .,*"[24] but unfortunately he failed to cite pages. He held, too, that " 'ratiocination' from simpler inductions, partly common to the followers of Fechner, and partly peculiar to Professor Delboeuf" confirmed his postulate.[25]

Edgeworth had, as a crowning similarity, a three-variable utility function that resembles the one he later used in his early discussions of economics. "F (xy)," Edgeworth writes, "is a unit's pleasure of consumption. . . ."[26] However, the x and y do not represent two goods as they did in his later work. Here the x stands as a parameter of the individual's capacity for pleasure, and y stands for the amount of means. Nonetheless, we must admit that Edgeworth had written down a version of one of the chief devices of the Marginal Utility School.

IV

What turned Edgeworth's interests towards economics? Perhaps it was in part the publication of three books in 1879. Two of these books are referred to numerous times in his *Mathematical Psychics*, which he published in 1881 and in which he first began to consider economic problems.[27] One of these was the second edition of Jevons' *Theory of Political Economy*. It probably came into Edgeworth's hands late in 1879. At least he said he did not know it earlier in the year.[28] From this book Edgeworth picked up the clues that led him to read Cournot, Gossen, and especially Walras, and to mention their names in the *Mathematical Psychics*. Edgeworth had, too, during this time, whatever personal counsel his neighbor Jevons in Hampstead could give him. Alfred Marshall's *Pure Theory of Domestic Value*, published in 1879, also exerted a strong influence on Edgeworth. Edgeworth referred to parts of this privately printed volume many times in *Mathematical Psychics* but never by the full title. Edgeworth also had a copy of Marshall's *Economics of Industry*, which came out in the same year, but his eye was taken by the curves and the propositions of the *Pure Theory of Domestic Values*, and not by the primer simplicity of the *Economics of Industry*.[29]

Edgeworth's interest in utility reached a peak in the *Mathematical Psychics* of 1881. In the years of the eighteen-eighties before he went to Oxford as a professor, he switched to statistics and, although he later returned to more strictly economic topics, he never again treated utility separately, and at length. The *Mathematical Psychics* reprinted his 1879 article on the "Hedonical Calculus" almost without change and supplemented it with a section "Economical Calculus" and "Appendices" which are new and largely economics.[30]

One of the problems Edgeworth wrote on in the "Economical Calculus" is the possibility of the measurement of utility. He must have taken his direction partly from his study of psychophysics and partly from his recent acquaintance with some of the literature of marginal utility where measurement was considered. On the question of measurement he provided three answers, all different: first, that the future will turn up some method of measurement not now known, as it has in other lines of study; second, that economists can do a great deal with unnumerical mathematics; and third, that the methods of psychophysics in measuring sensations lend themselves to adaptation to the problems of measurement in economics.

Of the three, Edgeworth gave least attention to the idea that the future may provide helpful methods of measurement as it has done in other sciences. Jevons had hinted as much and Edgeworth merely

101

assented. "There is, no doubt, much difficulty here," Edgeworth wrote in one of his appendices, "and the risen science is still obscured by clouds; and hedonism may still be in the state of heat or electricity before they became exact sciences, as described by Professor Jevons."[31]

Edgeworth made more of the idea that a good deal of mathematical reasoning about economic problems involves only "unnumerical" mathematics, that it involves only the notion that "a quantity is *greater* or *less* than another, *increases* or *decreases*, is *positive* or *negative*, a *maximum* or *minimum*. . . ."[32] In support of this argument Edgeworth cited the "father of Mathematical Economics," A. A. Cournot.[33]

Neither the view that the future will provide measurement nor the view that economics does not need cardinal measurement, satisfied Edgeworth, and he recommended at two places in the *Mathematical Psychics* that economists apply the devices of psychophysics to economics.[34] Here he brought psychophysics into one of its few contacts with economics.[35] Edgeworth accepted Jevons' idea that utility has two dimensions, the dimensions of intensity and of time. "The unit in each dimension"—Edgeworth added what Jevons had not said—"is the just perceivable increment."[36] He next turned to the necessary discussion of the similarity, for counting purposes, of the different and separate "just perceivable units," a discussion that comes up whenever Fechner's attempt to measure psychological quantities arises as a topic for debate. In the early part of the *Mathematical Psychics* he accepted the view that the equality of the different units has no proof, though the equality evidently holds true anyway. "The implied equation to each other of each *minimum sensible* is a first principle incapable of proof. It resembles the equation to each other of undistinguishable events or cases, which constitutes the first principle of the mathematical calculus of *belief*. It is doubtless a principle acquired in the course of evolution. The implied equatability of time-intensity units, irrespective of distance in time and kind of pleasure, is still imperfectly evolved. Such is the unit of *economical* calculus."[37] Later he stated a hesitant, and tentative, proof of the equatability of "just perceivable units," which runs as follows: "For if possible let one just perceivable increment be preferred to another. Then it must be preferred in virtue of some difference of pleasurability (non-hedonistic action not existing, or not being pertinent to the present inquiry). But, if one of the increments exceeds the other in pleasurability, then that one is not a *just perceivable* increment, but consists of at least *two* such increments."[38] But Edgeworth had no faith in his argument, for he added apologetically that "of course such a way of turning the subject has no pretence to *de*duction. The stream of thought 'meanders level with its fount'."[39]

So Edgeworth retreated to the view that necessity compels the consideration of the "just perceivable increments" as equal and relied again on support for the view on his earlier argument that a similar axiom underlies the theory of probabilities: "Turn the matter as we please, there must, I think, be postulated some such equation as the above, which may be compared, perhaps, to the first principle of probabilities, according to which cases about which we are equally undecided, between which we perceive no material difference, count as equal; a principle on which we are agreed to act, but for which it might be hard to give a reason."[40]

All these reflections on the measurability of utility echo the debates in psychophysics that had gone on for twenty years. To these Edgeworth added other speculations on the subject. He thought that perhaps we only require that in the future in some perfect world the increments equal each other. "Indeed," he wrote, "the equation, or equatability, in question exists not so much in fact as in the limit of perfect evolution."[41] He knew, too, that the *time* dimension of utility shares the same position as to the comparability of the "just perceivable units" as does the *intensity* dimension. He entertained, and then rejected, the idea of introducing a second time dimension into utility so that utility would have "three dimensions, namely, objective time, subjective time, and intensity."[42]

He suggested, in the next paragraph, that instead of adding a dimension, "probably it is more competent to consciousness to combine into a single mark the two considerations of rate and intensity."[43] After a short, unfruitful example of measurement he concluded that "the comparison of pleasures as to quantity is here admitted to be vague; not vaguer perhaps than the comparisons made by an examiner as to excellence, where numerical marks are usefully employed."[44] He finally turned from the imperfections of reality to the flawlessness of the imagination and asked the reader "to imagine an ideally perfect instrument, a psychophysical machine, continually registering the height of pleasure experienced by an individual, exactly according to the verdict of consciousness, or rather

103

diverging therefrom according to a *law of errors.*"[45] From topic to topic Edgeworth wandered suggestively but inconclusively.

V

Edgeworth turned from the subject of measurability to that of the interpersonal comparability of utility. Here he found the same sort of difficulties that he had met in the measurement of the utility of an individual. Again he resorted to an axiom, or rather extended his previous axiom to read: "Any just perceivable pleasure-increment experienced by any sentient at any time has the same value."[46] Over this assumption in its extended form, as in its simpler, Edgeworth found that there hung "the primal mystery of an ultimate axiom." He called the extended axiom that involves interpersonal comparisons, the *utilitarian* principle, while he named the simpler axiom the *economic* principle. He met the objection that only an inference gives the "just perceivable increment" in the case of the *utilitarian* principle by stating that "greater uncertainty of hedonimetry in the case of others' pleasures may be compensated by the greater number of measurements, a wider average; just as, according to the theory of probabilities, greater accuracy may be obtained by more numerous observations with a less perfect instrument."[47]

VI

The part of the *Mathematical Psychics* that Edgeworth wrote after 1879, both after he had read the second edition of Jevons' *Theory of Political Economy* and Alfred Marshall's two privately published pamphlets on the theory of value, and after this reading had led him to explore Walras, Gossen, and Cournot, contrasts with what he had done earlier without any aid. It took Jevons to put him on the track that led him to economic solutions. These economic solutions involve marginal utility. Yet we may remark safely that marginal utility does not by any means form the central intent of Edgeworth even in the strictly economic parts of the *Mathematical Psychics,* for although he used marginal utility in his analysis, he actually turned in this part of his book from a consideration of psychics to the new problem of determining the equilibrium of different market forms of exchange, or, as he called them, of "contract."[48]

Edgeworth began his study of "contract" with the consideration of Jevons' case of two individuals who exchange two goods. He made a noteworthy change when he combined the total utility of both goods for an individual in the same function instead of using a separate function for each good as Jevons had. He specified this change in the following words: "More generally. Let P, the utility of X, one party, = F (xy), and Π, the utility of Y, the other party, = Φ (xy)."[49] The only advantage of this procedure which he mentioned is that the "inquiry suggested at p. 34, near foot, could not have been suggested by Professor Jevons' formula." This reference turns out to concern the second cross derivative or, in other words, the change in the marginal utility of one good per unit change in the amount of the other good consumed. In his later writings Edgeworth used the signs of these second cross derivatives to define the relation of independence, of complementarity, or of substitutability between the two goods. In the *Mathematical Psychics,* however, he did not mention this specific use of these cross derivatives.

Another consequence of the type of utility function that Edgeworth chose to employ was his introduction of the indifference curve. Historians properly give Edgeworth credit for the first use of this device. His principal graph illustrating this idea shows the contract curve of exchange between Friday, who brings labor to the market,

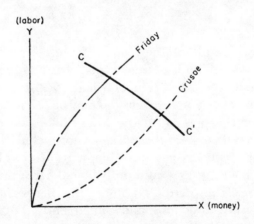

and Robinson Crusoe, who brings money to pay as wages. The "available portion of the contract-curve lies between two points . . . which are respectively the intersections with the contract curve of the *curves of indifference* for each party drawn through the origin."[50]

105

Edgeworth measured Robinson Crusoe's money on the x-axis and Friday's labor on the y-axis. The dotted indifference curve belongs to Robinson Crusoe; the dot-dash-dot curve belongs to Friday. Robinson Crusoe's dotted curve relates the amount of money he would give to get a certain amount of labor from Friday. Friday's dot-dash-dot curve relates the amount of labor he would perform to obtain a certain amount of wages. Although Edgeworth did not represent them in any of his graphs, a family of indifference curves for Crusoe and a family for Friday fill the plane. The higher the curve for Robinson Crusoe, the more satisfaction he receives; the lower the curve of Friday, the more enjoyment he receives. The loci of the points of tangency of the two families trace out the contract curve cc', although Edgeworth did not draw this construction.

Indifference curves of the form that Edgeworth used here did not catch on in economics perhaps because, since they were based on utility functions, they offered no advantage over the direct use of utility curves. Also the inadequacies of Edgeworth's exposition of his own ideas may have played a part. A weaker reason for their subsequent neglect lies in the circumstance that Edgeworth's indifference curves, compared with those now used, have an asymmetrical twist. The indifference curves now used relate the different quantities of both goods that the individual holds, not the quantity he would give up to get quantities of the second good.

VII

Perhaps as a result of the many references in the volume to Jevons and Marshall, both of these economists reviewed the *Mathematical Psychics*. We considered Marshall's well-known and favorable review earlier.[51] No one seems to know of Jevons' equally favorable review which appeared at the same time.[52] Even the bibliography in Jevons' *Letters & Journal* does not include it. "Whatever else readers of this book may think about it," Jevons began his appraisal of the book, "they would probably all agree that it is a very remarkable one."[53] Jevons did not notice the change that Edgeworth made in his utility functions, and consequently did not comment on its implications or advantages. In fact, Jevons said most about the conclusions of the "Utilitarian Calculus" and hardly anything about Edgeworth's "Economical Calculus." Jevons also took the opportunity to regret Edgeworth's obscure style and to request that he mend his ways in the future.[54] It is perhaps likely that Edgeworth de-

106

veloped his style in imitation of that of the brilliant and precocious Alfred Barratt, whose writings read quite like Edgeworth's. Jevons' stricture may have had some temporary effect, for his articles written immediately thereafter have a very plain style indeed in comparison and lack totally the dress of metaphor, classical quotation, and enigmatic statement. But soon he reverted to his former ways.

VIII

Edgeworth's first article after 1882 that had any direct economic import introduced Edgeworth's ideas on index numbers.[55] Utility, of course, bears upon the subject of index numbers. Edgeworth made the bearing plain when he stated the problem as "a *quæsitum* which may be defined as such that the total utility which a person would derive from a certain income at the former of the two epochs under consideration, is equal to that which he would derive at the latter epoch from the same quantity of money multiplied by the sought number."[56] Here Edgeworth gives the first express connection of utility with index numbers. His article, however, does not mainly concern this connection. In 1887, Edgeworth again took up the same subject.[57] Here he spoke of the "margin of final utility," a strange combination of Jevons' "final" and the term "margin" which eventually replaced it. Edgeworth's use of the word "margin" in this report to the British Association for the Advancement of Science, although it did not appear in print until the next year, must be one of the first public uses of the word in anything like its modern context.

IX

In 1887, Edgeworth published his least-known work, a pamphlet with the title *Metretike: or the Method of Measuring Probability and Utility*.[58] This pamphlet certainly concerns utility but probably in a way more significant personally to Edgeworth than to any of his readers. It is of some interest at the present time because of the use of probability in the measurement of utility, but the interest can only be an indirect one. Edgeworth explored here the axioms that he believed to underlie the two, to most people quite removed, subjects of probability and utility. Edgeworth had toyed with the topic before when he sought support for the measurement of utility by Fechner's method and when he considered interpersonal comparisons of utility.[59] He thought of utility and probability as "sister

107

sciences, whose character cannot be fully understood until their mutual relation is considered."[60] His views on this relation never spread, because other writers failed to find this "general similarity" and "partial identity" between probability and utility either real or helpful. Moreover, Edgeworth had by 1887 reverted to his most obscure style, and very possibly he lost most of the readers he might have had before they read very far. Edgeworth wrote a short summary of the pamphlet for *Mind*;[61] but no one else prepared a review for any of the journals. His entire discussion lies in areas twice removed from economics: once, since it treats utility generally; and twice, because it concentrates on the axioms underlying utility. Consequently, Edgeworth never connected his considerations with the body of economic literature or marginal utility, although by this time he knew well the works of Jevons, Walras, and many of the predecessors.

X

Edgeworth was elected President of Section F of the British Association for the Advancement of Science in 1889. He opened his presidential address by recalling that Jevons had submitted a paper to the same section a quarter of a century earlier, and by announcing that he intended to "consider the justice of the unfavorable verdict which our predecessors appear to have passed on the mathematical method introduced by Jevons."[62] Since Jevons' paper had launched his discussion of marginal utility as well as his views on the mathematical method, Edgeworth considered utility as well as mathematics. He explained only briefly the connection of marginal utility with the problem of valuation, for he said: "I shall not be expected here to dwell on a subject which has been elucidated in treatises of world-wide reputation, such as those of Professors Marshall, Sidgwick, Walker, and I would add Professor Nicholson's article on Value in the 'Encyclopædia Britannica'."[63] Edgeworth thus apparently hoped to indicate that the idea of marginal utility had spread throughout the field of economics, for he mentioned none of the pioneers at this point. But we must note that of these four writers, only Marshall gave any considerable space before 1889 to the elucidation of the idea of marginal utility.

Despite his disclaimers of intent not to dwell on utility he did treat the subject off and on throughout the address. And in the process of his discussion Edgeworth named a good many of the earlier writers on utility: Dupuit, Gossen, Walras, and Menger. Edgeworth also referred to Böhm-Bawerk and to Wicksteed and to the work of the Austrian School. Here Edgeworth displayed fully at a public professional meeting the names of the members of the Marginal Utility School, not as novelties, but as accepted and valuable parts of economics. His address signaled that an end had come to the period during which economists wrote of the idea of marginal utility only on rare occasions and as an innovation.

Chapter XII

JOHN BATES CLARK

I

John Bates Clark is often discussed in the history of marginal utility, not only because histories of economic thought usually credit him with spreading the doctrine in the United States, and with adding ideas thereto, but also because historians frequently mention him as an independent discoverer of the idea itself, although a discoverer at a date many years after Jevons, Menger, and Walras. These references to Clark as an independent discoverer of marginal utility date from the first complete account of its place in the histories of economic thought.[1] Most recent histories repeat the same claim.[2] J. M. Clark carried the idea of his father's originality a step farther by offering the following explanation of how easily his father could frame a marginal utility theory without Jevons' help:

> As already noted, Clark formulated a marginal-utility theory of value, later than Jevons and other originators of such theories, but apparently independently. The materials for such a theory stood ready in the classical economics, which left a challenge in the unsolved problem of the relation between utility and exchange value, and fell back, in Ricardo's case, on a labor theory, which turned into a cost-of-production theory after Ricardo had accepted the idea that labor cost alone does not determine the rates at which things tend to exchange for one another. The classical economics also included the concept of rational weighing of utilities, and the marginal method, the two needing only to be put together to produce a marginal-utility theory.[3]

Even the Society of Economic Sciences of Vienna, when it welcomed Clark as an honorary member, cited him as "one of the men to whom it has been given to discover, independently of other seekers, the new concepts which for half a century have constituted the basis for the development of economic theory. . . ."[4] His own colleagues at Columbia University thought likewise.[5] As in the case of Alfred Marshall, some historians of economic thought have not commented on J. B. Clark's right as an independent discoverer of marginal utility, but none have sought to contradict this right.

II

We will examine here this unanimous claim and will begin with an account of Clark's early life. Only a few years separate the birth dates of J. B. Clark (1847), Edgeworth (1845), and Marshall (1842). The year after the publication of Jevons' *Theory* and Menger's *Grundsätze* in 1871, while Edgeworth continued to study at Oxford and while Marshall taught at Cambridge, J. B. Clark graduated from Amherst and from there went to Germany for further study in economics. He spent the years from the end of 1872 until 1875 mainly at Heidelberg but partly (six weeks) at Zurich. Of all his professors, Karl Knies at Heidelberg influenced him most.[6] Despite the fact that the Historical School flourished in Germany and that Knies belonged among its followers, Heidelberg and Knies could not have discouraged marginal utility analysis particularly, not only because J. B. Clark survived his influence, but also because no sooner had Clark gone than Friedrich von Wieser and Eugen Böhm-Bawerk arrived and made their reports to Knies' seminar that inaugurated their careers as leading members of the Austrian Marginal Utility School. Knies himself added a footnote reference on Jevons' *Theory* and examined Walras' *Éléments* over several pages in the second edition (1883) of *Die politische Oekonomie vom geschichtlichen Standpuncte*.[7] His interest, however, in both concerned chiefly the mathematical method, not the use of utility in economic analysis. Wieser reported to his seminar on the relation between cost and value, and Böhm-Bawerk read a paper on capital theory.[8] Karl Menger's *Grundsätze* had influenced both of these reports. It is striking that three of the outstanding figures in the spread of marginal utility economics should pass through Heidelberg within a space of a few years.

Later, J. B. Clark perhaps attributed too much influence to Karl Knies when he credited him with "suggestions" that led him "to seek to discover a unit, by which all varieties of wealth might be measured."[9] Clark never singled out these "suggestions" of Knies, nor, of course, did he describe the path over which they took him on the way to his discovery of marginal utility.

III

J. B. Clark published his first article on economics, "The New Philosophy of Wealth," as soon as he returned to the United States to teach at Carleton College.[10] It contains no reference to any idea similar to *marginal* utility, although it does concern itself almost wholly with the concept of utility. It shows no trace of the work of

111

any of the pioneers. It deals with the problem of the nature of wealth. In this analysis Clark made only a meager beginning in utility theory when he showed an interest in departing from the implications of the labor theory of value and displayed a leaning toward utility. But he gave no indication of a realization that the use of utility without a knowledge of the importance of marginal utility to the economic problem leads nowhere. His claim as an independent discoverer of marginal utility cannot rest on the use of utility in his first publication. On the other hand, it certainly proves beyond doubt that Clark had not profited from the discussions of Jevons, Menger, or Walras before this time.

Toward the end of 1877, Clark followed his initial article with another that also touched on the idea of utility, an article which shows most clearly the influence of Karl Knies.[11] Clark investigated, in this paper, the nature of man, on the presumption that political economy misrepresents him as "too mechanical" and "too selfish," as "actuated altogether too little by higher psychological forces," and as too separate from the society of which he forms a part.[12] In connection with the analysis of man, Clark introduced a long discussion of "wants." This discussion connects in many ways with the idea of utility. Clark came closest to considering diminishing marginal utility when he examined the satiability of wants. He said that the lower wants are completely satiable and the higher ones indefinitely expandable.[13] Consequently, in neither of these extreme and vague cases do wants decline noticeably as a man increases his consumption. Between these two extremes, however, lie wants that decrease in intensity as the quantity of the goods available for their satisfaction increases. Here we find J. B. Clark's first statement of any kind that approaches the idea of diminishing marginal utility: "Wants of this medium sort are indefinitely expansive but decrease in intensity as the desired objects are supplied. Pleasures of this kind tend to cloy. The first gratification is an object of intenser desire than the second, and the second than the following. An indefinite number of such acquisitions would each afford some gratification, but in diminishing degree."[14]

Clark connected, too, his reflections on wants with the purchases of the consumer and thus with the pricing system. At the beginning he gave the following table:

"A, B, C, D, E = Different objects of desire.

5, 4, 3, 2, 1 = Relative intensity of the different desires."[15]

This table does not carry any idea of diminishing marginal utility, since each of the objects differs in kind from every other. Clark assumed that it applies to all consumers and that it regulates the order of their purchases. If the price does not permit the consumption of all of the goods by all of the individuals, then the price must fall. The depth of the necessary fall in price depends on the nature of the goods.

These two articles of Clark's were at best hardly more than a promise of a future consideration of marginal utility. Clark had let utility or wants dominate the center of the stage in this second article as he had done in the first. He never displayed any knowledge either by direct or indirect reference to any earlier writings on marginal utility, in particular to Jevons, Menger, and Walras. His discussion in terms of "wants" or "desire" rather than of "utility" reflected the many sections on this subject in the German literature insofar as it had a source in the work of earlier economists.

IV

Four years passed before Clark again wrote on the subject of utility. In the meantime he had expressed himself on the livelier topics of socialism, communism, and the ethics of business.[16] The article on which his principal claim to recognition as an early independent discoverer of marginal utility rests appeared in the *New Englander* in July, 1881, with the title of "The Philosophy of Value."[17] Clark said that this article grew from a dissatisfaction with the literature on value. At the beginning of his article he complained that "it is certain that in all that has been written on this much elucidated theme, a statement of the real nature of the thing discussed is not to be found."[18] In the very next paragraph he repeated the same idea when he asked "how large a mass of literature . . . [a reader] may patiently read through without satisfying himself exactly what value is."[19] And he ended his introduction with the statement that "he may search economic literature in vain for a satisfactory formula for value in the generic."[20] Clark probably did not intend to speak precisely when he referred to the "mass of literature." At least nothing in the remainder of this article, or in Clark's writing generally, suggests that he appreciated or wished any high degree of bibliographic thoroughness. His article really displays, not the acquaintance with the economic literature on the subject of

113

value to which he alludes, but instead a complete unfamiliarity with the new and promising literature in the field.

Clark's first attempt to bring "society" into a connection with the problem of value marks one important difference between his writing on utility and that of his contemporaries. This device caught on later with other American economists and served to distinguish the American School from the Austrian School.[21] Clark doubtless brought this characteristic of his doctrine back from his study in Germany, where it had a long history and where it played a part in the work of his teacher, Karl Knies.[22] After having disposed of his new ideas of the relation of society to value, Clark looked at the connection between utility and value. He began with Adam Smith's paradox of the diamonds and the water and discovered the solution in the idea of marginal utility. Here is his complete statement of this discovery:

> We must now make a distinction which, so far as I am aware, has never before been applied in political economy, but one which, as I hope to show, is absolutely essential to clear reasoning in this department of the science. . . .
> The one mode of estimating gives a measure of what may be termed absolute utility; and, in the case of air, this is indefinitely great. The other estimate measures what may be termed effective utility; and, in the case of air, this is nothing. Effective utility is, then, power to modify our subjective condition, under actual circumstances, and is mentally measured by supposing something which we possess to be annihilated, or something which we lack to be attained.
> Now, is it not this the utility with which political economy has to deal; and is it not the former, or absolute utility, that with which actual treatises have dealt? Moreover is not the difference radical, and the failure to distinguish it ruinous to any philosophy?[23]

No one could point out the significance of the difference between marginal and total utility more forcefully than did J. B. Clark in this key passage. On these paragraphs rests Clark's main claim to the independent discovery of the idea of marginal utility and of the realization of its importance. Clark staked his own claim to originality in the first sentence of the quotation when he said that he knew of no other writer on political economy who had made the same distinction previously.

Clark proceeded from the simple example of the measurement of marginal or effective utility of air, simple since air has no marginal utility, to the measurement of marginal utility in the more complicated case of drinking water, more complicated since drinking water has some marginal utility. Take away a glass of drinking water from the individual and his satisfaction decreases, both because of the "sacrifice of replacing the water," and because of the possible "inferiority of that which was brought in its stead."[24] Utility appears thus as not directly measurable, but measurable only through the inconvenience of effort and the possible lessened satisfaction from the substitute good.

Clark applied the same train of reasoning to a more important category of goods, the various articles that any individual buys in a market. Again Clark did not measure marginal utility directly. In the case of a coat Clark stated that "the removal of a coat lessens the owner's enjoyment, not by the difference between his condition with such a garment and his condition with none, but by the difference between the sum of his enjoyments, had the coat not been taken, and the sum after the necessary sacrifice shall have been made to replace it, and the substitute, perfect or imperfect, shall have been brought into use."[25] Clark would have done better to insist on a direct measurement of marginal utility, rather than to attempt to bring in, as more realistic, some variant of the earlier economists' idea of sacrifice. We can only interpret him as measuring the marginal utility of any good by the marginal utility of the money income of the individual, making allowance, at the same time, for the imperfection of the substitutions. This interpretation cannot give satisfaction, for the marginal utility of money income must depend on the marginal utility of goods, not the other way around.

V

J. B. Clark used his 1881 essay, without substantial alteration, as a chapter in his first book, *The Philosophy of Wealth: Economic Principles Newly Formulated,* which he published in 1886.[26] He incorporated, in the same book, the two essays that the *New Englander* had published in 1877, and that contained his early and partial views on utility and value, but with more alteration and rearrangement. The review of this book by Henry C. Adams pointed out the resemblance between Clark and Jevons. "For those who are acquainted with the writings of Professor Jevons there is little new in this chapter," Adams wrote, "but those who appreciate Professor Jevons will gladly see his views again brought into prominence."[27] No doubt Adams' statement jolted Clark, who used most of the preface to the

115

second edition to disclaim any dependence on Jevons; and to maintain the independence of his thought, Clark wrote:

I comply with the suggestion of a friendly critic in stating the relation which the theory of value advanced in the fifth chapter of this book bears to that of Professor Jevons. My theory was attained independently, very long ago, but proved to coincide with that of Professor Jevons in the general fact of establishing a close connection between utility and value in exchange, and in regarding utility as subject to mental measurements. In some more specific points it resembled that theory without quite coinciding with it. It has been published without change in any of these respects. Features of the theory which I still venture to regard as my own are the identification of value in all its forms with measure of utility, the distinction between absolute and effective utility, and the analysis of the part played by society as an organic whole in the valuing processes of the market.[28]

Clark made further comment on the difference between his viewpoint on marginal utility and that of Jevons in a letter to Professor T. Miyajima in 1927.[29] Jevons, in Clark's opinion, assumed that the individual adds to his consumption and that the "last or 'final' increment consumed is the one that figures in the adjustment of values." In contrast, Clark imagined that the individual has a complete stock of the good already in his possession, and that the individual estimates its value by what he would have to go without in order to replace any part of his supply. But clearly the difference between the valuation process of an individual who has already acquired his stock of goods, and that of an individual engaged in acquiring a stock cannot materially affect the outcome. Clark agreed. "It amounted to a *final utility* theory," Clark concluded his description of his own theory, "but was cast in a somewhat different form."

Other indications in his later work point to the fact that Clark thought that his early theory differed from those of Jevons, Menger, and Walras in more ways than it actually did. The explanation for this belief in some sense might lie in the fact that Clark did not read Jevons or Menger or Walras carefully even after he had the similarity of their writings pointed out to him. Consequently, he never knew, at first hand, what they wrote. Indirect evidence of this circumstance is the fact that Clark never mentioned any of the three in his subsequent writings, except to disclaim having read them before 1881. And we may note too that people who knew him well pointed out that he read little on any subject, for good reasons. On this point Alvin Johnson said: "His health was never good and the few hours he could give to study seemed most usefully employed in an examination of concrete facts and in the elaboration of his own theoretical system. Professor Giddings once told me that when the translations of Wieser's and Böhm-Bawerk's great works first appeared he tried to interest Clark in them, as affording striking parallels to Clark's own system. In vain. Clark read these works after some years but never took any serious interest in differentiating his own position from that of the Austrians."[30] Clark's strength evidently came from his own thought, and he apparently gained no help, or even inspiration, from the works of other writers on economics. This characteristic of his personality supports the view that, when he first wrote of utility and value, he did so without knowledge of what the three pioneers of the Marginal Utility School had written on the subject.

After the publication of the second edition of *The Philosophy of Wealth,* Clark did not return to the subject of the connection of marginal utility with the theory of value until 1892, by which time the Marginal Utility School enjoyed an international reputation. Clark had one good opportunity to comment on marginal utility during this period, for he prepared a long review of Alfred Marshall's *Principles,* but he failed to utilize the occasion, never once bringing the word "utility" into his discussion.[31] In later years J. B. Clark added a number of new amendments to the marginal utility theory of value.

Chapter XIII

P. H. WICKSTEED

I

Unlike Marshall, Edgeworth, and J. B. Clark, who all have some claim to originality in the use of marginal utility, Philip Henry Wicksteed plays largely the role of disciple and figures mainly in the history of marginal utility as a forceful teacher who contributed markedly, in the eighteen-eighties, to a number of persons who made good use of the doctrine.

We do not know the initial circumstances that drew Wicksteed's attention to Jevons' *Theory*. Wicksteed settled in London in 1874.[1] For over twenty years he held the post of minister in the Little Portland Street Unitarian Church. Jevons arrived in London in 1876, two years after Wicksteed's arrival, and retained his residence there until his death in 1882. Possibly Jevons and Wicksteed had some association during the years 1876-82 when both lived in London, but no record remains of the nature of this association. In fact their paths had crossed many years before when both attended University College. Lionel Robbins said that Wicksteed had purchased a copy of the second edition of Jevons' *Theory* in 1882 and that the "marginal annotations on almost every page show how profoundly and how extensively he had meditated on its doctrines."[2] Perhaps this was Wicksteed's first glimpse of Jevonian economics; at least Wicksteed's first publication on economics came in 1884.

II

The Economic Circle, the group before which Wicksteed first expounded his views on Jevons, played a significant role in the spread of the idea of marginal utility, and thus in the history of economics in the England of the eighteen-eighties. Unfortunately the history of this important organization remains, to this day, unclear in detail. The few references made to it lie scattered. All the members died without publishing any substantial account of its history. Its beginning was connected, in several ways, with the nonconformist religion of the time. Perhaps it had a connection with the Bedford Chapel Debating Society sponsored by Stopford Augustus Brooke, a minister who caused a considerable stir at the beginning of the eighteen-eighties by seceding from the Church of England. At least some of the members of the Bedford Chapel Debating Society (Sidney Webb, Bernard Shaw, Graham Wallas, and Henry Ramié Beeton) belonged also to the Economic Circle.[3]

C. H. Herford gave the following account that also involved Stopford Brooke: "Stopford Brooke, at Bedford Chapel, to whose ministrations he [Wicksteed] had turned for refuge, presently himself showed symptoms of the same heresies. And among the young men studying under him at Manchester College some keen minds were also discussing the ideas of Henry George. This was of importance, for it is, in fact, to their initiative that we owe the foundation of the 'Economic Circle'. . . ."[4] This group of nonconformist theological students of Manchester College, who had had their social curiosity aroused by the recent lectures of Henry George in London, obtained from the start the services of Wicksteed, who, according to Herford, responded "to their appeal, requiring them, however, to equip themselves for the purpose with the instrument of mathematical analysis provided by Jevons."[5] Herford mentioned the names of only a few of the Manchester College men, and none of those mentioned need concern us.

In March of 1884, Henry Ramié Beeton became a member of the Economic Circle. The members of the Circle first met Beeton at a meeting of the Hampstead Liberal Club, where both he and Wicksteed spoke in approval of Henry George.[6] That meeting marked "the beginning of a lifelong friendship" between Beeton and Wicksteed.[7] It marked, also, an important milestone in the spread of the idea of marginal utility, for Beeton gave Wicksteed valuable support in many ways. Beeton had a number of successful business interests. He had a membership in the London Stock Exchange, he took an active and profitable part in the budding electrical business of the eighteen-eighties, and at the end of his life he moved from London and turned to the pursuit of agriculture. But he always had, too, the time and means to enjoy such activities as the writing of pamphlets on bimetallism and the cultivation of the society of economists.[8] James Bonar said that he "was one of those whose influence is greater than his fame."[9]

III

In October, 1884, the Economic Circle again gathered strength when it transferred its meetings to Beeton's home and added new

119

members, among whom were Herbert Somerton Foxwell, Francis Ysidro Edgeworth, and Sidney Webb.[10] Wicksteed continued "as an ardent investigator who had now found a unique opportunity of pressing the economic problem home to the core."[11] In this same month and year, Wicksteed wrote his first article on the subject of economics. It appeared in the organ of the Marxian Social Democratic Federation, the propagandist magazine *Today*.[12]

The article attempts a refutation of the essential point of Marx's economics, his theory of surplus value. Wicksteed attempted to destroy the idea of surplus value by the proof that the value of a good depends, not on the amount of labor used to produce it, but on its marginal utility. Wicksteed expressly invoked the use of Jevons' methods in his refutation of Marx. "It is the complete and definitive solution of the problem thus presented which will immortalize the name of Stanley Jevons," Wicksteed said, "and all that I have attempted or shall attempt in this article is to bring the potent instrument of investigation which he has placed in our hands to bear upon the problems under discussion."[13] The two years that he had spent on the study of Jevons bore fruit.

Wicksteed's argument against Marx runs as follows. Labor, as well as commodities, must depend for its value on the marginal utility of the labor or, more literally, on the marginal utility of the product of the labor. Now the key point remains that the value of goods and the value of labor under the marginal utility theory do not come into correspondence with the amounts of labor involved in their production in the axiomatic fashion that they do in a labor theory of value. Their values, under the marginal utility theory, do not correspond except on the supposition that labor can flow *either* to the production of goods, *or* to the production of labor, a circumstance impossible unless "slave-breeding is possible."[14] It does not suffice to stress marginal utility, rather than labor cost, as a theory of value to refute Marx, for Marx's theory of surplus value still stands if the values of goods and labor remain proportional to the amounts of labor necessary for their production, for any reason whatsoever. Wicksteed's refutation of Marx consisted in showing that this proportionality would result only under unusual circumstances. Wicksteed by his introduction of marginal utility probably cast a shadow, too, over all of Marx, and not just over surplus value, since Marx based all his value theory and thus all of "scientific socialism" on a labor theory of value.

IV

Wicksteed's article irritated the Marxians, especially their leader, Henry Mayers Hyndman, who, although he did not reply to Wicksteed, continued all his life to do all he could to discredit Jevons and marginal utility.[15] The answer to Wicksteed finally came from the aspiring young socialist George Bernard Shaw, after some hesitation on his part, and after he realized that none of his socialist friends and acquaintances knew any more about the subject than he did. " 'I read Jevons,' he afterwards wrote, 'and made a fearful struggle to guess what his confounded differentials meant; for I knew as little of the calculus as a pig does of a holiday.' "[16] Years later Shaw wrote that his reply "was not bad for a fake. . . ."[17] Towards the end of his reply Shaw regretted "that the utility of space at the margin of supply; the obscurity of the Jevonese language; and the extreme unpopularity of our subject, have compelled me to put forward a counterblast to Mr. Wicksteed rather than a thorough analysis and discussion of his interesting contribution."[18]

Essentially Shaw attempted no more than skirmishes against Wicksteed's position. He said openly that he had "not the slightest intention here of defending Karl Marx against Mr. Wicksteed."[19] Shaw even felt that Marx might have a good deal of the Jevonian theory of utility tucked away in the yet unpublished volumes of *Das Kapital,* a circumstance that would make any defense of Marx against Wicksteed useless. He realized, too, the peculiarity of putting Marx "on the side of the standard English school of Adam Smith, Ricardo, Mill, and Cairnes . . ." to defend him "as against Cournot, Jevons, Walras, Professor Marshall, and Mr. J. [F.] Y. Edgeworth. . . ."[20] Shaw treated the whole controversy as one within the ranks of the socialists, and as one "which seems . . . of great interest because it is one on which Socialists, without at all ceasing to be Socialists, are sure to divide very soon. . . ."[21] Shaw admitted that his knowledge of economics did not prepare him for the rebuttal. He added that he was "not mathematician enough to confute Mr. Wicksteed by the Jevonian method."[22] Slight wonder, with all this hesitancy, that the several paragraphs of Shaw's "counterblast" directed specifically at the utility theory of value fail to convince the reader. In fact, we wonder to what extent, at the time that Shaw prepared this reply, he admittedly wished to refute Wicksteed and to retain his belief in Marx. Of course, Shaw said that "I do not

121

mind admitting that a certain weight will be removed from my mind when the attack is repulsed, and the formerly pellucid stream of the Ricardian labour value theory has deposited the mud which the late Stanley Jevons stirred up in quantities which, though expressed by differentials, were anything but infinitely small."[23] But quite possibly Shaw had tired already of socialists who "often dogmatize intolerably on the subject of what Marx taught, or what they suppose him to have taught, on the subject of value. . . ."[24] If Shaw had not already gone covertly over to Wicksteed's side, why did he write that "in my opinion [Wicksteed has] . . . acted wisely as well as written ably in leading the assault which must have been made sooner or later upon the economic citadel of Collectivism"?[25] Stripped of its asides, Shaw's article really says nothing in favor of Marx's labor theory of value, and not much more against Jevons' final utility.

Shaw evidently thought that he had found a weak point in Wicksteed's and Jevons' reliance entirely on utility to explain value. He thought that they should have included costs, evidently rejecting or not understanding their explanation of how costs influence utility through the effect on supply. He illustrated his objection with the example of a world where everyone has all the beef that he can consume at a particular time, and where consequently the value of meat has sunk to zero. In this situation Shaw concluded that "the utility of beef will then be at zero; the choicest undercut will be as valueless as it is in heaven, no matter how much labour its production may have cost. Utility, then, is evidently a condition of value."[26] So far Shaw had found in favor of Jevons and Wicksteed. Now Shaw supposed that everyone in the community becomes so hungry that the utility of beef rises from "nothing to everything," and concluded that, under these circumstances, the value will not rise equally and that it will rise only "to the cost of catching, killing, and cooking a cow: not a farthing higher."[27] If it does rise higher no one will pay the higher price but will "catch, kill, and cook for himself. . . ."[28]

He put too strict a construction on the Jevonian proposition that price will be proportional to marginal utility and erroneously presumed that the following example of monopolistic price discrimination does not accord with Jevons' or Wicksteed's conclusions: "To half-a-dozen travellers dying of thirst, but having unequal possessions, half-a-dozen draughts of water would possess equal utility; yet a Jevonian sheikh with command of the water would receive different quantities of commodity for each draught."[29] Also he found a soft spot in utility analysis in the circumstance that an individual frequently does not wish to consume all goods and thus cannot equate prices and marginal utilities. This example, of the "family Bible and dozens of brandy," came from Wicksteed: "The price of neither would be raised or lowered by one farthing if Mr. Wicksteed suddenly got tired of the Bible and became a dipsomaniac. Apart from that, his nearest teetotal neighbor would probably give more money for a Bible than for a dozen hogsheads of brandy; whilst the nearest drunkard would eagerly offer a dozen Bibles for a single bottle of brandy, if the ratio of exchange were determined by the utility of the commodities. But as the rain falls alike on the just and the unjust, so is the price of Bibles and brandy the same to Mr. Wicksteed and his neighbors, though the utility differs in each of their cases."[30] Jevons had tried to amend his original system to take the case in which an individual consumes none of a good into account.

Shaw had insisted that Wicksteed be permitted a rejoinder. It came quickly and was short. In it Wicksteed reasserted the importance of his first article by maintaining that it endeavored to show that the keystone of the arch of Marx's system "is not sound."[31] He treated Shaw pleasantly and with consideration. He met squarely the argument that cost, as well as utility, affects the price of beef, by pointing out that "it is only by producing more beef, and thus at the same time increasing its total and lowering its final utility, that the increased facilities of beefmaking can produce any effect on the price whatever."[32] He avoided the main issue in the case of the "extortionate sheikh," but pointed out the consumer's surplus enjoyed by some of the travelers, and he said nothing about the case of the indivisible goods and the corresponding difficulty of connecting them with ratios of marginal utility as seen in the "family Bible and dozen of brandy" example.

V

This interchange with Wicksteed drew Shaw into the Economic Circle that was meeting every other week at H. R. Beeton's house. One of the members described Shaw's entrance into their discussions in this manner:

123

He stood up with red hair and beard, in a grey suit (most of the company being in evening dress), and chaffed both Wicksteed and the rest of us with an audacious wit, sometimes too pointed to be entirely relished. "You fellows," he declared, "have been talking a great deal about 'choice.' You would know better what choice is, if, like me, you had every night to 'choose' between a bit of fire and a bit of supper before you went to bed." And as to "curves", the "curves of supply and demand" had much less to do with a man's control of the market, than the curves of his profile. He himself had earned only £100 in the previous twelve months, whereas, with our host's resolute curve of the chin, he would be making £10,000 a year. And he proceeded to illustrate his point, amid the embarrassed laughter of the company, by drawing their own profiles in lively caricature on the blackboard.[33]

Shaw said that after he had gained an entry to this circle he "held on to it like grim death until after some years it blossomed out into The Royal Economic Society; founded the Economic Journal; and outgrew Beeton's drawingroom."[34]

At the time that Shaw joined the Economic Circle it included among its members Wicksteed, Edgeworth, Webb, Foxwell, and Beeton. Other members who had already joined it or who soon joined it were, according to Herford, A. E. Emslie (the artist who painted Wicksteed's portrait and made an etching of one of the meetings of the Economic Circle that he sent out with an invitation to view the portrait) and Stopford Brooke.[35] Archibald Henderson, the biographer of Shaw, added the names of Alfred Marshall, William Cunningham, and George Armitage-Smith.[36] The Economic Circle evidently had less effect on this last group than on the members of the circle mentioned earlier. The work of William Cunningham showed no influence from the Economic Circle. Alfred Marshall must have played a minor role in the group, since he did not live in London. G. Armitage-Smith found a slight use for marginal utility in the courses of lectures he delivered in 1892 for the London Society for the Extension of University Teaching,[37] and in another course of lectures that he delivered two years later he made even more specific references to utility.[38]

The Economic Circle continued to meet for five years. It must have played an important part in the cultivation of the use of marginal utility and a lesser part in the determination of the course that economic study subsequently took. We may list a number of specific consequences that followed in some part from the discussions in the Economic Circle: the adoption of Jevonian economics rather than Marxian economics by the Fabians; the formation of the British

Economic Association, later the Royal Economic Society, in 1890; the creation of the Junior Economic Club, later the Economic Club, at the University of London; and the publication in 1888 of Henry Philip Wicksteed's *The Alphabet of Economic Science*. Let us consider each of these.

VI

The organization, "The Fellowship of the New Life," from which the Fabian Society grew, commenced to meet October 24, 1883, only slightly before the first meeting of the Economic Circle.[39] Some of the dissatisfied members of this group, under the influence of Marx's writings, established the Fabian Society as an independent organization at their meeting of January 4, 1884.

George Bernard Shaw first attended a meeting of the Fabian Society on May 16, 1884. He was elected a member on September 5, 1884, and elevated to the Executive Committee on January 2, 1885. Between the time that Shaw became a member and the time that he appeared on the Executive Committee, he had engaged in the controversy with Wicksteed over Marx and had begun to attend the meetings of the Economic Circle in Hampstead.

Shaw's appearance in the Economic Circle marked its first connection with the Fabian Society. Other connections followed when the Fabian Society elected Sidney Webb a member on March 20, 1885, and Graham Wallas in April, 1886. The three main links of the Economic Circle to the Fabian Society—George Bernard Shaw, Sidney Webb, and Graham Wallas—also had another meeting ground, the Hampstead Historic Society. This society began "near the close of 1884 or the beginning of 1885 . . . as a sort of mutual improvement society for those ambitious Fabians who desired to read, mark, learn and inwardly digest Marx and Proudhon."[40] The spirit of Jevons shows here, too, for Shaw wrote that they disputed as to whether the value of vases was fixed by "their 'cost of production on the margin of cultivation, or by the "final utility" of the existing stock of vases.' "[41] They held their meetings every other week, the weeks when the Economic Circle did not meet.

From Wicksteed at the Economic Circle, George Bernard Shaw supposedly brought the marginal utility economics of Jevons to the Fabian Society. Shaw himself wrote that he had put himself "into Mr. Wicksteed's hands and became a convinced Jevonian, fascinated by the subtlety of Jevons' theory and the exquisiteness with which it adapted itself to all the cases which had driven previous economists, including Marx, to take refuge in clumsy distinctions between use value, exchange value, labour value, supply and demand value, and the rest of the muddlements of that time."[42] Although Shaw obtained the central drift of Jevons' economics, he must have missed many of the details because of his lack of understanding of rudimentary mathematics. As late as 1887, Shaw pretended not to understand how an expression such as "$2a + 3b$" could have any meaning.[43]

Shaw contributed two articles touching on marginal utility to the *Pall Mall Gazette* for 1886 and 1887. He reviewed Jevons' *Letters & Journal* on May 29, 1886.[44] Of the second contribution to the *Pall Mall Gazette* Shaw said, "An untimely attack of sunspots on Hyndman's part exasperated me to the point of falling on him furiously in a correspondence in the *Pall Mall Gazette,* (May 1887)."[45] Both Hyndman and Mrs. Besant joined in the discussion.[46]

Shaw put his knowledge of Jevons and marginal utility again actively into practice on the occasion of the translation of the first volume of Marx's *Das Kapital* in 1887 into English because, as he said, "the danger of allowing the public to believe that Socialism, or even Marx's own historical and social generalizations, stood or fell with his chapters on value. . . ."[47] Shaw spread his review over three issues of the *National Reformer*.[48] The first notice highlights the strength of Marx as depending on his view of capitalism as a passing social condition and on his belief in the equality of man. At the end Shaw promised "in a future article, to deal with the apparent mistakes of Marx, which promise to be almost as fruitful of controversy in the near future as the mistakes of Moses."[49]

The second installment of Shaw's review of Marx's *Das Kapital* concerns almost nothing except a long analysis of the error that Marx made by accepting the labor theory of value. Shaw excused Marx for accepting the labor theory of value as a dogma, since he could not have foreseen that Jevons' utility theory would replace it: "Marx's omission to give the *rationale* of his dogma can hardly be condemned as unwarrantable. When a theorem has been proved so often that all the world cries 'agreed!' the theorem becomes an axiom. There are axioms of ours which are still theorems to our mothers, and blasphemies or paradoxes to our grandmothers. Marx may have thought that his Ricardian theorem . . . might by this time be advanced as an axiom."[50] Shaw quickly pointed out, how-

126

ever, that the "reasoning that satisfied Ricardo and Marx did not satisfy Jevons; and whatever be the upshot, the Marxite of today must not expect his master's axiom to be admitted now as it would have been in the middle of the century."[51] Marx, Shaw asserted, made his first error and thus committed himself to the use of a labor theory of value when he considered utility as "specific" to each certain good but not "abstract" (comparable as between any two goods), while he held as both "specific" and "abstract" the labor involved in the production of each good. Shaw pointed out that "abstract" utility, especially "final abstract utility," serves much better to determine value than "abstract labor."

The third installment of Shaw's review contains less about Marx's theory of value, for it concerns more particularly the question as to whether surplus value arises from capital as well as labor. But it has, nonetheless, many references to Jevons and the utility theory of value and ends with this strong recommendation: "My last word for the present is—Read Jevons and the rest for your economics; and read Marx for the history of their working in the past, and the condition of their application in the present."[52]

The *Fabian Essays,* first published in 1889, set the tone held during the subsequent development of the Fabian Society. In them, Shaw said that "the abstract economics of the *Fabian Essays* are, as regards value, the economics of Jevons."[53] Jevons, to be sure, does receive more attention than Marx. Shaw's first essay has a complete exposition of a utility theory of value illustrated by examples.[54] "Some economists," he writes, in an ingenious if not accurate explanation of the term "marginal utility," "transferring from cultivation to utility our own metaphor of the spreading pool, call final utility 'marginal utility'." All in all, Shaw gave here a compact, clear exposition of the relation of marginal utility to the theory of value at a time when a reader could find few other expositions. He showed that the efforts of Wicksteed and Jevons had produced a respectable result.

Shaw had delivered his second essay initially on September 7, 1888, at the meeting of the British Association for the Advancement of Science. Two friends from the Economic Circle, F. Y. Edgeworth and H. S. Foxwell, read papers at the same meeting on the same day.[55] The papers of W. L. Rees and Henry Sidgwick completed the program. Shaw's paper, which seems rather tame today, evidently had an electric effect at the time, especially on Henry Sidgwick.

127

Here are two quite different versions of the effect. Twenty-eight years later Shaw himself wrote the following account of the occasion:

As late as 1888 Henry Sidgwick, a follower of Mill, rose indignantly at the meeting of the British Association in Bath, to which I had just read the paper on The Transition to Social-Democracy, which was subsequently published as one of the Fabian Essays, and declared that I had advocated nationalisation of land; that nationalisation of land was a crime; and that he would not take part in a discussion of a criminal proposal. With that he left the platform, all the more impressively as his apparently mild and judicial temperament made the incident so unexpected that his friends who had not actually witnessed it were with difficulty persuaded that it had really happened.[56]

Sidgwick gave the following quite different account, in which no indignation shows at all, in the notation in his diary made under the date of September 8:

The most interesting thing at my Section (Economic Science) was the field day on Socialism which we had yesterday. The Committee had invited a live Socialist, redhot "from the streets," as he told us, who sketched in a really brilliant address the rapid series of steps by which modern society is to pass peacefully into social democracy. . . . How exactly this seizure of urban rents was to develop into a complete nationalisation of industry I could not remember afterwards, but it seemed to go very naturally at the time. There was a peroration rhetorically effective as well as daring. . . .

Altogether a noteworthy performance:—the man's name is *Bernard Shaw*: Myers says he has written books worth reading.[57]

This second essay by Shaw gives a very brief attention to Jevons and his refutation of the labor theory of value, before he turned to his more exciting topic of social change.

George Bernard Shaw evidently never lost sight, in some sense, of final utility, although he used it but infrequently after the end of the eighteen-nineties, for he included an allusion to it in a postscript to the 1948 edition of the *Fabian Essays,* written at the age of ninety-one.[58] On the other hand, the two prominent members of the Economic Circle who also belonged to the Fabian Society, Graham Wallas and Sidney Webb, never at any time gave any direct hint in their writings that Wicksteed had influenced their modes of thought by teaching them the economics of Jevons. Doubtless the simple explanation of the avoidance by the Fabians of any direct contact with the idea of the theory of marginal utility after the early days with Wicksteed lies in the nature of the subsequent activities and interests of this group. They had practical programs to accomplish immediate ends and never wasted their energies in unscrambling ideological conflicts. George Bernard Shaw, in speaking of the Webbs, expressed the range and character of their viewpoint when he said that the Webbs had ". . . no time for argybargy as between Marx's Hegelian metaphysics and Max Eastman's Cartesian materialism. The question whether Socialism is a soulless Conditioned Reflex à la Pavlov or the latest phase of The Light of the World announced by St. John, did not delay them; they kept to the facts and the methods suggested by the facts."[59] What practical advantage, if any, did the Fabians get from Jevons? Jevons did give them a means in the early days, when necessary, to confront the arguments of the group in England that allied itself with Marx, and at the same time to leave themselves free to accept such parts of Marx as appealed to them. H. M. Hyndman, who ably led the Marxian Social Democratic Federation, composed a violent attack on final utility that he read before the Political Economy Circle of the National Liberal Club, which shows well how irritating the Marxians found the references to Jevons and final utility given by the Fabians.[60]

VII

The Economic Circle also had some part in the formation of the British Economic Association. Two of the members of the group that met on the afternoon of November 21, 1890, to discuss the formation of an economic society or association, Henry Higgs and Shaw, specified the connection between the Economic Circle and the British Economic Association.[61] We also note in the list of those present at the organizational meeting the following people who were allied with the Economic Circle: H. R. Beeton, Professor Edgeworth, Professor Foxwell, Professor Alfred Marshall, and Mr. George Armitage-Smith.[62] Wicksteed and William Cunningham received nominations to the committee formed to draft the rules of the organization.[63] The "Report of the Proceedings at the Meeting which Inaugurated the British Economic Association" has only a concealed reference to the Economic Circle in the section that speaks of the need for meetings of economists as shown by "private meetings and discussions on the subject in Oxford, Cambridge, London, and possibly elsewhere. . . ."[64]

129

Another club established in 1890, the Junior Economic Club (later the Economic Club), also must have sprung from the Economic Circle, since its initial membership included many of the known members of the group. It apparently filled a local need in London for the occasional meeting together of economists that the gatherings at H. R. Beeton's had supplied, but that the British Economic Association had not furnished, since the latter did little more than publish the *Economic Journal*. Of the original members of the Junior Economic Club the following belonged in some sense and at some time to the Economic Circle: H. R. Foxwell, F. Y. Edgeworth, H. R. Beeton, Philip Wicksteed, and Alfred Marshall.[65]

Chapter XIV

WICKSTEED'S *ALPHABET*

I

At one of the meetings of the Economic Circle in 1888, Wicksteed read the "last sheets of the book which was to be the first fruit of their meetings, and was shortly afterwards published under the title of *The Alphabet of Economic Science*."[1] Wicksteed dedicated it to Henry Ramié and Elizabeth Beeton "and to the friends who, in the enjoyment of their genial hospitality, have met to discuss the principles set forth in these pages" as the "first-fruits of their counsel and assistance."[2] In this way a side result of the Economic Circle was the first systematic book-length exposition of the idea of marginal utility in England following the publication of Jevons' *Theory* in 1871.

Wicksteed gave in the Preface an historical sketch of the development of the Marginal Utility School, relying largely on Jevons' *Theory* and *Letters & Journal*. He added to Jevons' account the name of Carl Menger as one of the co-discoverers of marginal utility in the early eighteen-seventies.[3] Seventeen years had passed after the publication of Menger's *Grundsätze* before anyone in England publicly recognized that his work essentially duplicated the books of Jevons and Walras written at the same time. Wicksteed noted, too, that Jevons never had known of Menger.

The *Alphabet* had at its beginning a forty-page explanation of mathematics. After Wicksteed discussed the general idea of a function, he showed that he could express the value-in-use of blankets, or water, or butcher's meat as a function of the quantity of the good in question in the possession of the individual. He, of course, knew that there would be some inconvenience with goods of which a consumer took only one, and he thought that the expression "value-in-use" or "utility" might well be replaced by some term devoid of ethical content such as "sum of advantages," "desiredness," "gratification," or "satisfaction."

II

When Wicksteed finally came around to expressing his utility function as a curve he encountered the problem of measurement for the first time. At this point he mainly assured the reader that he could not regard the objection to measurement as "formidable," cited the part of the book ahead at which he would consider the problem more fully, and suggested that "it may be observed that since satisfaction is certainly capable of being 'more' or 'less', and since the mind is capable of estimating one satisfaction as 'greater than' or 'equal to' another, it cannot be theoretically impossible to conceive of such a thing as an accurate measurement of satisfaction, even though its practical measurement should always remain as vague as that of heat was when the thermometer was not yet invented."[4]

When Wicksteed later in the book returned to the problem of measurement he first pointed out that, since we could distinguish between more or less satisfaction that we obtain from additional quantities of different goods, we can regard these satisfactions "as theoretically *reducible to a common measure,* and consequently capable of being measured off in lengths, and connected by a curve with the lengths representing the quantities of commodity to which they correspond."[5] He gave the illustrations of the comparisons we make between china and linen, fresh air and friendship, residence within reach of our friends and the British Museum and residence in the country with fresh air and fresh eggs, space for books and time for a journey to the library.

Wicksteed even suggested the use of "a given amount of work as the standard unit by which to estimate the magnitude of satisfaction," and illustrated how he might express the utility of different numbers of tons of coal by the lifting work he would do willingly in order to acquire another hundredweight. Wicksteed pointed out that we need not use "lifting work" as a measure necessarily, would not, in fact, had we not grown accustomed to it, but that he could use any other kind of work. "In academical circles," Wicksteed explained, "it is not unusual to take an hour of correcting examination papers as the standard measure of pleasures and pains."[6] The measurement must, of course, assume that the "hedonistic value" of the work remains constant. To illustrate the process of measurement Wicksteed gave an example of a person who measures his total utility, y, for linen, x, selecting the unit of y as the satisfaction that he would undergo 500 foot-tons of work to obtain. For the first unit of x he would do 3,300 foot-tons of work, and consequently he measured the y as 6.6; for the second unit of x he would do 1,750 foot-tons of work, and consequently his y increased to 10.1 for the $2x$; and in the same way it rose to 12.3 for $3x$.

Wicksteed evidently believed, erroneously, that he had provided an adequate method of measuring utility, for he said "that though we have imagined an ideally perfect and exact power of estimating what one would be willing to do under given circumstances in order to secure a certain object of desire, yet there is nothing theoretically absurd in the imaginary process; so that the construction of economic curves may henceforth be regarded as theoretically possible."[7] And at another place he said that "there is no absurdity involved in speaking of so many units of gratification."[8] The impossibility of Wicksteed's method of measurement comes from the assumption that the "hedonistic value" of the work done remains constant. He would have had no more real difficulty in imagining the *direct* measurement of the utility than in "imagining an ideally perfect and exact power of estimating what one would be willing to do under given circumstances in order to receive a certain object of desire...." His analytical procedure yields information adequate for the partial construction of an indifference map. The other of the pair of quantities in the indifference map cannot have a uniform value no matter what the quantity that the person has, or it affords a direct measure. Of course Wicksteed could obtain a definite figure in foot-tons, but if he had begun when his individual had already done a greater number of foot-tons of work (unless the individual never tired), he would have obtained another set of measurements that differed from the first set in no simple fashion. The first set would resemble the second set only ordinally; a resemblance that does not constitute measurement as usually construed.

Wicksteed invited the reader to construct curves for himself for some "article such as coffee or tobacco." He told the individual to ask himself "how much work he would do for a single cup or pipe per week or per day sooner than go entirely without, how much for a second, etc., and dotting down the results, [to] see whether they seem to follow any law and form any regular curve."[9] Although a person can construct curves of this kind for himself if he has sufficient imagination, and although these curves may serve a useful purpose for many kinds of problems, they do not give a satisfactory measurement of utility.

133

III

Having disposed of the problem of measurement, Wicksteed contended that the total utility curve always reaches a maximum and then descends until it eventually becomes negative.[10] There follows a solid twenty-page introduction to calculus that contains no reference at all to any economic problem.[11] When he returned to the economic interpretation of the curves he called the slope of the curve the "marginal effectiveness" or "marginal usefulness" of the good in question.[12] This change from "final" to "marginal" became a permanent change in terminology after it caught on. Wicksteed did not indicate why he regarded "marginal" as superior to the word "final" or "terminal," nor did he give any hint that he obtained it from anyone else or even that he used it as a literal translation of Wieser's *Grenznutzen*. It simply suddenly appeared in the pages of the *Alphabet*. Probably Wicksteed experimented with the term in the Economic Circle and found it satisfactory; at any rate he used it frequently and with confidence.

After Wicksteed defined his basic concepts he proceeded to elaborate the use of them to a degree to which no one hitherto had done. He commenced with the distinction between the uses to which we put total utility and marginal utility as a guide to our actions and thoughts, the crucial distinction that underlies the work of Jevons, Menger, and Walras.[13] Wicksteed illustrated the principles by which men divide their hours between alternative employments.[14] He had, too, a consideration of the circumstances that would cause a marginal utility curve to shift, as well as an examination of the principal types of shift that might occur.[15]

At no place did Wicksteed have in mind a utility function which relates the interdependence of the utilities of different goods. Why did Wicksteed continue to construe the total utility that an individual enjoys as the sum of the utilities from the separate utility functions for each good, rather than as a single utility function in which all the separate commodities enter as variables, when Edgeworth had earlier shown the way to the more general function? Wicksteed knew the *Mathematical Psychics* well enough to quote it and ought to have felt an interest in any differences between his exposition and Edgeworth's, but he never did.[16] Edgeworth, of course, attended meetings of the Economic Circle and could have raised the point had he felt anxious to do so. Apparently he never did to the degree necessary to impress his objections on Wicksteed; whether because he did not consider the distinction important, or whether his well-known indifference again triumphed here over his sense of importance, we do not know. Edgeworth had a further opportunity to speak out on the subject had he wished to do so, for he wrote one of the few reviews of the *Alphabet* to appear, a review which, although in general most favorable, did include criticisms.[17] Yet here Edgeworth never mentioned the subject of the form of the utility function. The fact that the many-variable utility function did not catch on with Wicksteed must have followed from the fact that no one in the Economic Circle, not even Edgeworth or Wicksteed himself, saw the significance of its use.

IV

The first part of the *Alphabet* deals with the individual and the second part with the relation between individuals. The second part begins with a number of strong statements on the impossibility of interpersonal comparisons of utility. Wicksteed said that the impossibility must "never be lost sight of on peril of a total misconception of all the results we may arrive at in our investigations . . .," that "by no possibility can desires or wants, even for one and the same thing, which exist *in different minds,* be measured against one another or reduced to a common measure . . .," that if three individuals desire a single good "no possible process can determine which of them desires it most . . .," that any use of interpersonal comparisons brings forth the "fatal objection that it must use as a standard of measurement something that may not mean the same in different minds to be compared . . .," and that it "is impossible to establish any scientific comparison between the wants and desires of two or more separate individuals."[18] Wicksteed then showed that the use of marginal utility in the explanation of exchange does not involve an interpersonal comparison, since it makes use only of the ratios of marginal utility which are comparable between persons.[19]

Nonetheless Wicksteed shared the belief that although he could not compare the marginal utility of an individual he could compare the *average* marginal utility of a group of individuals. "But if we take into account the principle of averages," Wicksteed said, immediately after remarking that we cannot even hold that a poor man values a shilling more than a rich man, "by which any purely personal variations may be assumed to neutralise each other over any considerable area, then we may assert that shillings either are or ought to be worth more to poor men than to rich."[20] Wicksteed specifically used this intergroup comparison of marginal utilities to argue, for the first time on these grounds, for "the more equal distribution of wealth. . . ."

After this examination of the possibility of intergroup comparisons, Wicksteed commenced a long section on the nature of a demand curve. The probability that he intended to use the demand curves in connection with intergroup comparisons appears at the outset. Wicksteed, using Cournot's medicinal-spring example, said that the price measures "the marginal utility of the water *to the community*."[21] In this way, through the medium of price, Wicksteed obtained a "collective or social" curve. By this time, beguiled by the substitution of groups for the individual, he had gone a long way from his original avoidance of interpersonal comparisons. Having gone this far, he even seemed willing to compare the utility curves of individuals, for he sketched the manner in which he could derive a total utility curve for the community from the separate demand curves of the individuals. For a single individual A who buys the medicinal water from the spring, "the total utility of the q quarts which A consumes in the year is made up of the whole sum he would have given for one quart rather than have none, *plus* the whole quantity he would have given for a second quart sooner than have only one $+ \ldots +$ the whole sum he gives for the qth quart sooner than be satisfied with $(q - 1)$."[22] Wicksteed willingly added together the total utility curves of A, B, C, etc., for a "grand total of the utility to the community of the whole quantity of water consumed." He had a sense of uneasiness in doing so, as well he might after his long and strong objection to interpersonal comparisons, for he remarked that he must neglect the fact "that they are not subjectively but only objectively commensurate with each other. . . ."

Wicksteed next turned his attention to a summary of the forces that direct the use of the productive resources in the community and showed that the direction always takes place toward the production of goods that have the greatest relative marginal utility as revealed by their prices. In this analysis, especially when he extended it to the case of many goods, it became evident that he had read Walras' *Éléments* by this time, although he never referred to the book itself.[23]

He included, too, a refutation of the labor theory of value, evidently directed more at Marx than at the English Classical School.[24] He called the labor theory of value a delusion and then continued to explain why serious thinkers had accepted it. Wicksteed had a view, too, as to why the marginal utility theory failed to win out handily over the delusions of the labor theory of value. He said that "it is quite easy to demonstrate the general theory of value to any housekeeper who has been accustomed to keep an eye on the crusts, even though she may never have had any economic training."[25] But unfortunately the class of people who study economics do not belong "to a class in whose daily experience its elementary principles receive the sharpest and most emphatic illustrations." Since they do not belong to the class of the "very poor or very careful," the students of economics think that experience contradicts the marginal utility theory of value. Wicksteed pointed out that, since the marginal utility theory holds that the marginal utilities of all goods stand in proportion to the commodities' prices, no one can have enough of any good that bears a price, or wish an additional shilling's worth of any one good more than another. The rich or the careless think that they have all of some goods that they want (such as bread), and they think, too, that they can name many goods which they would desire above all others; therefore, they can say that experience for them flatly contradicts the conclusions of the marginal utility theory of value. One can imagine that these arguments came up in the discussions of the Economic Circle and that the painstaking answers that Wicksteed gave were developed at that time as counterarguments. Wicksteed had no trouble in showing that the apparent contradictions of the theory of marginal utility by experience came mainly from the bugbear of divisibility, added to somewhat by "tradition and viscosity."[26]

Certainly in more ways than one the *Alphabet* provides a landmark in the extension of the use of marginal utility in the analysis of economics, as well as in the publication of many new ideas. Yet the book did not succeed. It never went into a second edition; no one translated it into another language; and not until recently was it reprinted.

At the time, the *Alphabet* did get a few reviews that spoke well of it. F. Y. Edgeworth reviewed it in the *Academy*. He approved of it generally and for the most part enthusiastically; but few people have the capacity to enjoy the sort of thing that appealed to Edgeworth. Eugen Böhm-Bawerk said that Wicksteed had the correct views so far as he could tell, but he admitted that he disapproved of the mathematics in the *Alphabet,* and implied that Wicksteed's mathematics might have concealed some of Wicksteed's errors from him.[27] Other prospective reviewers must have found it too much for them.

Chapter XV

GERMAN JOURNAL LITERATURE AND MENGER'S PUBLICATIONS, 1871-1889

I

No one in France or Germany reviewed Jevons' *Theory* in 1871. Similarly Walras' *Éléments* was overlooked in England and Germany in 1874.[1] Menger's *Grundsätze* stood in similar national isolation in 1871 and received only German reviews. The Germans in 1871 had four professional journals in the field of economics, of which three noticed Menger's *Grundsätze*.[2]

The *Vierteljahrschrift für Volkswirtschaft und Kulturgeschichte* gave Menger's *Grundsätze* by far the longest review.[3] It began by noting the increased activity in Austria in economics since the War of 1866 and by praising the high quality of the work done by the younger Austrian economists. With all his good-will, however, the reviewer did not recognize Menger's *Grundsätze* as an innovation in the theory of value. He included two long quotations in his review. The first, taken from Menger's preface, concerns the method that Menger had intended to employ. He agreed with Menger's method. The reviewer quarreled with the second quotation, one that states Menger's characteristic division of goods into different orders. In his conclusion the reviewer cautiously reserved judgment on the worth of the book until he could see the continuation that Menger promised.

Menger fared no better in the next longest review, the review that Friedrich Hack prepared for the *Zeitschrift für die gesammte Staatswissenschaft*.[4] Hack, like the anonymous reviewer, had a charitable attitude toward Menger. He called the *Grundsätze* one of the best books appearing on economics in recent times, and expressed the wish that the promised second volume would follow quickly. Despite his good intentions, Hack clearly missed the central idea of the book and consequently failed to describe or appraise it accurately. The revolution in value theory lost one of its first opportunities to gain support, not because the reviewer opposed it, but because he did not understand it. In the last of the three reviews, again an anonymous one, the reviewer deplored the writing of short

139

textbooks on economics by young men.[5] Needless to say, this approach did nothing to herald the new spirit in economics. The review gave little idea of what the book contained and absolutely no hint of the final merit of its contents.

II

Anyone can read the German journals on economics, the best specialized journals in the world in that period, from the time of the reviews to the end of the seventies without coming across any direct reference to the idea of marginal utility. Wilhelm Lexis first interrupted this silence when he reviewed Léon Walras' *Mathematische Theorie der Preisbestimmung der wirtschaftlichen Güter* for the *Jahrbücher für Nationalökonomie und Statistik* in 1881.[6] The reader has no doubt, after Lexis' summary, that Lexis understood and appreciated the use of marginal utility. However, he did not associate Walras' work with Menger's *Grundsätze*. Doubtless he failed to make the connection because he had not read Menger, even though he later had some reputation for a wide knowledge of economic literature.[7] Nothing more appeared until Böhm-Bawerk's important article in 1886. It gave a thoroughgoing, clear explanation of marginal utility theory and will be discussed later at length.[8]

In 1889 Julius Lehr wrote the next substantial article on the subject of marginal utility.[9] Lehr had the ability and the willingness to use mathematics. Further, he was acquainted with and cited all the essential previous literature on the subject; in fact the article in a way served as a review of some of the more recent books. The following year, Heinrich Dietzel published a similar article, with the title "Die klassische Werttheorie und die Theorie vom Grenznutzen."[10] Here for the first time the phrase "marginal utility" appeared in the title of an article. The issues sharpened in this article, which drew subsequent replies by Rudolf Auspitz, Böhm-Bawerk, Julius Lehr, and Robert Zuckerkandl.

The scarcity of journal articles in German on marginal utility in the years from 1871 to 1889 did not follow wholly from an anti-theoretical bias of the editors. Several theoretical articles even appeared on the subject of value. They did not, however, mention marginal utility. For example, Julius Wolf wrote an article in 1886 which, although it cited Jevons' *Theory* and Menger's *Grundsätze*,[11] discussed the subject of value for almost fifty pages without ever referring to marginal utility. An article in the same journal the next year by F. W. Gärtner did not come any closer.[12] A third article, even longer than the others, followed in the next year (1888), and, although it mentioned marginal utility and referred to Böhm-Bawerk, Wieser, and Jevons, it would remain quite complete as an article if it had not referred to marginal utility and if it had skipped Jevons and the Austrians entirely.[13]

III

Carl Menger had begun to lecture at the University of Vienna in 1872. He became an associate professor the next year and a full professor in 1879. He retired in 1903 and died in 1921. We intend to follow here only the first two decades of his university career for the purpose of observing his further connections with the idea of marginal utility. As in the case of Jevons and Walras, Menger published very little on the subject after the early eighteen-seventies. The first things that he wrote after the *Grundsätze* were a group of twenty-five articles, mostly book reviews, prepared for the *Wiener Abendpost* from 1873 to 1875. None of these, from their nature, contained anything on utility. One of the reviews is of J. E. Cairnes' *Essays in Political Economy*,[14] a book which did not offer him any opportunity to comment on value theory. Had he waited until 1874 to review Cairnes' *Some Leading Principles of Political Economy Newly Expounded,* a volume which contains a refutation of Jevons on utility, he might have been drawn to the support of his English contemporary. He also narrowly missed contact with one of his predecessors when he reviewed, in 1875, Gyula Kautz's *Entwickelungs-Geschichte der volkswirtschaftlichen Ideen in Ungarn.* Had he had enough interest to look carefully at the early work of Kautz, *Die geschichtliche Entwickelung der National-Oekonomik und ihrer Literatur,* he might have seen the reference to Gossen and thus have anticipated Adamson's discovery of this writer by several years.[15]

Menger published nothing in the years between the writing of these newspaper articles and reviews and the appearance, in 1883, of his *Untersuchungen über die Methode der Socialwissenschaften und der politischen Oekonomie insbesondere.* This volume has no direct connection with his *Grundsätze.* It did, however, serve indirectly to publicize the *Grundsätze,* for it drew attention to Carl Menger in a way, and to an extent, that his earlier book never had. The German professors reacted strongly, if naturally, to Menger's criticisms

141

especially after he replied to the initial reviews the next year with his *Die Irrthümer des Historismus in der deutschen Nationalökonomie.* As a result, the Austrians felt some cohesion among themselves. Thereafter the term "Austrian School" fitted them better. The Germans pulled as hard in the other direction, with the consequence, according to Hayek, that even "thirty years after the close of the controversy Germany was still less affected by the new ideas now triumphant elsewhere, than any other important country in the world."[16]

We must not, however, overestimate the part that marginal utility played in any increased feeling of unity that came to the Austrians at this time. From Menger's review on October 12, 1884, in the *Wiener Zeitung,* we can see that we should be cautious of the growing literature of the Austrian economists.[17] He pointed out that Austria had never before had an output of economic literature of equal quantity. But Menger never connected his own name with the movement, nor did he give any account of its genesis. Although he emphasized, at the beginning of his review, the role of the Austrians in opposing the historical method, he hardly gave so much as a hint of the part played by marginal utility. He had plenty of opportunity to do so, for he had a paragraph on Wieser's *Über den Ursprung und die Hauptgesetze des wirtschaftlichen Werthes,* a book that expounds in detail Menger's ideas on value and that contains Wieser's first use of the word *Grenznutzen.* His later reviews of Austrian literature have the same characteristics. He published one in 1886,[18] and another in 1889.[19] The last review is especially disappointing in that it never connects the many excellent books written on marginal utility in that year either with that subject or with Menger himself.

In general we can say that, although Menger talked about the Austrian School, no one could gather from his words in any of his publications after 1871 down to his death that the Austrian School had the slightest connection with the Marginal Utility School. He either did not admit the connection, or wished to minimize it, or took it for granted. Similarly, Menger never admitted publicly any kinship with Walras or with Jevons.

Chapter XVI

FRIEDRICH VON WIESER

I

One of the first public signs of any considerable interest in Menger's *Grundsätze* was the publication of Friedrich von Wieser's *Über den Ursprung und die Hauptgesetze des wirtschaftlichen Werthes* thirteen years after Menger had first written.[1] The story of Wieser's connection with marginal utility and thus the story of the events that led up to the writing of this book has been told many times.[2] In brief, the account runs as follows. His father had been a successful government official, an occupation the son intended to follow. In school and at the University of Vienna, which he entered in 1866, he had Böhm-Bawerk as a classmate and friend. Wieser studied jurisprudence and especially enjoyed its history, an aspect on which he thought economics ought to throw light. However, the economics that Lorenz von Stein taught at the University of Vienna did not satisfy him. Neither, on the other hand, did the economics of Adam Smith, Ricardo, or Marx. He graduated in 1872, and during that same year both he and Böhm-Bawerk found in Menger's *Grundsätze* exactly the kind of economics they thought to be most useful.

This course of events in the usual account of Wieser's life has a breathtaking, adventitious quality. It seems too remarkable to be true. The most implausible part of the whole account is Wieser's and Böhm-Bawerk's rejection of Lorez von Stein's brand of economics and their acceptance of Menger's at an age when both had barely passed twenty-one, and in a period when almost no one else had the insight to see this superiority. Morgenstern put the usual interpretation of the reported reaction of these two young Austrians quite clearly: "Economics had their [Wieser's and Böhm-Bawerk's] sympathies always; but *the* economics taught at Vienna at this critical time—Lorenz von Stein—had nothing to say to them. At this critical time of dissatisfaction Carl Menger's *Grundsätze der Volkswirtschaftslehre* came into their hands and indicated the solution. The 'Archimedian point' had been found and a basis had been given them upon which they could erect their own structure independently."[3] The primary source for this account is in Wieser's autobiographical notes.[4] In these Wieser, writing fifty years after the occasion, made a dramatic story of the events. He could not help idealizing, in retrospect, the events of his youth. To a critical eye at the present, with a realization of how lukewarm the general reception of the work of the pioneers was, the account seems too perfect.

Having completed his studies at the university, Wieser, together with Böhm-Bawerk, worked for the Austrian government for three years. It took two traveling scholarships, *Reisestipendien*, to pluck Wieser and Böhm-Bawerk out of the offices of the government and send them back to academic life and to such subjects as the theory of value. This time they turned toward the universities of Germany where the Historical School flourished. We know little of what they did during these two academic years spent at Heidelberg, Jena, and Leipzig except that they read highly significant papers before Knies' seminar at Heidelberg in 1876: highly significant in that they both foreshadowed the direction that their work took in later years, and in that they both showed the influence of Menger. Knies' seminars, even though presumably advancing the historical method, could not have been too hostile to the idea of marginal utility and of deductive work generally. Both Wieser and Böhm-Bawerk submitted these papers they had written for Knies' seminar when they applied for the renewal of their traveling scholarships in 1876.[5] Astonishingly enough, Menger was unenthusiastic about Wieser's paper. Wieser's seminar paper was not published until 1929.[6] It has the descriptive title "Über das Verhältnis der Kosten zum Wert." It does not expressly mention Menger's *Grundsätze,* or, for that matter, any other piece of economic literature. It does, however, reveal the clear influence of Menger, for it states that the paper has the purpose of showing how the application of "goods of the higher order" affects the value of "goods of the lower order." It showed that concern with utility, and especially with the relation of utility and cost, that Wieser was never to lose.

After their two years of study, both Böhm-Bawerk and Wieser returned to their government jobs. But they did not stay long. Their study in the German universities had increased their desire for an academic career. For a brief time they served as *Privatdozenten* at the University of Vienna. Böhm-Bawerk left first to take a professorship at Innsbruck. Wieser moved to the University of Prague in 1884.

Wieser had submitted his first book, *Über den Ursprung und die Hauptgesetze des wirtschaftlichen Werthes*, as a *Habilitationsschrift* at the University of Vienna.[7] He divided it into four chapters, the first of which discusses the idea and nature of value, commencing with a consideration of the uses of the term "value" in everyday speech. The second chapter outlines the basic conditions necessary to the determination of value, an outline which, in sum, amounts to a general statement of the economic problem. Only in the third chapter does the reader come to the problem of the *origin* of value, a part of the subject announced in the title of the book, and here he finds that value originates in utility and not in cost of labor. The fourth and last chapter, which includes one hundred of the 220 pages in the book, contains the principal laws of value that are proposed in the title. Wieser gave the chief law of the determination of value as the Law of Marginal Utility. He proceeded to show that costs have a meaning only in the sense of an alternative foregone, and he dealt with the division of the produce among the factors that contribute to its production. Menger, himself, had foreshadowed or expressly stated the leading ideas found in this long final chapter. Since Wieser took up all these problems in much greater detail five years later, we will postpone a discussion of them until we discuss that period.

This first book of Wieser's received no notices or reviews outside Germany and only two in the German journals.[8] In one of these Dietzel called attention to the fact that it is an unusual book in that it is a book by a German author of over two hundred pages that does not have a single footnote in it. Wieser did not need footnotes at this time, for he wrote with almost a complete lack of bibliographic aids. In the entire book he mentioned only Jevons and Menger. But even this is an advance over his paper of 1876, in which he mentioned no one. Of course Menger's influence shines from every page despite the absence of chapter and verse citations. At only one place, cited later, does the book show any especial indebtedness to Jevons. At this time he evidently did not know of Walras' connection with utility.

The book is a landmark in the history of marginal utility because in it Wieser introduced the word *"Grenznutzen,"* a term that Wicksteed later translated into "marginal utility." He had limped through his earlier paper without its help. In fact, he went more than halfway through his first book before he introduced the term. He made the introduction specifically as a translation of Jevons' "terminal utility" or "final degree of utility." Wieser introduced this expression in the following sentence: "Ich werde im Folgenden den für den Werth der Gütereinheit entscheidenden Güternutzen, weil er an der Grenze der wirtschaftlich zugelassenen Verwendungen steht, den wirtschaftlichen Grenznutzen oder auch kurzweg den Grenznutzen nennen (vergl. die Ausdrücke "final degree of utility" und "terminal utility" bei Jevons)."[9] Wieser specifically said that he used this new word because the unit of the good stands at the *Grenze* of economic employment. But did not the whole idea come to him through the suggestion of Jevons' phrase "terminal utility"?[10] In fact, how else could he have translated it more neatly? If we can allow that Wieser translated Jevons' expression "terminal utility" to get *"Grenznutzen,"* then we have the English phrase "marginal utility" only because *"Grenznutzen"* when translated back into English came out as "marginal utility" rather than "terminal utility," by which it went in. Wieser himself, after he once introduced the term, used it repeatedly through the remainder of his book. One wonders how he managed to express himself in the first half of the book and in his paper of 1876, since he evidently found a handle for his key idea most useful. Wieser continued to make constant use of the term *"Grenznutzen"* after 1884 and other writers took it up also.

Beside introducing the word *Grenznutzen* Wieser's first book probably had little influence. The style of all Wieser's writings diminished their effectiveness, presenting a real obstacle to their being understood. Two different aspects of his style created special difficulty. In the first place, he dealt almost wholly in general or nonspecific terms. He would use the word "object" in preference to "food," and the word "food" in preference to "fruit," and the word "fruit" in preference to "apple." However laudable his generality, it does burden the reader. And in the second place, he included among the significant parts of his analysis an unusual number of related but unnecessary statements, marked off in no way, so that the reader never knows whether the sentence he begins will convey a relevant idea or simply the most obvious kind of information. The following example typifies the latter kind of sentence, evidently introduced for the sake of completeness: "Suppose a person wishes to acquire an object, no matter what, he will not, however strong his desire, agree to pay *any* price that may be asked."[11] We could not possibly raise a doubt regarding this proposition. Wieser not only introduced this sentence, but followed it with another that stated the same proposition in another way.

Another reason why Wieser's *Über den Ursprung und die Hauptgesetze des wirtschaftlichen Werthes* did not impress readers was that it avoided personalities and strong statements. It has a timeless, unreal quality that tends to subdue argument, and the circumstances it describes have no definite geographical bearing. Since they could happen anywhere, at any time, they seem to take place nowhere. The book sets out to prove that value lies only in the minds of men, and yet it never refers to anything resembling a man at any place; Wieser gives to persons the most impersonal treatment possible. Add to these circumstances the fact that the book has few sharp memorable sections that the reader can carry with him and we have marshaled reasons enough to explain its lack of success. It did not fail in the sense that anyone at the time openly condemned it, or in the sense that today a reader can easily pick flaws in it. It failed in the sense that only with difficulty can one bring together today as much as two or three pages of comment on it, outside of two initial reviews, that show any understanding of the nature of its contents.

III

During his first five years at Prague Wieser worked on his next book, *Der natürliche Werth* (1889), which helped to gain him a promotion to *ordentlicher Professor*.[12] It received the usual few reviews. Only one German, Werner Sombart, undertook to assess the book and he found nothing good.[13] Certainly no one could say that by 1889 the Germans received the idea of marginal utility cordially. The French in 1889 gave Wieser similar treatment: one unfavorable review.[14] Only the Americans and the English applauded *Der natürliche Werth,* mostly after the English translation with the title *Natural Value* appeared. However, F. H. Giddings did write four pages on the German edition that showered it with compliments.[15]

In contrast with Wieser's book of 1884, *Der natürliche Werth* shows a detailed familiarity with the history of marginal utility theory.[16] Wieser realized that many of the early writers on marginal utility did not succeed very well; but he admired them anyway and

147

selected for special commendation Auguste Walras, Condillac, Genovesi, and Senior.[17] He listed four writers who worked out the theory of utility independently, and he showed separately the reasons for which he thought Menger surpassed the other three—Gossen, Jevons, and Léon Walras. Some of these reasons reveal salient characteristics of Wieser's methods of thought. Even his short comment on Gossen, the comment that Gossen of all the early writers "is, on the whole, the most imperfect . . ." uncovers in Wieser that perfectionist attitude that led him to turn every detail of the idea over in his mind, even at the risk of wearying his audience, so that he could say finally of his own exposition "that no value theory has ever yet been put forward more complete and exhaustive in external form and treatment."[18] Walras' analysis suffered in Wieser's eyes from "the preponderance of the mathematical element."[19] Here we meet another continuing aspect of all Wieser's work. His training did not prepare him in any of the essentials of mathematics. He had, as a result, a continuing suspicion of those who did use mathematics, and a feeling he could accomplish as much as they, or perhaps more, without the use of mathematics. Wieser's only criticism of Jevons is that he is superficial in comparison with Menger, who, according to Wieser, started "from a more general conception of value."[20]

All of the parts of *Natural Value* deal in some considerable degree with the introduction of the idea of marginal utility into the problem of the determination of value. The main treatment of marginal utility in value theory comes in the first section. The second part deals with "Natural Value," an idea for which Wieser named the book, and its relation to exchange value and to value in a socialist state. Then, after the long section on "imputation" (two-fifths of the book)[21] Wieser came back to the topic of his first paper, the relation of costs to value, which constitutes a third section on value. And he finished with a short section on the use of marginal utility value theory in relation to the economics of the State, particularly taxation and government expenditures—a section obviously inspired by Wieser's associate at the University of Prague, Emil Sax, who had handled the subject two years before in his *Grundlegung der theoretischen Staatswirtschaft*.

IV

Wieser began by expressing the hope that he could present a

148

theory of value which would reconcile all the apparent contradictions brought up in the past against a utility theory. Goods have value, Wieser said, because they satisfy wants, and the fact that desire decreases when the amount consumed increases Wieser christened Gossen's Law, a law which, he added, holds "of all emotions, from hunger to love."[22]

Wieser next said what little he had to say on the subject of measurement of satisfaction. He presumed some ability to measure, as the following quotation shows: "If we were to follow out the course of satisfaction of a want, and mark every separate act of satisfaction with the value that accompanied it, we should obtain a diminishing scale, the zero of which would be reached with full satisfaction or 'satiation' while its higher point would correspond with the first act of satisfaction."[23] Wieser apparently found two obstacles in the way of obtaining a scale of measurement: exactness and commonness. He said little about the lack of a common scale. He never made clear whether he had in mind applying the word "commonness" to different goods or to different people. He did accept an approximation to exactness, for he suggested that the scale of measurement consist in "the possibility of distinguishing between one hundred different degrees of intensity of desire. . . ."[24] Needless to say, measurement requires neither accuracy of any given degree nor commonness of any kind, howsoever much it profits from both in ordinary application.

When Wieser examined the form of the utility function, which he did to a very limited extent, not only did he have in mind, at the time of examination, a discontinuous utility function, perhaps on the ground mentioned before that a consumer can discriminate between relatively few intensities of satisfaction, but he also appeared to think that everyone else had or ought to have a like view. As a consequence, he took Jevons and others to task for implying "that it is necessary to keep strictly in every branch of expenditure to the same degree of satisfaction, the same level, the same marginal utility."[25] To accommodate his discontinuous functions Wieser restated the principle of the best division of income among expenditures to read that "in all employment as low a marginal utility [should] be reached as is possible without necessitating the loss, in some other employment, of a higher utility."[26] His antipathy toward continuous functions rested more on his lack of ability to see that the assumption of continuity only idealizes a part of the real world, than on anything else. Howsoever willingly he idealized in other directions, he resisted continually the idea of continuity, at some cost to his analyses. It reflects one way in which some training in mathematics could have helped him, and one way, accordingly, in which Jevons and Walras remain his superiors.

Wieser not only understood the marginal utility theory of value in the sense that Jevons, Menger, and Walras did, but had original and different ideas of his own on particular aspects of the subject. One set of views peculiarly his own concerns the "future satisfactions of want." On this subject he disagreed at a distance and expressly with Jevons, but closer at hand, though not by name, with Böhm-Bawerk. His position, contrary to that of both, is that people do not generally value future wants less than present wants. He admitted that primitive people do not value the future appropriately, but he insisted that economically advanced people learn to do so. He pointed out especially that people learn to keep their stock of capital intact. He specifically denied the relevance of the weakness of future desires to the problem of capital and interest, basing his denial on the ground that interest "is not in the least a sign of a defective economy."[27]

Another of Wieser's original insights on the problems of utility was his notion of the value of the entire stock of a good to a consumer. He measured total value by the product of the value of a single unit of the good, i. e., the marginal utility of the stock, and the number of units in the stock. "In a word," Wieser wrote, "the value of a supply of similar goods is equal to the sum of the items multiplied by the marginal utility."[28] Wieser required two chapters to clear up in his own mind all the perplexities introduced by this particular idea of a total quantity of value. The first of these perplexities has received the name "Wieser's Paradox." The paradox lies in the circumstance that, given his definition of value, after a point in the increase of the quantity of good the value commences to decrease. It would be truly paradoxical if, when we had all of a good we desired, its value to us would be nil. Wieser resolved his own paradox by pointing out that value has not only a positive element, i. e., the circumstance that each additional good reduces the utility attributed to the earlier goods, but also a negative element, i.e., the circumstance that each additional good reduces the utility attributed to the earlier goods. A quicker resolution than the unsatisfactory one Wieser supplied involves the rejection of Wieser's

150

unfruitful conception of total value. Wieser must himself have felt dissatisfied with his resolution, for he hastened to assure his readers that in human economics, our consumption lies almost entirely in the range where an increase in consumption would increase total value, and that therefore well-being and value would correlate positively in the future.[29]

Wieser followed the discussion of his paradox with a consideration of the so-called "antinomy of value," a phrase that goes back to Proudhon and that has a relation to the paradox. The apparent contradiction is that if value (total value of the kind Wieser uses) guides our lives, then it "would be expedient for every one, not only from a moneymaking and selling point of view, but in his own private economy . . . to convert superfluity into want, and want into greater want, in order to create and increase value."[30] Wieser gave the sensible answer that *utility* rather than *value* guides our actions. What, then, does *value* do? Wieser replied that, since total value and total utility, in general, move in the same direction and since we can measure total value but not total utility, "Transactions which commend themselves in consideration of their utility, commend themselves also in consideration of their value."[31] We end by measuring total utility in the coin of price and quantity figures. He rejected Proudhon's conclusion that the discord can be resolved only by a socialist organization of society.

V

Wieser probably named his book *Natural Value* because he thought that title expressed the most original and valuable part of the book. His idea, as events turned out, did not prove useful, and, accordingly, the idea and term never entered into the writings of later economists. Wieser was not even clear as to what he meant by "natural value." It seems most likely that he thought of it as an ideal. He evidently thought of natural value as the value that would arise when everybody has the same purchasing power, and, presumably, also the same tastes, so that the exchange value would coincide with the utility of every individual.[32] Wieser never stated his definition in these terms, but what he did say comes in the end to these same conditions. For example, he stated that the value of the isolated individual discussed in the first part of the book is natural value.[33] In the society of this single individual everyone certainly has the same income and the same tastes. He also said that the value

151

in a communist state, a state again where incomes and tastes of all individuals would be identical, would be natural value.[34] Certainly natural value does not exist, and Wieser admitted that it "is doubtful whether it can ever be more than a dream."[35] He advised us to "content ourselves with imagining it, and it will be an excellent aid in realising what would remain of our present economy if we could think away private property, as well as all the troubles which are a consequence of human imperfection."[36] Presumably inequality of income goes out the window when private property disappears, and differences in taste vanish with the abolition of human imperfections. Clearly, natural value appealed to Wieser in some ideal and unreal sense.

Actually, since Wieser could not put his idea of natural value to very good use, he left it stranded in the middle of his volume. His purpose in developing the idea arose from the twofold circumstance that, as he believed, marginal utility guides or ought to guide all our conduct, and that he had no measure of utility. Consequently he tied the marginal utility to a concept that he could measure. Value corresponds to marginal utility only under certain conditions, the conditions that he called "natural value." He could measure objective value and thus, insofar as natural value prevails as objective value, he could measure utility. He wished so far as possible to show that the exchange value found in the real world always comes reasonably close to natural value, and thus that our actual guides to economic conduct usually serve a good purpose. But he fell short of his wish. All that remained of the idea has little practical bearing; consequently later writers passed over it. Wieser set forth the same idea again in his book *Theorie der gesellschaftlichen Wirtschaft* in 1914, this time under a different name, but with no more recognition.

VI

A favorite topic of Wieser was the relation of utility and cost. We must note that Wieser regarded value from a viewpoint different from that of most economists today. He sought to discover the cause of value, while today most economists seek to lay out the circumstances that simultaneously determine all relevant economic quantities without probing into the complex to select any particular part as the cause of the results in any other part. A general equilibrium theory of value includes within itself all forces that affect value, but it does not label any one set as the cause.

Wieser followed Menger in the belief that utility, properly understood, *caused* value. He realized, however, that other students found the cause in a different place, especially in costs of some kind, particularly labor costs. Wieser knew, further, that these costs existed and that they played some part in the economic world. He saw, too, that Menger did not deal with them in the *Grundsätze*. To repair this omission by Menger, to show the relation of utility, the true cause of value, to costs, Wieser wrote the paper for Knies' seminar and now again came back to the subject in *Natural Value*.

Wieser's rejection of labor cost as an element in the determination of value followed logically enough from the kind of economy that he had in mind at the time of his analysis. At most points in his discussion, Wieser thought of value as arising in the simplest kind of situation, a consumers' market with given stocks of the commodities in the hands of the sellers. In a market of this kind labor cost, or any other kind of cost, clearly could not enter into value calculations, for the basic reason that no labor, or other productive effort of any kind, took place. The utility conditions and the given conditions of supply alone rule the exchange value or any other kind of value, in a market where only the consumers' interests govern. When driven to include the circumstances of production in his model, Wieser did so in such a way that labor cost played a limited role. Throughout his work on value he almost always thought of the quantity of labor as a fixed quantity, whenever he went so far as to relate production to his model. Since he did so the labor cost always entered into his analysis as a constant and, as such, Wieser did not regard it as a cause.

Wieser did rig a case, and a very unlikely one, in which he thought that the labor cost caused value. It is an absurd situation in which labor can and does produce so much of all goods that their marginal utilities all fall to exactly zero. This case must assume that the marginal utility of leisure is zero. In this case the goods would be valuable, Wieser thought, since if any labor were given up some want would not be fulfilled. But marginal utility could not express this positive value, since it would equal zero. Wieser concluded that we never find these conditions under which the labor theory of value holds and that, therefore, utility always regulates value.[37]

Wieser's *Natural Value* remained his principal contribution on the subject of value. In the next few years he turned out two articles designed to help spread the correct views of value to the United

States, but, after that, he did not touch the subject again for twenty-five years.[38] Hayek said that after "fifteen years of intensive work devoted to highly difficult problems, a status of exhaustion finally sets in, which for many years made the continuation of theoretical studies impossible."[39] We may doubt whether the publication of two small volumes in fifteen years could have exhausted him, but we cannot doubt that he quit value theory at this time and never again returned to it at the same level and with the same singleness of purpose with which he had conducted his investigations up to 1889.

Chapter XVII

EUGEN VON BÖHM-BAWERK

I

Eugen von Böhm-Bawerk already has entered this account of the rise of the Marginal Utility School in connection with the discussion of Friedrich von Wieser. Böhm-Bawerk's association with marginal utility comes second to that of Wieser only because he concentrated somewhat less on the subject than did Wieser. He made use of the idea, however, a great deal, introducing it even when he pursued his favorite topic of capital and interest.

Böhm-Bawerk followed the same path as Wieser for his first thirty years.[1] He was associated with Wieser in school, the University of Vienna, the discovery of Menger's *Grundsätze* in 1872, the entrance into the Austrian civil service, the two years' study in Germany at Heidelberg, Jena, and Leipzig, and the return to the Austrian civil service. The most notable difference for us was that while Wieser wrote his seminar paper for Knies on the relation of value and cost, Böhm-Bawerk wrote his on capital and interest. In 1881, at the age of thirty, the two friends parted for the first time. In that year he left Vienna for the University of Innsbruck with his wife, Friedrich von Wieser's sister, whom he had married the year before.

II

Böhm-Bawerk had quit government work in 1880 to become a *Privatdozent* at the University of Vienna. In order to qualify he wrote and later had published in Innsbruck in 1881 his *Rechte und Verhältnisse vom Standpunkte der volkswirtschaftlichen Güterlehre*.[2] The topic of his first book required that he make decisions on the nature of an economic good, a subject for which his reading of Menger's *Grundsätze* had prepared him. The specific goods he investigated include credit, patents, and goodwill, all of which, he decided, do not generally fit into the category of economic goods. Reviewers examined the volume at reasonable length in the German periodicals.[3] Although Böhm-Bawerk's first book did serve to emphasize the utility aspect of goods, it gave no evidence that its author understood the importance of marginal utility. In the *Rechte und Verhältnisse* he made no reference to Jevons or to Walras. We can clearly see that Böhm-Bawerk's interests in 1881 were not in the marginal utility theory of value.

III

In his first book Böhm-Bawerk unveiled his plan to investigate further the problems of capital and interest.[4] In partial fulfillment he completed three years later the first volume of *Kapital und Kapitalzins*, a volume which amounts to a history of the theory of capital and interest.[5] It has as little to do as his first book with the value problem. It did take him through a great deal of economic literature and brought him into contact with Jevons' *Theory*, but he did not, at this time, associate Jevons with Menger. Walras' *Éléments*, despite its long sections on capital theory, was not among the books that Böhm-Bawerk cited. Very probably Walras temporarily remained hidden from Böhm-Bawerk, since Böhm-Bawerk included him in later editions of *Kapital und Kapitalzins*, for the same reason that he remained hidden from many other people—namely, because his use of mathematics hid the other aspects of his work. Böhm-Bawerk missed a good opportunity in 1884 to connect the three pioneers together. But the truth is that up to this time he had shown little interest in marginal utility theory. No one who read Böhm-Bawerk's first two books would suspect that anyone would ever list him among those who were to do most to advance the marginal utility theory. Certainly the reviewers had not linked his work with any particular theory of value.[6]

IV

Two years later, in 1886, Böhm-Bawerk interrupted his studies on capital and interest to publish his most important work on value theory, a work that marked him as a member of the Marginal Utility School. It was a two-part article that appeared in the leading German technical economic journal.[7] It set out to expand the theory and introduced few new ideas. Why did Böhm-Bawerk stop his other studies to deliver this study of value? Perhaps the publication by his close friend, Friedrich Wieser, of the *Ursprung und Hauptgesetze* in 1884 stimulated him, or his own work on capital and interest may have led him in this direction, or perhaps some combination of the two brought it about. At any rate it was the first long clear presentation of the idea of marginal utility in any German journal. It was in a convenient place for all who had an interest in economics to see, and it shortly stirred up a controversy.

With very few alterations he incorporated this article in the second volume of *Kapital und Kapitalzins* in 1889.[8] This made the idea of marginal utility again available to Germans in an elementary form. He set it in the midst of his analysis of capital and interest, with the explanation that the reader needs to know about value in order to understand the rate of interest. Most readers, however, would not need for this purpose so extensive a treatment. The later discussion by Böhm-Bawerk of capital and interest makes some use of the idea of marginal utility but hardly a sufficient use to warrant the time a reader would have to give to the subject. In truth, Böhm-Bawerk probably unconsciously used the occasion of the publication of his book on capital and interest to aid in the spread of the marginal utility theory.

V

Böhm-Bawerk's explanation of marginal utility followed Menger's and Wieser's closely in all particulars. This adherence shows quite clearly in his refusal to think of goods as completely divisible. He divided goods, but he always had a limit beyond which he would not go. He often limited divisibility in a common-sense customary fashion even when the good has no physical characteristics to interfere. He used, for example, slices of bread but not half slices, quarter slices, etc. More often he framed his examples in terms of goods such as "horses," where units of "half-horses" or "third-horses" would have had a ludicrous aspect.

As a result of the limitations he placed on divisibility he had a set of problems that Jevons and Walras avoided, and he occupied a good deal of space in their discussion. He wrote a chapter on "complications," most of which would have disappeared if he had accepted the idea of complete divisibility. His section on price uses repeatedly the completely Böhm-Bawerkian term of "marginal pairs" of buyers and sellers, pairs which diminish in importance as the size of the unit exchanged grows smaller. The following sentences give an idea of the time that Böhm-Bawerk spent on notions that derive their entire content from the size of the units he used in analysis:

Suppose that in one branch of employment there are four opportunities, indicated, according to importance, by the figures 10, 8, 6, 4; and that in another branch there are four opportunities, indicated by the figures 9, 7, 5, 3; and suppose that a man possesses in all five individual goods; there is no doubt that the five goods will be allotted to the opportunities 10, 9, 8, 7, 6, and that the last figure (which, accidentally, belongs to the first branch of employment) is the real marginal utility and determines the value of the good, while the employment that comes next in the second branch, that indicated by the figure 5, must, according to our formula, become the "pseudo-marginal utility."[9]

Needless to say, no other writer copied his use of the term "pseudo-marginal utility."

VI

Böhm-Bawerk never committed himself on the problem of the measurability of utility. For the most part he restricted his discussion to the ordinal aspect of quantity, but his restriction follows more from his desire to present his analysis in the simplest possible terms than from any view that the cardinal aspect cannot fit the case. In the following sentences he showed a willingness to adhere to an ordinal view of utility measurement: "It is a familiar fact that our wants vary very greatly in importance. We are accustomed to rank them according to the seriousness of the consequences which their non-satisfaction has on our well-being."[10] He differentiated between the rank of classes of goods, as in the statement that " 'needs of subsistence' come far and away before the desire for tobacco . . .," as well as between the rank of the different items of goods within a particular class. Böhm-Bawerk's analogy between utility and geography reveals the degree to which he often went to confine his analysis in ordinal terms: "It is very much the same as if a geographer were one time to arrange the Alps, Pyrenees, and Harz by their height as mountain ranges, and another time were to arrange their single summits."[11] He talked of "scales" thereafter. He presented a table in the manner of Menger in which he assigned numbers to all the units of all of the goods; but the numbers only guide the consumer in his choices and never tell him of the amount of utility he obtains.[12] Of course since Böhm-Bawerk showed in this table and elsewhere that the consumer esteems each addition to a good less than he does the one before (diminishing marginal utility), he opens the way to cardinal measurement. But Böhm-Bawerk at this point only opened the way; he never required the consumer to perform the operations that would yield cardinal quantities.

Böhm-Bawerk, in fact, did not turn from an ordinal view of utility until he came to the question of complementary goods. Here he felt compelled to treat cardinally his numbers that represent marginal utilities. He appeared unaware that he was using these numbers differently than before. He supposed, here, that "three goods, A, B, and C, in cooperation afford a marginal utility of 100; that A by itself has a marginal utility of 10, B by itself of 20, and C by itself of 30. . . ."[13] This is a new tone in Böhm-Bawerk. These quantities do not look like the indicators of rank Böhm-Bawerk had dealt with previously. Böhm-Bawerk soon showed that he considered them differently, too, for he at once began to add and subtract with them in order to obtain the value of the complementary goods, these operations clearly betraying the circumstance that he no longer dealt with ordinal measurement only.

VII

For the most part Böhm-Bawerk had no need for interpersonal comparisons of utility and consequently usually proceeded in his analyses as though he thought them impossible. Doubtless he would not have said, under usual circumstances, that the marginal utility of a good to a given person exceeds the marginal utility of the same good to another person. Yet he did admit to differences in the marginal utility of income to the rich and the poor, concluding his observations on this subject with the following common-sense observation: "We would scarcely compare the state of mind of a poor clerk, who received his month's salary of £5 on the first day of the month and lost it on his way home, with that of the millionaire who dropped the same sum. To the former the loss would mean most painful privation over a whole month; to the latter it would only involve the want of some idle luxury."[14]

Böhm-Bawerk also compared his own theory of value with the widely held and quite opposite opinion that costs in some form determine the value of the good. He followed here the lead that Menger had given, and he doubtless profited from the elaboration of the subject that Wieser had made. For productive factors that can make only one specific good, he pointed out, no one questions that the value of the good determines the worth or cost of the productive factor. "That Tokay is not valuable because there are Tokay vine-

159

yards," Böhm-Bawerk concludes, "but that the Tokay vineyards are valuable because Tokay has a high value, no one will be inclined to deny. . . ."[15] But where a single factor contributes to the production of many different consumer goods, this circumstance "gives the appearance of the contrary, and a little consideration shows this to be an appearance and nothing more."[16] The cost in this case corresponds with the least marginal utility the factor produces in any of the products. "As the moon reflects the sun's rays on to the earth, so the many-sided costs reflect the value, which they receive from their marginal product, on to their other products."[17]

VIII

Böhm-Bawerk followed Menger in his discussion of price determination. The buyers and the sellers in this analysis go into the varying market situations with prices in their minds at which they will buy and sell. They exchange solely in order "to better their economical condition. . . ."[18] Here an analysis of exchange in terms of utility ought to submit the necessary conditions of the maximum utility or advantage in terms of marginal utility and price. Both Walras and Jevons gave such a presentation. Böhm-Bawerk did not, as Menger did not. Böhm-Bawerk had discovered Jevons' *Theory* by this time and had looked at parts of it, and he probably knew something about Walras' *Éléments,* too. But he never followed their procedures in any way in the consideration of price.

As a result of this limitation in his analysis, Böhm-Bawerk made only a weak connection between his theory of price and his analysis of utility and value. In fact the term "marginal utility" occurs but infrequently in his discussion of price and then in a not very helpful fashion. At first, he limited the connection to an analogy, since, in his discussion, the margin *determines* both value and price.[19] "But," he concluded, "this analogy does not exhaust the connections between price and subjective value."[20] He added nothing further beyond saying that "it is the relation of the subjective valuation of commodity and price-equivalent which decides the persons who may consider it worth their while to compete, either as buyers or sellers. . . ."[21]

Chapter XVIII

MINOR MEMBERS OF THE AUSTRIAN SCHOOL

I

During the years from 1871 to 1889 the School of Vienna had connected with it a total of nine economists in addition to its leader, Menger, and his two foremost disciples, Wieser and Böhm-Bawerk.[1] The lives of most of these lesser Austrian economists have an impressive similarity. Their careers were cut so closely to the pattern of those of Menger, Wieser, and Böhm-Bawerk that there is no wonder that they had similar ideas. Seven of the nine, Gustav Gross, Johann von Komorzynski, Victor Mataja, Robert Meyer, Eugen Philippovich von Philippsberg, Emil Sax, and Robert Zuckerkandl, each obtained a degree in law, *Doktor der Rechte*, and then spent a few years outside the university, typically in the service of the government. Subsequently each wrote a book to qualify *(habilitieren)* himself as a lecturer *(Privatdozent)* at the University of Vienna. Thereafter, although they continued to occupy some post with the government,[2] they maintained at the same time a connection with an Austrian university, the University of Vienna usually. Most of them joined the *Gesellschaft oesterreichischer Volkswirte*.[3] Later they published other books, in part in order to encourage their advancement in the universities where each rose first to *ausserordentlicher Professor* and later sometimes to *ordentlicher Professor*. The following table presents a summary of the principal dates in the careers of ten of the twelve early members of the Austrian School.[4]

The two remaining members of the School of Vienna were Rudolf Auspitz and Richard Lieben. Neither of them attended the University of Vienna, obtained a *Doktor der Rechte*, became a *Privatdozent*, or qualified as a professor. They had quite different backgrounds and careers. They shared with the Viennese economists already mentioned only the circumstance that they lived, at about the same time, in Vienna and that they had an interest in economics, particularly in the application of the idea of marginal utility to the theory of value.

In age they came nearest to Menger, with Rudolf Auspitz' birth, July 7, 1837, a few years earlier than Menger's and Richard Lieben's birth, October 6, 1842, a few years later. Their taste in study turned,

161

FACULTY IN ECONOMICS AT THE UNIVERSITY OF VIENNA, 1871-1889

Name	Birth	Doktor der Rechte	Privat-dozent	Ausserordent-licher Professor	Ordentlicher Professor	Death
Carl Menger	February 23, 1840	1867 (Krakau)	1872-73	1873-79	1879-1903	February 26, 1921
Friedrich von Wieser	July 10, 1851	1875	1883-84	1884-89 (Prague)	1889-1903 (Prague) 1903-1922 (Vienna)	July 22, 1926
Eugen von Böhm-Bawerk	February 12, 1851	1875	1880	1881-84 (Innsbruck)	1884-89 (Innsbruck) 1905-14 (Vienna)	August 27, 1914
Gustav Gross	June 12, 1856	1878	1884-98	1898-1920		1932
Johann von Komorzynski	1843	1868	1890-1903	1903-11		1911
Victor Mataja	July 20, 1857	1885	1885-90		1890-92 (Innsbruck)	1933
Robert Meyer	January 8, 1855	1877	1884-91	1891-1901		June 10, 1914
Eugen Philippovich von Philippsberg	March 15, 1858	1882	1884	1885-88 (Freiburg)	1888-93 (Freiburg) 1893-1917 (Vienna)	June 4, 1917
Emil Sax	February 8, 1845	1868 (?)	1871 (?)	1879-80 (Prague)	1880-93 (Prague)	March 25, 1927
Robert Zuckerkandl	December 3, 1856	1879	1886-94	1894-96 (Prague)	1896-1926 (Prague)	May 28, 1926

not to law and political science, but instead to the physical sciences.[5] They consequently began their studies with more mathematical facility than the other Viennese economists had.[6] After finishing their technical training, they became businessmen.[7] Auspitz also engaged in politics and concluded a career of thirty years in parliament before his death, March 8, 1906. Lieben died on November 11, 1919. Both belonged to the *Gesellschaft oesterreichischer Volkswirte.*

II

It is astounding how little of the large literary output of the nine minor writers has the slightest bearing on marginal utility when it is considered that they are often banded together as part of the Marginal Utility School.[8] Two of them said absolutely nothing about marginal utility. Four others said very little. Only Sax, Auspitz, and Lieben wrote very much on the subject.

Gustav Gross and Victor Mataja are the two who never so much as mentioned the idea of marginal utility in any of their voluminous writings. They have a right to an inclusion in the School of Vienna principally in that they said nothing in conflict with its views on marginal utility. They had little temptation to do so because their interests kept them out of areas in which they might have had use for such contrary beliefs as the labor theory of value.

Gross's first theoretical book, *Die Lehre vom Unternehmergewinn* deals wholly with profits: their nature; justification; and social significance.[9] In treating these topics he could have referred to marginal utility but he did not do so. His only reference to the *Grundsätze* has no connection with utility.[10] At about the same time Gross prepared the article, "Karl Marx" for the *Allgemeine Deutsche Biographie*,[11] of which he published somewhat later an expanded version.[12] Here he took up, quite sympathetically, Marx's theory of value in detail.[13] Although he criticized Marx for not considering the usefulness of a good in his discussion of exchange value, and although he cited both Knies' and Schäffle's criticisms of Marx's labor theory of value,[14] he at no place either mentioned Menger or brought out anything like the idea of marginal utility in his restrained corrections of Marx.

Gustav Gross' third book, *Wirtschaftsformen und Wirtschaftsprinzipien*,[15] gave him every opportunity to make use of any ideas on marginal utility he had acquired by 1888. He did not utilize the opportunity. He discussed, in a general way, exchange and price, and he connected Menger with the discussion by reference to the *Grundsätze,* but he never came closer to the core of the marginal utility analysis than to join the needs of the exchanging individuals in a loose fashion to the evaluations the individuals put on the goods.

None of Gross's later publications have any more direct relation to marginal utility.[16] Consequently it is difficult to see how Wilhelm Weber could state that Gross was "von *Menger* beeinflusst."[17] Of course we do not know what Gross taught in his course at the University of Vienna. In the list given below,[18] we see that during this period he frequently taught the basic course, *Nationalökonomie,* along with Menger, Wieser, Philippovich, and Mataja. His views on marginal utility must therefore not have conflicted with theirs.

The case of Victor Mataja[19] parallels that of Gustav Gross. Like Gross, Mataja first published a short book on profits that contains nothing to link him with Menger's views or with marginal utility economics.[20] It served as a *Habilitationsschrift* that gained him a position with the University of Vienna, which in turn led to a professorship at Innsbruck from 1890 to 1892. In his later years he became *Honorar-Professor* at the University of Vienna but apparently without doing much teaching. As with Gross, he taught courses that might have held some reference to utility, but this is an assumption.[21] Mataja in later years developed an especial interest in advertising and wrote a book on the subject. We might anticipate that he would touch on utility, since advertising tampers to the advantage of the firm with the native utility of the individual, but the connection does not appear. His book on advertising has an extended bibliography that contains no trace of anyone's writings on the subject of marginal utility.[22] Mataja published a number of other books and wrote considerably for different journals, but none of his contributions show any interest that might connect them with Menger, Böhm-Bawerk, or Wieser.[23] He had a wholly different set of interests in such things as advertising, retailing, installment buying, and insurance.

III

Robert Meyer is the first of the group of members of the Austrian School who wrote a little on the subject of marginal utility. His solitary article on the subject concerns Simon Nelson Patten's "Law of the Increasing Variety of Consumption."[24] Here he showed a firm understanding of the idea of marginal utility and an ability to use it in the analysis of economic phenomena. He did not mention Menger, but he did refer to Wieser, Auspitz, Lieben, and Böhm-Bawerk. Meyer had not touched on the topic of utility earlier.[25] He may, of course, have used the idea in his lectures at the University of Vienna, but no record of such use remains.[26] His later writings were concerned mainly with public finance.[27]

The second minor member of the Austrian School to write a little, but not much, on the subject of marginal utility was Johann von Komorzynski. He had published nothing during the twenty years between the time when he contributed to the controversy on value that stimulated Menger to begin his writing and the year that he offered his *Der Wert in der isolirten Wirthschaft* as a *Habilitationsschrift* at the University of Vienna.[28] We do not know what led this forty-six year old Viennese lawyer to return to the university, but we do see that he had kept abreast the developments in marginal utility economics. Böhm-Bawerk found his book, which Komorzynski dedicated to Menger, entirely in the spirit of marginal utility theory.[29] Komorzynski attempted to contribute an original proof that the theory of value rightly applied only to reproducible goods and services and not to unique goods. He based his reasoning on an assumption of the incomparability of the satisfaction derived from different kinds of goods.[30] For this reason Othmar Spann listed Komorzynski as the first "outspoken opponent" of the Marginal Utility School.[31] Yet no one could rank him as a severe opponent, for he never again offered a criticism.[32]

A third Austrian economist who devoted a part of his writing to marginal utility was Robert Zuckerkandl. His *Zur Theorie des Preises, mit besonderer Berücksichtigung der geschichtlichen Entwicklung der Lehre*[33] has a chapter on subjective theories of value. The book, however, does not serve as a plea for such theories. Zuckerkandl began to show the party spirit of the Austrian School, for he displayed more willingness to defend Menger against Jevons and Walras than to praise the merits of a subjective theory of value. However faulty the book may seem now as an evaluation of the group of economists to which the author himself belonged, for the time its account was good. At least J. B. Clark, in his review of it, said that "the book constitutes an especially good introduction to the writings of recent economists of the Austrian school."[34]

Robert Zuckerkandl returned more frequently to the subject of marginal utility in his subsequent writings than did the other minor members whose works we have examined.[35] He commenced with a reply to Heinrich Dietzel's energetic criticisms of the theory in 1890,[36] reviewed William Smart's *An Introduction to the Theory of Value on the Lines of Menger, Wieser, and Böhm-Bawerk*,[37] incorporated the idea of marginal utility in his lectures on *Volkswirtschaftslehre* that he gave at Prague,[38] wrote in 1910 an article on Menger celebrating the latter's seventieth birthday,[39] and contributed an article, "Preis," to the *Handwörterbuch der Staatswissenschaften* that made use of the idea of utility.[40] From 1910 to his death in 1926 he did not again write on the subject.

Eugen Philippovich von Philippsberg was the last of the Austrian professors of economics usually included within the lists of the members of the Marginal Utility School who wrote something but not much on subjective value theory. He published nothing on marginal utility until 1893, several years beyond the period under investigation.[41] As he himself told, although he had studied at Vienna from 1879 to 1885, he had fallen wholly under the influence of Lorenz von Stein and had known Carl Menger only as the tutor of the Crown Prince Rudolf.[42] He came to what leanings he had away from the Historical School and toward the Marginal Utility School after he had read Böhm-Bawerk's *Kapital und Kapitalzins* at the time the second part of it appeared in 1889.[43] We include him here principally because his *Grundriss der politischen Oekonomie*[44] became the best-known general treatise in German on economics in the following generation, a main source for many Germans of their knowledge of marginal utility economics. The principal German reviews, however, never mentioned the idea of marginal utility.[45]

IV

Emil Sax is associated with the Austrian School more often than anyone else except Menger, Wieser, and Böhm-Bawerk. The sketchy character of our information on his life prevents us from ascertaining when he became acquainted with Menger's *Grundsätze* and consequently when he began to learn of marginal utility. He may have read it in the early seventies while a *Privatdozent* at the University of Vienna, but it certainly had no pronounced influence on him for a long time afterward.

The publications of Sax in the five years before he went to Prague in 1879 had a descriptive, historical, and analytical tone that had no connection with the work of Menger.[46] His first book published five years after he settled in Prague did show Menger's clear influence, but of his *Untersuchungen* rather than his *Grundsätze*.[47] Here he treated the subject of method exclusively and not the subject of value.[48] He made, consequently, no use of the idea of marginal utility.

In 1887 Sax published his *Grundlegung der theoretischen Staatswirtschaft*,[49] the book that shows his complete acceptance of marginal utility as a useful concept. This was the year after Böhm-Bawerk had revealed his similar intense interest in the theory of marginal utility. From this date on, Sax clearly belonged to the Marginal Utility School. We should remember, however, that he went his way on the path of economics for sixteen years after the publication of Menger's *Grundsätze* before he ever made use of its precepts.

We ought to guard against thinking of Sax's *Grundlegung* too strictly in terms of what historians of economic thought set down as its central purpose. For example, Alexander Gray, who says that "a fourth writer [Sax] claims, and can hardly be refused, inclusion among the original founders," made the following statement: "The State may take, and apply to less urgent purposes, money which might have been more profitably employed by the taxpayer. This is indeed a rather dowdy old truth, which, however, is clearly capable of being neatly dressed in a chic Viennese confection. A discussion of this aspect of the question was the peculiar contribution of Emil Sax in his *Grundlegung der theoretischen Staatswirtschaft* (1887). He applied Austrian thought to the economics of the State, and in particular used it to develop a theory of taxation."[50] True enough! But anyone who expects Sax's *Grundlegung* to deal mostly with taxation and the state will be surprised by the book itself. It contains many things, including a little on taxation, and much on the marginal utility theory of value.

This book by Sax succeeded only moderately well from any standpoint.[51] It never reached a second edition but it was translated into Italian.[52] Its reception displeased Sax, and it is said that he resigned his professorship at the University of Prague and at the age of forty-eight went into retirement in Italy partly for this reason.[53]

Looking at the book we can see that Sax might well have expected great things from it. He considered it an original work of importance.[54] It tried to do, and he thought it succeeded in accomplishing, the difficult task not only of presenting a theory of political science on the same level and with the same method by which Menger had produced a theory of economics, but also of connecting it with the theory of economics, so as to make the social sciences into a whole.

Although it had not accomplished the grand end Sax had in mind, his *Grundlegung* nevertheless gave a push to the marginal utility theory of value. The volume does not immediately reach this subject. The first book, which investigates the idea of individual and collective action, their interrelations, their history, and their connection with *Egoismus* and *Altruismus,* has no bearing on marginal utility. Nor does the second book, which gives a doctrinal history of the views of economists on the economic role of the state. Only after continuing through a long discussion on the elements of human economy (such things as trade, property, the division of labor) and through a general discussion of wants, goods, and labor (where we begin to reach the outskirts of the ideas of Menger, Wieser, and Böhm-Bawerk), and upon arriving at the middle of the book itself, does the reader come to the subject of value and the use of marginal utility in the determination thereof. Sax credited Menger with the discovery of the relation of marginal utility to value, and Wieser with the choice of the word *"Grenznutzen."*[55] He discussed the law of diminishing marginal utility.[56] The final half of the book first examines the relation of social wants to individual value and then turns to such subjects as capital and costs. At the end of his book comes the discussion of taxation that uses utility and that has attracted such attention.

Sax returned to the subject of marginal utility only twice after his *Grundlegung* had appeared. In 1889, he mentioned it in an address that he published, *Die neuesten Fortschritte der nationalökonomischen Theorie.*[57] And he made use of it in his long article on progressive taxation (1892).[58]

V

Auspitz and Lieben published their *Untersuchungen über die Theorie des Preises* in 1889.[59] They had written nothing that foreshadowed its appearance. Auspitz had published a good deal on economics after the middle of the eighteen-seventies but wholly on popular subjects.[60] Lieben evidently had done no writing for publication before this date. In the preface the two authors state that their interest began ten years earlier, but they do not say what brought it about or what kept it alive in the interval.[61] We know, however, again from the preface that they had acquired by 1888 an acquaintance with the literature on utility theory that must have equaled that of any other economist. Evidently they knew of the work of Thünen, Cournot, Dupuit, Gossen, Jevons, Léon Walras, Menger, Wieser, Böhm-Bawerk, and Launhardt. They had an advantage over all other Austrian writers in that they possessed both the ability to read the mathematical sections of Thünen, Cournot, Gossen, Jevons, Walras, and Launhardt, and the willingness to do so.

As an example of book production, the *Theorie des Preises* ought to command respect.[62] Its use of utility theory is as outstanding as the form of the book. It utilizes the idea on a scale and with a degree of care not duplicated in the work of any other economists of the time, except Wicksteed. Its authors combined a perfect understanding of much of what had been written earlier, their mathematical facility, their worldly experiences, and their ingenuity into an elaborate exposition of consumption economics. It did not have the impact it ought to have had, not only because it contained more mathematics than the Austrian and other economists of the time could tolerate, but also because its authors had no connection with the University of Vienna. It also contained some annoying faults.

Auspitz and Lieben evidently began in their own mind, although not in their book, with the whole of the consumption and the production of an individual in view for a specified and long period of time, a year. They gave as their most general statement of the relationships the massive function $z = \phi\,(v_a,\ e_a,\ g_a,\ f_a,\ s_a,\ tg\xi_a;\ v_b,\ e_b,\ g_b,\ f_b,\ s_b,\ tg\xi_b,\ \ldots\ v_n,\ e_n,\ g_n,\ f_n,\ s_n,\ tg\xi_n;\ \mu)$.[63] In this expression the annual satisfaction z of an individual depends on six aspects of the n goods in the economy, and upon the stock of money μ. These aspects are: the anticipated prices of each good $tg\xi$, the quantity of each good consumed v or produced e by the individual; and three different $(g,\ f,\ s)$ non-consumption uses of the goods. This long expression, which lumps together satisfactions of every kind whether in consumption or production, certainly transcends in generality all pictures of utility relationships given either before its time or later, but it has the disadvantage of including too much.[64] As soon as Auspitz and Lieben commenced to talk about any aspect of utility, they of course appropriately spoke of simpler functions derived from their basic function.

They began with a description of collective total utility curves.

They turned, only later, to the individual curves and the method by which they are compounded into collective curves.[65] The collective curve, like the individual curve, starts at the origin, rises to a zenith, and then approaches a vertical asymptote.[66] This curve evidently traces the addition to the sum of the z's (in their basic functions) due to the uses of the specified good and on the assumption that the prices, but not the quantities of the other goods, as well as the desires of the individuals, remain constant. As with the individual utility curve, the collective curve is constant in terms of the annual consumption. We may note also that, unlike most utility curves, the goods referred to may be either consumed or used in production. The authors measure utility by the sum of money just necessary to compensate the individuals for the loss of the given amount of the good. This curve is used in conjunction with the symmetrical collective total cost function to determine the price of the good and the amount of the consumers' rent.

The next section includes a long discussion of the manner in which utility curves change as the *Lebensweise* of an individual alters. The *Lebensweise* changes whenever any other condition (besides the quantity of the good in question) changes essentially—an admittedly somewhat vague and also amazing concept. The representation of all the total utility curves of a good for the different possible *Lebensweisen* gives a graph as below.[67] The envelope curve

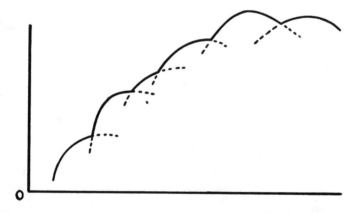

drawn to these curves measures the maximum utility available to the individual when he can make the necessary adjustments in all aspects of his life. No one has used curves of this nature in connection with utility except Auspitz and Lieben, although similar curves with respect to production, which Auspitz and Lieben also employed, and which are sometimes called "planning curves," have found wide adoption.

Auspitz and Lieben also introduced the *Lebensgenusskurve*.[68] This enjoyment curve differs from the utility curve only in that it is not zero for a zero consumption of the good, but equals whatever total satisfaction would result if the consumer had none of this good to consume throughout the year. In other words, the *Lebensgenusskurven* show the total satisfaction that the individual in question obtains, not merely that part resulting from the good under consideration. Enjoyment plus the initial satisfaction equals utility.[69] Auspitz and Lieben investigated at length the many influences on the slope of the *Lebensgenusskurve*.

We might imagine that this book would have pleased all the other members of the Marginal Utility School. At least we could expect that Léon Walras, who could follow the mathematics in parts that might be obscure to the more literary members of the School of Vienna, would have recognized the value of their work and be grateful for the support it gave his own, especially since it paid him such high compliments and in part used his method of general equilibrium. Our expectations would not be fulfilled, for not only did the other members of the Marginal Utility School fail to show any enthusiasm but Walras even wrote an unfavorable review of the book.[70] Walras apparently did not examine it thoroughly. At least none of his observations extend beyond the first chapter. And in his comments on this chapter he contented himself with a recital of seven numbered errors and permitted himself no word of praise. Insofar as his strictures concern utility, Walras charged that Auspitz and Lieben fell into the same error that he had charged Dupuit with in his *Éléments*, the error of confusing the demand curve with a utility curve. In a reply to Walras' criticisms, Auspitz and Lieben pointed out that they assumed the individual's valuation of money or *numéraire* constant, as well as all other prices fixed, in which case, according to Walras' suppositions, the utility curve and the demand curve coincide.[71] Auspitz and Lieben held that Walras had obtained his result only because he had used a utility curve with a single argument, the quantity of the good, while their utility functions had as their arguments, the quantities of *all* goods and of *numéraire*.

Two other people, Vilfredo Pareto and Irving Fisher, felt the influence of Auspitz and Lieben at this time. Pareto joined in the dispute between Walras and the two Austrians.[72] He also mentioned the *Theorie des Preises* at the beginning of his important series of articles that ran under the general title of "Considerazioni sui principii fundamentali dell' economia politica pura," where he said that it showed how the theory "dell' economia matematica possano practicamente usari nello studio dei prezzi."[73]

Louis Suret made a French translation of the *Theorie des Preises* in 1914.[74] Irving Fisher wrote the only American review of the translation. In this he acknowledged "his own keen sense of obligation to the original book to which in fact he owes his first real stimulus to the serious scientific study of political economy."[75] He had said much the same thing earlier when he wrote, in the preface to his *Mathematical Investigations in the Theory of Value and Prices*, that "the two books which have influenced me most are Jevons: '*Theory of Political Economy*' and Auspitz und Lieben: '*Untersuchungen ueber die Theorie des Preises*'."[76]

The *Untersuchungen über die Theorie des Preises* also received some high praise in later years. Schumpeter said, "Even now it offers to the student a wealth of ideas and suggestions as yet but partially utilized."[77] And Hutchison made a similar appraisal when he remarked that "no work in our period, not even Marshall's or Pareto's, contains a greater number of precise and original contributions to the pure analysis of the individual consumer and firm, and to the clarification of the main assumptions. . . ."[78]

Chapter XIX

ECONOMICS AT THE UNIVERSITY OF VIENNA

I

We have examined in some detail the writings of the economists associated with the School of Vienna during the period from 1871 to 1889, to discover the nature and extent of their views on the subject of marginal utility. Let us now look at the teaching at the University of Vienna both to determine the extent that the professors of those days taught the new doctrine, and to decide what factors explained the rise of a Marginal Utility School in that university.

Nothing about the Austrian universities seems calculated to turn out economists of any school whatsoever. The Austrian universities taught economics only in the *Rechts- und staatswissenschaftliche Facultät,* usually the faculty with the largest number of students.[1] As a result, a student who studied any economics would receive the degree of *Doktor der Rechte* instead of the *Doktor der Philosophie* that he would have received in most German universities. Nor could the student have specialized in economics at the university during this time as he could have at some German universities. All the students had to take a prescribed course that had in it a minimum amount of economics. The *Doktor der Rechte* degree supposed a residence for four years of two semesters each during which the student had to pass three examinations but did not write a thesis. The first examination covered canon, Roman, and German law. The second examination concerned Austrian law. The third examination consisted of statistics, general economics, and public finance.[2]

The following courses provided the instruction given in economics from 1876 to 1889.[3]

Major Courses

General Economics (*Nationalökonomie*). This principal course in economics was usually taught in the winter semesters in two sections which met five times a week. In all the winter semesters from 1876-77 to 1884-85 Menger taught one of the sections and Stein the other (perhaps from 1873 to 1876 also). In 1885 Stein retired. Menger continued to teach one section each winter semester all the remainder of the period in question (to 1890). The other winter semester sections were taught in 1886-87 by Gross, in 1888-89 by Brentano and Gross, and in 1889-90 by

173

Miaskowski. They were also taught in the following summer semesters: in 1880 by Böhm-Bawerk; in 1884 by Wieser and Gross; in 1885 by Gross and Philippovich; in 1886 by Mataja; and in 1887 by Gross.

Public Finance (*Finanzwissenschaft*). This second important course in economics was usually taught in the summer semester in two sections which met five times a week. Stein and Menger each taught a section from 1877 to 1884 (perhaps also from 1873 to 1877). Menger continued through the eighteen-eighties to give a section in each summer semester. Meyer taught in the winter semester 1884-85, the summer semester 1885, and the winter semester 1887-88. Brentano taught in the summer semester 1888.

Menger's Seminar (*Übungen in Nationalökonomie und Finanzwissenschaft*). It met twice a week in the summer semesters from 1877 to 1889. Probably it was also held in the winter semesters of 1876-77 and 1877-78.

Minor Courses

The History of Economic Thought (lectures twice a week given under various titles and with different contents): *Geschichte der Nationalökonomie* (Philippovich, winter semester 1884-85; Zuckerkandl, winter semester 1887-88 and summer semester 1888; both Zuckerkandl and Meyer in winter semester 1888-89); *Geschichte der Nationalökonomie seit Adam Smith* (Mataja, winter semester 1884-85); and *Geschichte des Communismus und Sozialismus* (Wieser, winter semester 1884-85; Mataja, winter semester of 1885-86 and 1886-87; and Gross, summer semester 1888).

Credit and Banking (*Credit und Bankwesen, Geld und Creditwesen, or Geld und Bankwesen*). Taught by Mataja in the summer semester 1885 and winter semester 1887-88, by Philippovich in the winter semester 1885-86, by Gross in the summer semesters of 1886 and 1889, and by Meyer in the summer semester of 1888.

Other courses given infrequently were: *Die Lehre von den Abgaben* (Meyer, summer semesters of 1884, 1887 and 1889); *Die Lehre von den Staatsschulden* (Meyer, summer semesters of 1886 and 1887); *Handels und Gewerbepolitik* (Gross, winter semesters of 1885-86 and 1887-88; and Mataja, summer semester of 1889); *Arbeiterschutzgesetzgebung* (Mataja, summer semester 1887; and Zuckerkandl, summer semester 1889, and winter semester 1889-90); *Verkehrswesen* (Gross, winter semesters of 1884-85, 1886-87, 1889-90); *Steuerwesen* (Mataja, summer semester 1888 and winter semester 1888-89); *Ueber Fabriksgesetzgebung* (Mataja, winter semester, 1885-86); *Die Ordnung des Staatshaushaltes und der Staatscredit* (Meyer, winter semester 1886-87); *Werth und Preis und die damit zusammenhängenden theoretischen Grundlehren* (Zuckerkandl, summer semester 1887); *Darstellung des Systems der englischen sogenannten Einkommensteuer* (Meyer, summer semester 1885); *Öffentliche Schulden* (Brentano, summer semester 1888); *Die gewerbliche Arbeiterfrage und die Socialpolitik in England und Deutschland*

174

(Brentano, winter semester 1888-89); *Handelspolitik, Theorie und Geschichte* (Zuckerkandl, winter semester 1889-90); and *Nationalökonomische Übungen* (Gross, winter semester 1888-89); *Handels und Zollpolitik* (Mataja, summer semester 1889); *Die Lehre von Credit* (Meyer, winter semester, 1889-90).

The University of Vienna had perhaps ten thousand students who went through this fixed program in the twenty years after 1871. They were the students who intended to enter the profession of law, the Austrian civil service, or business. None of them came to the university with the especial intention in mind of studying the subject of economics. For the most part they attended the lectures which would prepare them for their examinations. Only a few listened to the *Privatdozenten* who delivered the few lectures in the minor courses. Perhaps it was to be expected that a handful would become absorbed in this incidental study that occupied a part of their curriculum, and would develop into the professors of the Austrian School.

What turned these few Viennese students from their intended professions to a lifelong study of economics? The other Austrian universities had similar requirements but did not turn out economists.[4] The French universities introduced economics into their law curriculum in the seventies but produced no school of economists thereby. The University of Vienna had two things that the other Austrian and the French universities lacked. They had a new doctrine to teach, one that economists of the future accepted. Other universities taught the doctrines of the past, doctrines that faded in the future. The Austrians could give their students in the seventies and the eighties a radically different viewpoint in economics that could increase in value as the years passed. Finally, the Austrians had the advantage of having a number of excellent teachers in economics whose sincerity and enthusiasm helped to turn a few students to the serious pursuit of economics.

II

Accounts of the teaching of economics at the University of Vienna around the end of the eighties and the beginning of the nineties by Ernest Mahaim (a Belgian), H. R. Seager (an American), and Henri Saint-Marc (a Frenchman) give a good contemporary picture of the situation. These students came to Vienna because word of the Austrian School had spread. But it was Menger's controversy over method with Schmoller, as much as his views on the theory of value, that attracted foreign students. Mahaim specifically mentioned "la grande question de la methode" as one of his main interests in Vienna.[5] Seager said that the eyes of the economists of all nations were directed toward Menger, Schmoller, Böhm-Bawerk, and Wagner.[6] St. Marc said that Menger occupied nearly the same position at Vienna that Schmoller did at Berlin.[7] All three of these visitors at Vienna thought highly of the professors of economics. Mahaim said that "c'était surtout la personnalité des professeurs qui nous appelait à Vienne."[8] He had an especially high regard for Menger, to whom he paid the following tribute: "Une de ses grandes qualités est, qu'avant d'être un savant, il est un pédagogue dévoué. Son enseignement se fait moins à l'université que chez lui. Il accueille avec affabilité tous ceux de ces élèves qui viennent lui demander des conseils; ils les dirige dans leurs recherches, discute pendant des heures les travaux qu'on vient lui soumettre. Il possède une bibliothèque qui est un trésor de merveilles et de raretés, et son grand plaisir est d'en mettre les richesses à la disposition de ses élèves."[9] Seager likewise gave Menger's teaching the highest praise:

One can scarcely say too much in praise of Professor Menger as a teacher. His great popularity with his students and the success that has attended his efforts to gather about himself talented young men, who sympathize with his fundamental views, are sufficient evidence of his genius in this direction. . . . To have access to such a collection of books [as Menger has in his personal library] is itself a boon of inestimable value; add to it the advice and guidance of such a man as Professor Menger, and the reader will understand some of the attractions which induce not a few economic students to come here to Vienna in preference even to going to Berlin.[10]

III

To what extent did peculiar national characteristics prevent the growth of the Marginal Utility School in Germany, France, and England and thus give Austria a comparative advantage? In Germany the Historical School, a school that had adopted an attitude hostile toward marginal utility, dominated all the university appointments during this time. An observer said that Schmoller, through a friend in the Ministry of Education, could stop the appointment of anyone unsympathetic with the Historical School, and consequently could prevent by this means an intrusion of marginal utility into the

German universities.[11] Doubtless this explanation overestimates Schmoller's personal power. It also implicitly overestimates the number of candidates who harbored a strong attachment to marginal utility and who coveted a professorship of economics in any of the approximately two dozen German universities.

In a very similar fashion a conservative, unyielding group controlled the French university professorships, a circumstance that drove Léon Walras to Switzerland. In comparison with the Germans, the French had few chairs of political economy in the universities until 1877, and consequently had even fewer opportunities to bar economists than the Germans. At this date they admitted (among many others) Charles Gide, who immediately wrote in praise of Jevons, and who used the idea of marginal utility in his textbooks. As in Germany, no large number of economists who might teach marginal utility economics in France could have been barred from teaching positions, for the reason that few French candidates for these posts had this qualification.

A like supposition holds that that nebulous body, the English Classical School, kept out professors in England who inclined toward marginal utility in order to uphold the labor theory of value, but this supposition has only a faint resemblance to the facts. Both Marshall and Edgeworth had obvious leanings toward marginal utility; yet they obtained, in these times, the two leading professorships of economics in England, those at Oxford and Cambridge. The marginal utility economists can have little complaint in England as to their treatment by their contemporaries.

In Austria itself, the opposition to marginal utility seems quite as formidable as anywhere else. The Austro-Hungarian monarchy of the eighteen-seventies and eighteen-eighties contained seven Austrian universities: Vienna, Prague, Innsbruck, Graz, Czernowitz, Cracow, and Lemberg. In the twenty years after 1870 the last four of these universities felt no effect of the rise of the Marginal Utility School. For that reason it is more strictly accurate to speak of the "School of Vienna" than the "Austrian School," even though several of the Viennese students did teach at Prague and Innsbruck. Not only is marginal utility confined largely to one of the Austrian universities (remembering that Prague and Innsbruck had participated to some degree) but even within the University of Vienna (and at Prague too) the administration tried to see to it that other views than those of the Marginal Utility School were presented. This was made possible by the circumstance that the Austrian universities had the policy of giving two sections of each required subject in economics, the student being free to enroll in either one. When Menger first commenced to lecture at the University of Vienna, Lorenz von Stein, a luminary with quite different views, held the other chair. After Stein retired in 1885, the authorities brought in August von Miaskowski and Lujo Brentano for the express reason that they held views in some ways opposite to Menger. Although neither stayed long at the University of Vienna, the circumstance that the university engaged their services suggests that even in Vienna marginal utility economists got something less than wholehearted welcome. In short, facts contradict the suggestion that the Austrian School arose because the national characteristics of economists opposed the new ideas elsewhere and encouraged them in Austria.

Chapter XX

LÉON WALRAS' LATER CONTRIBUTIONS

I

The twenty-two years that Léon Walras spent in teaching, before he retired in 1892, established the Lausanne School. Note the limited sense of the word "School" in this context. At first it consisted entirely of Léon Walras. Then later, in succession, came Vilfredo Pareto, Pascal Boninsegni, and Firmin Oulès. None of the successors of Léon Walras at Lausanne, and accordingly none of the successive heads of the Lausanne School, had ever studied at Lausanne. In this respect Lausanne differed from the Austrian School, where the professors, almost to a man, had their academic origins in Vienna. The Lausanne School did not spread its ideas by direct teaching. No important economist obtained any part of his inspiration or views by study at the University of Lausanne. Instead, the doctrine spread through an audience which read the works of Walras or Pareto miles from Switzerland. All the attention that Walras gave to the students in his classes came to little compared to the results that he obtained from his books and articles.

The School of Lausanne has many distinguishing characteristics. In any list of its attributes there is no doubt that its use of marginal utility ranks high. As a consequence we might expect that Walras gave marginal utility a good deal of attention after he published the *Éléments,* and we will now examine the extent to which he fulfilled our expectations.

II

In 1878, Gerolamo Boccardo added to his *Biblioteca dell' economista* a translation of the four *Mémoires* under the title *Teoria matematica della ricchezza sociale.* He included the correspondence between Walras and Jevons with respect to the originality of their ideas, which had appeared earlier in the *Journal des économistes.* With both Jevons' *Theory* and the central parts of Walras' *Éléments* in Italian, and with a commentary by Jevons and Walras on the development of the idea included, Italian economists had the new ideas on marginal utility before them in an easily available form. A German translation by Ludwig von Winterfeld of the same four

179

Mémoires followed in 1881, with the title *Mathematische Theorie der Preisbestimmung der Wirthschaftlichen Güter.*[1] It seemed to have had a negligible effect on German economic thought, but at least Wilhelm Lexis read it and wrote a long review.[2] A few years later a French edition appeared, supplemented by two articles on money and one on land nationalization.[3] It was the second book published in French that used marginal utility theory extensively in connection with an explanation of value. As an illustration of how little it furthered the cause of marginal utility we note that Charles Gide's review of the book did not mention the portions that have a connection with utility.[4] He worried about the mathematics and noticed the newer sections on the livelier topics of money or land reform at the end of the book. Other French readers evidently did likewise.

One of the few new things that Walras published on the subject of utility was the part of the correspondence between himself and Jevons on the origin of their ideas on value.[5] The nature of this correspondence, as well as its form, could have attracted many readers who might have avoided a more rigorous mathematical statement.

A second occasion on which Walras wrote on utility in connection with a relatively attractive subject came with the publication of his study of Gossen.[6] In the course of the paper, Walras not only provided the main known facts on the life of Gossen but also set forth, not Gossen's claim to originality, but his own. Walras said that he shared the human weakness of wishing to attach his name "à quelque résultat important."[7] Consequently after receiving the letter informing him of the discovery of Gossen's work, he was "quelque peu inquiet de savoir ce qui me resterait en propre" after Gossen's claims had been satisfied.[8] He concluded that, although Gossen may have anticipated all or most of Jevons' discoveries as Jevons says that he did, Gossen had not anticipated his own. On his good fortune he wrote jubilantly that he had carried his analysis to a point that Gossen had not attained and thus had retained his priority for a good part of his discovery.[9]

Walras accepted completely Gossen's and Jevons' priority in the use of utility. He retained credit for extending the conditions of exchange to many exchangers, for treating the prices of the factors of production more thoroughly, especially for considering the general case in which the producers hire the use of productive services and sell the finished product to the consumers, and for the use of marginal utility in the consideration of his theory of capital. He finished by extending his thanks to Gossen and Jevons, who "en me dérobant le point de départ de toute l'économie politique pure, ont eu la délicatesse de me laisser à peu près entièrement en possession de toutes les déductions ultérieures."[10]

III

The next year, 1886, Léon Walras again put the idea of marginal utility before economists who read French when he published his *Théorie de la monnaie*.[11] Walras, Menger, and Jevons spent more time on, and published more about, the subject of money than on any other subject during the years after they had published their major treatises on economics. Of the three, only Walras introduced the idea of marginal utility into his monetary writings. Walras' *Théorie de la monnaie* played a significant role in the history of the spread of marginal utility theory, since in it Walras announced his discovery that Menger had used the idea of marginal utility. Walras had been led to correspond with Menger several years earlier in 1883 by d'Aulnis de Bourrouil. In the exchange of letters at this time the discussion was confined principally to the problem of method, and nothing was made of the similarity in the use of marginal utility.[12] Walras first had his mind definitely focused on Menger's employment of marginal utility by Böhm-Bawerk in 1886. After Walras had finished his *Théorie de la monnaie* and had had it printed, he received from Böhm-Bawerk an offprint of his article "Grundzüge der Theorie des wirtschaftlichen Güterwerts."[13] As a consequence Walras wrote a foreword for the already printed book in which he characterized the state of marginal utility theory in 1886.[14] Among those who had leaned toward the idea of marginal utility Walras listed the Austrians: Menger, Wieser, and Böhm-Bawerk. He did not mention Menger as a third discoverer or rediscoverer in the seventies of utility theory, but at least he had become aware that Menger, along with Böhm-Bawerk and Wieser, dealt with marginal utility. Menger had sent Walras a copy of the *Grundsätze* in 1883. However, it made no impression on Walras. Nor was Walras influenced by the earlier publication of Böhm-Bawerk or, even more unfortunately, by Wieser's *Ursprung und die Hauptgesetze des wirtschaftlichen Werthes*.

Böhm-Bawerk evidently learned of Walras' interest in marginal utility by some means other than through reading Walras' article on

181

Gossen in 1885, for he did not mention Gossen in this important work on value that he wrote in 1886. "Quand il se sera renseigné à cet égard," Walras wrote about Böhm-Bawerk, "il reconnaîtra combien l'absence d'une mention du nom et du livre de cet auteur constitue une lacune regrettable. . . ."[15]

The receipt of the offprint of the article by Böhm-Bawerk stirred Walras' hopes for the success of the marginal utility doctrine. Walras provided a list of the economists who had accepted in some degree the validity of the use of marginal utility in economic analysis. The list contained not only the names of Menger, Wieser, and Böhm-Bawerk, but also of N. G. Pierson (whom he had learned of from Böhm-Bawerk's article), Alfred Marshall, Henry Sidgwick, H. S. Foxwell, F. Y. Edgeworth, P. H. Wicksteed, J. d'Aulnis de Bourouill, H. B. Greven, Francis A. Walker, Charles Gide, Wilhelm Launhardt, and G. B. Antonelli.[16] Walras' consideration of this list led him to refer to the group as a "School," the first time that anyone had applied this designation to those who made use of marginal utility in the discussion of value. "L'essentiel est qu'une école se forme," wrote Walras, "sur le terrain de notre théorie de la valeur et de l'échange; or cette école tend évidemment de jour en jour à se constituer. . . ."

Walras also outlined the direction in which the school should march. Theory, Walras said, should throw light on applied economics and thus should help in framing economic reforms. Walras thought that he, and the others who knew the secret of marginal utility, could judge of reforms in a way that neither the socialists nor the conservatives could match.[17] With this end in mind he worked on the taxation of land values in a progressive society and upon the problem of money. Thus this discussion revealed one avowed reason that Walras did not continue with theoretical problems after 1877, and consequently one reason that he never returned to any extent to a consideration of marginal utility. He did not come back to theoretical economics or to marginal utility because he thought that he had developed those tools sufficiently to spend his time best in the use of them.

Accordingly Walras wrote his book on money as an argument for monetary reforms. He based his reforms on the analysis of exchange which, in turn, rested on utility. Consequently, he opened his *Théorie de la monnaie* with a sketch of his whole system that gave due prominence to the ideas of *raretés*. In this sketch he could not resist the impulse to give marginal utility a special place as a *cause*, instead of treating it in the way his system implies that he should treat it, as one of many variables, simultaneously determined. In other words, when he thought of the utility functions as exogeneous, he gave them a special place of honor among the exogeneous parts of his system. We would expect this kind of treatment of marginal utility, or of the utility function, on the part of Menger, who began his *Grundsätze* with a reference to cause and effect, but it startles us to find the same vein in Walras, who represents a quite contrary viewpoint. Walras could not keep away from cause and effect in the *Éléments,* and he shows no intention to mend his ways in the *Théorie de la monnaie.* "Cela revient à dire qu'à l'état d'équilibre de l'échange et de la production," Walras said, "le prix des services est déterminé par le prix des produits (et non pas le prix des produits par le prix des services), et que le prix des produits est determiné par la condition de satisfaction maxima des besoins qui est ainsi la condition fondamentale de tout l'équilibre économique."[18]

In consequence of the key role that marginal utility played in his system, Walras gave a basic explanation of the idea. He began by describing a curve that traced the *intensités des derniers besoins satisfaits,* or the *raretés,* as a function of the quantity consumed. The curves that he drew to describe these functions differ from the similar curves that he had drawn in the first edition of the *Éléments.* In the *Éléments* Walras drew linear utility curves, a shape that Jevons criticized as misleading. In the *Théorie de la monnaie* Walras drew a concave curve, a convex curve, and curves with both concave and convex segments, but avoided linear curves.[19] In an unpublished letter, he explained to Jevons that he changed them to avoid the impression that the *rareté* varied with changes in the quantity according to some simple law.[20]

Walras brought out, in his explanation in the *Théorie de la monnaie,* most of the problems concerning marginal utility that he had tackled in the *Éléments.* He mentioned the problem of the measurement of utility and stated that the fact that he could not measure utility "n'importe pas pour la théorie qui n'a besoin que de la concevoir et non de la measurer."[21] Walras spoke of indivisible goods, but added that, for the sake of simplicity, he intended to discuss only goods for which the individual can change his consumption by infinitely small quantities. As in the *Éléments* Léon Walras called the integral of the curve *l'utilité effective,* and stated the condition for maximizing *l'utilité effective* of all the goods in terms of

183

the relations of the prices of the goods and their *raretés*. He mentioned, too, the difficulty that arises, in his equilibrium conditions, when an individual consumes none of a good.

His entire elementary discussion of marginal utility followed on the same lines that he had chosen in the *Éléments*. He introduced only one addition, the idea of average *raretés*. Jevons had averaged utility in the *Theory*, but Walras had not in the 1874 portion of the *Éléments*.[22] Walras made his introduction of the idea of an average, a dangerous procedure generally, since, in some degree, it must involve interpersonal comparisons, without any explanation and without much advantage to his argument. He only said, "On sait que la proportion des raretés moyennes serait la même que celle des raretés individuelles."[23] The use of $R_b, R_c, \ldots$ for the average utility of the goods $B, C, \ldots$ did permit him some economy of space in writing his equilibrium conditions as $P_b = R_b/R_a$, $P_c = R_c/R_a$, $\ldots$ instead of specifying the maximizing conditions for each of the individuals. But he gained nothing else from it.

IV

In the preface to his *Théorie de la monnaie* Walras noted that the first edition of the *Éléments* was almost exhausted. However, he did not publish the second edition until 1889. One of the classes he taught was required to read the *Éléments*. Evidently the students had had difficulty with the notation, for Walras added to the second edition an initial section designed to explain his mathematical procedures, the second lengthy attempt to explain mathematics to students of economics.[24]

The preface to the second edition relates some of the history of the use of marginal utility in economic analysis.[25] Walras supplemented it with a few pages in the text that acquaint the reader with the writing of Jevons, Gossen, and Menger.[26] Here for the first time he set down his realization that Menger shared on an equal footing the discovery of the use of the idea of marginal utility, a point not mentioned a few years before in his book on money.

Léon Walras in 1889 retained the optimistic note, in his discussion of the future of the use of marginal utility, that he first expressed in the preface to the *Théorie de la monnaie*. He said that he could add to the list of names that he had given earlier of professors who taught the doctrine. He did not do so, however, but listed instead the places at which they taught: Dublin, Louvain,

Würzburg, and Bordeaux. Walras introduced many changes in the second edition of the *Éléments*, but only a few of these concern marginal utility. He pointed out what he considered the main addition, a further discussion of the maximum conditions in the case of a discontinuous utility curve.[27] In the first edition Walras had mentioned the case of indivisible goods.[28] In the second edition he examined the exchange of a good that has a continuous utility curve for a good with a discontinuous curve.[29] Walras showed that a very close approximation to his equilibrium conditions held in the case of discontinuous goods.

Walras added to the second edition several sections calculated to sharpen his exposition by the use of a more precise mathematical notation, and in doing so he brought in more direct mathematical procedures. They may have helped those who had a mathematical bent, but they could only further dismay the reader who had found the mathematical reasoning of the first edition difficult to follow.[30]

In one of his sentences Walras made a curious change that Jaffé interpreted as showing "that the principle of maximization of utility in exchange, which had been enunciated as a broad empirical observation in the first edition, was reduced to a hypothetical proposition in the second and subsequent editions."[31] The two sentences follow:

FIRST EDITION[32]	COMMON TO BOTH FIRST AND SECOND EDITIONS	SECOND EDITION[33]
On est fondé à dire en principe qu'il opérera		En supposant qu'il opère
	l'échange de manière à satisfaire la plus grande somme totale de besoins possible	
et que, par conséquent,		il est certain que,
	P_a étant donné, d_a est déterminé	

Walras made another change of this kind. His statement of the equilibrium condition of exchange in the first edition reads that the exchangers "obtiennent" the greatest satisfaction.[34] In the second edition Walras changes "obtiennent" to "peuvent obtenir."[35] These verbal changes certainly bear out Jaffé's interpretation. Yet had Walras intended any serious alteration in his doctrine he ought to have impressed the nature of the change more forcibly on the reader. Very probably no one noticed these changes until Jaffé had his

185

attention drawn to them in the process of collating the different editions of the *Éléments*.

Walras included in the second edition of the *Éléments* the idea of average *raretés* which he had first used in the *Théorie de la monnaie*. The only advantage that it gained him was the conservation of notation.[36]

Chapter XXI

CHARLES GIDE AND A FRENCH CONTROVERSY OVER VALUE

I

Charles Gide made a bolder attempt to spread the idea of marginal utility than any other French writer during the seventies or eighties. He began his attempt with an article on Jevons' *Theory* that he sent to the *Journal des économistes* in 1881.[1] He also incorporated in 1884 the idea of marginal utility into his new and successful textbook on economics.

He had fewer results than he might have anticipated, but the blame falls on Gide himself, for quite probably no one followed his lead because his lead itself faltered. His article stimulated a discussion of the theory of value that continued for seven years, mostly in the *Journal des économistes*. But the discussion he generated never seized on the essentials of value theory as Jevons had seen them and certainly did not convert any of the economists in the controversy to the marginal utility theory. Nonetheless, the position of Gide and the nature of his attempt make desirable a consideration of his comments and of the results that developed therefrom.

II

Charles Gide entered the teaching of economics in 1877 to fill one of the chairs of economics created when the French government made political economy a compulsory subject for the law degree. At this time his only training in economics consisted, according to his necrographer, in his reading of a set of the complete works of Bastiat given him by his uncle on the occasion of his final degree. Consequently, Gide had a fresh viewpoint on economics.

Gide recognized specifically, in his article on Jevons, both the sad state of affairs in French economics and the need to take into account such writers as Jevons. At a time when French economists did not practice self-examination Gide made the following caustic inventory of French interests and tastes in the field of economics: "On s'occupe de statistique, de démographie, de finances, de législation économique, de sociologie peut-être, de tout ce qui ressemble à de l'économie politique sans en être, mais quant à des discussions sur les notions de l'utilité et de la valeur, sur la nature du capital et du travail, telles que celles que traite exclusivement l'ouvrage de M. Jevons, il est entendu que ce sont là des questions scolastiques qui ne sont plus de notre temps."[2] As an illustration of this state of affairs Gide cited the neglect by the French of Jevons' *Theory*. Gide pointed out that the first edition had appeared ten years earlier, that a second edition had come out in 1879, that not only did the French lack a translation but that no one in France ever had reviewed the book in any detail, and that none of the recent textbooks mentioned Jevons. Gide seemed more determined to disagree with his French colleagues, however, than to agree with Jevons. Gide first strongly approved Jevons' contention that the method of deduction suits economics better than the method of induction. He used this conclusion to wave aside the Historical School that had claimed supporters in France.[3] But when he came to Jevons' further methodological proposition that economic investigations must utilize the methods of mathematics, since economics involves quantities, Gide joined his French colleagues in protest. Mathematics irritated Gide as it did and does many other people partly, at least, and understandably, because it makes unintelligible what the author says.

Gide recognized that the theory of value formed "la partie capitale" of Jevons' *Theory*. He clearly understood the central idea of the connection of the "final degree of utility" to value and he presented it in such a way that no one could miss the point. In Gide's statement the French had as early as 1881, in a wholly non-mathematical form, and in a quite available place, a brief statement of the marginal utility theory of value. Gide immediately blemished his exposition of this theory with a damaging criticism. Readers probably gained the impression, since Gide inserted his exposition of the marginal utility theory between his strictures on mathematics and his criticism of Jevons' utility theory, that a student could pass up a book of this kind, with its obvious faults, at no great loss.

In support of his adverse judgment of Jevons' utility theory of value, Gide mustered two principal objections. He first objected that, since Jevons could not measure independently the final degree of utility, he had no way of ascertaining whether the exchange rates of goods do stand to each other in the suggested relation. If Jevons could not measure them directly, he argued, according to Gide, in a circle when he implied the ratios of the final degrees of utility from

the ratios of the exchange values.[4] Actually no circularity or inde-
terminateness exists in Jevons' system of equations. If it did, it
would have no connection with the problem of measurement. Gide's
lack of understanding of Jevons' mathematics led him to raise a
fictitious difficulty.

The second objection of Gide to Jevons' utility theory has a
wholly different basis. Gide objected to the use of the word "utility,"
since it has a popular connotation and would lead to continual mis-
understandings. Gide proposed as a remedy, not an alternate word
such as he advocated later, but a return to the expression that "la
valeur dépend à la fois de l'utilité et de la rareté. . . ."[5] Gide could
not have thought seriously that he provided a solution through this
suggestion taken from Bastiat, especially since he himself used the
expression "final degree of utility" in his own text.

Three years later Charles Gide published the first modern textbook on economics in France, a textbook that used the idea of marginal utility in its discussion of value.[6] For a long time this text remained the only one in French that contains anything like an adequate exposition of marginal utility.

III

Gide's paper on Jevons started a long discussion on the subject
of value in the *Journal des économistes*. This discussion well illustrates how little marginal utility influenced the theory of value
in France during the eighties, for, although the discussion commenced with the ideas of Jevons and Walras, and did occasionally
return to them, it revealed that the participants really never understood or appreciated the new ideas. The discussion began at once.
Ad. Blaise (des Vosges) corresponded with Gide immediately after
the publication of Gide's article and the *Journal d_s économistes*
published the letters in December, in 1881.[7] Blaise missed Gide's
explanation of marginal utility and its application to the theory of
value, even though Gide had given the explanation most clearly. He
interpreted Gide as saying that Jevons had determined value by
utility, and Walras by *rareté,* and that both authors had only half the
truth. Gide did say something like this, but fortunately he also
said more. Gide answered Blaise appropriately and showed that the
quantity of the good influences value only through its influence on
the marginal utility of the good. These two letters are a futile interchange. Blaise could not possibly understand the idea of marginal

utility. Gide understood clearly enough but could make no impression on Blaise and even seemed in need of adding some courage to his own convictions.

Almost a year later, Marcel Mongin, who joined the *Faculté de droit* at Dijon in 1877 at the same time that Gide went to Montpellier, published an article on value. Mongin used Gide's article as a starting point only.[8] He hoped to bring forth an acceptable theory of value, since he thought that Gide had shown that Jevons' would not bear scrutiny.[9] The point of interest here concerns the lack of understanding of the marginal utility theory in France in 1882, the year that Jevons died, rather than the particular solution that Mongin proposed. Mongin's entire article does not indicate that he had any inkling of the circumstances that Jevons' innovation consisted in the use of the idea of the margin (in later terms) and not in the application of utility to the analysis of value.

This article brought on an interchange between E. Martineau[10] and Mongin[11] which had nothing directly to do with the marginal utility theory of value, but which discussed value theory, and which again showed how little economics at the time depended on anything that Jevons or Walras had done.[12]

Hippolyte Dabos gave the theory of value a lengthy treatment in a pamphlet issued in this period.[13] In it he aimed to go over in detail all parts of the controversy beginning with the publication of Gide's article in 1881 in order to point out the errors contained in them and to prepare the way for an exposition of his own views. The details of this mass refutation would exhaust any reader today, as it possibly did most readers in 1886, and will detain us only because, and to the extent that, Dabos set forth his views on Jevons. Dabos came to the staggering conclusion that "la théorie de Stanley Jevons n'apporte, en fait de valeur, dans le domaine de la science économique, ni vérité nouvelle, ni fragment de vérité: elle ne fait qu'accroître le nombre des confusions existantes."[14] He evidently reached this conclusion simply by reading Gide's paper on Jevons, not by reading Jevons' *Theory* itself. Dabos, for some reason, would have nothing to do with Jevons' consideration of utility as a function of quantity. He said: "Cette proposition que *l'utilité est une fonction de la quantité* constitue donc une erreur absolue. L'utilité des choses est indépendente de la quantité: elle n'est pas moindre avec une quantité considérable, elle n'est pas plus grande avec une quantité moindre . . . un habit, un morceau de pain, ne sont pas d'autant plus utiles qu'ils sont plus rares: ils ne nourrissent pas mieux, ils ne préservent pas plus efficacement des intempéries lorsqu' ils sont rares que lorsqu' ils sont abondants. Leur utilité est la même dans les deux cas."[15] Here reigns complete misunderstanding. Lacking, perhaps, any basic idea of utility in any sense as a quantity and not having specifically any idea of total utility as dependent on quantity, he clearly could not understand the more difficult idea of the marginal utility decreasing as the quantity of the good increases. Dabos' pamphlet again stirred controversy, but the results proved no more revealing than before. Houdard reviewed Dabos' pamphlet,[16] Dabos replied,[17] and Houdard answered.[18] Th. Mannekin took Dabos' side,[19] and Dabos replied to his suggestions.[20]

What purpose does an account of this long drawn-out, sterile dispute on the subject of value between long-forgotten writers on economics hope to serve in a history of marginal utility theory? The account, as we have seen, hardly mentions the concept of marginal utility even though it starts from the intention of Gide to introduce Jevons to the French. The introduction of the controversy has not been intended to direct attention to Gide's concern over Jevons so much as to emphasize again how far away from the acceptance or understanding of the doctrines of Jevons, Menger, and Walras the French economists stood, not only all during the eighteen-seventies, but all during the eighteen-eighties as well. The last two letters to the editor of the powerful *Journal des économistes* came at the middle of 1888, seventeen years after 1871. Their authors, insofar as their contents go, could as well have written them seventeen years before 1871. Only one of the numerous persons in the controversy had read Jevons, and he seemed torn between accepting and rejecting him. Only Gide and Dabos examined Jevons' doctrines. Nor did any of these writers ever speak of the opinions of Léon Walras, or connect him with Jevons, even though he had numerous writings on the subject in French. Walras could well complain of the conspiracy of silence against him. No one of the disputants had read Walras with any understanding; only Gide mentioned his name. Evidently none of them had heard of Menger or any of the later Austrians. Aside from Gide's initial exposition, no one showed even a vague familiarity with the idea of marginal utility; nor did any other writers in France have any more advanced views on this part of the subject of economics.[21] In 1889, France lacked anything that resembled modern economics.

Chapter XXII

ÉMILE DE LAVELEYE

I

Beside Charles Gide, and of course Léon Walras, only Émile Louis Victor de Laveleye, among the French-speaking economists in the generation following 1870, gave any sign of an ability or willingness to use the idea of marginal utility. Laveleye, a professor at Liége, used something akin to marginal utility to refute Marx in his *Le Socialisme contemporain* in 1881, and repeated somewhat the same ideas in his *Éléments d'économie politique* in 1882. He used, however, only a rough approximation of the idea of marginal utility in both of these places.

His *Le Socialisme contemporain* had a wide audience, for it went through many editions.[1] It also had success abroad.[2] Laveleye introduced utility as a means to escape from Marx's argument on surplus value. He concluded his review of Marx's argument with the statement: "As we read Marx's book and feel ourselves shut up within the iron bars of his logic, we are, as it were, a prey to a nightmare, because, having admitted his premises, which are borrowed from the most undoubted authorities, we know not how to escape from his conclusions . . . it is not easy to release ourselves, and if we admit the theory of value circulated by Smith, Ricardo, Bastiat, and Carey, we cannot do so without contradicting ourselves."[3]

Laveleye escaped from his Marxian "nightmare" by throwing overboard the value theory of Smith, Ricardo, Bastiat, and others. "The fundamental error of Marx," he asserted, "lies in the idea he conceives of value, which, according to him, is always in proportion to labour."[4] Instead of labor, Laveleye substituted utility as having the most telling relation to value. This substitution has importance only because, to make it effective, Laveleye twisted the customary version of utility into something sufficiently like the idea of marginal utility.

Laveleye explained and elaborated the same example of water that had served before to refute the utility explanation of value. Notice that he did not offer the authority of Jevons or of Walras in support of his contention. Instead of citing authorities, he himself claimed originality when he said that the customary refutation of a utility theory of value by the "water example" relies on an ambiguity of language, "which has never been exposed."[5] Notice too that, although Laveleye in a sense did use marginal utility to explain value, he did so only in the crudest terms.

In his explanation he pointed out that people use *utility* in two senses, in a *general* sense and in a *specific* sense. Though, of course, Laveleye did not say so, these senses accord approximately with *total* utility and *marginal* utility. Thus when one writer says that water has great utility he means utility in the *general* or *total* sense; while when another says that water has little or no utility, he means utility in the *specific* or *marginal* sense. Let Laveleye himself explain this *specific* utility to which he referred and to which he ascribed the value of a good: "When it is said that water has no value, a specific portion of water is intended; and in this sense it has also very little utility. What is the value of a pail of water at the river bank? Nothing beyond the trouble of fetching it. . . . In the middle of Sahara, to the traveller who cannot at any price obtain it elsewhere, it would be worth all the money in the world."[6] While anyone could improve upon this paragraph as an exposition of the idea of marginal utility, everyone must admit that Laveleye stated here the essentials of the idea. Laveleye did not undertake his refutation of Marx with the thoroughness or skill with which a few years later Wicksteed, Shaw, and other Fabians in England brought the same kind of an argument to bear on Marx, but, in comparison with other French economists of his time, he does stand out for his understanding of marginal utility.

Laveleye's *Éléments d'économie politique* gained as great a success as his book on socialism. It had many editions and many translations, including an American translation. It repeats the same arguments on value as are found in the *Le Socialisme contemporain*, again using the water example.[7] In the preface the author said that Stanley Jevons and M. P. Marshall had been helpful. Although he did not specify, he undoubtedly had in mind Stanley Jevons' *Primer of Political Economy*, translated into French in 1878, rather than Jevons' *Theory of Political Economy*, and certainly he alluded to *The Economics of Industry* of Alfred and Mary Paley Marshall.[8] Neither of these volumes, of course, contained much to help him in his exposition of a utility theory of value.

193

Chapter XXIII

ÉMILE LEVASSEUR AND AUGUSTE OTT: FRENCH CRITICS OF MARGINAL UTILITY

I

Evidently the French did not neglect marginal utility because they had a specific objection to it. Only on two occasions did French writers on economics object strongly and openly to the use of marginal utility in economic analysis during the years from 1870 to 1889. The earlier objection came from Émile Levasseur, the later from Auguste Ott.

Levasseur raised his objection at the time of Léon Walras' first official statement of his views on marginal utility, in Walras' paper read, on the 16th and 23rd of August, 1873, to the Académie des Sciences Morales et Politiques. Here we concern ourselves solely with the reception of Walras' paper by the Académie. Jevons thought that his similar paper had fallen on deaf ears.[1] Walras knew that his paper had an audience, for, after Walras completed his reading, Levasseur announced that, at the next meeting, he would present his objections to the communication. He did so at the meeting of August 30. Two other members of the Académie, Auguste Valette and Louis François Michael Raymond Wolowski, added comments of their own.[2] Walras probably did not attend the meeting, since the *Compte-rendu* contains no record of any replies. The remarks of Levasseur, Vallette, and Wolowski on the utility aspect of Walras' paper provide evidence of the immediate reaction of members of the Académie to the new idea of marginal utility. In general, the opinion of the three members was unfavorable, although Valette attempted to bring in some support, which Levasseur, in turn, quickly rejected.

II

The criticism of Levasseur really did no credit to his understanding of either the paper that Walras had just read or of the nature of mathematics and economics. He began with the criticism, made many times before and since, that, because needs and desires do not lend themselves to measurement, mathematics has no relation to them. A too simple view of mathematics, and of measurement, underlies this criticism. Levasseur concluded sweepingly that "ses courbes sont sans fondement, . . . peu solide, sont fausse, dangereuse. . . ."[3] He evidently believed that the danger consisted in the false sense of precision that the mathematical apparatus conveyed to the reader.

Levasseur did not rest, however, with this single criticism. His second objection reveals his failure to understand the nature of Walras' utility functions. Levasseur said that "desire" does not increase and decrease according to the rules that Walras had laid down, that "needs" fluctuate from high to low according to many and diverse circumstances. To all of this Walras could not have helped agreeing unless Levasseur intended to convey the notion that, for all practical purposes, the shape of the utility function varies so continually and erratically as to preclude its use in analysis. But Levasseur's example shows that he did not dispute Walras' tacit assumption of the reasonable stability of human desires and wants. Levasseur gave, as an example of the fluctuation of needs, the circumstance that the intensity of desire for wheat during a famine exceeds many times the intensity of desire for wheat in a period of abundance. His example of wheat during the famine illustrates, rather than offers a criticism of, Walras' idea of a utility function.

At another point, Levasseur implied that the theory of Walras oversimplifies. But he offered no further support for his contention.[4] Levasseur also criticized the idea of *rareté* that Léon Walras had borrowed from his father, and by his criticism displayed that he had not caught from Walras' reading of his paper the unusual sense in which Léon Walras used this term. Léon Walras, perhaps, could only blame himself for Levasseur's misunderstanding, for he had taken, without sufficient warning, a word with a quite common meaning and had given it an equally uncommon interpretation. Levasseur concluded his remarks with the statement that an economist could use the geometric method as a means of demonstration but not as an instrument of investigation.

At this point, in the first colloquy in France on the subject of the relation of marginal utility to value, Valette objected that a person who buys a good does not care whether much or little labor is required to produce it and that labor creates value but does not regulate its amount. Levasseur replied that buyers often do take account of the amount of labor, that even if they do not the sellers do, and the true character of economics, which we should hold as a moral that the labor cost provides the minimum toward which competition drives the price.

The discussion concluded with the remarks of Wolowski, who approved the position taken by Levasseur and added that, in considering economics as an exact science, Léon Walras misconstrued science that has man both for its point of departure and for its end.

Léon Walras never commented directly on these expressed views of Levasseur and Wolowski. However, he said later that "L'Académie accueillie cette communication de la façon la moins favorable et la moins encourageante."[5] In the face of such a discouraging reception Walras showed a considerable steadfastness in continuing with the preparation of the book that he published the next year.

III

Evidently Levasseur retained his original impression of the slight worth of marginal utility theory throughout the remainder of his long life. However, he never touched on the idea of marginal utility at any place in his later work. The English translation of his principal textbook on economics appeared in 1905, partly rewritten by the author for the translator.[6] It gave absolutely no sign of recognition of marginal utility. The next year he wrote an article on the evolution of economic and socialist doctrines in France during the Third Republic which treats the Historical School but pays no heed to the Marginal Utility School.[7] In Levasseur's account France seems to have no connection with the marginal utility movement, nor even any interest in it.

An ironical sequel to Émile Levasseur's lack of interest in marginal utility, and especially with the Walrasian version thereof, came near the end of his life. In 1909 the professors and economists of the universities of France sent Léon Walras an *Hommage* that contained the following rhetorical question: "Comment serait-il possible que l'esprit français, si épris de clarté, d'unité, de logique, n'eût pas été séduit—du jour ou il l'aurait comprise—par la belle ordonnance du système économique de Walras, de ce système qui embrasse tout le monde économique et dans lequel une même formule enferme le prix de tous les produits et la valeur de tous les services?"[8] Who would never have asked this question, but who could have answered it better than anyone else in an objective sort of way? Certainly

196

Émile Levasseur, the member of the Académie who rose with his sheaf of objections to Walras' system at the meeting the week following Walras' initial presentation of the core of his ideas on economics, the man who, throughout his long and active career in economics in France, apparently never absorbed a drop from the Walrasian spring. Yet ironically, Levasseur's name tops the list of the signers who sent to Walras this *Hommage,* with its pointed and meaningful inquiry.

IV

The second critic, Auguste Ott, expressed his opinion on marginal utility at the very end of the eighteen-eighties. Ott had switched from history to economics in 1848, at the age of thirty-four. He wrote for the *Journal des économistes* at various occasions after 1865 on a variety of subjects. He showed no especial interest, however, in theoretical parts of economics in general, and marginal utility theory in particular, during the seventies and eighties. He had published a *Traité d'économie sociale* in 1851, of which he prepared a second edition in 1892.[9] He had commented on marginal utility first when, in 1889, he unexpectedly reviewed for the *Journal des économistes,* Wieser's *Der natürliche Werth* that had just appeared, and Böhm-Bawerk's *Geschichte und Kritik der Kapitalzins-theorien* which had come out five years earlier.[10]

Ott read Wieser with sufficient care to get the main idea of his theory of value. He translated Wieser's term *Grenznutzen* into French as *la valeur-limite.*[11] But Ott saw no advantage in the idea. Everyone, Ott pointed out, knows that more is taken by the consumer as the price falls. Ott charged that Wieser had associated this recognized fall in price with a fall in usefulness, and had derived his conclusions from this association. Ott thought that this association confused value-in-exchange with the totally different idea of value-in-use. In what essential way had Ott believed that value-in-exchange differs from value-in-use? He never said directly. He spent half a page showing that, although the utility of successive additions to a stock of water, shoes, books, or wheat diminishes, the earlier units in the stock retain their original importance, a proposition that Wieser would not deny. Ott emphasized this circumstance, which means only that both marginal and total utility exist as facts, in the following passage: "Dans ma bibliothèque se trouve un livre qui me sert tous les jours et m'est d'une grande utilité. Estimons la valeur de cet

197

usage à 10. Il me vient par un hasard dix autres exemplaires du même ouvrage. Est-ce que par suite l'utilité du livre sera réduite à zéro? Ce livre ne me servira-t-il plus à rien? Je pourrai disposer il est vrai de 10 exemplaires, mais l'un des 11 que je possède aura toujour la valeur d'utilité 10."[12] Perhaps Ott protested unconsciously against the reduction in importance of *total* utility that took place with the discovery of the idea of *marginal* utility. But this protest, while perhaps warranted, hardly justified his extreme statement that Wieser's theory of value "doit être considérée comme illusoire et rester confinée dans les livres des auteurs qui l'ont imaginée."[13]

V

Ott also reviewed the second edition of Léon Walras' *Éléments* in 1890 for the *Journal des économistes,* a journal which had not carried a review of the first edition of the book. It made some amends for the omission by giving the second edition a seventeen-page review.[14] This review shows that Ott had studied the book with care. It must have exercised his mind considerably to go through the pages of mathematical economics at the age of seventy-five, since nothing in his earlier writing indicates any interest in mathematics.

Ott did not, however, pretend to criticize the book as a mathematician, but only as an economist. As an economist he could not hide his distrust of the use of mathematics in economics. Ott gave an accurate description of Walras' curves that relate functionally the quantity of a good to what Walras had called its *rareté,* and then gave a paragraph-long characterization of the term *rareté* as "ce singular abus des mots."[15] He went on to sketch clearly the manner in which Walras, in his model, obtained the equilibrium price that maximizes the satisfaction of the consumer. Although Ott explained Walras' arguments well, he objected to them. "Mais sans la discuter dans ses points particuliers," he said, "je dirai qu'elle manque par la base et que ce n'est ni l'utilité ni la quantité des marchandises offertes et demandées qui, dans le plus grand nombre des cas, constituent la valeur d'échange."[16]

Ott first objected to the kind of situation that Walras had postulated, a situation in which the individuals come to the market with their wares and in the market decide, in the light of the exchange rates, how much of their wares to keep for their own use and how much to exchange. The circumstances that Walras had described might, Ott admitted, fit a savage and barbarous tribe at the beginning of history, but it could not fit the present society that employs money and makes use of the division of labor, and in which accordingly the traders come to market expecting to sell *all* their stock of goods, and not with the artificial problem of what proportion to retain for their own use. The trader, Ott insisted, sells the goods he brings to market without paying any attention to the needs they satisfy. Here Ott made his only reference to anything like marginal utility when he said that the buyers do not ask that the traders offer the second half of the goods at a lower price than the first half because the first half could satisfy the buyers' most intense wants. "Celui qui fait un bon dîner," Ott added as an illustration, "paie ordinairement plus cher les boissons et les mets de la fin du repas que ceux du commencement."[17]

His next argument rests on the alleged fact that, in an advanced society, production adapts itself to needs and that usually the quantity of goods produced exceeds the quantity the consumer can buy. Ott inferred from producers' difficulty in selling their wares that the quantity of goods produced usually exceeds the quantity needed. He argued that this meant that marginal utility for most goods is zero and hence cannot be instrumental in determining value. In Ott's view, the amount of labor used in production regulates value in all cases except under conditions of partial monopoly. As a clinching argument against the marginal utility theory of value, Ott brought in the quite unrelated circumstance that demand requires that the buyer have not only the need but also sufficient purchasing power to satisfy his need.[18]

All these arguments of Ott have no weight. They require no skill or special understanding to answer. Yet no one answered them in the *Journal des économistes,* and they stood as the final view of the official French School on marginal utility economics at the end of the eighteen-eighties.

Chapter XXIV

MARGINAL UTILITY IN THE FRENCH ECONOMIC JOURNALS AND MANUALS, 1871-1889

I

France had several journals specializing in economics that regularly reviewed important foreign and French books and that might have evaluated the first editions of Jevons' *Theory*, Menger's *Grundsätze*, and Walras' *Éléments*.[1] But only one of the journals reviewed any of these books.

Charles Letort wrote the only French review of any of the first editions of the pioneering works in marginal utility of Jevons, Menger, and Walras.[2] Letort's review of Walras' *Éléments* does not mention marginal utility, confining itself to a discussion of the mathematical method. In the course of his discussion the reviewer referred to Jevons' *Theory* (of which he could find no copy for consultation) and to Dupuit's writings, but in both of these cases, as with Walras himself, the use of marginal utility made no impression on him. Here we have the peculiar circumstance that the only French reviewer of the foremost pioneering book in France on the subject of marginal utility had not, in the whole of his review, ever mentioned the subject of marginal utility.

Two later books by Jevons and Walras fared no better. The second edition of Jevons' *Theory* prompted an unsigned review which did not mention utility and which used all of its short space to criticize adversely the employment of mathematics in economics.[3] Even Charles Gide, when he reviewed Walras' *Théorie mathématique de la richesse sociale*, which had reprinted as its first part Walras' earliest publications on marginal utility, dwelt mainly on the impracticality of the mathematical method in economics. Gide says nothing of marginal utility.[4] His omission is notable, since two years earlier he had published an article on Jevons, and had included in his textbook the only secondary account of marginal utility to appear in any language for many years. Apparently he did not see the same thing in Walras' exposition that he had seen in Jevons', even though Jevons and Walras already had drawn attention to the identical nature of their ideas in correspondence reprinted in the very book that Gide reviewed.

200

The French economists knew Jevons, not for his connection with marginal utility but for his advocacy of the mathematical method, an advocacy in which they bracketed him with Walras. They knew, too, about his work in applied fields such as money, the price level, commercial crises, and coal. Jevons' obituary notices in France show the kind of reputation he enjoyed and reveal that his reputation did not include his work in utility.[5] French economists knew as little about Carl Menger during the seventies and the eighties as about Jevons. The *Grundsätze* was not reviewed in France, just as it had not been in England. Perhaps the fact that Menger wrote in German and published in 1871 deterred French editors from offering the book for review, but doubtless, too, other circumstances contributed. French economists knew Menger's reputation in some degree after 1890, but they quite possibly did not know his *Grundsätze,* at least at first hand, until much later, for Bernard Lavergne says in his doctoral thesis of 1910, "Malheureusement cet ouvrage est excessivement rare, il semble qu'il n'en existe aucun exemplaire en France; les bibliothèques publiques n'en possèdent, à notre connaissance, aucun."[6]

II

No one of the French texts and manuals of the writers other than Gide and Laveleye ever mentions the idea of marginal utility. A reader of French general compendiums on the subject of economics would be most certain to miss any reference to the concept. Few circumstances show more clearly how inadequately the dates of 1871 and 1874 indicate the time when the Marginal Utility School began. As a typical French textbook we can examine Joseph François Garnier's *Traité d'économie politique,* which led all the other French manuals of the time in popularity. Of Garnier's *Traité,* a contemporary economist wrote: "This work alone would have made the name of Garnier famous. It forms in reality an encyclopaedia of economic science; methodical order and deep knowledge of the subject being alike conspicuous in it. And it should be added that the author has shown a perfect power of appreciating those opinions which are opposed to his scientific convictions."[7] Garnier's "perfect powers" of appreciation did not extend to marginal utility, for neither the revised and augmented eighth edition published in 1880, the year before Garnier's death, nor the ninth edition for which A. Liesse prepared the revision in 1889, contained a single mention of the idea.[8]

Other ambitious manuals displayed the same neglect. Paul Cauwès' *Précis du cours d'économie politique,* a two-volume work of which the first edition came out in 1879-80, a revised and enlarged edition in 1881-82, and an expanded four-volume edition in 1893, contains a reference to both Jevons' *Theory* and Walras' *Éléments* in the first edition and adds Menger's *Grundsätze* in the third, but shows no trace of the influence of these three books in any of the editions.[9] Paul Leroy-Beaulieu brought out his *Précis d'économie politique* in 1888, a work which contains no hint of marginal utility.[10] Yet eight years later the same author, in his four-volume *Traité théorique et pratique d'économie politique,* made extensive use of marginal utility.[11] Another standard text of the period, the *Manuel d'économie politique* of Henri Joseph Léon Baudrillart, which began publication in 1857, has no more on utility in the fifth edition of 1883 than it had in the first.[12] The same lack of attention is found in the important texts of Alfred Jourdan.[13] Yves Guyot,[14] Ferdinand Jacques Hervé-Bazin,[15] and Maurice Block.[16]

Chapter XXV

MARGINAL UTILITY IN HOLLAND AND
ITALY

I

Outside of the literature in English, French, and German, we find recognition of the use of marginal utility in economics during the seventies and the eighties only in Dutch and Italian. No writers in the Scandinavian or Slavic languages contributed to the rise of the Marginal Utility School. Spain and Portugal also offered nothing. And, of course, the whole movement confined itself to Europe and the United States. Economics of this kind had not extended to Asia, Africa, or South America.

Both Jevons and Walras noticed the interest of the Dutch and Italians in the idea of marginal utility and had somewhat exaggerated notions of its reception in these small countries. Walras mentioned Professors N. G. Pierson of Amsterdam, H. B. Greven of Leiden, W. C. Mees of Amsterdam, H. P. G. Quack and J. d'Aulnis de Bourouill of Utrecht, and Alberto Errera, G. B. Antonelli, Gerolamo Boccardo, G. A. Zanon, and A. Zambelli, all of Italy.[1] Jevons had listed all of these except Greven, Mees, Quack, and Antonelli.[2]

II

Johan d'Aulnis de Bourouill preceded all other Dutch writers in the recognition of the marginal utility theory of value. He had an early familiarity both with Jevons' *Theory* and with Walras' 1873 paper. In fact, d'Aulnis de Bourouill first called Walras' attention to Jevons and then later introduced Walras to Menger. He also corresponded with Jevons both before and after he published his dissertation, the first published reference in Dutch to the work of Jevons and Walras.[3] He did much more than anyone else to make the international scope of the Marginal Utility School known.

We have no idea of the circumstances that led d'Aulnis de Bourouill to turn to marginal utility as a dissertation topic at the University of Leyden.[4] Perhaps he was indebted to H. P. G. Quack, then at Utrecht, whom Jevons mentioned as favorably disposed towards the new economics. Quack had become a professor at Utrecht in 1868 at the age of thirty-four and left the university in 1877 for the Nederlandsche Bank.[5] Johan d'Aulnis de Bourouill succeeded him as professor of economics at the University of Utrecht in 1878. Nothing that Quack wrote has any imprint of marginal utility economics in it. D'Aulnis de Bourouill's work with marginal utility ceased after the publication of his thesis. He continued to teach at the University of Utrecht until 1917 and he lived until 1930.[6]

N. G. Pierson, another of the supposed Dutch converts, spent most of his time in business and banking but also taught in Amsterdam from 1877 until 1884. After he left teaching he first became the president of the Nederlandsche Bank and then went into the service of the Dutch government. He had too many and too diverse interests to spend much time on the subject of value theory, especially after he stopped teaching. Although Pierson never became a complete convert to the new economics he received credit at home for spreading the idea of marginal utility. A Dutch economist wrote that "Pierson was one of the first economists to accept the theory of value of the Austrian School. . . ."[7] A contemporary said that, through Pierson's work, "the latest improvements in economic theory, initiated by Jevons, Menger, and others, and their application to problems of distribution, have penetrated wide circles of readers."[8]

H. B. Greven, professor of economics at Leyden from 1880 to 1915, an associate and disciple of N. G. Pierson and a collaborator with d'Aulnis de Bourouill, perhaps also came within the group of Dutch professors who received marginal utility with favor. The Dutch had an excellent periodical in economics, *De Economist,* which began in 1852, flourished in the seventies and eighties, and continues down to the present. Only once, in the twenty years before 1889, did this journal take notice of any part of the literature of marginal utility. In it, Greven gave a short review of Philip Wicksteed's *Alphabet of Economic Science* in 1889.[9]

Besides the notice, however slight, of these economists in the lists of Jevons and Walras, at least one other Dutch economist accepted the idea of marginal utility. Anthony Beaujon followed Pierson as professor of political economy at Amsterdam in 1885. He also taught statistics in the same university. During this period he published nothing to indicate an interest in marginal utility, but in 1890, the year of his death, he contributed an article to the *Revue d'économie politique* that shows his understanding of, and sympathy with, the literature on marginal utility.[10] Since in the article he spoke of teaching some of the ideas connected with marginal utility in his course for several years, we may assume that he had expounded such ideas in Amsterdam before 1889.

Toward the close of the eighteen-eighties several Dutch economists began to use marginal utility theory as a justification for progressive taxation. N. G. Pierson and Anthony Beaujon may have stimulated them to turn their talents in this direction, for the development centered in Amsterdam. P. W. A. Cort van der Linden, M. W. F. Treub, and H. J. Tasman published at this time on marginal utility in connection with the subject of taxation. The outstanding performance, however, came from A. J. Cohen Stuart. Cohen Stuart published his doctoral dissertation, *Bijdrage tot de theorie der progressieve inkomstenbelasting,* in 1889.

III

Of the Italians whom Jevons and Walras looked to in the eighteen-seventies for support of their system, a considerable number never fulfilled their initial promise. Andrea Zambelli, who wrote about Walras' *Éléments* in the *Rassegna di agricoltura, industria e commercio* in 1876, published nothing further on economics. After Alberto Errera, on the other hand, reviewed the *Éléments* for *La Perseveranza,* Errera continued to write on economic topics. In fact, Léon Walras reviewed two of Errera's books.[11] But Errera did not return to theoretical economics and consequently never wrote on utility theory or mathematical economics. Giovanni Antonio Zanon corresponded with Alberto Errera about Walras in the *Rassegna di agricoltura, industria e commercio* in 1874, but gave no further help in spreading the idea of marginal utility in Italy. Luigi Bodio, a correspondent of Jevons, became a government statistician and took no time from his official duties to follow whatever initial interest he had had in utility.

Only Gerolamo Boccardo did anything to further the acceptance of marginal utility. Boccardo certainly helped Walras and Jevons by translating into Italian both Walras' four principal memoirs and Jevons' *Theory,* and by publishing both works in the third series of the *Biblioteca dell' economista.* Boccardo's aid probably came as a result of his tolerant attitude toward dissenters, however, rather than from any especial appreciation that he had for the work of the members of the Marginal Utility School. Consequently Boccardo lent no active support to the Marginal Utility School in Italy. Achille Loria commented as follows on Boccardo's unwillingness to champion any particular doctrine: "In no phase of his being and doing did he ever appear as a combatant, or as an investigator of thorny questions, or as the standard-bearer of a theory or a school."[12] None of Boccardo's later writings show any trace of marginal utility. Jevons and Walras could well feel disappointment with the work of this Italian writer, whom they had counted on as an early adherent.

Perhaps the first notable result of Boccardo's translation of Walras and Jevons into Italian came with the publication of Giovanni Battista Antonelli's *Sulla teoria matematica della economia politica* in 1886.[13] Antonelli, who had studied mathematics at the Scuola Normale Superiore di Pisa, prepared this pamphlet of thirty-one pages in the year that he took his degree. It received little notice until comparatively recently, even though Jevons did include it in his bibliography of mathematical economics.[14] Antonelli not only gave an accurate picture of marginal utility but also made an addition to utility theory, an addition that no one recognized at the time or, for that matter, for many years thereafter. He added what we now term the "integrability condition."[15] In a world prepared to accept the simpler forms of the marginal utility theory only at a slow pace, the introduction of Antonelli's succinct exposition of the mathematical theory had no effect. And the addition of the integrability condition, an aspect of economics little understood even now, had less influence.

Luigi Cossa played a part in helping to spread the idea of marginal utility, although, at the same time, he opposed the extended use of utility in economics and consequently could not accept the new ideas with enthusiasm. Cossa first published his *Guida allo studio dell' economia politica* in 1876 and first revised it in 1878.[16] This *Guida*, to which Jevons gave approval in his preface to the English translation, surveys all economic literature and reveals how slight an effect marginal utility had on economic thought in Italy. Cossa did not mention utility in his survey. He came closest to doing so when he said that Jevons and Walras arrived "at almost identical results in the *theory of exchange*."[17] He linked the name of J. d'Aulnis de Bourouill and G. Boccardo to those of Walras and Jevons, but he did not refer to Carl Menger. In 1892 Cossa issued a third edition of the *Guida*. Comparison of the contents of this expanded third edition, which has the new title *Introduzione allo studio dell' economia politica,* shows that an appreciation both of marginal utility and of the Marginal Utility School, absent in the middle of the seventies, came to Italy in the eighties.[18] In 1892 Cossa associated Jevons with utility, whereas in his earlier book he had not done so. Most important of all, Cossa had discovered Menger and the Austrian School by 1892, though in 1876 he had not so much as cited Menger. He listed the names and principal accomplishments of Friedrich Wieser, Eugen Böhm-Bawerk, Emil Sax, Robert Zuckerkandl, Johann Komorzynski, Victor Mataja, Gustav Gross, and Eugen Philippovich. He also brought into the discussion what he called "the Austrian theory of the margin of utility."[19] Cossa qualified his approval of the Austrian School and the utility theory of value.

Cossa also gives the names of most of the other followers of the three pioneers: Rudolf Auspitz and Richard Lieben, whom he listed as from Germany rather than Austria; d'Aulnis de Bourouill and Cohen Stuart from Holland; P. H. Wicksteed from England; and G. B. Antonelli and Maffeo Pantaleoni from Italy. Cossa said that Marshall "adopts from Jevons the theory of a final degree of utility, which he prefers to call marginal utility, and then straightway he points out that this notion of marginal utility both explains and also completes the current account of the cost of production, although not a few have undertaken to oppose the two ideas."[20] But, although he called attention to the principal books of J. B. Clark and F. Y. Edgeworth, Cossa connected neither of these economists with the Marginal Utility School.[21]

IV

Maffeo Pantaleoni, the economist who worked hardest to launch marginal utility analysis in Italy, did not appear on the scene until the end of the eighteen-eighties.[22] He had a cosmopolitan background. His mother was an English or Irish woman, educated in Germany and Italy. Maffeo Pantaleoni himself studied in Germany before graduating in law from the University of Rome, and he later lectured at Geneva for three years. His cosmopolitanism explains his easy access to foreign literature and economics, especially to the writings of the Austrian School and of Jevons.

Pantaleoni published his *Principii di economia pura* in 1889.[23] It showed how completely he accepted the views of the Marginal Utility School. In it he expressed a familiarity with almost every work that had touched on utility before 1889.[24] Pantaleoni's mind mirrored other people's writings. In this book we see flawless reflections of the ideas of the many other writers he had studied. He commenced with a lengthy consideration of psychological hedonism, which he identified with the desire for self-preservation. He gave in detail his conclusions on diminishing marginal utility, calling it a fundamental law, and acknowledging his indebtedness to Gossen, Dupuit, and Jennings. He defended Gossen's use of linear functions, since we "know next to nothing of the rapidity with which real hedonic curves decline . . .," although he himself used non-linear curves.[25] Menger also influenced him, for he adopted Menger's table and assigned, as did Menger, "an arbitrary numerical index, say 10" to indicate the strength of the first aliquot part of the good most wanted.[26]

Pantaleoni was influenced by Richard Jennings as much as by anyone else on the subject of utility. He received more cordially, appreciated more fully, and extended farther the ideas of Jennings on the nature and subdivision of wants than any writer before or since, including even Jevons. Pantaleoni accepted Jennings' distinction between primary wants (such as hunger or thirst) and secondary wants of which the satisfaction comes through one of the five senses. Along with Jennings he pointed out that the law of diminishing marginal utility for goods satisfying primary wants will be different from what it would be for goods satisfying secondary wants, in that the curves will differ little among individuals for primary wants, while they could be very different for secondary wants.

Pantaleoni urged the importance of the determination of the extent that consumption of particular goods will change as income changes, an extent that hinges on the character of the utility curves. In this regard he came to think of an individual's utility curves as irreversible. He explained this irreversibility as follows:

Suppose that the scale of wants of the *homo œconomicus*, at a given moment, is constituted in order of importance by the wants *a, b, c, d,* and that subsequently he is enabled to satisfy new wants, and does so in the order in which they stand, *e, f, g, h.* But now, since he has tasted the satisfactions *e, f, g, h,* and has become accustomed to them, his absolute scale of wants for the future may have been modified so as to be constituted by *b, c, f, g, a, d, e, h.* In other words, the commodities he has consumed and the interval that has elapsed between the time when his means were less and the time when they became more, operate as alternative factors on the scale of importance of his wants. Now, suppose a diminution of his means to supervene: evidently he will act in accordance with the *new hedonic scale* in the retrenchment of his enjoyments.[27]

Pantaleoni also introduced an idea of a marginal utility curve that rose before it began to diminish. He gave the following explanation: "If we suppose a first and infinitely small portion, the satisfaction we shall derive from it will be imperceptible, and will be expressed accordingly by a very short ordinate. We may therefore at once assume that every curve representing the degrees of utility of any commodity commences with zero, and rises rapidly to the culminating point, after which it declines more or less slowly, according to the nature of the commodity concerned."[28] Not many writers drew marginal utility curves before 1889. No one drew them with an initial section of increasing marginal utility. Pantaleoni's explanation discloses that a flaw in his logic, rather than a difference in opinion, underlies the rising section of his curve. The consumer perhaps derives an "imperceptible" satisfaction from an "infinitely small portion" whether he consumes the small portion first or last. In no case, does the length of the ordinate depend on the size of the increment added, for the length of the ordinate depends on the ratio of the increment added to the increment of utility experienced. This ratio may well decline from the beginning.

Chapter XXVI

PORTRAYAL OF THE RISE OF THE MARGINAL
ULILITY SCHOOL IN HISTORIES OF
ECONOMIC THOUGHT

I

Every history has been developed by individuals. The development probably most often begins as a sketchy statement composed by some person who is partisan to the idea. This statement is later repeated and amplified by other people who turn it into a standard form that everyone afterwards accepts without question. This certainly was the course that the history of the idea of marginal utility took.

Let us begin by looking at the form which the standard version of the history of marginal utility eventually assumed. The usual account of the history of marginal utility almost always begins by saying that William Stanley Jevons, Carl Menger, and Léon Walras simultaneously and independently discovered marginal utility in the early years of the eighteen-seventies. It comments that the appearance at nearly the same time of the idea in the three widely separated cities of London, Vienna, and Lausanne later caused astonishment and led to the explanation that conditions of the times must have compelled the development. The standard history usually contains the comment that the advent of the Marginal Utility School marked the beginning of modern economics, in that it shifted the attention of economists from cost, or more specifically labor cost, to marginal utility in the explanation of value, and from nature to man in the wider picture. It dates the beginning of "subjective" or "psychological" economics from this time. The standard account of the rise of the Marginal Utility School cites a number of other writers who played a part as forerunners of the revolution and proceeds cautiously, in conclusion, to describe the works of those who follow in the footsteps of the pioneers.

Without question, this version of the history of the Marginal Utility School, which all writers have come to accept, accurately reflects the occurrences in this field after 1871 in all details. Predecessors abounded (they always have); a revolution took place (if we do not insist on a definition of a revolution that excludes its going practically undiscovered for twenty years, until, in fact, one of its heroes had died); and other economists followed the leaders (but not until after a long time, of course). However, the same materials can provide a number of quite different accounts, equally accurate in a factual sense, by appropriate shifts in selection or emphasis.

II

It is interesting and perhaps profitable to examine several of these ways in which the history of the discovery of marginal utility could be written. As one variation, the account might emphasize the simultaneous, independent discovery of marginal utility, not by Jevons, Menger, and Walras in the eighteen-seventies but by Dupuit, Gossen, and Jennings in the middle of the eighteen-fifties. This would move the beginning of the modern period in economics back from 1871 to 1854. Each of the writers mentioned did not publish his initial article or book on the subject in 1854, but neither did Jevons, Menger, and Walras each publish their initial articles in 1871. Everyone knows, but customarily overlooks, when stating the standard versions of the history of marginal utility, the dates at which the triumvirate first publicly announced their discovery: 1862 (Jevons); 1871 (Menger); and 1873 (Walras). These dates reveal no more simultaneity than those of Dupuit (1844), Gossen (1854), and Jennings (1855). No one denies that the exposition and understanding of the later group (Jevons, Menger, and Walras) surpassed that of the earlier trio (Dupuit, Gossen, and Jennings). But, for that matter, Wicksteed, Wieser, and Pareto also understood marginal utility better and expounded it more thoroughly than did Jevons, Menger, and Walras. Of course, credit came to Jevons, Menger, and Walras somewhat sooner than to Dupuit, Gossen, and Jennings, but not as much sooner as people sometimes think. And probably, in general, Wicksteed, Wieser, and Pareto leaned more heavily on the writers of the early eighteen-seventies than the writers of the eighteen-seventies had leaned on anyone, though we must remember that Jevons acknowledged help from Jennings and that Walras quoted Dupuit. Whatever one says about the group in the eighteen-seventies in support of the claim that they represent the founders of marginal utility theory holds to a surprising degree for the writers of the eighteen-fifties. It would not force the facts to put the beginning of the Marginal Utility School near the middle of the century. The

211

standard account sets it twenty years later; the standard account has weight and support; and twenty years later it doubtless will stay.

If 1854 does not suit as a substitute for 1871, perhaps 1890 will do better as a starting place for the history of marginal utility. A history emphasizing that date would start with the statement that around 1890, economists in Austria, England, the United States, and Switzerland began the widespread use of marginal utility in economic analysis that continues in some form in world economics down to the present day. In Austria its employment centered in the influential writings and teachings of Wieser and Böhm-Bawerk, in England in Wicksteed and Marshall, in the United States in Fisher and Clark, and in Switzerland in Pareto. A generation earlier, this account could continue, the publications of Jevons, Menger, and Walras had foreshadowed the work of the writers in the nineties. But the works of these three writers, the alternative version could point out, had received scant attention until the end of the eighties, and might have fallen into total oblivion had not work on marginal utility begun to flourish at London, Cambridge, Vienna, and Lausanne, and in the United States. The alternative account could survey the long list of predecessors going back to Dupuit, Jennings, and Gossen and to the influence of the first two of these on Jevons and Walras. And, of course, before 1855, and as far back as economic thought stretches, the predecessors of the predecessors set down similar ideas in various contexts and with various degrees of thoroughness.

Still another version of the history of the Marginal Utility School, instead of emphasizing a special date (1854, 1871, or 1890) as the date at which the idea really began to take hold, could deny the relevancy of any single year to the history and could stress instead the hypothesis that articles on utility appeared very evenly throughout all periods of writing on economics and that the proportion of all economic theorizing given over to the subject of utility has changed less than people think. Or, if the proportion of total economic writing on the subject of utility had increased, a variant of this version could assert, the increase from generation to generation took place gradually and never experienced any sudden spurts worthy of historical attention.

Or an author could write a history of a thoroughly artificial, yet factually correct and to some people very satisfying, kind in which he pointed out that almost every ten years beginning in 1834 there

212

had occurred an event in the history of the Marginal Utility School that made the years in between seem pale ones: 1834, Lloyd; 1844, Dupuit; 1854, Gossen; 1862, Jevons; 1874, Walras; 1884, Wieser (1894 and 1904 lie in the period without heroes, when absorption of the doctrine by the profession at large constitutes the main circumstance in the history of the doctrine); 1914, Slutsky; 1924, Frisch; 1934, Lange; and 1944, Neumann and Morgenstern. This apparent periodicity probably says nothing more than that utility analysis has gone on for a long time.

As said before, the present standard version of the history of the Marginal Utility School, which places the reader near 1871 in the company of Jevons, Menger, and Walras, and directs him to look backward at the predecessors and forward to the successors, doubtless has as much in its favor as any of the alternatives mentioned above, if not more. Perhaps for this reason the standard version continues to hold the field without challenge from any rival histories.

III

This standard version of the history of the Marginal Utility School appears to us today as simple, true, and almost obvious. It did not appear, however, in this way to people of the generation that followed 1870. Almost no one, in these years, realized the fact that a revolution had taken place in economics in the sense in which later historians of thought described it. No one completed a standard version of events of the revolution until the middle of the eighteen-eighties. And yet another twenty years had passed before historians of economic thought generally accepted this version. The history of the Marginal Utility School provides a good example of how slowly ideas form, and of how slowly they spread after formation.

We will now trace the slow course taken in the development of the standard version of the history of the Marginal Utility School. The first step in investigating the history of the subject was the search for predecessors. Jevons, Menger, and Walras all set down a number of writers to whom they were indebted in various degrees for their ideas. The second step was a more difficult one. It consisted in the arrival at the realization that Jevons, Menger, and Walras had published books on the subject of marginal utility at approximately the same time. This step required a recognition of such simple things as the facts that the three books written by Jevons, Menger, and Walras existed, and that (among other things) they all treated es-

213

sentially the same subject. This was not as easy as it now would seem. Because of the dissimilarity in method and terminology and because of the fact that few economists kept abreast of the international literature, for almost fifteen years after 1871 no one recognized the similarity of these books written by the authors in three different languages. Jevons, for example, despite his strong bibliographic interest in marginal utility and despite his numerous contacts with the world of economics, died in 1882 without ever knowing that Carl Menger had written a book on utility theory in 1871 of so similar a nature to his *Theory* that historians would thereafter bracket Menger's name with his own in discussions of the history of economic thought.

Apparently Léon Walras in his *Théorie de la monnaie* first linked publicly the names of Jevons, Menger, and Walras in 1886. Other writers make the same linkage among the three writers in all the major languages after 1886 and before 1890. But as late as April, 1885, in his study of Gossen, Léon Walras had related the ideas of Gossen to those of Jevons, but not to those of Menger. Nor had Walras ever mentioned Menger in print previously. He had been brought in touch with Jevons in 1874 by Johan d'Aulnis de Bourouill, who also introduced him to Menger in 1883. But Walras did not really appreciate Menger until later.[1]

In Austria, public recognition that the trio had simultaneously discovered the marginal utility theory of value proceeded no more rapidly. Menger had had early correspondence with d'Aulnis de Bourouill, who in turn had introduced him to Walras; he subsequently corresponded with Walras. Yet it probably did not become clear to him that he was a member of a trio until after Walras had sent him a copy of the *Théorie de la monnaie,* containing the first published statement of the similarity of the three men's views. Walras also wrote Menger a letter in 1887 in which he said, "Nous sommes plusieurs (Jevons, vous et moi) qui sommes arrivés indépendamment les uns des autres à la même conception. . . ."[2] Menger evidently spread the word. In 1887 Emil Sax gave the first printed statement in German of the connection of Walras and Jevons with Menger. In the same place he called attention to Gossen, and listed Pierson and Böhm-Bawerk as followers.[3] The next year Friedrich von Wieser gave the history of marginal utility in even more detail.[4] Yet only four years before, in 1884, Wieser had cited only Menger and Jevons.[5] And in Böhm-Bawerk's highly important journal article

214

on utility published in 1886 Walras did not appear in his true role as an independent discoverer of the idea of marginal utility. The Austrians had thus known for long that Jevons and Menger had something in common. They should have known, too, that Jevons had identified his ideas completely with those of Walras. They should have concluded that Menger had much in common with Walras also, but they never did.

We cannot ascertain with any more certainty the date of the introduction into England of the idea that Jevons, Menger, and Walras all wrote essentially about the same thing. All three appear in the bibliography of the third edition (1888) of Jevons' *Theory*. Philip Wicksteed in the preface to his *Alphabet* (1888) gave an excellent account of the development of marginal utility theory in its standard form that includes, of course, the recognition of the similarity of viewpoint of Jevons, Menger, and Walras. And in 1890, Alfred Marshall acknowledged the similarity in his *Principles,* where, with his own adornments, he recounted the history of marginal utility in a footnote, reciting the list of predecessors and ending with a muster of Jevons, Menger, and Walras.[6] We know, of course, that Jevons—who died in August, 1882—did not know of Menger's *Grundsätze*.[7] Much later (1888) James Bonar, who should have known if anyone did, wrote an article, "The Austrian Economists and Their View of Value," for the *Quarterly Journal of Economics,* in which he spoke of Jevons in connection with the Austrians but did not allude to Walras.

IV

Once economists recognized that the books of Jevons, Menger, and Walras had a remarkably similar theme, the question of the independence of their views came up. This question raised no difficulties. As soon as Jevons confronted Walras with his claim of priority, Walras admitted that Jevons' work obviously came first in time, but he insisted on the complete independence of his own work.[8] In turn, Jevons admitted that Walras developed his theories independently of his own.[9] Jevons, of course, had not known of Menger's *Grundsätze* and consequently never passed judgment on its originality. When Walras learned of his Austrian contemporary he evidently accepted the *Grundsätze* as a wholly independent version of the marginal utility theory.[10] Menger never gave public sanction to the other two members of the trio; in fact, he hardly mentioned the name of Jevons or Walras in print at any time.[11] One reason for this silence on the place of Jevons and Walras in the discovery of marginal utility by Menger followed from the circumstance that Menger, who lived much longer than the other two pioneers, wrote substantially nothing on economic theory during the final thirty years of his life. Perhaps we can take his silence as approval of their claims to originality. Or perhaps Menger's disciple, Wieser, spoke with sufficient authority in behalf of their independence.[12] In short, by 1890, the three pioneers or their disciples expressly had recorded the fact that even though they had reached similar ends, they had reached the ends independently.

Really a reading of the volumes themselves precludes any thought that they lack originality. Their great differences in details of construction and interpretation should indicate to anybody that the three volumes did not influence each other. These differences, however great though they now seem, did not prevent all writers at the time from feeling that someone must have copied from someone else. The differences in the dates of publication and the circumstance that the books treated the same subjects generally led Maffeo Pantaleoni to bring a charge of plagiarism against Menger.[13] But shortly afterwards the abundance of evidence to the contrary convinced Pantaleoni of his error, and he accordingly withdrew his charge.[14]

Really the pioneers gave each other astonishingly little attention even after they recognized their similarities. Actually, no one of the three pioneers considered any doctrinal differences between himself and either of the other two. In the second edition of his *Theory* Jevons made no use of any of the ideas of Walras. In fact, Jevons did not mention Walras' name in the text of the second edition of the *Theory*, although he referred to Walras in the "Introduction" and in the bibliography that he attached as an appendix. Walras did not change the second edition of his *Éléments* to include any comments on the different problems raised by Menger and Jevons. Menger never republished the *Grundsätze*, and nowhere else did he examine any differences between himself and the other two innovators of marginal utility theory.

V

Of all the general histories of economic thought published between the years 1870 and 1890, only one mentioned marginal utility:

the history that John Kells Ingram published at the end of the period.[15] He connected only Jevons with utility, never noticed Menger, and brought in Walras[16] and Gossen[17] only as economists who had used mathematics. In the first publication of his history in book form he wrote:

His [Jevons'] conception of "final utility" is ingenious. But it is no more than a mode of presenting the notion of price in the case of commodities homogeneous in quality and admitting of increase by infinitesimal additions; and the expectation of being able by means of it to subject economic doctrine to a mathematical method will be found illusory. He offers (*Theory of Political Economy*, 2d ed., p. 103) as a result of a hundred pages of mathematical reasoning what he calls a "curious conclusion" (*Fortnightly Review* for November 1876, p. 617), in which the "keystone of the whole theory of exchange and of the principal problems of economics lies." This is the proposition that "the ratio of exchange of any two commodities will be the reciprocal of the ratio of the final degrees of utility of the quantities of commodity available for consumption after the exchange is completed." Now as long as we remain in the region of the metaphysical entities termed utilities, this theorem is unverifiable and indeed unintelligible, because we have no means of estimating quantitatively the mental impression of final, or any other, utility. But when we translate it into the language of real life, measuring the "utility" of anything to a man by what he will give for it, the proposition is at once seen to be a truism. What Jevons calls "final utility" being simply the price per unit of quantity, the theorem states that, in an act of exchange, the product of the quantity of the commodity given by its price per unit of quantity (estimated in a third article) is the same as the corresponding product for the commodity received—a truth so obvious as to require no application of the higher mathematics to discover it.[18]

This exposition by Ingram is offered in full because of its place as the first evaluation of marginal utility in a general history of economic thought. Ingram treated the history of marginal utility in a very unhistorical and most deductive manner for a writer who abhorred deduction and preached the supremacy of the historical method.

Only two other histories of economic thought published between 1870 and 1890 mention the names of Jevons, Menger, or Walras, and neither of these lists all three of the writers.[19] Neither connects any one of the three with marginal utility. A number of other histories published during the period do not so much as allude to any one of the so-called founders of the Marginal Utility School. The following authors of histories written during this period completely ignore Jevons, Menger, and Walras: Eugen Dühring,[20] Francesco Mariotti,[21] Heinrich Contzen,[22] Moritz Meyer,[23] Charles Périn,[24] Hugo Eisenhart,[25] and Gustav Cohn.[26]

Appendix:

TREATMENT OF MARGINAL UTILITY IN THE HISTORIES OF ECONOMIC THOUGHT AFTER 1890

I

No history of economic thought gave a complete account of the Marginal Utility School in the twenty years from 1890 to 1909. Maurice Block's *Les Progrès de la science économique depuis Adam Smith* presented the fullest view.[1] He scattered his discussion throughout two volumes, overlooked Gossen, and neglected Walras in the first edition; nevertheless for almost twenty years his work remained the most complete statement of marginal utility theory in any general history of economic thought. The only other early sympathetic account, short and confined to England, was in L. L. Price's durable *A Short History of Political Economy in England from Adam Smith to Arnold Toynbee.*[2]

Two other histories of this period, Luigi Cossa's *Introduzione allo studio dell' economia politica,*[3] and Henry Dunning Macleod's *The History of Economics,*[4] did not consider the idea of marginal utility a fortunate one for the progress of economics and therefore elected to give it only slight treatment. A further history barely mentioned marginal utility.[5] No other history published from 1890 to 1909 contained any references to the theory, and if any of them remarked on the three founders of the Marginal Utility School, it did so only to connect them with some other subject, such as mathematical economics or the historical method.[6]

If little progress was made in the incorporation of the Marginal Utility School in the general history of economic thought up to 1909, at least specialists in the historical development of economics added to the knowledge of the predecessors of the school during this period. Auguste Dubois studied the predecessors in the eighteenth century.[7] Vincenzo Tangorra examined the use of utility by the classical Italian economists.[8] Alfred Pringsheim translated Daniel Bernoulli's work on marginal utility from Latin into German, and Ludwig Fick provided an historical introduction.[9] A study by Arthur Ruppin investigated the possibility of including Johann Heinrich von Thünen among the predecessors.[10] But the most important work in this line was E. R. A. Seligman's discovery of the work of W. F. Lloyd.[11] Seligman gave Lloyd full credit: "It will come as a surprise to many to be informed that the theory of marginal utility is, after all, an English discovery, and that what is a virtually identical doctrine was advanced by Professor Lloyd in 1834, a decade before Dupuit, two decades before Gossen, and considerably more than a generation before its rediscovery by Jevons, Menger, and Walras."[12] Along with his outstanding discovery Seligman also shepherded the following writers into the utility camp: John Craig, Edward Rogers, Samuel Bailey, Charles Francis Cotterill, Mountifort Longfield, and Isaac Butt. These discoveries of Seligman had an influence on the history of economic thought, as they should have had, but not the complete effect he contemplated when he urged that "we should no longer speak of the Austrian Theory of Value."[13]

Specialized histories of the theory of value began to appear during the period, and some of them contained good versions of the standard history of marginal utility.[14] Eugène Petit wrote the longest and best of these as a part of the thesis he submitted at the University of Paris in 1897.[15] Other fairly adequate treatments were given in the histories of value of Rudolf Kaulla,[16] Lujo Brentano,[17] and Bernhard Rost.[18] They added nothing new to the discussion of the Marginal Utility School. In addition, historical accounts of the School appeared in dictionaries of economies.[19]

II

The complete incorporation of the story of the rise of the Marginal Utility School into the general histories of economic thought, and the subsequent appearance of special histories treating some part of the development of marginal utility theory comprise the two principal attainments after 1909.

Three histories of economic thought share the credit for the earliest acceptance of the standard account of the predecessors, the revolution, and the followers:[20] the *Histoire des doctrines économiques* (1909) of Charles Gide and Charles Rist,[21] Lewis Haney's *History of Economic Thought* (1911),[22] and Othmar Spann's *Die Haupttheorien der Volkswirtschaftslehre* (1911).[23] What led these three to introduce marginal utility? In general it was the pressure to fill the gap after 1871, which widened each year, and which hitherto had had little in it save an account of the Historical School. In particular, Gide had had an early interest in Jevons that predisposed him towards utility. Spann lived in Vienna and could not avoid marginal analysis, and Haney must have felt the strong interest in the United States already current among economists. Since these three histories were best-sellers for a long time, they wielded an enormous influence. All other histories were forced to compete with them. After they showed the way, nearly all the later histories followed.

Of the more than twenty histories to come out between the two world wars, eleven rank as major full-length histories of economic thought.[24] At least these eleven still remained in print in 1950. That leaves at least an equal number of smaller, less influential histories of economic thought published in the years from 1911 to 1940 that went out of print before 1950.[25] Some of the shorter histories contain adequate standard accounts of the history of marginal utility, e. g., Schumpeter's and Salin's, but most of them have imperfections and omit salient details in their accounts.

All eleven major histories of economic thought carry substantial reports of the development of the Marginal Utility School that follow the pattern of the standard version. When the history proceeds chronologically, the topic of marginal utility falls generally at the very end of the book. In fact, these histories read as though only a short flirtation with the historical method, a socialistic aberration or two, and the acceptance of marginal utility intervene between the demise of the Classical School and the present.

These eleven writers show, of course, numerous and notable differences in the treatment of the Marginal Utility School. Boucke gave it the heaviest emphasis. His treatment stands forth as a sound standard version of the history spun out to great length and embellished with numerous, and generally sage, observations. Peck's account perhaps contains as high a percentage of interpretive material as does Boucke's and certainly higher than that of any of the others. Whittaker divided his history by topics. He selected marginal utility as one of the topics and gave it the standard treatment. Scott emphasized the Austrians and never mentioned Walras. Mitchell, Roll, Ferguson, and Gray all presented adequate standard accounts. Gonnard showed as little interest in the idea of marginal utility as anyone. But even Gonnard gave a clear picture of the main outlines of the history of marginal utility.

During the war years of the early forties, manuscripts accumulated, since publishing stood still. After the war, publishers found a brisk demand for books, especially textbooks. Consequently the number of histories of economic thought multiplied when peace came. The decade after 1943 saw over twenty new or revised histories of economic thought published.

The publishers of several older, successful histories of economic doctrine brought out new and, in some cases, revised editions.[26] The revisions leave the treatment of the history of the Marginal Utility School totally unchanged. During this same period about a dozen slight or somewhat incidental histories came onto the market, each of which contains some fragment of the standard version of marginal utility.[27]

There came, too, a burst of different, new, and important histories near the beginning of the nineteen-fifties, marking the first substantial change in histories of economic thought for forty years. They outmoded the books of Gide and Rist, Haney, and Spann which have served so well for so long. The main difference in the new histories lies in their expansion of the part of the book given to the more recent developments in economics. Their change follows a straightforward, obvious, and overdue pattern. The change reflects the international needs of economics, as did the change in the histories around 1910, for the authors of these histories write in English, French, Italian, German, and Dutch. In a number of these new histories the authors change the emphasis so markedly that the account of the history of marginal utility, instead of resting near the end of the volume, now begins before the middle of the book, leaving as much space for the developments in economics since the seventies as that taken by all the discussion of events before 1870.[28] And even in the others the discussion of the revolution of the three pioneers comes soon after the middle.[29]

The histories of value, already discussed for earlier periods, continued to come out in diminished numbers, and poorer quality, through the twenties, but none added anything new to the orthodox account of the development of marginal utility theory.[30] The accounts in the economic encyclopedias became longer.[31] The journal articles on marginal utility published during this period, although primarily analytical, threw some light on the history of marginal utility.[32] A detailed study of the predecessors appeared.[33] One can obtain a good view of the extent that marginal utility enters economics throughout the world from a survey made of the state of economics in seventeen countries in 1927.[34] It shows that in almost every country marginal utility provides one of the main topics of discussion among economists.

But the fact that monographs began to appear devoted exclusively to the history of marginal utility overshadows all other developments in this final period. This stage of monographic histories must comprise the final stage in the development of any idea. Otto Weinberger wrote the first of these, *Die Grenznutzenschule,* in 1926.[35] It follows the standard account, going back to the sources in each case. Friedrich von Hayek, in a review of the book, complained that it did not live up to its title, since most of the book covers the work of the predecessors and the pioneers and very little of it deals with the Marginal Utility School.[36] Gaëtan Pirou supplied two books, *L'Utilité marginale* in 1932, and *Les Théories de l'équilibre économique: L. Walras et V. Pareto* in 1934, which he reprinted often and which, despite the circumstance that they split the pioneers into two camps and that the last volume contains extraneous matter, present a good deal of material on the history of marginal utility.[37] Edward Francis Schröder's *The Marginal Utility Theory in the United States of America* (1947) treats a special part of the history.[38] By far the best purely historical account of marginal utility to come out at any time is the history contained in the two articles on "The Development of Utility Theory" written by George J. Stigler for the *Journal of Political Economy* in 1950. Stigler limited his historical research to the principal writers and to selected topics, but within the confines of that double limitation he presented an excellent historical account. For the first time in the historical treatment of marginal utility, Stigler examined the ideas that arose during and after the time of Pareto, and for the first time in an historical discussion he covered subjects such as the measurability of utility.

223

References

CHAPTER I

1. William Stanley Jevons, *The Theory of Political Economy* (London: Macmillan and Co., 1871); 2d rev. ed., 1879; 3d ed., 1888; 4th ed., 1911, 5th ed., 1957. Translations: *La Théorie de l'économie politique*, trans. H. E. Barrault and Maurice Alfassa (Paris: V. Giard et E. Brière, 1909); *La Teorica dell' economia politica* in Gerolamo Boccardo, *Biblioteca dell' economista*, 3ª Ser., II (1878), 173-312; *Teoria della economia politica ed altri scritti economici* (Torino: Unione tip.-editrice torinese, 1947: *Die Theorie der politischen Ökonomie*, trans. Otto Weinberger (Jena: Gustav Fischer, 1924); translated into Japanese by Shinzo Koizumi, Chikuma Terao, and Kiyoshi Nagata in 1913.

Carl Menger, *Grundsätze der Volkswirtschaftslehre* (Vienna: W. Braumüller, 1871); 2ⁿ Aufl. with an introduction by Richard Schüller, ed. Karl Menger, the son of Carl Menger (Wien: Hölder-Pichler-Tempsky, 1923). The London School of Economics reprinted the first edition as No. 17 in the "Series of Reprints of Scarce Tracts in Economics and Political Science," in 1934. Translations: *Principii fondamentali di economia*, translated by Gavino Alivia with the collaboration of R. Broglio d'Ajano under the direction of Maffeo Pantaleoni for the supplement of the *Giornale degli economisti* (1906-07) and later published in a single volume with a preface by Pantaleoni (Imola: P. Galeati, 1909); again under the direction of Pantaleoni the second edition was translated by R. Broglio d'Ajano and N. Bonelli under the title *Principii fondamentali di economia politica* (Bari: Gius. Laterza & Figli, 1925); *Principles of Economics*, trans. James Dingwall and Bert F. Hoselitz, with an introduction by Frank H. Knight (Glencoe, Ill.: Free Press, 1950); translated into Japanese by Takuma Yasui in 1937.

Léon Walras, *Éléments d'économie politique pure: ou, théorie de la richesse sociale* (Lausanne: L. Corbaz & Cie, 1874-77); 2ᵉ éd., 1889; 3ᵉ éd., 1896; 4ᵉ éd., 1900; ed. définitive, 1926 (reprinted, 1951). Translations: *Elements of Pure Economics: or the Theory of Social Wealth*, trans. William Jaffé (London: Allen and Unwin, 1954); in part translated into Japanese by S. Tezuka in 1933.

2. J. A. La Nauze, "The Conception of Jevons's Utility Theory," *Economica*, N. S., XX (1953), 356-58.

3. *Letters & Journal of W. Stanley Jevons*, ed. Harriet A. Jevons (London: Macmillan and Co., 1886), pp. 151-52.

4. See Ross M. Robertson, "Jevons and His Precursors," *Econometrica*, XIX (1951), 232-38, for a discussion of the dependence of Jevons in his utility theory on other writers.

5. E. R. A. Seligman, "On Some Neglected British Economists,"*Economic Journal*, XIII (1903), 356-63, 525-33; Marian Bowley, *Nassau Senior and Classical Economics* (London: G. Allen & Unwin, Ltd., 1937), chap. II; R. D. Black, "Trinity College, Dublin, and the Theory of Value, 1832-1863," *Economica*, N. S., XII (1945), 140-48.

6. *Letters & Journal of W. Stanley Jevons*, p. 5.

7. W. Stanley Jevons, *Political Economy* (New York: American Book Company, 1878), p. 5.

8. [Richard Whately (Abp. of Dublin)], *Easy Lessons on Money Matters for the Use of Young People* (London: John W. Parker, 1833), pp. 32-33.

9. Charles Oman gave a short account of the peculiar role of nineteenth century professors at Oxford in *Memories of Victorian Oxford* (London: Methuen & Co., 1941), pp. 258 ff. William Whewell, a Master at Cambridge with a strong interest in economics, presented the whole array of reasoning underlying the English scheme of university education at the time in *On the Principles of English University Education* (2d. ed.; London: John W. Parker, 1838), and explains the minor part played therein by the professor (pp. 66-70). James Edwin Thorold Rogers, later a Drummond Professor of Political Economy, outlined the same system with particular reference to Oxford at a later date in *Education in Oxford: Its Methods, its Aids, and its Rewards*

(London: Smith, Elder & Co., 1861). A book prepared to guide students through Oxford (Montagu Burrows, *Pass and Class*. *An Oxford Guide-Book through the Courses of Literae Humaniores, Mathematics, Natural Science, and Law and Modern History* [Oxford: J. H. & J. Parker, 1860]) has the same evaluation of the place of the professor in the system of English university education. At times the universities stood the investigation of Parliament. The following report on Oxford at many points refers to the negligible part taken by the professor in the nineteenth century in England: Great Britain, Oxford University Commission, *Report of Her Majesty's Commissioners Appointed to Inquire into the State, Discipline, Studies, and Revenues of the University and Colleges of Oxford: Together with the Evidence, and an Appendix* (London: Her Majesty's Stationery Office, 1852). From a consideration of this report on Oxford came Henry Halford Vaughan's *Oxford Reform and Oxford Professors* (London: John W. Parker and Son, 1854), which defended the professors and which drew forth Edward Bouverie Pusey's *Collegiate and Professorial Teaching and Discipline, in Answer to Professor Vaughan's Strictures, Chiefly as to the Charges against the Colleges of France and Germany* (Oxford and London: John Henry Parker, 1854).

10. Samuel Leon Levy, *Nassau W. Senior: The Prophet of Modern Capitalism* (Boston: Bruce Humphries, 1943), p. 114.

11. [N. W. Senior], "Report—On the State of Agriculture," *Quarterly Review*, XXV (1821), 466-504.

12. Richard Whately, *Elements of Logic* (London, B. Fellowes, 1826).

13. Nassau W. Senior, *An Outline of the Science of Political Economy* (London: Printed by W. Clowes and Sons, 1836), p. 133. This is an offprint of the article "Political Economy" that had appeared in the *Encyclopaedia Metropolitana*. To a considerable extent it puts in print the earlier lectures of Senior (S. Leon Levy [ed.], Senior's *Industrial Efficiency and Social Economy* [New York: Henry Holt and Company, 1928], II, 383).

14. *Ibid.*

15. Terence Wilmot Hutchison, *A Review of Economic Doctrines, 1830-1929* (Oxford: Clarendon Press, 1953), pp. 16-17; also in "Insularity and Cosmopolitanism in Economic Ideas, 1870-1914," *American Economic Review, Papers and Proceedings*, XLV (1955), 5.

16. J. A. La Nauze, "Jevons in Sydney," *Economic Record*, XVII (1941), 41-42.

17. J. R. Hicks, "Léon Walras," *Econometrica*, II (1934), 339-40 n.

18. Dionysius Lardner, *Railway Economy: A Treatise on the New Art of Transport* (London: Taylor, Walton, and Maberly, 1850), p. 223.

19. *Annales des ponts et chaussées. 1ʳᵉ partie: Partie technique . . . Mémoires et documents*, 2ᵉ Sér., VIII (1844), 1-68, 332-75.

20. *Letters & Journal of W. Stanley Jevons*, p. 101.

21. *Ibid.* This was probably a cliché of the time to which Jevons fortunately fell victim, as did Walras.

22. *Ibid.*, p. 116.

23. *Ibid.*, p. 119.

24. London. University. University College. *Calendar for the Session MDCCCLX.-LXI* (London: Walton and Maberly, n. d.), p. 19.

25. *Ibid.*

26. *Ibid.*, p. 74. Herbert H. Cozens-Hardy won the "Prize and 1st Certificate," "2nd" went "to a student whose Envelope was not returned to the Office," and Jevons shared "3d" with Marcus Nathan Adler.

27. *Letters & Journal of W. Stanley Jevons*, p. 154.

28. *Dictionary of National Biography*, LIX, 34.

29. London. University. University College, *Calendar for the Session MDCCCLX.-LXI*, p. 167. The examination consisted of sixteen questions: two on the nature of

wealth, four on wages and profits, six on money and banking, two on taxation, and two on miscellaneous subjects.

30. Emil Kauder, "The Retarded Acceptance of the Marginal Utility Theory," *Quarterly Journal of Economics*, LXVII (1953), 564-75.

31. *Ibid.*, p. 570.

32. George Chandler, *William Roscoe of Liverpool* (London: B. T. Batsford, 1953), p. xxxiv.

33. Mrs. Thomas Jevons, *Sonnets, and Other Poems, Chiefly Devotional* (London: Simpkin, Marshall, and Company, 1845), p. 26.

34. Jevons, *Theory*, 2d ed., p. xxvii.

35. *Ibid.*, 1st ed., p. 33.

36. W. S. Jevons, "Notice of a General Mathematical Theory of Political Economy," *Report of the Thirty-Second Meeting of the British Association for the Advancement of Science; Held at Cambridge in October 1862. Notices and Abstracts of Miscellaneous Communications to the Sections* (London: John Murray, 1863), p. 158.

37. As was clearly the case with W. E. Hearn and Daniel Bernoulli and undoubtedly with many of the others to whom he expressed indebtedness.

38. Hugh Hale Bellot, *University College, London, 1826-1926* (London: University of London Press, 1929), p. 25.

39. *Ibid.*, p. 423.

40. Charles Milner Atkinson, *Jeremy Bentham: His Life and Work* (London: Methuen & Co., 1905), p. 208.

41. *Letters & Journal of W. Stanley Jevons*, p. 154.

42. Cf. T. W. Hutchison, "Bentham as an Economist," *Economic Journal*, LXVI (1956), 288-306.

43. Jevons, *Theory*, 1st ed., pp. 64-65.

44. Richard Jennings, *Natural Elements of Political Economy* (London: Longman, Brown, Green and Longmans, 1855). Richard Jennings (1814-91) attended Cambridge, entered the law, and then evidently, as a member of the landed gentry, divided his time between his seat at Gellydeg, Carmarthenshire, and his London address. We have no knowledge of the source of his interest in economics or how he came to abandon the subject as suddenly as he had taken it up.

45. *Social Delusions concerning Wealth and Want* (London: Longman, Brown, Green and Longmans, 1856).

46. *Supra*, p. 1.

47. Cairnes, as Jevons did, noticed only Jennings' *Natural Elements* in his *The Character & Logical Method of Political Economy* (London: Longman, Brown, Green, Longmans, and Roberts, 1857) and possibly noticed it, in part, because both his and Jennings' books have the same publisher. Cairnes published this book to fulfill his first publication requirement as a Whately Professor. Cairnes mentioned Jennings in connection with the accordance of "theory" with "reality" (*ibid.*, p. 47 n.), on the subject of the use of mathematics (*ibid.*, p. 81 n.), and on the concern of economists with "mental principles as premises to be reasoned upon" (*ibid.*, pp. 180-83). But he never pointed out his own divergence from Jennings on the subject of value nor, of course, did he mention marginal utility.

48. Richard Jennings attended Trinity College, Cambridge, during the time when William Whewell was master.

49. Jennings, *Natural Elements of Political Economy*, p. 35.

50. Jevons, *Theory*, 1st ed., p. 18.

51. Jennings, *Social Delusions concerning Wealth and Want*, p. 12.

52. *Ibid.*, p. 13 n.

53. Jevons, *Theory*, 1st ed., pp. 65-68.

54. Jennings, *Natural Elements of Political Economy*, pp. 208-09.

55. Jevons, *Theory*, 1st ed., p. 166.

56. Jennings, *Natural Elements of Political Economy*, pp. 22-23.

57. Jennings, *Social Delusions concerning Wealth and Want*, p. 78.

58. Jennings, *Natural Elements of Political Economy*, pp. 34, 171, 140, 191, and 216; Jennings, *Social Delusions concerning Wealth and Want*, p. 106.

59. Two other English thinkers who wrote on psychology in the midpart of the nineteenth century published their books at practically the same time as Jennings published his and consequently did not influence him: Alexander Bain's *The Senses and the Intellect* (London: J. W. Parker and Son, 1855), and *The Emotions and the Will* (London: J. W. Parker and Son, 1859); and Herbert Spencer's *Principles of Psychology* (London: Williams & Norgate, 1855). It is a question whether Jevons knew the work of these writers, since he never mentioned them. Bain was quite close at hand, however, having become an examiner at the University of London in 1857.

CHAPTER II

1. *Letters & Journal of W. Stanley Jevons*, p. 155.

2. *Ibid.*, p. 157.

3. *Ibid.*, p. 169.

4. *Ibid.* The paper probably was read at the next to the last meeting on October 7, 1862.

5. *Ibid.*, p. 175.

6. Keynes in an article on Jevons notes the presence of Marshall in Cambridge at this time and states that "Marshall was an undergraduate in his first year" (J. M. Keynes, "William Stanley Jevons," *Journal of the Royal Statistical Society*, XCIX [1936], 532). Keynes missed by a year, for Marshall began his study at Cambridge the year before.

7. "Notices and Abstracts of Miscellaneous Communications to the Sections," *Report of the Thirty-second Meeting of the British Association for the Advancement of Science* (London: John Murray, 1863), pp. 158-59. J. M. Keynes wrote that "the paper attracted no attention whatever and was not printed, the Secretary of the British Association writing to him that 'a further explanation and publication of the above-mentioned theory is deferred until a more suitable period for establishing a matter of such difficulty' " (J. M. Keynes, "William Stanley Jevons," *Journal of the Royal Statistical Society*, XCIX [1936], 532). The British Association did publish a summary which gave a sufficiently full view of what the whole paper contains.

8. XXIX (1866), 282-87. He had occupied himself in these intervening years with other matters, among which his own establishment as a professor at Owens College, Manchester, held a central place. Partly as a means of advancing himself in this academic work he published three books during this interval: *A Serious Fall in the Value of Gold Ascertained, and Its Social Effects Set Forth* (London: Edward Stanford, 1863); *Pure Logic; or the Logic of Quality apart from Quantity: with Remarks on Boole's System, and on the Relation of Logic and Mathematics* (London: Edward Stanford, 1864), and *The Coal Question, an Enquiry Concerning the Progress of the Nation, and the Probable Exhaustion of our Coal-Mines* (London: Macmillan and Co., 1865).

9. *Ibid.*, p. 282.

10. *Ibid.*

11. *Ibid.*, p. 283.

12. *Letters & Journal of W. Stanley Jevons*, p. 151.

13. "Notices and Abstracts of Miscellaneous Communications to the Sections," *Report of the Thirty-second Meeting of the British Association for the Advancement of Science*, p. 159.

14. *Journal of the Royal Statistical Society*, XXIX (1866), 283.

15. *Ibid.*

16. *Ibid.*, p. 285.

17. *Ibid.*

18. *Ibid.*

19. 3ᵉ Sér., IV (1866), 89.

20. During these four years he was kept busy by the work connected with his professorship in Owens College and by his marriage on December 19, 1867. The two books that he published in these intervening four years concern logic, rather than economics. His periodical publications lie mainly in the field of applied economics, for he deals in them with the coal question, money, and taxation.

21. "Notices and Abstracts of Miscellaneous Communications to the Sections," *Report of the Fortieth Meeting of the British Association for the Advancement of Science* (London: John Murray, 1871), pp. 178-87.

22. *Letters & Journal of W. Stanley Jevons*, p. 251.

23. Jevons, *Theory*, 4th ed., p. lvii.

24. J. M. Keynes, "William Stanley Jevons," *Journal of the Royal Statistical Society*, XCIX (1936), 533 n.

25. "Trade-Unions: How Far Legitimate," *North British Review*, XLVIII (1868), 1-34.

26. *Ibid.*, p. 24.

27. "The Graphic Representation of the Laws of Supply and Demand, and their Application to Labour," *Recess Studies*, ed. Alexander Grant (Edinburgh: Edmonston and Douglas, 1870), pp. 151-85.

28. "On the Principles Which Regulate the Incidence of Taxes," in Fleeming Jenkin, *Papers, Literary, Scientific, &c.* (London: Longmans, Green, and Co., 1887), II, 109-10.

CHAPTER III

1. The following references provide most of the information on Carl Menger available: *Wer ist's?*, ed. Herrmann A. L. Degener (5ᵉ Ausg.; Leipzig: H. A. Ludwig Degener, 1911), p. 945; Friedrich Wieser, "Karl Menger," *Neue Österreichische Biographie* (Vienna: Wiener Drucke, 1923), I, 84-92, reprinted in Friedrich Wieser, *Gesammelte Abhandlungen* (Tübingen: J. C. B. Mohr, 1929); Robert Zuckerkandl, "Carl Menger," *Deutsches biographisches Jahrbuch* (1927), III, 192-200; F. A. von Hayek, "Introduction" to the reprint of Menger's *Grundsätze*, London School of Economics and Political Science, "Reprints of Scarce Tracts in Economics and Political Science," No. 17, reprinted as "Carl Menger," *Economica*, N. S., I (1934), 393-420; George J. Stigler, "The Economics of Carl Menger," *Journal of Political Economy*, XLV (1937), 229-50.

2. Menger, *Grundsätze*, 2ᵉ Aufl., pp. v-vi.

3. Wieser, "Karl Menger," *Gesammelte Abhandlungen*, p. 117.

4. Menger, *Grundsätze*, trans. Dingwall and Hoselitz, p. 49.

5. Menger refers in the 1871 edition of the *Grundsätze* (p. 78 n.) to the "Theorie d. Werthes, Dorpater Univ. Progr. 1852" of E. Friedlander. A second reference (p. 110) in the 1871 edition has a slightly different form from the first: "Die Theorie des Werthes; Dorpater Univ. Schr. 1852." In the Dingwall and Hoselitz translation the reference (p. 292) reads as the " 'Theorie des Werthes,' *Dorpater Universitäts Program, 1852*," and a footnote states: "We were unable to locate this item. We suspect, however, that Menger's reference is to the following work: Dorpat, Kaiserliche Universität, *Facultätsschriften der Kaiserlichen Universität Dorpat, dargebracht zur Feier ihres fünfzigjährigen Bestehens, etc.* Dorpat, 1852 (see *Catalogue of the Printed Books in the Library of the British Museum*, London, 1881-1900, I, 202)." The copy in the library at the University of Kansas has the title, *Die Theorie des Werths* (Dorpat: Druck von H. Laakmann, 1852).

A. E. F. Schäffle, "Die ethische Seite der nationalökonomischen Lehre vom Werthe," *Akademisches Programm zur Feier des Geburtsfestes Sr. Majestät des Königs Wilhelm* (Tübingen, 1885-86), I, 184-195.

Hermann Roesler, "Zur Theorie des Werthes," *Jahrbücher für Nationalökonomie und Statistik,* XI (1868), 279-313, 406-19. Menger also cites a second article of Roesler's, "Zur Theorie des Preises," *Jahrbücher für Nationalökonomie und Statistik,* XII (1869), 81-138.

Otto Michaelis, "Das Kapitel vom Werthe," *Vierteljahrschrift für Volkswirtschaft und Kulturgeschichte,* I (1863), 1-28.

Arnold Lindwurm, "Die Theorie des Werthes," *Jahrbücher für Nationalökonomie und Statistik,* IV (1865), 165-218.

Karl Knies, "Die nationalökonomische Lehre vom Werth," *Zeitschrift für die gesammte Staatswissenschaft,* XI (1855), 421-75.

Johann Komorzynski, "Ist auf Grundlage der bisherigen wissenschaftlichen Forschung die Bestimmung der natürlichen Höhe der Güterpreise möglich?" *Zeitschrift für die gesammte Staatswissenschaft,* XXV (1869), 189-238.

6. James Dingwall and Bert F. Hoselitz give most accurately in the index of their translation of Menger's *Grundsätze* the page references to the seven writers.

7. Both Menger and Jevons collected books systematically. Partly as a result of this interest they came to know a good deal about the literature of their subject and as a consequence of their knowledge could give a long list of writers whom we now identify as early members of the utility school. Menger, who lived much longer than Jevons, managed to gather together a library which, in 1911, he estimated to contain 25,000 volumes and which he considered the most complete collection on economics in private hands. (See the letter from Menger which Feilbogen published as part of a footnote of his article "L'École Autrichienne d'économie politique" in the *Journal des économistes,* 6ᵉ Sér., XXXI [1911], 56-57.) After his death, a Japanese university bought Menger's economics collection and moved it to Tokyo, where the university published a catalog of the collection under the title of *Katalog der Carl Menger—Bibliothek in der Handels—Universität Tokio* (Tokio: Bibliothek der Handels —Universität Tokio, 1926). His collection on philosophy was brought to this country by his son and is at present stored at the Midwest Inter-Library Center in Chicago.

8. [Siegmund] Feilbogen, "L'École Autrichienne d'économie politique," *Journal des économistes,* 6ᵉ Sér., XXXI (1911), 56-57.

9. F. A. von Hayek, "Carl Menger," *Economica,* N. S., I (1934), 396.

10. Cournot wrote two other and later books strictly on the subject of economics; both popularize the *Recherches.*

11. Menger's *Grundsätze,* of course, has no trace of Cournot in the way that Walras' *Éléments* has. Whatever the influence on Menger of reading Cournot (granted the implication of Menger's letter to Feilbogen), it does not result in any obvious effect on his writings. At one place we may imagine Cournot's influence on Menger's *Grundsätze:* when Menger uses the example of a mineral spring (*Grundsätze,* trans. Dingwall and Hoselitz, p. 110), which, of course, recalls Cournot.

Chapter IV

1. "Principe d'une théorie mathématique de l'échange," *Journal des économistes,* 3ᵉ Sér., XXXIV (1874), 20.

2. Léon Walras, "Un Initiateur en économie politique: A. A. Walras," *La Revue du mois,* VI (1908), 182. For additional information on Antoine Auguste Walras see Louis Modeste Leroy, *Auguste Walras: sa vie, son œuvre* (Paris: Librairie Générale de Droit et de Jurisprudence, 1923); Étienne Antonelli, "Un Économiste de 1830: Auguste Walras," *Revue d'histoire économique et sociale,* XI (1923), 516-38, an article in which Antonelli reviews Leroy's book cited above; "Lettres inédites de et à Léon Walras." *La Révolution de 1848,* IX (1912-13), 179-98, 286-309, 367-82, and 427-46; X (1913-14), 138-56, 231-53, 327-43, 405-31, and 508-25; and Gaston Leduc, "Introduction" in Auguste Walras, *De la nature de la richesse et de l'origine de la valeur* (Paris: Librairie Félix Alcan, 1938).

3. Leduc, "Introduction," in Auguste Walras, *De la nature de la richesse et de l'origine de la valeur*, 1938 reprint, p. 9.

4. Auguste Walras, *De la nature de la richesse et de l'origine de la valeur*, 1938 reprint, p. 53.

5. *Mercure du XIXᵉ siècle*, XXVIII-XXX (1830).

6. Évreux: Ancelle, 1831. The 1938 reprint of this first book on economics by Auguste Walras contains a biographical study by Gaston Leduc; a few unpublished notes of Jean Baptiste Say; a reprint of Auguste Walras' "Mémoire sur l'origine de la valeur d'échange" which he presented September 15, 1849, to the *Académie des sciences morales et politiques;* numerous notes on the texts by Gaston Leduc; and a preface by Gaëtan Pirou.

7. "Esquisse d'une théorie de la richesse," *Revue de Caen,* Avril, 1844, pp. 337-49, and Mai, 1844, pp. 381-94; "Mémoire sur l'origine de la valeur d'échange ou exposition critique et réfutation des opinions les plus accréditées chez les économistes sur cette question," *Compte rendu des séances et travaux de l'académie des sciences morales et politiques,* 15 Septembre, 1849, pp. 201-33; and *Esquisse d'une théorie de la richesse: Discours prononcé le 19 décembre 1863 à l'ouverture du cours d'économie politique professé à Pau* (Pau: Vignancourt, 1863).

8. Paris: Guillaumin et Cie, 1849.

9. Auguste Walras, *De la nature de la richesse et de l'origine de la valeur,* 1938 reprint, pp. 9, 11, 18.

10. *Ibid.,* pp. 91-92.

11. *Ibid.,* p. 175.

12. *Ibid.,* p. 176.

13. *Ibid.,* p. 270.

CHAPTER V

1. Léon Walras, "Un Initiateur en économie politique: A. A. Walras," *Revue du mois,* VI (1908), 181.

2. "Lettres inédites de et à Léon Walras," *La Révolution de 1848,* IX (1912-13), 190.

3. Léon Walras, "De la propriété intellectuelle: position de la question économique," *Journal des économistes,* 2ᵉ Sér., XXIV (1859), 392-407.

4. *Ibid.,* p. 395.

5. Léon Walras, *L'Économie politique et la justice: examen critique et réfutation des doctrines économiques de M. P. J. Proudhon: précédés d'une introduction à l'étude de la question sociale* (Paris: Guillaumin et Cie, 1860). Walras had published the part of this book that contains his discussion of value earlier in the year as an article "Philosophie des sciences économiques" (*Journal des économistes,* 2ᵉ Sér., XXV [1860], 196-206).

6. *Ibid.,* p. xxx. See also pp. 7-10, 75-76, 103.

7. *Ibid.,* p. lvii. See also pp. 9, 17.

8. Paris: Guillaumin et Cie, 1861.

9. *Ibid.,* p. vi.

10. "Lettres inédites de et à Léon Walras (suite)," *La Révolution de 1848,* X (1913-14), 148-50.

11. *Ibid.,* pp. 149-50.

12. No library in the United States has a file of this periodical. Georges Lutfalla published Walras' review as one of the appendices to the reprint of Augustin Cournot's *Recherches sur les principes mathématiques de la théorie des richesses* (Paris: Marcel Rivière, 1938).

13. Léon Walras, *Études d'économie sociale* (Lausanne: F. Rouge, 1896), pp. 28-29.

14. Walras, *Éléments,* 1ᵉʳᵉ éd., 27ᵉ Leçon.

15. *Ibid.,* pp. 385-88.

16. Étienne Antonelli, "Léon Walras et sa correspondance avec Augustin Cournot et Stanley Jevons," *Econometrica*, III (1935), 126.
17. *Letters & Journal of W. Stanley Jevons*, p. 366.
18. "Principes d'une théorie mathématique de l'échange," *Comptes-rendus des séances et travaux*, Janvier, 1874, pp. 97-116. It also was published in the *Journal des économistes*, 3ᵉ Sér., XXXIV (1874), 5-21. For an account of the reception of the paper by the members of the *Académie* see *infra*, pp. 194 ff.
19. Walras, *Éléments*, 1ᵉʳᵉ éd., p. 79.
20. Léon Walras, "Principes d'une théorie mathématique de l'échange," *Journal des économistes*, 3ᵉ Sér., XXXIV (1874), 16.

CHAPTER VI

1. *Infra*, pp. 134, 145-46.
2. Menger, *Grundsätze*, trans. Dingwall and Hoselitz, pp. 118-19.
3. For a slightly different interpretation see the translators' comments, *ibid.*, p. 118 n.
4. *Ibid.*, pp. 123-25.
5. *Ibid.*, p. 125.
6. Jevons, *Theory*, 1st ed., p. 44.
7. *Ibid.*, p. 46.
8. *Ibid.*, p. 62.
9. Walras, *Éléments*, trans. Jaffé, p. 118.
10. *Ibid.*, p. 505.
11. *Ibid.*, p. 119.
12. For a statement of the usual objections to this procedure see E. H. P. Brown, *The Framework of the Pricing System* (London: Chapman & Hall, 1936), pp. 53-55.
13. Jevons, *Theory*, 1st ed., p. 157. See *supra*, pp. 18-19, for a discussion of the terms he employed in his early writings.
14. Menger, *Grundsätze*, trans. Dingwall and Hoselitz, p. 57.
15. Walras, *Éléments*, trans. Jaffé, p. 239.
16. Jevons, *Theory*, 1st ed., p. 74.
17. Walras, *Éléments*, trans. Jaffé, p. 67.
18. Jevons, *Theory*, 1st ed., pp. 73-74.
19. *Ibid.*, p. 74.
20. *Ibid.*, p. 130.
21. Menger, *Grundsätze*, trans. Dingwall and Hoselitz, p. 228.
22. *Ibid.*, pp. 228-29.
23. Jevons, *Theory*, 1st ed., pp. 118-19.
24. Walras, *Éléments*, trans. Jaffé, pp. 145, 175.
25. Menger, *Grundsätze*, trans. Dingwall and Hoselitz, pp. 118, 140, 145, 162.
26. Jevons, *Theory*, 1st ed., p. 57.
27. *Ibid.*, p. 120.
28. *Ibid.*, pp. 125-27.
29. Walras, *Éléments*, trans. Jaffé, p. 95.
30. *Ibid.*, p. 577.
31. Menger, *Grundsätze*, trans. Dingwall and Hoselitz, p. 183 n.
32. *Ibid.*, p. 125.
33. Walras, *Éléments*, trans. Jaffé, p. 117. See *supra*, p. 38, for his earlier comments on the problem of measurability.
34. *Ibid.*, p. 126.
35. *Ibid.*, pp. 445-46.
36. Jevons, *Theory*, 1st ed., p. 9.
37. *Ibid.*
38. *Ibid.*, p. 11.

39. *Ibid.*, p. 12.
40. *Ibid.*
41. *Ibid.*, p. 13.
42. *Ibid.*
43. *Ibid.*, pp. 12-13.
44. *Ibid.*, p. 14.
45. *Ibid.*
46. *Ibid.*, pp. 18-23.
47. *Ibid.*, p. 19.
48. *Ibid.*
49. *Ibid.*, pp. 19-20.
50. *Ibid.*, p. 35.
51. *Ibid.*, p. 36.
52. *Ibid.*, pp. 53-54.
53. *Ibid.*, pp. 140-42.

CHAPTER VII

1. Jevons, *Theory*, 1st ed., p. 21.
2. Menger, *Grundsätze*, trans. Dingwall and Hoselitz, p. 299.
3. Walras, *Éléments*, trans. Jaffé, p. 511.
4. Jevons, *Theory*, 1st ed., p. 21.
5. *Ibid.*, p. 88.
6. *Ibid.*, p. 96.
7. *Ibid.*, p. 98.
8. *Ibid.*, pp. 100-01.
9. *Ibid.*, p. 137.
10. Menger, *Grundsätze*, trans. Dingwall and Hoselitz, p. 299.
11. *Infra*, pp. 184, 186.
12. Menger wrote on complementarity but confined his discussion to producers' goods. (Cf. Menger, *Grundsätze*, trans. Dingwall and Hoselitz, pp. 63, 84-87, and 157-65.) He also commented on substitute goods but avoided the problem by the reduction of all the substitutes to a single good on the basis of technical qualities (*ibid.*, p. 143). Jevons spoke of beef and mutton as substitutes but gave them separate utility functions (Jevons, *Theory*, 1st ed., pp. 127-30). Walras never considered complementary or substitute relationships even incidentally.
13. Jevons, *Theory*, 1st ed., p. 62.
14. Walras, *Éléments*, trans. Jaffé, pp. 568-69. Walras changed the shape of these curves in the second edition.
15. *Ibid.*, pp. 443-45.
16. Jevons, *Theory*, 1st ed., pp. 93-94.
17. *Ibid.*, p. 93.
18. Walras, *Éléments*, trans. Jaffé, p. 117.
19. Menger, *Grundsätze*, trans. Dingwall and Hoselitz, pp. 82-83.
20. Jevons, *Theory*, 1st ed., p. 54.
21. *Ibid.*, p. 91.
22. Both Menger (*Grundsätze*, trans. Dingwall and Hoselitz, p. 130), and Jevons (*Theory*, 1st ed., p. 68), did mention the family or household but never gave them utility functions. Jevons could have considered the family or household when he developed his idea of a "trading body," but he did not.
23. Walras, *Éléments*, trans. Jaffé, p. 445. See also p. 175, where Walras compares the fortunes of the rich and poor in such a way as to imply diminishing marginal utility of income.
24. Jevons, *Theory*, 1st ed., pp. 154-55.
25. *Ibid.*, p. 133.

26. *Ibid.,* pp. 112-13.
27. *Ibid.,* p. 126.
28. Menger, *Grundsätze,* trans. Dingwall and Hoselitz, p. 80. See also pp. 95-96, 114, 131, 182, and 192.
29. Jevons, *Theory,* 1st ed., p. 44.
30. Walras, *Éléments,* trans. Jaffé, p. 121.
31. *Ibid.,* p. 202.
32. Menger, *Grundsätze,* trans. Dingwall and Hoselitz, p. 149.
33. Jevons, *Theory,* 1st ed., p. 160.
34. *Ibid.,* p. 159.
35. Menger, *Grundsätze,* trans. Dingwall and Hoselitz, p. 219.
36. Walras, *Éléments,* trans. Jaffé, pp. 115 ff.

CHAPTER VIII

1. November 4, 1871, p. 590.
2. LV (January, 1872), 244.
3. American edition, XCVII (January, 1872), 102-03.
4. Besides the reviews examined here, Jevons mentions a review in the *Evening Standard* for December 17, 1871 (*Letters & Journal of W. Stanley Jevons,* p. 275).
5. November 15, 1871, p. 7.
6. November 22, 1871, p. 7.
7. December 16, 1871, p. 3.
8. "Jevons on the Theory of Political Economy," *Saturday Review,* XXXII (November 11, 1871), 624-25. Jevons wrote to J. d'Aulnis de Bourouill on July 7, 1874, that "as to the reviews in the English periodical journals, that in the *Saturday Review* of 11th November 1871 is the most important, and indeed the only one requiring any attention." Jevons placed the critical level of this review above that of the later review by Alfred Marshall in the *Academy,* for he wrote in the same letter to d'Aulnis de Bourouill that there "was indeed a review in the *Academy . . .* but though more fair than that of the *Saturday Review,* it contained no criticism worthy of your notice" (*Letters & Journal of W. Stanley Jevons,* p. 309). In contrast, F. Y. Edgeworth, in his presidential address delivered to Section F of the British Association in 1889, referred to the "remarkable review of Jevons' *Theory* in the *Academy . . ."* (*Papers Relating to Political Economy* [London: Macmillan and Co., 1925], II, 276 n.).
9. "New Theories in Political Economy," *Fortnightly Review,* N. S., XI (January, 1872), 71-76.
10. *Academy,* III (April 1, 1872), 130-32. Reprinted in *Memorials of Alfred Marshall,* ed. A. C. Pigou (London: Macmillan and Co., 1925), pp. 93-99. The *Memorials* also has a "Comment on the above Review in an undated MS. found among Dr. Marshall's Papers."
11. *North American Review,* CXIV (April, 1872), 435-40.
12. *Memorials of Alfred Marshall,* pp. 99-100.
13. *Academy,* XVI (July 26, 1879), 59-60.
14. The short account in the *Westminister Review* (American edition, CXIII [January, 1880], 106) deals mostly with utility and ends with the statement that Jevons "will certainly deserve the gratitude of English economic students for having laboured so earnestly to enlarge their field of view." A longer review in the *Popular Science Monthly* (XVI [March, 1880], 699-701) provides a fuller exposition of the connection of utility with value and concludes that the value of the theory "is for economists to decide, but it can be studied with interest and profit by all who desire to know one of the directions in which present economic inquiry is tending" (*ibid.,* p. 701).

Chapter IX

1. *Letters & Journal of W. Stanley Jevons*, pp. 268-70.
2. *Ibid.*, p. 269.
3. *Ibid.*
4. *Ibid.*
5. *Ibid.*
6. *Ibid.*
7. W. Stanley Jevons, *The Principles of Science: A Treatise on Logic and Scientific Method* (New York: Macmillan and Co., 1874), I, 386.
8. "Théorie mathématique de l'échange.—Question de priorité," *Journal des économistes*, 3ᵉ Sér., XXXIV (1874), 419.
9. *Ibid.*
10. *Letters & Journal of W. Stanley Jevons*, p. 302.
11. *Ibid.*
12. *Ibid.*, pp. 302-03.
13. "Théorie mathématique de l'échange.—Question de priorité," *Journal des économistes*, 3ᵉ Sér., XXXIV (1874), 419-22.
14. *Letters & Journal of W. Stanley Jevons*, pp. 305-06.
15. 3ᵉ Sér., XXXIV, 417-22.
16. *Letters & Journal of W. Stanley Jevons*, pp. 309-11.
17. *Ibid.*, p. 320.
18. *Ibid.*
19. *Ibid.*, p. 321.
20. *Journal of the Statistical Society*, XXXVII (1874), 478-88.
21. *Letters & Journal of W. Stanley Jevons*, p. 326.
22. *Ibid.*, p. 327.
23. *Ibid.*, p. 331.
24. *Ibid.*, p. 332.
25. Published later in W. Stanley Jevons, *The Principles of Economics*, pref. Henry Higgs (London: Macmillan and Co., 1905), pp. 187-206.
26. *Letters & Journal of W. Stanley Jevons*, p. 366.
27. *Ibid.*, pp. 387-88.
28. *Ibid.*, p. 389.
29. *Ibid.*, p. 390. See *infra*, pp. 180-81, for an account of Walras' reception of the news.
30. Jevons, *Theory*, 2d ed., pp. xii-xiii.
31. *Ibid.*, p. x.
32. *Ibid.*, pp. 85-90, 110-15, 205-09.
33. *Ibid.*, pp. 137-45.
34. *Ibid.*, p. 215.
35. London: Macmillan and Co., 1905.

Chapter X

1. Alfred Marshall, "On Mr. Mill's Theory of Value," *Fortnightly Review*, N. S., XIX (1876), 591-602.
2. *Ibid.*, pp. 593 n., 598.
3. Alfred Marshall and Mary Paley Marshall, *The Economics of Industry* (London: Macmillan and Co., 1879). Two later editions that contain no change whatever in content followed, the second in 1881, and the third in 1885.
4. The London School of Economics reprinted this paper as part of "No. 1 in Series of Reprints of Scarce Tracts in Economic and Political Science" in 1930. J. M. Keynes in his "Alfred Marshall, 1842-1924" said that it "must have been substantially complete about 1873. . ." (*Memorials of Alfred Marshall*, ed. A. C. Pigou [London: Macmillan and Co., 1925], p. 23). Keynes gave no evidence in support of this state-

ment. Marshall had not completed it entirely at this early date, however, for *The Pure Theory of Domestic Values* contains one reference (p. 3 n.) to Marshall's 1876 article on Mill. Of course Marshall may well have added the reference after the completion of the rest of his manuscript.

5. Marshall, *The Pure Theory of Domestic Values*, p. 20.

6. Marshall placed the apostrophe after the "s" whenever he used the expression *consumers' rent* in *The Pure Theory of Domestic Values* even when he referred to a single individual's rent. Later, in the *Principles*, he used both *consumer's rent* and *consumers' rent*. Also in the first edition of the *Principles* Marshall began to replace the word *rent* with the word *surplus*. Edwin Cannan noticed the peculiarity of the position of the apostrophe in "consumers' rent" and remarked that he "looked through five editions of the *Principles* without discovering whether Marshall preferred 'consumer's' or 'consumers' " (Edwin Cannan, "Alfred Marshall, 1842-1942," *Economica*, IV [1924], 259).

7. Marshall, *The Pure Theory of Domestic Values*, p. 21.

8. *Ibid.*

9. *Ibid.*, p. 22.

10. *Ibid.*

11. *Ibid.*

12. *Ibid.*

13. *Ibid.*, p. 37.

14. A. and M. P. Marshall, *Economics of Industry*, pp. 69-70.

15. *Ibid.*, p. 70.

16. *Ibid.*, p. v.

17. *Ibid.*, p. 148.

18. Keynes, "Alfred Marshall, 1842-1924," *Memorials of Alfred Marshall*, p. 38.

19. "Alfred Marshall, the Mathematician, as Seen by Himself," *Econometrica*, I (1933), 222.

20. *Memorials of Alfred Marshall*, p. 66.

21. F. W. Taussig, "Alfred Marshall," *Quarterly Journal of Economics*, XXXIX (1924), 1.

22. *Academy*, XIX (1881), 457.

23. Alfred Marshall, "Note by Professor Marshall," *Quarterly Journal of Economics*, I (1887), 359-61.

24. Alfred Marshall, *The Present Position of Economics: An Inaugural Lecture given in the Senate House at Cambridge 24 February, 1885* (London: Macmillan and Co., 1885).

25. *Ibid.*, p. 29.

26. *Ibid.*, p. 31.

27. Maffeo Pantaleoni, *Principii di economia pura* (Firenze: G. Barbèra, 1889), p. 96 n.

28. *Letters & Journal of W. Stanley Jevons*, p. 331.

29. *Ibid.*

30. *Ibid.*, pp. 408-09.

31. H. S. Foxwell, "The Economic Movement in England," *Quarterly Journal of Economics*, II (1887), 88.

32. Talcott Parsons, "Wants and Activities in Marshall," *Quarterly Journal of Economics*, XLVI (1931), 103.

33. *Memorials of Alfred Marshall*, pp. 21-22.

34. "William Stanley Jevons, 1835-1882: A Centenary Allocution on his Life and Work as Economist and Statistician," *Journal of the Royal Statistical Society*, XCIX (1936), 516-48.

35. *Ibid.*, p. 533.

36. *Ibid.*

37. *Ibid.*, p. 535.

38. *Ibid.*, p. 536. Marshall enjoys a reputation for having anticipated Jevons in his lectures. He also has the reputation for delivering lectures so unsystematically

that we may wonder if it matters what he revealed. Keynes thought that the "informality" of his lectures may have increased as time went on, but he admitted that "in 1906 . . . it was impossible to bring away coherent notes" (*Memorials of Alfred Marshall*, p. 51). Others contributed to the same impression. "Under some blanket title," D. H. Macgregor wrote, "he talked, with complete discontinuity between one lecture and another, on any matter of economic interest that had occurred to him on the way to his class, or that the morning paper had suggested" ("Marshall and His Book," *Economica*, N. S., IX [1942], 313). Because of this "informality" or "discontinuity," the lectures of Marshall ought not to receive much emphasis, in comparison with his written work, as a means of spreading his doctrines or views.

39. *Ibid.*, p. 549.

40. *Ibid.*, p. 550.

41. *Academy*, III (1872), 131.

42. Alfred Marshall, *Principles of Economics* (London: Macmillan and Co., 1890), I, x n.

43. *Ibid.*, 2d ed., I, xiv n.

44. *Ibid.*, p. 184 n.

45. William Jaffé, "Unpublished Papers and Letters of Léon Walras," *Journal of Political Economy*, XLIII (1935), 202.

46. Jevons, *Theory*, 1st ed., p. 157.

47. *Academy*, III (1872), 131.

48. *The Pure Theory of Domestic Values*, p. 21; *The Economics of Industry*, p. 69; *Principles of Economics*, 1st ed., p. 155.

49. *Memorials*, pp. 412-13.

50. *Supra*, p. 84.

51. *Memorials*, p. 416.

52. "Alfred Marshall, the Mathematician, as Seen by Himself," *Econometrica*, I (1933), 221.

53. Joseph Dorfman, "The Seligman Correspondence III," *Political Science Quarterly*, LVI (1941), 407.

54. A. Marshall, "Graphic Representation by Aid of a Series of Hyperbolas of some Economic Problems Having Reference to Monopolies," *Proceedings of the Cambridge Philosophical Society* (October 20, 1873), pp. 318-19.

55. *Supra*, pp. 22-23.

56. *Academy*, III (1872), 132.

57. *Political Science Quarterly*, LVI (1941), 409.

58. *Ibid.*, p. 410. In a footnote the editor noted that Marshall erred, since he had also reviewed Edgeworth's *Mathematical Psychics*.

59. Joseph A. Schumpeter, "Alfred Marshall's *Principles*: A Semi-Centennial Appraisal," *American Economic Review*, XXXI (1941), 238.

60. Whewell might well have influenced Marshall. Both Marshall and Whewell were in Cambridge at the same time, and Marshall could scarcely have ignored Whewell's great fame and many spectacular accomplishments. Those accomplishments included work in both mathematics and in economics, two subjects in which Marshall either had or acquired an interest. It cannot help striking the student as peculiar that Marshall never mentioned Whewell. "It is very surprising," Hutchison said at the beginning of a long footnote on the relation of Marshall and Whewell, "that no reference ever seems to have been made by Marshall to the pioneer essays in Mathematical Economics of William Whewell, Master of Trinity" (T. W. Hutchison, *A Review of Economic Doctrines 1870-1929* [Oxford: Clarendon Press, 1953], p. 64 n.).

61. G. F. Shove, "The Place of Marshall's *Principles* in the Development of Economic Theory," *Economic Journal*, LII (1942), 313.

62. *Ibid.*, p. 315.

63. *Ibid.*, pp. 315-16.

64. *Ibid.*, p. 295.

65. *Ibid.*

66. P. 418. Why should Marshall call reconciliation "trumpery" when applied to his own book and yet praise the same quality in Adam Smith? Adam Smith's chief work, Marshall wrote, "was to combine and develop the speculation of his French and English contemporaries and predecessors as to value" (*Principles,* 1st ed., p. 57).

67. 1st ed., p. xii.

68. L. L. Price, "Notes on a Recent Economic Treatise," *Economic Journal,* II (1892), 30.

69. L. L. Price, *A Short History of Political Economy in England: From Adam Smith to Arnold Toynbee* (London: Methuen and Co., 1891). The same quotation remains in the fifteenth edition of this book, which Price had published in 1937.

70. Luigi Cossa, *An Introduction to the Study of Political Economy,* revised by the author and translated from the Italian by Louis Dyer (London: Macmillan and Co., 1893), p. 360.

71. Lewis H. Haney, *History of Economic Thought* (3d ed.; New York: The Macmillan Company, 1936), p. 694.

72. Alexander Gray, *The Development of Economic Doctrine* (London: Longmans, Green and Co., 1931), p. 364.

73. Edmund Whittaker, *A History of Economic Ideas* (New York: Longmans, Green and Co., 1940), p. 453.

74. Eric Roll, *A History of Economic Thought* (rev. and enlarged ed.; New York: Prentice-Hall, 1942), p. 436.

75. *Ibid.,* p. 437.

76. John Fred Bell, *A History of Economic Thought* (New York: The Ronald Press, 1953), p. 575.

77. Philip Charles Newman, *The Development of Economic Thought* (New York: Prentice-Hall, 1952), p. 279.

78. *Ibid.*

79. *Ibid.,* p. 284.

80. *Ibid.,* p. 285.

81. See Émile James, *Histoire des théories économiques* (Paris: Flammarion, 1950), p. 173; Alfred Kruse, *Geschichte der volkswirtschaftlichen Theorien* (Munich: Richard Pflaum, 1948), p. 161; Jenny Griziotti Kretschmann, *Storia delle dottrine economiche* (Torino: Unione Tipografico-Editrice Torinese, 1949), pp. 370-71; and Emil Kauder, "The Retarded Acceptance of the Marginal Utility Theory," *Quarterly Journal of Economics,* LXVII (1955), 570.

CHAPTER XI

1. Allyn A. Young, *American Economic Review,* 4th Ser., XV (1925), 721-24; Irving Fisher, *Quarterly Journal of Economics,* XL (1926), 167-71; Arthur C. Pigou, *Economic Journal,* XXXV (1925), 177-85; Edwin Cannan, *Economica,* V (1925), 332-33; Joseph Schumpeter, "Edgeworth und die neuere Wirtschaftstheorie," *Weltwirtschaftliches Archiv,* XXII (1925), 183-202.

2. The following include the longer and better-known of these necrologies: John Maynard Keynes, "Obituary: Francis Ysidro Edgeworth, 1845-1926," *Economic Journal,* XXXVI (1926), 140-53; James Bonar, "Memories of F. Y. Edgeworth," *Economic Journal,* XXXVI (1926), 647-53; L. L. P[rice], "Obituary, Francis Ysidro Edgeworth," *Journal of the Royal Statistical Society,* LXXXIX (1926), 371-76; Oskar Morgenstern, "Francis Y. Edgeworth," *Zeitschrift für Volkswirtschaft und Sozialpolitik,* N. F., V (1927), 646-52; Otto Weinberger, "Francis Ysidro Edgeworth: Ein Nachruf," *Jahrbücher für Nationalökonomie und Statistik,* CXXIV (1926), 205-17; and Charles Gide, "Nécrologie: Le professeur Edgeworth," *Revue d'économie politique,* XL (1926), 1217-18.

3. J. M. Keynes, "Francis Ysidro Edgeworth," *Dictionary of National Biography, 1922-1930* (Oxford: Oxford University Press, 1937), pp. 284-85.

4. Pp. 570-71. The article bears the signature "T. Y. Edgeworth," instead of "F. Y. Edgeworth."

5. II (1877), 167-86.

6. Oxford: James Parker and Co., 1877. See also the review of *New and Old Methods of Ethics* in *Mind*, III (1878), 146-47.

7. *Mind*, III (1878), 146.

8. *Ibid.*, p. 147.

9. *History of Economic Thought*, 3d ed., pp. 581-82.

10. *Journal of Political Economy*, LVIII (1950), 375-77.

11. Edward Bradford Titchener, *Experimental Psychology* (New York: The Macmillan Company, 1905), II, Part II, xx.

12. Ernst Heinrich Weber, *De Pulsu, Resorptione, Auditu et Tactu* (Leipzig: C. F. Koehler, 1834). Weber republished this as the first part of his *Annotationes Anatomicae et Physiologicae* (Leipzig: C. F. Koehler, 1851). He incorporated his findings also in his article "Der Tastsinn, und das Gemeingefühl," written for Rudolf Wagner's *Handwörterbuch der Physiologie* (Braunschweig: Friedr. Vieweg, 1846), III, 481-588. Notice that the same firm published Gossen's *Entwicklung* eight years later.

13. Titchener, *Experimental Psychology*, II, Part II, xx-xxii.

14. L. L. Thurstone in his experimental derivation of the constants in an indifference function made use of the measurement of satisfaction or utility in a manner comparable to Fechner's. "In the measurement of satisfaction," Thurstone writes, "we shall imply throughout that it is accomplished in terms of the subjective unit of measurement, the discriminal error. . . " (L. L. Thurstone, "The Indifference Function," *Journal of Social Psychology*, II [1931], 140-41). Thurstone found also that the equation that relates the quantity of satisfaction to the amount of good consumed "is certainly no stranger in psychophysics. It is our old friend, Fechner's law" (*ibid.*, p. 142).

15. Gustav Theodor Fechner, *Elemente der Psychophysik* (2ᵉ Aufl.; Leipzig: Breitkopf & Härtel, 1889), II, 549. Jevons, *Theory*, 1st ed., pp. 154-55.

16. See especially Sully's *Sensation and Intuition: Studies in Psychology and Aesthetics* (London: H. S. King & Co., 1874), and his review of Wilhelm Wundt's *Grundzüge der physiologischen Psychologie* in *Mind*, I (1876), 20-43.

17. Edgeworth, *New and Old Methods of Ethics*, p. ii.

18. James Sully, *My Life & Friends: A Psychologist's Memories* (New York: E. P. Dutton, 1918).

19. *Ibid.*, p. 164.

20. See James Sully, "Civilization and Noise," *Fortnightly Review*, XXX (1878), 704-20.

21. Sully, *My Life & Friends*, pp. 177-79.

22. *Mind*, IV (1879), 394-408.

23. *Ibid.*, p. 397.

24. *Ibid.*

25. *Ibid.*

26. *Ibid.*, p. 400.

27. *Mathematical Psychics: An Essay on the Application of Mathematics to the Moral Sciences* (London: C. Kegan Paul & Co., 1881).

28. *Ibid.*, p. 34 n.

29. The Library of the University of Kansas has a copy of the first edition of Alfred Marshall's *Economics of Industry*, with F. Y. Edgeworth's name and address (5 Mt. Vernon, Hampstead) on the title-page and with numerous annotations in Edgeworth's handwriting throughout.

30. Edgeworth added a sentence to the footnote on p. 57 of *Mathematical Psychics* and by accident or design he omitted a paragraph from p. 404 of *Mind*.

31. Edgeworth, *Mathematical Psychics*, p. 98.

32. *Ibid.*, p. 2.

33. *Ibid.*, p. 83.

34. *Ibid.*, pp. 7-8, 99.

35. Only the association of the ideas of Weber and Fechner with economics by F. A. Lange in his *Die Arbeiterfrage in ihrer Bedeutung für Gegenwart und Zukunft* (Duisberg, 1865) came earlier.

36. Edgeworth, *Mathematical Psychics*, p. 7.

37. *Ibid.*

38. *Ibid.*, p. 99.

39. *Ibid.*

40. *Ibid.*, p. 99.

41. *Ibid.*, p. 100.

42. *Ibid.*

43. *Ibid.*

44. *Ibid.*, p. 101.

45. *Ibid.*

46. *Ibid.*

47. *Ibid.*, p. 102.

48. *Ibid.*, p. 20. Edgeworth's use of the word "contract" stemmed perhaps from his legal training. (He signed the *Mathematical Psychics* as "Barrister-at-Law.") No one had used it in this sense earlier in economics and no one followed Edgeworth in his use.

49. *Ibid.*

50. *Ibid.*, p. 29.

51. *Supra*, pp. 62-64.

52. *Mind*, VI (1881), 581-83.

53. *Ibid.*, p. 581.

54. *Ibid.*, p. 583.

55. "On the Method of Ascertaining a Change in the Value of Gold," *Journal of the Statistical Society*, XLVI (1883), 714-18.

56. *Ibid.*, p. 714.

57. *Report of the Fifty-seventh Meeting of the British Association for the Advancement of Science* (London: John Murray, 1888), pp. 263-65.

58. London: The Temple Company [1887].

59. *Supra*, p. 103.

60. Edgeworth, *Metretike*, p. 1.

61. F. Y. Edgeworth, "The Method of Measuring Probability and Utility," *Mind*, XII (1887), 484-85. A. L. Bowley has the only secondary account of Edgeworth's relation of utility and probability in his chapter in *F. Y. Edgeworth's Contributions to Mathematical Statistics* (London: Royal Statistical Society, 1928) on "Probability in Statistics and Utility in Economics."

62. *Report of the Fifty-ninth Meeting of the British Association for the Advancement of Science* (London: John Murray, 1890), p. 671.

63. *Ibid.*

Chapter XII

1. Lewis H. Haney, *History of Economic Thought* (New York: The Macmillan Company, 1911), p. 521, and Charles Gide and Charles Rist, *Histoire des doctrines economiques* (Paris: L. Larose & L. Tenin, 1909), p. 607 n.

2. Eric Roll, *A History of Economic Thought* (rev. ed.; New York: Prentice-Hall, 1942), p. 467; John Fred Bell, *A History of Economic Thought* (New York: The Ronald Press, 1953), p. 527; T. W. Hutchison, *A Review of Economic Doctrine, 1870-1929* (Oxford: Clarendon Press, 1953), p. 255.

3. John Maurice Clark, "J. M. Clark on J. B. Clark," in Henry William Spiegel, *The Development of Economic Thought* (New York: John Wiley & Sons, 1952), p. 605.

4. *John Bates Clark: A Memorial* (Privately printed, 1938), p. 21.

5. *Ibid.*

6. Frances Aurelia Toyer, *The Economic Thought of John Bates Clark,* a dissertation in the Department of Economics, submitted in partial fulfillment of the requirements for the degree of Doctor of Philosophy at New York University, December 1951. This thesis pays but slight attention to J. B. Clark's connection with marginal utility. Cf. pp. 15-16.

7. Karl Knies, *Die politische Oekonomie vom geschichtlichen Standpunkte* (Braunschweig: C. A. Schwetschke und Sohn, 1883), pp. 500-07.

8. F. A. von Hayek, "Friedrich Freiherr von Wieser," in Friedrich Freiherr von Wieser, *Gesammelte Abhandlungen* (Tübingen: J. C. B. Mohr, 1929), p. viii.

9. John Bates Clark, "The Unit of Wealth," *Staatswissenschaftliche Arbeiten: Festgaben für Karl Knies zur fünfundsiebzigsten Wiederkehr seines Geburtstages* (Berlin: O. Haering, 1896), p. 1. Since Eugen v. Böhm-Bawerk also contributed an essay, two out of the five essays in this *Festgabe* for a famous member of the German Historical School came from equally famous members of the opposing school, the Marginal Utility School.

10. *New Englander,* XXXVI (1877), 170-86. This journal provided one of the few outlets for serious articles in economics at the time in the U. S. It later became the *Yale Review.* In its early days, theological interests played a large part in its policy (it sold at lower rates to students in theological seminaries), and must have made it partial to Clark's writings, which initially leaned in this direction.

11. "Unrecognized Forces in Political Economy," *New Englander,* XXXVI (1877), 710-24.

12. *Ibid.,* p. 712. This idea that Clark expounds here holds a central position in the work of Karl Knies. (Cf. Hans Gehrig, "Karl Gustav Adolf Knies [1821-98]," *Encyclopaedia of the Social Sciences,* VIII, 580-81.)

13. *Ibid.,* p. 714.

14. *Ibid.*

15. *Ibid.,* p. 720.

16. "Bibliography of the Writings of John Bates Clark: Articles in Newspapers, Magazines, etc.," *Economic Essays Contributed in Honor of John Bates Clark* (New York: The Macmillan Company, 1927), p. 339.

17. N. S., IV, 457-69.

18. *Ibid.,* p. 457.

19. *Ibid.*

20. *Ibid.,* p. 458.

21. B. M. Anderson, *Social Value* (Boston: Houghton Mifflin, 1911), particularly chap. i.

22. Hans Gehrig, "Karl Gustav Adolf Knies (1821-98)," *Encyclopaedia of the Social Sciences,* VIII, 580.

23. John B. Clark, "The Philosophy of Value," *New Englander,* N. S., IV (1881), 461-62.

24. *Ibid.,* p. 463.

25. *Ibid.*

26. John B. Clark, *The Philosophy of Wealth: Economic Principles Newly Formulated* (Boston: Ginn & Co., 1886). A second edition has a preface dated Feb. 2, 1887. Clark rewrote only one paragraph (pp. 83-84) in *The Philosophy of Wealth.* The rewritten paragraph concerns "social value." The rewriting does not change its meaning noticeably.

27. Henry C. Adams, *Political Science Quarterly,* I (1886), 688.

28. John B. Clark, *The Philosophy of Wealth* (2d ed.; Boston: Ginn & Co., 1887), p. vii.

29. Joseph Dorfman, *The Economic Mind in American Civilization,* III (New York: The Viking Press, 1949), iii in the Appendix.

30. Alvin Johnson, "John Bates Clark, 1847-1938," *American Economic Review,* XXVIII (1938), 427.

31. "Marshall's Principles of Economics," *Political Science Quarterly,* VI (1891), 126-51.

CHAPTER XIII

1. For details of Wicksteed's career consult Charles Harold Herford, *Philip Henry Wicksteed: His Life and Work* (London: J. M. Dent & Sons, 1931). This volume contains an appraisal of Wicksteed's economics by Lionel Robbins (pp. 228-47), reprinted from *Economica,* X (1930), 245-58.

2. *Ibid.,* p. 229.

3. Lawrence Pearsall Jacks, *Life and Letters of Stopford Brooke* (London: John Murray, 1917), II, 359. Jacks also mentioned William Clarke, Sir William Collins, Frank Wright, Michael Davitt, Herbert Burroughs, and John Muirhead as members of the Bedford Chapel Debating Society. William Clarke gave a short account of the meetings of the "debating society over which Mr. Brooke used to preside, and at which I was a pretty regular attendant . . . " in his article on "Stopford A. Brooke," *New England Magazine,* III (October, 1890), 239. Brooke mentioned Beeton in a letter of January 29, 1886, quoted by Jacks (p. 378).

4. Herford, *Philip Henry Wicksteed,* pp. 205-06.

5. *Ibid.,* p. 206.

6. Foxwell had known H. R. Beeton as early as 1879, when Beeton had attended some extension lectures that Foxwell gave in Hampstead. See Audrey G. D. Foxwell, "Herbert Somerton Foxwell: A Portrait," *The Kress Library of Business and Economics* (Boston: Baker Library, Harvard Graduate School of Business Administration, 1939), p. 8.

7. Herford, *Philip Henry Wicksteed,* p. 207.

8. J[ames] B[onar], "Obituary: Henry Ramie Beeton," *Journal of the Royal Statistical Society,* N. S., XCVII (1934), 693-94. Beeton evidently limited his writing to three pamphlets on bimetallism that he published in the years 1894-95: (1) *A Comment upon Mr. Sellar's Essay against Bimetallism,* 1894 (7 pp.), another issue of which has the title *Mr. H. R. Beeton's Comment upon Mr. Sellar's Essay against Bimetallism and Mr. Sellar's Reply,* 1894 (10 pp.); (2) *The Case for Monetary Reform,* 1894 (48 pp.); (3) *Bimetallism: Its Advantages and What We Suffer by the Loss of it, etc.,* 1895 (24 pp.).

9. *Ibid.*

10. Herford, *Philip Henry Wicksteed,* p. 207.

11. *Ibid.*

12. Philip Henry Wicksteed, "Das Kapital: A Criticism," *Today: The Monthly Magazine of Scientific Socialism,* N. S., II (1884), 388-409. This periodical began publication in 1883; the *International Review* superseded it in 1889 but lasted for only three issues. The following reprints give easier access to this article of Wicksteed as well as to George Bernard Shaw's reply and Wicksteed's subsequent rejoinder: Appendix II of Herford's *Philip Henry Wicksteed;* the "Selected Papers and Reviews" in Philip Henry Wicksteed, *The Common Sense of Political Economy and Selected Papers and Reviews on Economic Theory,* edited with an introduction by Lionel Robbins (London: George Routledge & Sons, 1933), II, 705-33; and *Bernard Shaw & Karl Marx: A Symposium, 1884-1889* (New York: Random House, 1930), pp. 11-99. The pages cited here refer to those in *Today.*

13. *Ibid.,* p. 399.

14. *Ibid.,* p. 408.

15. See especially Henry Mayers Hyndman, "Final Futility of Final Utility," in National Liberal Club: Political and Economic Circle, *Transactions* (London: P. S. King & Son, 1895), II, 118-33, reprinted as chapter xi in Hyndman's *The Economics of Socialism* (Boston: Small, Maynard & Co., 1921).

16. Archibald Henderson, *George Bernard Shaw: His Life and Works* (Cincinnati: Stewart & Kidd Co., 1911), p. 156.

17. Edward Reynolds Pease, *The History of the Fabian Society* (London: A. C. Fifield, 1916), p. 261.

18. George Bernard Shaw, "The Jevonian Criticism of Marx (A Comment on the Rev. P. H. Wicksteed's Article)," *Today: Monthly Magazine of Scientific Socialism*, N. S., III (1885), 26. For more easily available reprints of this article see footnote 12 of this chapter.

19. *Ibid.*, p. 23.

20. *Ibid.*, p. 22.

21. *Ibid.*, p. 23.

22. *Ibid.*

23. *Ibid.*, p. 22.

24. *Ibid.*

25. *Ibid.*

26. *Ibid.*, p. 24.

27. *Ibid.*

28. *Ibid.*

29. *Ibid.*, p. 26.

30. *Ibid.*, p. 25.

31. Philip Henry Wicksteed, "The Jevonian Criticism of Marx: a Rejoinder," *Today: Monthly Magazine of Scientific Socialism*, N. S., III (1885), 177-79. For a list of reprints of Wicksteed's "Rejoinder" see footnote 12 of this chapter.

32. *Ibid.*, p. 177.

33. Herford, *Philip Henry Wicksteed*, pp. 208-09.

34. Archibald Henderson, *Bernard Shaw: Playboy and Prophet* (New York: D. Appleton and Co., 1932), p. 223.

35. Herford, *Philip Henry Wicksteed*, p. 210.

36. Henderson, *George Bernard Shaw: His Life and Works*, p. 158.

37. G. Armitage-Smith, *Syllabus of a Course of Lectures on Social and Economic Problems (Being a Discussion of Some Economic Aspects of Socialism)* (London: Co-operative Printing Society Limited, 1892), p. 9.

38. G. Armitage-Smith, *Syllabus of a Course of Twelve Lectures on the Production and Distribution of Wealth* (London: W. Bishop, 1894), pp. 5-6.

39. Pease, *The History of the Fabian Society*, pp. 28 ff.

40. Henderson, *Bernard Shaw: Playboy and Prophet*, p. 163. Edward R. Pease, who belonged to "The Hampstead Historic" puts the date at which it began as in "1885 or early in 1886" (*The History of the Fabian Society*, p. 64).

41. *Ibid.*

42. Pease, *The History of the Fabian Society*, p. 261.

43. Henderson, *Bernard Shaw: Playboy and Prophet*, p. 221 n.

44. *Pall Mall Gazette*, May 29, 1886, p. 5.

45. "Bluffing the Value Theory," *Bernard Shaw & Karl Marx: A Symposium 1884-1889*, p. 182.

46. Henderson, *George Bernard Shaw: His Life and Works*, p. 164. Henderson gives the following bibliography of articles on utility in the *Pall Mall Gazette* (*ibid.*, p. 165 n.): "Marx and Modern Socialism" (May 7, 1887), p. 3; Hyndman's reply (May 11), p. 11; Shaw's rejoinder, "Socialists at Home" (this heading doubtless a jibe of the editor) (May 12), p. 11; Hyndman's rejoinder (May 16), p. 2; Mrs. Besant's article on the same subject (May 24), p. 2.

47. *Bernard Shaw & Karl Marx: a Symposium, 1884-1889*, p. 182.

48. N. S., L (August 7, 1887), 84-86; N. S., L (August 14, 1887), 106-08; N. S., L (August 21, 1887), 107-08. Reprints of these three notices appear in *Bernard Shaw & Karl Marx: A Symposium, 1884-1889*, pp. 103-71. Pages here cited refer to the original articles.

49. *National Reformer*, N. S., I (August 7, 1887), 86.
50. *Ibid.* (August 14, 1887), 106-08.
51. *Ibid.*
52. *Ibid.* (August 21, 1887), 118.
53. Pease, *The History of the Fabian Society*, p. 261.
54. Bernard Shaw and others, *Fabian Essays* (Jubilee ed.; London: George Allen & Unwin, 1948), pp. 12-17.
55. *Report of the Fifty-eighth Meeting of the British Association for the Advancement of Science* (London: John Murray, 1889), pp. 760-63.
56. Pease, *The History of the Fabian Society*, pp. 258-59.
57. A[rthur] S[idgwick] and E[leanor] M[ildred] S[idgwick], *Henry Sidgwick: A Memoir* (London: Macmillan and Co., 1906), pp. 497-98.
58. *Fabian Essays*, Jubilee ed., p. 228.
59. G. Bernard Shaw, "The Webbs," in Sidney and Beatrice Webb, *The Truth about Soviet Russia* (New York: Longmans, Green and Co., 1942), pp. 12-13.
60. H. M. Hyndman, "The Final Futility of Final Utility," in National Liberal Club, Political Economy Circle, *Transactions* (London: P. S. King & Son, 1895), II, 118-33.
61. Henry Higgs, "Obituary: Henry Ramie Beeton," *Journal of the Royal Statistical Society*, XCVII (1934), 693; Henderson, *Bernard Shaw: Playboy and Prophet*, p. 223.
62. "The British Economic Association," *Economic Journal*, I (1891), 3.
63. *Ibid.*, p. 13.
64. *Ibid.*, p. 2.
65. C. E. Collet, "Professor Foxwell and University College," *Economic Journal*, XLVI (1936), 617.

CHAPTER XIV

1. Herford, *Philip Henry Wicksteed*, p. 211.
2. Philip Henry Wicksteed, *The Alphabet of Economic Science* (London: Macmillan and Co., 1888), p. v.
3. *Ibid.*, p. xii.
4. *Ibid.*, p. 15.
5. *Ibid.*, p. 53.
6. *Ibid.*
7. *Ibid.*, p. 54.
8. *Ibid.*, p. 40.
9. *Ibid.*, pp. 54-55.
10. *Ibid.*, pp. 15-19.
11. *Ibid.*, pp. 19-39.
12. *Ibid.*, pp. 40-41.
13. *Ibid.*, pp. 46-52.
14. *Ibid.*, pp. 58-61.
15. *Ibid.*, pp. 62-67.
16. *Ibid.*, p. 136.
17. *Academy*, XXXV (1889), 71.
18. Wicksteed, *The Alphabet of Economic Science*, pp. 68-69.
19. *Ibid.*, pp. 69-86.
20. *Ibid.*, p. 86.
21. *Ibid.*, p. 96.
22. *Ibid.*, p. 99.
23. *Ibid.*, pp. 113 ff.
24. *Ibid.*, pp. 117-24.
25. *Ibid.*, p. 127.
26. *Ibid.*, pp. 128-32.

27. Eugen von Böhm-Bawerk, "Aus der neuesten nationalökonomischen Litteratur Englands und Nordamerika's," *Jahrbücher für Nationalökonomie und Statistik*, N. F., XVIII (1889), 676.

CHAPTER XV

1. In 1877, on the occasion of the publication of the second part of Walras' *Éléments*, a review appeared in the *Zeitschrift für die gesammte Staatswissenschaft* signed "W," doubtless written by Bela Weiss (XXXIII [1877], 547-48). The reviewer dealt mostly with the mathematical method and promised to go into the subject more exhaustively elsewhere. Weiss later wrote an article "Die mathematische Methode in der Nationalökonomie" for the *Jahrbücher für Nationalökonomie und Statistik* (XXXI [1878]), which treated Jevons and Walras from the standpoint of method but not of content.

2. From the standpoint of the treatment of theoretical economics, the *Jahrbücher für Nationalökonomie und Statistik* ranks first among the German journals. Bruno Hildebrand founded it at Jena in 1863. Later, Johannes Conrad took Hildebrand's place as editor. A still older journal, the *Zeitschrift für die gesammte Staatswissenschaft* began in 1844 and had a changing board of editors. A third journal, the *Jahrbuch für Gesetzgebung, Verwaltung and Volkswirtschaft*, doubtless has a reputation as the most controversial of all the German journals, for it served as the unofficial organ for the Historical School, having as editors from 1871 to 1876, Franz Joachim Wilhelm Philipp von Holtzendorff and Lujo Brentano, and from 1880 and for a long time thereafter, Gustav Schmoller, who exercised such an influence on its character that it became known by the short title of *Schmollers Jahrbuch*. Only the *Vierteljahrschrift für Volkswirtschaft und Kulturgeschichte*, which Julius Faucher edited with the assistance of many others, including Emil Sax, failed to survive down to the present.

3. XXXV (1871), 194-205.

4. XXVIII (1872), 183-84.

5. *Jahrbücher für Nationalökonomie und Statistik*, XVIII (1872), 342-45.

6. Wilhelm Lexis, "Zur mathematisch-ökonomischen Literatur," *Jahrbücher für Nationalökonomie und Statistik*, N. F., III (1881), 427-34. Lexis' review also includes an account of Walras' "Théorie mathématique du prix des terres et de leur rachat par l'état," which has little to do with utility.

7. Pierre Victor Henri Saint-Marc, *Étude sur l'enseignement de l'économie politique dans les Universités d'Allemagne et d'Autriche* (Paris: L. Larose et Forcel, 1892), p. 68.

8. *Infra*, pp. 156 ff.

9. "Wert, Grenzwert und Preis," *Jahrbücher für Nationalökonomie und Statistik*, N. F., XIX (1889), 17-56.

10. *Jahrbücher für Nationalökonomie und Statistik*, N. F., XX (1890), 561-606.

11. "Zur Lehre vom Werth," *Zeitschrift für die gesammte Staatswissenschaft*, XLII (1886), 415-63.

12. "Ueber die wirtschaftliche Natur des Geldes mit besonderer Berücksichtigung der verschiedenen Wertbegriffe," *Zeitschrift für die gesammte Staatswissenschaft*, XLIII (1887), 417-73.

13. William Scharling, "Werttheorien und Wertgesetz," *Jahrbücher für National-ökonomie und Statistik*, N. F., XVI (1888), 417-37, 513-62.

14. "Anhang: Verzeichnis der Schriften Carl Mengers," *The Collected Works of Carl Menger* (London: The London School of Economics, 1935), IV, 328.

15. *Supra*, p. 74.

16. Friedrich von Hayek, "Carl Menger," *Economica*, N. S., I (1934), 407.

17. Pp. 3-5.

18. Carl Menger, "Nationalökonomische Literatur," *Wiener Zeitung*, 14 Jänner, 1886, pp. 3-4, and 15 Jänner, 1886, pp. 2-3.

19. Carl Menger, "Nationalökonomische Literatur in Oesterreich," *Wiener Zeitung*, 7 März, 1889, pp. 2-4, and 8 März, 1884, pp. 2-4.

CHAPTER XVI

1. Eugen von Böhm-Bawerk's *Rechte und Verhältnisse vom Standpunkte der volkswirtschaftlichen Güterlehre* (Innsbruck: Wagner, 1881) had confined its treatment to the application of marginal utility to a particular problem.

2. Wilhelm Vleugels, "Friedrich von Wieser (1851-1926)," *Encyclopedia of the Social Sciences* (New York: The Macmillan Company, 1935), XV, 419-20; Hans Mayer, "Friedrich Wieser zum Gedächtnis," *Zeitschrift für Volkswirtschaft und Sozialpolitik*, N. F., V (1927), 633-45, also in *Neue österreichische Biographie* (Vienna: Amalthea Verlag, 1929), VI, 180-98; Evald Schams, "Friedrich Freiherr von Wieser und sein Werk," *Zeitschrift für die gesamte Staatswissenschaft*, LXXXI (1926), 432-48; Oscar Morgenstern, "Friedrich von Wieser, 1851-1926," *American Economic Review*, XVII (1927), 669-74; Joseph A. Schumpeter, "Friedrich von Wieser," *Economic Journal*, XXXVII (1927), 328-30, reprinted in *Ten Great Economists: from Marx to Keynes* (New York: Oxford University Press, 1951), pp. 298-301; Friedrich A. von Hayek, "Friedrich Freiherr v. Wieser," *Jahrbücher für Nationalökonomie und Statistik*, 3ᵉ Folge, LXX (1926), 513-30, also in Friedrich Wieser, *Gesammelte Abhandlungen* (Tübingen: J. C. B. Mohr, 1929), pp. v-xxiii, also translated and abridged somewhat in Henry William Spiegel, *The Development of Economic Thought: Great Economists in Perspective* (New York: John Wiley & Sons, 1952), pp. 554-67; Wilhelm Vleugels, "Friedrich Wieser (1851-1926)," *Kölner Vierteljahrshefte für Soziologie*, VI (1927), 213-16; L[udwig] E[lster], "Friedrich Wieser," *Handwörterbuch der Staatswissenschaften* (4ᵉ Aufl.; Jena: Gustav Fischer, 1928), VIII, 1048-49.

3. Oscar Morgenstern, "Friedrich von Wieser, 1851-1926," *American Economic Review*, XVII (1927), 669.

4. *Neue österreichische Biographie* (Vienna: Wiener Drucke, 1923), I, 84-92. Wieser gave other biographical incidents in "Arma virumque cano," *Festschrift zur Hundertjahrfeier des Schottengymnasiums* (Vienna, 1907), and in Friedrich von Wieser, *Das Gesetz der Macht* (Vienna: Julius Springer, 1926), p. v.

5. Friedrich A. von Hayek, "Friedrich Freiherr von Wieser," in Wieser, *Gesammelte Abhandlungen*, p. xi.

6. Wieser, *Gesammelte Abhandlungen*, pp. 377-404.

7. Vienna: Alfred Hölder, 1884.

8. H. Dietzel, *Jahrbücher für Nationalökonomie und Statistik*, N. F., XI (1885), 161-62; A. E. F. Schäffle, *Zeitschrift für die gesammte Staatswissenschaft*, XLI (1885), 450-54.

9. Wieser, *Über den Ursprung und die Hauptgesetze des wirtschaftlichen Werthes*, p. 128.

10. At least Wilhelm Lexis held the opinion that Wieser translated Jevons' "final degree of utility" into Grenznutzen (*Jahrbuch für Gesetzgebung, Verwaltung und Volkswirtschaft im Deutschen Reich*, XIV [1890], 290).

11. Friedrich von Wieser, *Natural Value*, ed. William Smart, trans. Christian A. Malloch (London: Macmillan and Co., 1893), p. 40. This is a translation of *Der natürliche Werth* (Vienna: Alfred Hölder, 1889), of which Wieser read the proofs. Unless otherwise noted page references are to the English translation.

12. *Ibid.*

13. *Jahrbuch für Gesetzgebung, Verwaltung und Volkswirtschaft*, XIII (1889), 1488-90.

14. *Journal des économistes*, 4ᵉ Sér., XLVI (1899), 282-86.

15. *Political Science Quarterly*, IV (1889), 681-84. The following notes and reviews appeared after the 1894 translation: *Political Science Quarterly*, IX (1894), 179; W. K. Firminger, *Economic Review*, V (1895), 423-27; A. C. Miller, *Journal of Political Economy*, II (1894), 308-09; and Arthur T. Hadley, "Recent Tendencies in

Economic Literature," *Yale Review,* III (1894), 252-53; David I. Green, "Wieser's Natural Value," *Annals of the American Academy of Political and Social Science,* V (1895), 512-30; F. Y. Edgeworth, *Economic Journal,* IV (1894), 279-85; *Westminister Review,* CXLI (1894), 211-12; and *Nation,* LVIII (1894), 448.

16. Wieser, *Natural Value,* pp. xxxii ff.
17. *Ibid.,* p. xxxiii.
18. *Ibid.,* pp. xxxiii, xxxv.
19. *Ibid.,* p. xxxiii.
20. *Ibid.,* p. xxxiv.
21. George J. Stigler reviewed and evaluated the idea of imputation in his *Production and Distribution Theories: The Formative Period* (New York: The Macmillan Company, 1941). "Imputation" *(Zurechnung)* is a subject connected with, but not directly concerned with, the ideas of utility and value.
22. Wieser, *Natural Value,* p. 10.
23. *Ibid.,* pp. 10-11.
24. *Ibid.,* p. 11.
25. *Ibid.,* p. 15.
26. *Ibid.*
27. *Ibid.,* p. 19 n.
28. *Ibid.,* p. 25.
29. *Ibid.,* p. 31.
30. *Ibid.,* pp. 32-33.
31. *Ibid.,* p. 33.
32. Friedrich von Hayek wrote that Wieser "calls 'natural value' that value which would prevail in a communist society, assuming complete absence of exchange and a central authority directing the entire economic process" (Spiegel, *The Development of Economic Thought,* p. 561). Surely Wieser did not intend to rule out exchange of all kinds.
33. Wieser, *Natural Value,* p. 60.
34. *Ibid.*
35. *Ibid.,* p. 61.
36. *Ibid.,* p. 61 n.
37. *Ibid.,* pp. 198-99.
38. "The Austrian School and the Theory of Value," *Economic Journal,* I (1891), 108-21; "The Theory of Value (a Reply to Professor Macvane)," *Annals of the American Academy of Political and Social Science,* II (1891), 600-28.
39. Spiegel, *The Development of Economic Thought,* p. 562.

CHAPTER XVII

1. Joseph A. Schumpeter, a great admirer of Böhm-Bawerk, wrote more about him than anyone else, much of it in the form of a tribute. He wrote his biography for the *Neue österreichische Biographie* (Vienna: Amalthea Verlag, 1929), II, 63-80, which Henry William Spiegel abridged and translated as part (pp. 569-79) of *The Development of Economic Thought* (New York: John Wiley & Sons, 1952). Schumpeter also wrote the longer and more eulogistic "Das wissenschaftliche Lebenswerk Eugen von Böhm-Bawerk" *(Zeitschrift für Volkswirtschaft, Sozialpolitik und Verwaltung,* XXIII [1914], 454-528), which, after its translation and abridgment, he published in *Ten Great Economists: from Marx to Keynes* ([London: George Allen & Unwin, 1952], pp. 143-90). Carl Menger and Friedrich von Wieser both lived to prepare obituaries of Böhm-Bawerk: Carl Menger in the *Almanach der Wiener Akademie der Wissenschaften* (1915); Friedrich von Wieser in the supplemented edition of *Palgrave's Dictionary of Political Economy* ([London: Macmillan and Co., 1925], I, 825-26). J. Bonar prepared the obituary notice for the *Economic Journal* (XXIV [1914], 648-50).
2. Innsbruck: Wagner, 1881. Reprinted in *Gesammelte Schriften von Eugen von*

Böhm-Bawerk, ed. Franz X. Weiss (Vienna: Hölder-Pichler-Tempsky A. G., 1924), I, 1-126.

3. Emil Struck published the most complete review in the *Jahrbuch für Gesetzgebung, Verwaltung und Volkswirtschaft im Deutschen Reich* (V [1881], 1290-1301). Heinrich Dietzel wrote the review for the *Zeitschrift für die gesammte Staatswissenschaft* (XXXVIII [1882], 771-73), and F. Kleinwächter for the *Jahrbücher für Nationalökonomie und Statistik* (N. F., IV [1882], 119-20).

4. Böhm-Bawerk, *Rechte und Verhältnisse.* Reprint in *Gesammelte Schriften,* I, 125-26.

5. *Kapital und Kapitalzins, Erste Abtheilung, Geschichte und Kritik der Kapitalzins-Theorieen* (Innsbruck: Wagner, 1884). English translation, *Capital and Interest, a Critical History of Economical Theory* (London: Macmillan and Co., 1890).

6. See reviews by Otto Pringsheim in *Jahrbuch für Gesetzgebung, Verwaltung und Volkswirtschaft im Deutschen Reich* (IX [1885], 314-17); Eduard Wiss in *Vierteljahrschrift für Volkswirtschaft, Politik und Kulturgeschichte* (LXXXVII [1885], 108-12); and R. F[riedberg]. in *Jahrbücher für Nationalökonomie und Statistik* (N. F., XII [1886], 77).

7. "Grundzüge der Theorie des wirtschaftlichen Güterwerts," *Jahrbücher für Nationalökonomie und Statistik,* N. F., XIII (1886), 1-82, 477-541. Reprinted in 1932 as "No. 11 in Series of Reprints of Scarce Tracts in Economic and Political Science" by the London School of Economics and Political Science.

8. Eugen von Böhm-Bawerk, *Kapital und Kapitalzins, Zweite Abtheilung, Positive Theorie des Capitals* (Innsbruck: Wagner, 1889). William Smart, the friend of marginal utility in England in the early nineties, had this volume translated into English in 1891, with the translated title, *The Positive Theory of Capital.* Subsequent citations and quotations come from this English translation. A French translation appeared in 1929.

9. *Ibid.,* p. 165.
10. *Ibid.,* p. 140.
11. *Ibid.,* p. 142.
12. *Ibid.,* p. 144.
13. *Ibid.,* p. 172.
14. *Ibid.,* p. 161.
15. *Ibid.,* p. 189.
16. *Ibid.*
17. *Ibid.*
18. *Ibid.,* p. 193.
19. *Ibid.,* p. 209.
20. *Ibid.,* p. 210.
21. *Ibid.*

CHAPTER XVIII

1. This count excludes five men who resided and taught during this time in the Austro-Hungarian capital, but who, for various reasons ought not to be included in the Vienna School. Lorenz von Stein served at the university from 1855 to 1885, but his work represents the economics of the earlier period. Both Lujo Brentano, who replaced Stein in 1888 but who remained for only a year, and August von Miaskowski, who succeeded Brentano in 1889, were from outside the influences of Menger and clearly do not belong to the Vienna School. Hermann Blodig, *Privatdozent der österreichischen Finanzgesetzkunde,* and Karl Theodor von Inama-Sternegg, *Honorar Professor der Staatswissenschaft,* taught at the university, but on the borderline of economics.

2. The two of the nine who did not serve the government in some capacity were Johann von Komorzynski (except that the 1911 edition of *Wer ist's* lists him as "Regierungsrat") and Emil Sax.

NOTES ON PP. 161-164

3. Carl Menger did not belong, nor did Johann von Komorzynski and Robert Zuckerkandl. Emil Sax, Gustav Gross, Victor Mataja, Richard Lieben, and Rudolf Auspitz belonged but did not take an active part in the organization. Wieser, Böhm-Bawerk, Robert Meyer, and Eugen Philippovich von Philippsberg were the more active members of the organization. This was the group that had as its official organ the *Zeitschrift für Volkswirtschaft, Socialpolitik und Verwaltung* (Hans Patzauer, "Chronik der Gesellschaft österreichischer Volkswirte [1875-1915]," Gesellschaft österreichischer Volkswirte, *Jahrbuch 1915* [Vienna: Manz, 1915], 160-69).

4. The degrees taken or the positions held are at the University of Vienna unless otherwise stipulated.

5. Rudolf Auspitz studied natural science in Vienna, Berlin, and Heidelberg. Richard Lieben followed a course in mathematics at the Polytechnic School in Vienna, and mathematics and engineering at Karlsruhe in 1860-62. Later he undertook further mathematical study with the physiologist, Ernst Fleischl. Otto Weinberger wrote a long interpretive article, "Rudolf Auspitz und Richard Lieben: ein Beitrag zur Geschichte der mathematischen Methode in der Volkswirtschaftslehre" (*Zeitschrift für die gesamte Staatswissenschaft*, XCI [1931], 457-92) of a kind denied to all the other minor writers of the School of Vienna.

6. The other Viennese economists obtained what mathematical preparation they had in the *Gymnasium*, a preparation which did not remain with them after their university years in a usable form. Several of them expressed a distaste for the use of mathematics in connection with economics.

7. Rudolf Auspitz founded one of the first sugar refineries in Austria, but Lieben played the more prominent role in business and finance. The marriage of Rudolf Auspitz to the sister of Richard Lieben gave them a family connection similar to the one of Böhm-Bawerk and Wieser.

8. For example, Gross was the only one of the group that Lewis H. Haney omitted in his *History of Economic Thought* (3d ed.; New York: The Macmillan Company, 1936), pp. 622-23.

9. Leipzig: Duncker & Humblot, 1884. Earlier he had published *Die Staatssubventionen für Privatbahnen* (Vienna: Alfred Hölder, 1882), an article, "Die Zeit in der Volkswirtschaft" (*Zeitschrift für die gesammte Staatswissenschaft*, XXXIX [1883], 126-65), and several book reviews in the *Jahrbücher für Nationalökonomie und Statistik* (N. F., VI [1883], 164-65, 166, 175-76, 186; N. F., VIII [1884], 272-73), none of which were in the spirit of the Marginal Utility School.

10. *Ibid.*, p. 173. He quoted Menger in a quite appropriate place in connection with an attempt to make clear the determination of price in the market. None of his discussion, however, bears any similarity to Menger's analysis; no one could tell from Gross's explanation that he had ever read Menger. He said that a consumer buys the goods in order to satisfy his needs, that the consumer's demand depends on the *"Heftigkeit"* of his needs and on the consumer's ability to pay. Some goods have so much *"Heftigkeit"* that ability to pay plays a minor part, as, for example, with needs the satisfaction of which provides for the physical existense of man. Therefore, if the entrepreneur varies the prices of these necessities, a particular and peculiar train of circumstances begins.

11. XX (1884), 541-49.

12. Gustav Gross, *Karl Marx: eine Studie* (Leipzig: Duncker & Humblot, 1885).

13. *Ibid.*, pp. 47 ff.

14. *Ibid.*, p. 78.

15. Leipzig: Duncker & Humblot, 1888.

16. Gustav Gross wrote very little on economics after 1888, mainly because his principal activities became political. He continued to teach at the University of Vienna until 1920 but became in 1889 a member of the *Reichsrat* and was in 1917-18 the last president of this same body. He contributed to the *Zeitschrift für Volkswirtschaft, Socialpolitik und Verwaltung* (I [1892], 279-87, and IV [1895], 177-81) as well as to the *Jahrbücher für Nationalökonomie und Statistik* (N. F., XVII [1888], 440-41;

N. F., XVIII [1889], 227-30; and N. F., XXI [1890], 189-92). Gross ceased to write on the subject of economics in 1895.

17. Hans Mayer, ed., *Hundert Jahre österreichischer Wirtschaftsentwicklung, 1848-1948* (Vienna: Springer-Verlag, 1949), p. 631.

18. *Infra*, pp. 173-75.

19. He was the brother of Emilie Mataja (pseud., "Emil Marriot"), a novelist, and of Heinrich Mataja, a Christian Socialist who took an active part in Austrian politics.

20. Victor Mataja, *Der Unternehmergewinn: ein Beitrag zur Lehre von der Gütervertheilung in der Volkswirtschaft* (Vienna: Alfred Hölder, 1884).

21. *Infra*, pp. 173-75.

22. Victor Mataja, *Die Reklame: eine Untersuchung über Ankündigungswesen und Werbetätigkeit im Geschäftsleben* (Leipzig: Duncker & Humblot, 1910).

23. For a bibliography of the writings of Victor Mataja to 1910 see the *Handwörterbuch der Staatswissenschaften* (3e Aufl.; Jena: Gustav Fischer, 1910), VI, 622-23. The only book he published between 1910 and his death in 1933 was the *Lehrbuch der Volkswirtschaftspolitik* (Vienna: Österreichische Staatsdruckerei, 1931), which he edited and to which he contributed the introduction and the section on population. The main articles on economics that he wrote during these last years were for the *Handwörterbuch der Staatswissenschaften*, both for the latter volumes of the third and for the fourth editions.

24. Robert Meyer, "Die zunehmende Mannigfaltigkeit der Consumtion," *Zeitschrift für Volkswirtschaft, Socialpolitik und Verwaltung*, II (1893), 385-418.

25. Earlier he had written *Die Principien der gerechten Besteuerung in der neueren Finanzwissenschaft* (Berlin: Wilhelm Hertz, 1884) and *Das Wesen des Einkommens: eine volkswirthschaftliche Untersuchung nebst einem Anhange* (Berlin, Wilhelm Hertz, 1887). In the second of these he showed a familiarity with the names of both the major and minor writers of the Marginal Utility School, but he did not use their central ideas in his book.

26. *Infra*, pp. 173-75.

27. His only later book was *Das Zeitverhältnis zwischen der Steuer und dem Einkommen und seinen Theilen: ein Beitrag zum österreichischen Steuerrechte und zur Lehre vom Einkommen* (Vienna: Manz, 1901). He published, in addition, book reviews in the *Zeitschrift für Volkswirtschaft, Socialpolitik und Verwaltung*: II (1893), 351-59; III (1894), 170-72, 471-75, and 629; IV (1895), 181-83; VI (1897), 322-25; and in the *Jahrbücher für Nationalökonomie und Statistik*; 3e Folge, IX (1895), 441-44; and 3e Folge, XIII (1897), 447-51. He also wrote a long article, "Die ersten Ergebnisse der Personaleinkommensteuer in Österreich," in the *Zeitschrift für Volkswirtschaft, Socialpolitik und Verwaltung*, VIII (1899), 23-83. He served as an editor of this journal from 1911 to 1914. He contributed the article "Begriff und Einteilung des Einkommens" to the *Handwörterbuch der Staatswissenschaften*, 2e Aufl., III (1900), 347-80.

28. Vienna: Manz, 1889.

29. *Zeitschrift für die gesamte Staatswissenschaft*, XLVI (1890), 596.

30. Neither Böhm-Bawerk nor Henri St.-Marc (*Revue d'économie politique*, IV [1890], 216-19), who also reviewed the book, agreed with Komorzynski's conclusions.

31. Spann, *The History of Economics*, pp. 263-64.

32. He dedicated his only subsequent book, *Die Nationalökonomische Lehre vom Credit* (Innsbruck: Wagner, 1903. 2e Aufl.; Innsbruck: Wagner, 1909), to Böhm-Bawerk. In it he only incidentally mentioned his earlier statement of opinion on value theory (1e Aufl., pp. 248-49). His principal articles in the *Zeitschrift für Volkswirtschaft, Socialpolitik und Verwaltung*, III (1894), 27-62; VI (1897), 242-99; and XIII (1904), 537-45, show almost no concern with marginal utility.

33. Leipzig: Duncker & Humblot, 1889.

34. *Political Science Quarterly*, V (1890), 171.

35. For a bibliography of his writings see *Handwörterbuch der Staatswissenschaften*,

3ᵉ Aufl.; VIII (1911), 1084, and Harold E. Batson, *A Select Bibliography of Modern Economic Theory, 1870-1929* (London: George Routledge & Sons, 1930), pp. 207-08. Two other books (mimeographed) not in the above bibliographies are *Volkswirtschaftslehre nach den Vorlesungen des Professor Dr. Zuckerkandl* (Prague, 1899), and *Volkswirtschafts-Politik nach den Vorlesungen des Prof. Dr. Zuckerkandl* (Prague, 1900).

36. Robert Zuckerkandl, "Die klassische Werttheorie und die Theorie vom Grenznutzen," *Jahrbücher für Nationalökonomie und Statistik*, N.F., XXI (1890), 509-19.

37. *Zeitschrift für Volkswirtschaft, Socialpolitik und Verwaltung*, I (1892), 371-72.

38. *Volkswirtschaftslehre nach den Vorlesungen des Professor Dr. Zuckerkandl*, pp. 252 ff.

39. *Zeitschrift für Volkswirtschaft, Sozialpolitik und Verwaltung*, XIX (1910), 251-64.

40. 3ᵉ Aufl., VI (1910), 1130-54.

41. Philippovich published a number of books during the latter part of the eighties, but only one of them has a general tone that might lead to the expectation of some expression of opinion on marginal utility. All the others have a more practical and descriptive outlook. His *Über Aufgabe und Methode der politischen Ökonomie* (Freiburg: J. C. B. Mohr, 1886), the inaugural lecture he delivered at Freiburg, could well contain references to utility. We ought to foresee, however, that Philippovich would mention Menger's *Untersuchungen* but not his *Grundsätze*. For a bibliography of his writings see Batson, *A Select Bibliography of Modern Economic Theory, 1870-1929*, pp. 196-200, or *Handwörterbuch der Staatswissenschaften*, 3ᵉ Aufl., VI, 1038.

42. Eugen von Philippovich, "Dr. Eugen von Böhm-Bawerk," *Zeitschrift für Volkswirtschaft, Sozialpolitik und Verwaltung*, XXIII (1914), 441-42.

43. He prepared a review of both volumes for the *Zeitschrift für die gesamte Staatswissenschaft*, XLV (1889), 568-74.

44. *Band I: Allgemeine Volkswirtschaftslehre* (Freiburg i. B. und Leipzig: J. C. B. Mohr, 1893).

45. Ludwig Elster, *Jahrbücher für Nationalökonomie und Statistik*, 3ᵉ Folge, VIII (1894), 449-53; August von Miaskowski, *Jahrbuch für Gesetzgebung, Verwaltung und Volkswirtschaft im Deutschen Reich*, XVII (1893), 919-22; and A. E. F. Schäffle, *Zeitschrift für die gesamte Staatswissenschaft*, XLIX (1893), 544-49. In contrast the non-German journals specifically approved the introduction of the idea of marginal utility into a general textbook (W. Caldwell, *Journal of Political Economy* [I (1893), 302-07]; H. R. Seager, *Annals of the American Academy of Political and Social Science*, IV [1893-94], 168-79; and Pierre Victor Henri Saint-Marc, *Revue d'économie politique*, VII [1893], 166-67).

46. For the most complete bibliography see the *Handwörterbuch der Staatswissenschaften*, 3ᵉ Aufl., VII, 191.

47. *Das Wesen und die Aufgaben der Nationalökonomie: ein Beitrag zu den Grundproblemen dieser Wissenschaft* (Vienna: Alfred Hölder, 1884).

48. *Das Wesen und die Aufgaben der Nationalökonomie* was reviewed at length by two German journals which examined it solely and properly as a part of the methodological dispute of the times. See Wilhelm Hasbach, "Ein Beitrag zur Methodologie der Nationalökonomie," *Jahrbuch für Gesetzgebung, Verwaltung und Volkswirtschaft im Deutschen Reich*, IX (1885), 545-57; and Heinrich Dietzel, *Jahrbücher für Nationalökonomie und Statistik*, N. F., VIII (1884), 498-500.

49. Vienna: Alfred Hölder, 1887.

50. Alexander Gray, *The Development of Economic Doctrine: An Introductory Study* (New York: Longmans, Green and Co., 1931), pp. 361-62.

51. Gustav Schmoller gave the book a respectful if unfavorable review (*Jahrbuch für Gesetzgebung, Verwaltung und Volkswirtschaft im Deutschen Reich*, XII [1888], 729-33. Böhm-Bawerk praised it generally but found fault with particular parts and judged its style "*schwer*" (*Zeitschrift für die gesamte Staatswissenschaft*, XLIV [1888],

157-64). An unsigned review gave it the least attention (*Vierteljahrschrift für Volkswirtschaft, Politik und Kulturgeschichte*, XCVI [1887], 259-70). Edmund James probably was the only reviewer outside Germany (*Political Science Quarterly*, V [1890], 166-69).

52. In Boccardo's *Biblioteca dell' economista*, 4ᵃ Ser.

53. Erwin von Beckerath, "Ein Nachruf auf Emil Sax," *Zeitschrift für Nationalökonomie*, I (1930), 348.

54. Wieser probably made the most use of Sax's *Grundlegung* when he employed a good part of the central idea with appropriate acknowledgments in Part II of *Der Natürliche Werth*.

55. Sax, *Grundlegung der theoretischen Staatswirtschaft*, p. 253.

56. *Ibid.*, p. 256.

57. Leipzig: Duncker & Humblot, 1889.

58. Emil Sax, "Die Progessivsteuer," *Zeitschrift für Volkswirtschaft, Socialpolitik und Verwaltung*, I (1892), 43-101.

59. Leipzig: Duncker & Humblot, 1889. The authors published separately in January, 1887, the first chapter of this book under the title *Zur Theorie des Preises* (Leipzig: Duncker & Humblot, 1887). Michael Hainish reviewed this initial publication in the *Jahrbuch für Gesetzgebung, Verwaltung und Volkswirtschaft im Deutschen Reich*, XI (1887), 727.

60. Otto Weinberger, "Rudolf Auspitz und Richard Lieben," *Zeitschrift für die gesamte Staatswissenschaft*, XCI (1931), 460-63.

61. Auspitz and Lieben, *Untersuchungen über die Theorie des Preises*, p. xxvi.

62. Its length, oversize pages, wide margins, large well-leaded type, good quality of heavy paper, cloth binding, and ninety carefully prepared diagrams, mostly in red and black, contrast with the similar aspects of the usual book on economics in this period, and reflect the superior business and social position of the authors.

63. Auspitz and Lieben, *Untersuchungen über die Theorie des Preises*, p. 459.

64. Auspitz and Lieben evidently had not known of F. Y. Edgeworth, who had related the utility of a good not only to the quantity of that particular good but to the quantity of other goods. At least they never mentioned him. And certainly they went far beyond Edgeworth. Neither Edgeworth nor Auspitz and Lieben gained acceptance for their increased generality.

65. Auspitz and Lieben, *Untersuchungen über die Theorie des Preises*, chap. ii.

66. *Ibid.*, p. 10.

67. *Ibid.*, p. 113.

68. *Ibid.*, pp. 137-97.

69. *Ibid.*, p. 149.

70. Léon Walras, "Observations sur le principe de la théorie du prix de MM. Auspitz et Lieben," *Revue d'économie politique*, IV (1890), 320-23.

71. *Revue d'économie politique*, IV (1890), 599-605.

72. "La teoria dei prezzi dei signori *Auspitz e Lieben* e le osservazioni del professore *Walras*," *Giornale degli economisti*, 2ᵃ Ser., IV (1892), 201-39. He returned to the same subject in the August issue of the same year with "Ancora della *Theorie des Preises* dei signori *Auspitz e Lieben*," p. 168.

73. *Giornale degli economisti*, 2ᵃ Ser., IV (1892), 390.

74. *Recherches sur la théorie du prix*, 2 vols. (Paris: M. Giard & É. Brière, 1914). The translation contains a few clearly indicated alterations, and has the diagrams removed from the body of the text and placed in the accompanying album (Vol. II). The success of the translation evidently suffered from the dislocations brought about by World War I.

75. *American Economic Review*, V (1915), 107-08.

76. Published in *Transactions of the Connecticut Academy of Arts and Sciences*, IX (1892), 2-124.

77. "Rudolf Auspitz, 1837-1906," *Encyclopaedia of the Social Sciences*, II, 317.

78. T. W. Hutchison, *A Review of Economic Doctrines, 1870-1929* (Oxford: Clarendon Press, 1953), p. 189.

CHAPTER XIX

1. Vienna. Universität. Akademischer Senate. *Geschichte der Wiener Universität von 1848 bis 1898* (Vienna: Alfred Hölder, 1898), p. 404. Medicine came second, philosophy third, and theology fourth.

2. *Ibid.*, pp. 136-37.

3. Vienna. Universität. *Öffentliche Vorlesungen an der k. k. Universität zu Wien* (Vienna: aus der k. k. Hof- und Staatsdruckerei). All the issues of this publication from 1879 to 1890 were inspected except for the winter semesters of 1881-82 and 1883-84.

4. The University of Vienna was the largest of the Austrian universities. Next in size came the University of Prague with about half the enrollment at Vienna. Graz was half as large as Prague, and Innsbruck half as large as Graz. Each of the other three, Czernovitz, Cracow, and Lemberg, had fewer students than Graz.

5. Ernest Mahaim, "L'Enseignement de l'économie politique à l'université de Vienne," *Revue de Belgique*, LXI (1889), 360.

6. H. R. Seager, "Economics at Berlin and Vienna," *Journal of Political Economy*, I (1893), 239.

7. Pierre Victor Henri Saint-Marc, *Étude sur l'enseignement de l'économie politique dans les universitées d'Allemagne et d'Autriche* (Paris: L. Larose et Forcel, 1892), p. 74.

8. *Op. cit.*, p. 360.

9. *Ibid.*, p. 363.

10. *Op. cit.*, p. 257.

11. M. Epstein, "Gustav Schmoller," *Economic Journal*, XXVII (1917), 437.

CHAPTER XX

1. Stuttgart: Ferdinand Enke, 1881.

2. "Zur mathematisch-ökonomischen Literatur," *Jahrbücher für Nationalökonomie und Statistik*, N. F., III (1881), 427-34.

3. Léon Walras, *Théorie mathématique de la richesse sociale* (Lausanne: Corbaz & Cie, 1883).

4. *Journal des économistes*, 4e Sér., XXIII (1883), 444-48.

5. *Supra*, pp. 71-72.

6. Léon Walras, "Un Économiste inconnu: Hermann-Henri Gossen," *Journal des économistes*, 4e Sér., XXX (1885), 68-90.

7. *Ibid.*, p. 74.

8. *Ibid.*, p. 75.

9. *Ibid.*, p. 76.

10. *Ibid.*, p. 79.

11. Lausanne: Corbaz & Cie, 1886.

12. Étienne Antonelli, "Léon Walras et Carl Menger à travers leur correspondance," *Économie appliquée*, VI (1953), 269-87.

13. Walras, *Théorie de la monnaie*, p. vi. Böhm-Bawerk sent only the first of the two parts in which he published the article, since Walras refers to the complimentary words at the article's end. Böhm-Bawerk published the part that has the complimentary closing remarks in the third issue of the *Jahrbücher für Nationalökonomie und Statistik* for 1886 and the second part in the last issue of the same year.

14. *Ibid.*, pp. v-xii.

15. *Ibid.*, p. vii n.

16. *Ibid.*, pp. vii-ix.

17. *Ibid.*, p. x.

18. *Ibid.*, p. 29.
19. *Ibid., Planche* I.
20. Quoted by William Jaffé in Walras, *Éléments*, trans. Jaffé, p. 568.
21. Walras, *Théorie de la monnaie*, p. 30.
22. *Supra*, p. 52.
23. Walras, *Théorie de la monnaie*, p. 35.
24. "Des fonctions et de leur representation géométrique: théorie mathématique de la chute des corps," *Éléments*, 2ᵉ éd., pp. 3-21. Philip Wicksteed's *Alphabet of Economic Science* contained the first attempt to teach mathematics to economists in order to enable them to understand economic theory. Walras dropped this introduction in the later editions when the book no longer served as a text.
25. Walras, *Éléments*, 2ᵉ éd., pp. vii-ix, xviii-xxiv.
26. *Ibid.*, pp. 188-92.
27. *Ibid.*, p. x.
28. Walras, *Éléments*, 1ᵉʳᵉ éd., p. 87.
29. Walras, *Éléments*, 2ᵉ éd., pp. 106-09.
30. *Ibid.*, pp. 105-06.
31. *Ibid.*, pp. 569-70.
32. Walras, *Éléments*, 1ᵉʳᵉ éd., p. 82.
33. Walras, *Éléments*, 2ᵉ éd., p. 100.
34. Walras, *Éléments*, 1ᵉʳᵉ éd., p. 99.
35. Walras, *Éléments*, 2ᵉ éd., p. 121.
36. Walras, *Éléments*, 2ᵉ éd., pp. 125, 138, and 256.

CHAPTER XXI

1. Charles Gide, "La Théorie de l'économie politique de M. Stanley Jevons," *Journal des économistes*, 4ᵉ Sér., XVI (1881), 179-91.
2. *Ibid.*, p. 180.
3. *Ibid.*, p. 181.
4. *Ibid.*, pp. 186-87.
5. *Ibid.*, p. 187.
6. Charles Gide, *Principes d'économie politique* (Paris: L. Larose et Forcel, 1884).
7. "Correspondance: La Valeur et le capital," *Journal des économistes*, 4ᵉ Sér., XVI (1881), 451-54.
8. Marcel Mongin, "Des éléments de la valeur," *Journal des économistes*, 4ᵉ Ser., XIX (1882), 369-80.
9. *Ibid.*, p. 369.
10. E. Martineau, "Correspondance: Qu-est-ce que la richesse?" *Journal des économistes*, 4ᵉ Sér., XX (1882), 239-44.
11. Marcel Mongin, "Correspondance: La Définition de la richesse," *Journal des économistes*, 4ᵉ Sér., XXI (1883), 276-83.
12. If the neglect of the Marginal Utility School at this time needed further confirmation it could be found in the articles of Beaurin-Gressier, "Correspondance: De la théorie de la valeur" (*Journal des économistes*, 4ᵉ Sér., XXI [1883], 445-49), of Jean Gustave Courcelle-Seneuil, "Richesses et valeur" (*Journal des économistes*, 4ᵉ Sér., XXII [1883], 5-17), and of Adolphe Houdard, "Théorie générale de la valeur" (*Journal des économistes*, 4ᵉ Sér., XXVII [1884], 321-26).
13. Hippolyte Dabos, *Le Dernier mot sur une controverse relative à la notion de valeur: Véritable théorie de la valeur* (Paris: Guillaumin et Cie, 1886). He had published an earlier pamphlet, *La Théorie de la valeur: Étude économique sur la notion de valeur: Qu'est-ce que la valeur?* (Paris: Guillaumin et Cie, 1879). Also he had followed the controversy in the *Journal des économistes* and had contributed "Correspondance: Examen d'une opinion économique relative à la valeur" (*Journal des économistes*, 4ᵉ Sér., XXV [1884], 98-107).

14. *Ibid.*, p. 13.
15. *Ibid.*, pp. 12-14.
16. *Journal des économistes,* 4ᵉ Sér., XXXVIII (1887), 450-53.
17. Hippolyte Dabos, "Correspondance: La Théorie de la valeur.—Réponse à M. Houdard," *Journal des économistes,* 4ᵉ Sér., XL (1887), 398-408.
18. Adolphe Houdard, "Correspondance: Le Théorie de la valeur.—I. Réponse à M. H. Dabos," *Journal des économistes,* 4ᵉ Sér., XLII (1888), 247-51.
19. Th. Mannekin, "Correspondance: La Théorie de la valeur.—Observations de M. Th. Mannequin," *Journal des économistes,* 4ᵉ Sér., XLII (1888), 99-101; Th. Mannequin, "Correspondance: La Théorie de la valeur," *Journal des économistes,* 4ᵉ Sér., XLII (1888), 404-06.
20. Hippolyte Dabos, "Correspondance: La Théorie de la valeur.—II. Réponse de M. Dabos aux observations de M. Th. Mannequin sur ma 'Théorie de la valeur'," *Journal des économistes,* 4ᵉ Sér., XLII (1888), 251-54.
21. Émile Laveleye, discussed in the next chapter, wrote in French, but lived in Belgium.

CHAPTER XXII

1. Brussels: Muquardt, 1881. 2ᵉ éd., 1883, 3ᵉ éd., 1885, 19ᵉ éd., 1896.
2. A Russian translation came out in 1882, an English translation in 1884 (Émile de Laveleye, *The Socialism of Today,* trans. Goddard H. Orpen [London: Field and Tuer, 1884]), and a German translation also in 1884 (*Die socialen Parteien der Gegenwort,* trans. Meinhard Eheberg [Tübingen: H. Laupp, 1884]).
3. Laveleye, *The Socialism of Today,* p. 32.
4. *Ibid.*, p. 34.
5. *Ibid.*, p. 36.
6. *Ibid.*
7. Emile de Laveleye, *Éléments d'économie politique* (2ᵉ éd.; Paris: Libraire Hachette, 1884), pp. 28-29.
8. *Ibid.*, p. iv.

CHAPTER XXIII

1. *Supra,* p. 16.
2. *Compte-rendu des séances et travaux de l'académie des sciences morales et politiques,* CI (1874), 117-20.
3. *Ibid.*, p. 117.
4. *Ibid.*, p. 119.
5. Walras, *Éléments,* 2ᵉ éd., p. xix.
6. Émile Levasseur, *Elements of Political Economy,* trans. Theodore Marburg (New York: The Macmillan Company, 1905).
7. Émile Levasseur, "Aperçu de l'évolution des doctrines économiques et socialistes en France sous la troisième république," *Comte-rendu des séances et travaux de l'académie des sciences morales et politiques,* CLXV (1906), 457-512, 577-602.
8. Firmin Oulès, *L'École de Lausanne* (Paris: Librairie Dalloz, 1950), p. 133.
9. Paris: Guillaumin, 1851, 2ᵉ éd.; Paris: Fischbacher, 1892.
10. 4ᵉ Sér., XLVI (1889), 282-92.
11. *Ibid.*, p. 283.
12. *Ibid.*, p. 285.
13. *Ibid.*, p. 286.
14. 5ᵉ Sér., I (1890), 98-114.
15. *Ibid.*, p. 108.
16. *Ibid.*, p. 109.
17. *Ibid.*, p. 110.
18. *Ibid.*, pp. 111-12.

CHAPTER XXIV

1. In France the *Journal des économistes* held first place among the economic journals of its time. It began as a monthly in 1842 and lived nearly a century, discontinuing publication in the early part of the nineteen-forties. It did not revive after the war. Joseph Garnier served as editor-in-chief from 1866 to 1881, and Gustave de Molinari held the same position from 1881 to 1909. Its list of contributors includes most of the important names in French economics.

A slightly older publication, the *Compte-rendu des séances et travaux de l'académie des sciences morales et politiques*, which began publication in 1840 and which continued until 1938, included a good many papers on economics, but, of course, published in other fields of the social sciences as well. The *Académie* represented the most conservative group among the French economists.

Paul Leroy-Beaulieu edited the *Économiste français* from its beginning in 1873 until his death in 1916. The journal itself continued publication until November, 1938. It began in frank imitation of the London *Economist* and, like the English journal, published from time to time articles and reviews of general theoretical economic interest.

The *Revue d'économie politique* was started toward the end of the period considered here (1887), and introduced a new note into French economic journals. The committee of editors included Charles Gide, Alfred Jourdan, Edmond Villey, and Léon Duguit. At present, it ranks as the oldest of the French publications in economics.

2. Charles Letort, "De l'application des mathématiques à l'étude de l'économie politique," *Économiste français*, 31 Octobre 1874, pp. 540-41.

3. *Économiste français*, 12 Juillet 1879, p. 47.

4. *Journal des économistes*, 4ᵉ Sér., XXII (1883), 444-48.

5. *Économiste français*, 2 Septembre 1882, pp. 296-97; *Annales de la société d'economie politique*, XIII (1880-82), 491; and *Journal des économistes*, 4ᵉ Sér., XIX (1882), 470.

6. Bernard Lavergne, *La Théorie des marchés économiques* (Paris: Arthur Rosseau, 1910), p. vii.

7. A. Courtois fils, "Joseph Garnier (1813-1881)," *Palgrave's Dictionary of Political Economy*, ed. Henry Higgs (London: Macmillan and Co., 1923), II, 185.

8. Joseph Garnier, *Traité d'économie politique, sociale ou industrielle* (8ᵉ éd.; Paris: Garnier frères, 1880), and *Traité d'économie politique* (9ᵉ éd.; Paris: Guillaumin et Cie, 1889).

9. Paul Cauwès, *Précis du cours d'économie politique* (Paris: L. Larose & Forcel, 1880), II, 712; Paul Cauwès, *Cours d'économie politique* (3ᵉ éd.; Paris: L. Larose & Forcel, 1893), IV, 610.

10. Paris: Ch. Delagrave, 1888.

11. I, 109-10; III, 28-44. (2ᵉ éd.; Paris: Guillaumin et Cie, 1896) .

12. Henri Joseph Léon Baudrillart, *Manuel d'économie politique* (5ᵉ éd.; Paris: Guillaumin et Cie, 1883).

13. Alfred Jourdan, *Cours analytique d'économie politique* (Paris: Arthur Rousseau, 1882); 2ᵉ éd., 1890.

14. Yves Guyot, *La Science économique* (Paris: C. Reinwald, 1881); 2ᵉ éd., 1887; 3ᵉ éd., 1907.

15. Ferdinand Hervé-Bazin, *Traité élémentaire d'économie politique* (Paris: V. Lecoffre, 1880); 2ᵉ éd.; 1885.

16. Maurice Block, *Petit manuel d'économie politique* (Paris: J. Hetzel, 1872); 9ᵉ éd., 1880.

CHAPTER XXV

1. Léon Walras, "Un nuovo ramo della matematica: dell' applicazione delle matematiche all' economia politica," *Giornale degli economisti*, III (1876), 2; *Théorie de la monnaie* (Lausanne: Corbaz & Cie, 1886), pp. viii-ix.

2. Jevons, *Theory*, 2d ed., pp. 307-09.

3. *Letters & Journal of W. Stanley Jevons*, pp. 309-11, 320-21, 325-27, 329-30, and 379-80.

4. Published as *Het Inkomen der Maatschappij* (Leiden, S. C. Doesburgh, 1874).

5. *Winkler Prins Encyclopaedie* (6ᵉ Druk; Amsterdam: Elsevier, 1952), XV, 706.

6. "Mr. Johan Baron d'Aulnis de Bourouill," *De Economist*, LXXIX (1930), 595-96.

7. H. W. C. Bordewijk, "Nicolaas Gerard Pierson (1839-1909)," *Encyclopaedia of the Social Sciences*, XII, 134.

8. H. B. G[reven], "Dutch School of Economists," *Palgrave's Dictionary of Political Economy*, I, 657.

9. *De Economist*, 1889, pp. 351-52.

10. Anthony Beaujon, "Á propos de la théorie du prix," *Revue d'économie politique*, IV (1890), 16-43.

11. *Journal des économistes*, 3ᵉ Sér., XXXVI (1874), 329-34.

12. Achille Loria, "Obituary: Girolamo Boccardo," *Economic Journal*, XIV (1904), 321.

13. Pisa: Folchetto, 1886. Reprinted in *Giornale degli economisti e annali di economia*, N. S., X (1951), 233-63.

14. For recent comments see Giovanni Demaria, "G. B. Antonelli, economista matematico ignorato," *Giornale degli economisti e annali di economia*, N. S., X (1951), 223-31; and Giovanni Ricci, "Commento alla memoria di G. B. Antonelli dell' anno 1886: 'Sulla teoria matematica della Economia politica'," *Giornale degli economisti e annali di economia*, N. S., X (1951), 264-97.

15. Antonelli, *Sulla teoria matematica della economia politica*, p. 16.

16. It was translated into English later. Luigi Cossa, *Guide to the Study of Political Economy* (London: Macmillan and Co., 1880).

17. *Ibid.*, p. 46.

18. The third edition was translated into both French and English: *Histoire des doctrines économiques* (Paris: V. Giard & E. Brière, 1899); *An Introduction to the Study of Political Economy* (London: Macmillan and Co., 1893).

19. *An Introduction to the Study of Political Economy*, p. 432.

20. *Ibid.*, p. 360.

21. *Ibid.*, pp. 357, 479.

22. On Pantaleoni's life and work see: P[iero] S[raffa] and Achille Loria, "Obituary: Maffeo Pantaleoni," *Economic Journal*, XXXIV (1924), 648-54; G. Del Vecchio and others in *Giornale degli economisti*, LXV (1925), 105-236; Gaëtan Pirou, "M. Pantaleoni et la théorie économique," *Revue d'économie politique*, XL (1926), 1144-65; Umberto Ricci, *Tre economisti italiani: Pantaleoni—Pareto—Loria* (Bari: Gius, Laterza & Figli, 1939), pp. 13-100; and Nicolò Campagna, *Il Pensiero di Maffeo Pantaleoni* (Messina: Liberia Editrice Antonino Sessa, n. d.).

23. Maffeo Pantaleoni, *Principii di economia pura* (Firenze: G. Barbèra, 1889). It had a second edition in 1894. Pantaleoni did not permit subsequent publication during his life, for he thought that Vilfredo Pareto's *Cours d'économie politique* had made it obsolete. A reprint did appear in 1931, seven years after Pantaleoni's death. The *Principii* has had three translations, one into English under the title *Pure Economics* (London: Macmillan and Co., 1898), one into Spanish, *Principios de economia pura* (Buenos Ayres: Perlado, Paez y Cia, 1918), and the last into Portuguese, *Principios de economia pura* (São Paulo, Athena editora, 1939).

24. Pantaleoni, *Principii*, 1889 ed., pp. 367-68.

25. Pantaleoni, *Principii*, English translation, p. 31.

26. *Ibid.*, p. 43.

27. *Ibid.*, p. 54 n.

28. *Ibid.*, p. 72.

CHAPTER XXVI

1. *Supra*, p. 71.

2. Étienne Antonelli, "Léon Walras et Carl Menger à travers leur correspondance," *Économie Appliquée*, VI (1953), 285-86.

3. Emil Sax, *Grundlegung der theoretischen Staatswirtschaft* (Vienna: Alfred Hölder, 1887), p. 250.

4. Friedrich von Wieser, *Der natürliche Werth* (Vienna: Alfred Hölder, 1889), pp. viii-xi. Wieser put the date of 1888 at the end of his preface.

5. Friedrich von Wieser, *Über den Ursprung und die Hauptgesetze des wirthschaftlichen Wertes* (Vienna: Alfred Hölder, 1884), p. vii.

6. Alfred Marshall, *Principles of Economics* (London: Macmillan and Co., 1890), I, 149 n. Marshall dropped this footnote in the second edition (1891) and never permitted it to reappear in the subsequent editions of the *Principles*. Perhaps partly to replace it Marshall introduced another footnote at a different point (pp. 158-59) in the second edition (1891) that mentioned Gossen and Dupuit (his name had not appeared in the first edition); that connected together Jevons, Menger, and Walras; and that listed as followers Böhm-Bawerk, Sax, Wieser, Pantaleoni, Edgeworth, Wicksteed, Auspitz, Lieben, and Launhardt. This footnote changed in subsequent editions. In the third edition of the *Principles* (1895) Marshall removed Sax's name and added those of Clark, Giddings, Patten, Greene, and Fisher (pp. 176-77). At the time of the fourth edition (1898) Marshall replaced the list of members of the school by a reference to Irving Fisher's bibliography which had appeared as an appendix to Bacon's translation of Cournot's *Recherches* (p. 176). Another reference to Jevons, Menger, and Walras in the first edition remained unchanged throughout the subsequent editions, although Marshall eventually shifted it from the main body of the book into the appendix. It comes at the end of Marshall's long "Note on Ricardo's Theory of Cost of Production in relation to value." The "Note" omits all reference to the usual predecessors and attempts instead to prove that David Ricardo knew all along everything important to know about marginal utility, although he failed to find the right words to express his ideas adequately. "Throughout the whole discussion," Marshall concluded, "he is trying to say, though (being ignorant of the terse langugage of the Differential Calculus) he did not get hold of the right words in which to say it neatly, that marginal utility is raised and total utility is lessened by any check to supply" (p. 531).

7. The bibliography in the third edition (1888) of Jevons' *Theory* lists Menger's *Grundsätze* as one of the books with which Jevons was not familiar (p. 283).

8. Léon Walras, "Théorie mathématique de l'échange.-Question de priorité," *Journal des économistes*, 3ᵉ Sér., XXXIV (1874), 417-22.

9. Jevons made the following statement in a letter written to Walras on May 30, 1874: "After receiving your very friendly letter of 23rd May, and after seeing a full statement of your mode of arriving at the equations of exchange, I cannot for a moment entertain the least doubt of the entire independence of your own researches as regard my own" (*Letters & Journal of W. Stanley Jevons*, p. 305).

10. Léon Walras, *Théorie de la monnaie* (Lausanne: Corbaz & Cie, 1886), p. viii.

11. Menger listed together the names of Böhm-Bawerk, Walras, Wieser, Pierson, Marshall, Gossen, and Jevons on the last page of a review of Gustav Schönberg's *Handbuch der politischen Oekonomie* in the *Zeitschrift für das Privat- und öffentliche Recht der Gegenwart*, which Hayek selected for inclusion (p. 31) in Vol. III of *The Collected Works of Carl Menger* (London: The London School of Economics, 1935), but he did not identify them in any way with the idea of marginal utility. Menger mentioned Walras' *Éléments* in his "Grundzüge einer Klassifikation der Wirtschaftswissenschaften" (*Jahrbücher für Nationalökonomie und Statistik*, N. F., XIX [1889], p. 468), which again does not mention marginal utility. Certainly Menger knew well the traditional history of marginal utility, since he lived down to a day when the standard history flourished, but he never commented on any of its aspects.

The history of economic thought interested him, as we see from the personal library on the subject that he collected, but it never interested him in such a way, or to such an extent, that he felt compelled to comment on either his role or the role of others in that history.

12. Wieser, *Der natürliche Werth*, p. ix.

13. Maffeo Pantaleoni, *Principii di economia pura* (Firenze: G. Barbèra, 1889), p. 121 n. Pantaleoni, after mentioning Menger's *Grundsätze* and giving the date as 1872, says that this work "ha soltanto il difetto di essere un *plagio dei più audaci delle pubblicazioni* del Cournot, Gossen, Jennings, e Jevons."

14. The second edition (1894) of the *Principii di economia pura* has a footnote (pp. 96-98) with the standard history in much detail and no mention of Pantaleoni's suspicion of Menger's plagiarism.

15. It began as the article "Political Economy" in the ninth edition of the *Encyclopaedia Britannica* in 1885. In a somewhat revised form Ingram published it in 1888 as *A History of Political Economy*, with a special American edition. A second edition appeared in 1907 in both the United States and England, and a "new and enlarged" edition came out in 1914 with supplementary chapters by William A. Scott to bring the book down to date. French, Spanish, German, Serbian, Russian, Italian, Czech, Polish, and Japanese translations came later. It must have provided the source for many people's knowledge of the history of economic thought.

16. J. K. I[ngram], "Political Economy," *Encyclopaedia Britannica* (9th ed.; New York: Charles Scribner's Sons, 1885), XIX, 396.

17. *Ibid.*, p. 386.

18. John Kells Ingram, *A History of Political Economy* (1st American ed.; New York: Macmillan and Co., 1888), pp. 233-34.

19. Of the two we know best, Luigi Cossa's *Guida allo studio dell' economia politica* (Milano: U. Hoepli, 1876) has a second edition in 1878. The English translation, *Guide to the Study of Political Economy* (London: Macmillan and Co., 1880), has a preface by W. Stanley Jevons that strongly recommends the book to the reader and that might lead one to look for a sympathetic account of the genesis of the Marginal Utility School. But Cossa included no such account. Cossa classified Jevons and Walras as members of the mathematical school and as co-founders of the theory of exchange, but he did not relate the idea of marginal utility to the mathematical school or the theory of exchange. He did not take note of Menger. Karl Walcker's *Geschichte der Nationalökonomie und des Sozialismus* appeared first in 1879, the second edition coming in 1884. This history gives little more than connected, brief comments on a series of books and authors—also a characteristic of Cossa's *Guida*. Walcker included Jevons in a list of authors of textbooks (p. 24). He directed attention to Menger's *Grundsätze* but did not analyze its contents (p. 66). Walcker omitted any reference to Walras or to marginal utility.

20. E[ugen] Dühring, *Kritische Geschichte der Nationalökonomie und des Sozialismus* (Berlin: Theobald Grieben, 1871). According to Oscar Morgenstern and Ewald Schams ("Eine Bibliographie der allgemeinen Lehrgeschichten der Nationalökonomie," *Zeitschrift für Nationalökonomie*, IV, [1933], 394), the publication of the first edition marks the beginning of the scientific period in the writing of the history of economic thought.

21. Francesco Mariotti, *Delle origini e dei progressi della scienza economica in Europa* (Imola: Ignazio Galeati, 1875).

22. Heinrich Contzen, *Geschichte, Literatur und Bedeutung der Nationalökonomie oder Volkswirtschaftslehre* (Cassel und Leipzig: Carl Maurer, 1876). A footnote reference in this volume to Léon Walras, which labels him a Swiss, hardly refers to his work. A second edition (Berlin: F. & P. Lehmann, 1881) does not extend the coverage of the first.

23. Moritz Meyer, *Die neuere Nationalökonomie in ihren Hauptrichtungen, auf historischer Grundlage und kritisch dargestellt* (Berlin: Stuhr'sche Buchhandlung, 1880).

24. Charles Périn, *Les doctrines économiques depuis un siècle* (Paris: V. Lecoffre, 1880).

25. H[ugo] Eisenhart, *Geschichte der Nationalökonomik* (Jena: Gustav Fischer, 1881). The expanded second edition (Jena: Gustav Fischer, 1891) also has no reference to Jevons, Menger, and Walras.

26. Gustav Cohn, "Geschichte der Nationalökonomie," *System der National-ökonomie*, I, 91-180. This volume has the separate title of *Grundlegung der National-ökonomie* (Stuttgart: Ferdinand Enke, 1885). An American translation appeared, *A History of Political Economy* (Philadelphia: American Academy of Political and Social Science, 1894).

APPENDIX

1. 2 vols.; Paris: Guillaumin et Cie, 1890. 2ᵉ éd., 1897.

2. London: Methuen & Co., 1891.

3. Cossa's *Introduzione* was translated into English as *An Introduction to the Study of Political Economy* (London: Macmillan and Co., 1893) and into French as the *Histoire des doctrines économiques* (Paris: V. Giard & E. Brière, 1899).

4. London: Bliss, Sands and Co., 1896. We perhaps ought not to think of this book as a history of economic thought despite its title.

5. Joseph Rambaud, *Histoire des doctrines économiques* (Paris: L. Larose & Forcel, 1899). 2ᵉ éd., 1902. 3ᵉ éd., 1909.

6. The four following histories of economic thought also appeared during this period: Hector Denis, *Histoire des systèmes économiques et socialistes* (Brussels: Charles Rozez, [1897]), of which an enlarged edition followed in 1904; Nikolai Khristïanovich Bunge, *Esquisses de littérature politico-économique* (Basle: Georg & Cie, 1898)—this French translation was published three years after the original Russian edition; Adolf Damaschke, *Geschichte der Nationalökonomie* (2ʳ Aufl.; Jena: G. Fischer, 1905); A[lfred Victor] Espinas, *Histoire des doctrines économiques* (Paris: Armand Colin et Cie, 1891). Morgenstern and Scham's bibliography cites a number of unobtainable Russian histories of economic thought both for this period and for the period after 1910. It is unlikely that they would contain any reference to marginal utility.

7. "Les Théories psychologiques de la valeur au XVIIIᵉ siècle," *Revue d'économie politique*, XI (1897), 849-61, 917-30.

8. Vincenzo Tangorra, "La Nuova teoria dell' utilità negli economisti classici Italiani," *Rivista di sociologia* (Dicembre, 1904).

9. *Die Grundlage der modernen Wertlehre: Daniel Bernoulli, Versuch einer neuen Theorie der Wertbestimmung von Glücksfällen (Specimen Theoriae novae de Mensura Sortis). Aus dem Lateinischen übersetzt und mit Erläuterungen versehen von Professor Dr. Alfred Pringsheim. Mit einer Einleitung von Dr. Ludwig Fick* (Leipzig: Dunker & Humblot, 1896).

10. Arthur Ruppin, *Die Wertlehre Thünen's und die Grenznutzentheorie* (Halle: S. Schlesingers, 1902).

11. The importance of W. F. Lloyd had received almost a page of clear description a few years before E. R. A. Seligman's article in T. S. Adams' "Index Numbers and the Standard of Value" (*Journal of Political Economy*, X [1901], 19). Lloyd's fame, however, dates from the publication of Seligman's articles.

12. E. R. A. Seligman, "On Some Neglected British Economists," *Economic Journal*, XIII (1903), 357-63.

13. *Ibid.*, p. 357.

14. A number of histories of value have as their most common defect in their accounts of the Marginal Utility School, outside of lack of appropriate emphasis, the total omission of any reference to Walras. This defect occurs in Robert Zuckerkandl's *Zur Theorie des Preises, mit besonderer Berücksichtigung der geschichtlichen Entwicklung der Lehre* (Leipzig: Duncker & Humblot, 1889); in Augusto Graziani's *Storia*

critica della teoria del valore in Italia (Milano: Ulrico Hoepli, 1889); in Augusto Montanari's *Contributo alla storia della teoria del valore negli scrittori italiani* (Milano: U. Hoepli, 1889); and in William Scharling's *Vaerdilaerens Udvikling 1871-1900* (Copenhagen: G. E. C. Gad, 1903). Giuseppe Ricca Salerno mentioned all of the pioneers of the early seventies and many of their predecessors and successors in "La Teoria del valore nella storia delle dottrine e dei fatti economici," *Atti della R. Accademia dei Lincei*, 5ª Ser., *Classe di scienze morali, storiche e filologiche*, I (1893). But the article fails to present any connected account. We find an earlier history of value of a limited kind that displays no awareness of the rise of the Marginal Utility School in Achille Loria's "La Teoria del valore negli economisti italiani," *Archivio giuridico*, XXVIII (1882).

15. Eugène Henri Joseph Petit, *Étude critique des différentes théories de la valeur (dans l'échange intérieur)* (Paris: Arthur Rosseau, 1897).

16. Rudolf Kaulla, *Die geschichtliche Entwicklung der modernen Werttheorien* (Tübingen: H. Laupp, 1906).

17. Lujo Brentano, "Die Entwickelung der Wertlehre," *Sitzungsberichte der Königlichen Bayerischen Akademie der Wissenschaften* (1908).

18. Bernhard Rost, *Die Wert- und Preistheorie, mit Berücksichtigung ihrer dogmengeschichtlichen Entwickelung* (Leipzig: Duncker & Humblot, 1908).

19. P[hilip] H. W[icksteed], "Final Degree of Utility," *Dictionary of Political Economy*, ed. R. H. Inglis Palgrave (London: Macmillan and Co., 1896), II, 59-61. And Friedrich von Wieser, "Grenznutzen," *Handwörterbuch der Staatswissenschaften* (Jena: Gustav Fischer, 1892), IV, 107.

20. The list omits P. A. Diepenhorst's *Voorlezingen over de Geschiedenis der Economie* (Utrecht: G. J. A. Ruys, 1910), since it does not compare with the other three in influence or in elaboration of treatment. Diepenhorst considered marginal utility mainly in the notes at the end of chap. iv.

21. Paris: L. Larose & L. Tenin, 1909.

22. New York: The Macmillan Company, 1911.

23. Leipzig: Quelle & Meyer, 1911.

24. The important histories of economic thought published from 1921 to 1940 appeared in the following order: Oswald Fred Boucke, *The Development of Economics, 1750-1900* (New York: The Macmillan Company, 1921); René Gonnard, *Histoire des doctrines économiques*, 3 vols. (Paris: Nouvelle Librairie Nationale, 1921-22); Paul Mombert, *Geschichte der Nationalökonomie* (Jena: Gustav Fischer, 1927); G. H. Bousquet, *Essai sur l'évolution de la pensée économique* (Paris: Marcel Giard, 1927); Alexander Gray, *The Development of Economic Doctrine* (London: Longmans, Green and Co., 1931); William A. Scott, *The Development of Economics* (New York: The Century Co., 1933); Harvey W. Peck, *Economic Thought and its Institutional Background* (New York: Farrar & Rinehart, 1935); [Wesley C. Mitchell], *Lectures on Current Types of Economic Theory*, 2 vols., mimeographed (New York, 1935; 2d ed., New York: Augustus M. Kelley, 1949); Erich Roll, *A History of Economic Thought* (London: Faber and Faber Ltd., [1938]); John M. Ferguson, *Landmarks of Economic Thought* (New York: Longmans, Green and Co., 1938); and Edmund Whittaker, *A History of Economic Ideas* (New York: Longmans, Green and Co., 1940).

25. Perhaps the most important of these shorter histories of economic thought is Joseph Schumpeter's "Epochen der Dogmen- und Methodengeschichte," which comes as part of the *Grundriss der Socialökonomik*, Abteilung I, Teil I (2ᵉ Aufl.; Tübingen: J. C. B. Mohr, 1914). It was recently translated into English by R. Aris under the title *Economic Doctrine and Method: An Historical Sketch* (New York: Oxford University Press, 1954). A most widely read volume, to judge from the number of editions and translations that appeared, was the history of economic thought written by Vakhan Fomich Totomiants. It first appeared in Russian. A French translation, *Histoire des doctrines économiques et sociales* (Paris, Marcel Giard, 1922), and an Italian translation, *Storia delle dottrine economiche e sociali* (Torino, Fratelli Bocca, 1922), soon

followed. A German edition, *Geschichte der Nationalökonomie und des Sozialismus,* was added in 1925.

The following shorter histories of economic thought came out during this time: Eugen Fridrichowicz, *Grundriss einer Geschichte der Volkswirtschaftslehre* (Munich: Duncker & Humblot, 1912), which provides little more than an annotated bibliography; Bernard Siegfried, *Repetitorium der Geschichte der Nationalökonomie* (2ᵉ Aufl.; Bern: Paul Haupt, 1922), of which the first edition came in 1919; Edgar Salin, *Geschichte der Volkswirtschaftslehre,* a part of the *Enzyklopädie der Rechts- und Staatswissenschaft* (Berlin: Julius Springer, 1923); Robert Wilbrandt, *Die Entwicklung der Volkswirtschaftslehre,* which serves as Vol. I of his *Einführung in die Volkswirtschaftslehre* (Stuttgart: Moritz, 1924); Theo Surányi-Unger, *Philosophie in der Volkswirtschaftslehre,* 2 vols. (Jena: Gustav Fischer, 1923-26), resembles many economic histories in that it has a series of chronologically arranged studies of eminent economists of which the one on "Carl Menger" discusses the standard account; Richard Kerschagl, *Volkswirtschaftslehre; eine Darstellung ihrer wichtigsten Lehrmeinungen* (Vienna: Manz, 1927); Paul Junker, *Geschichte der Volkswirtschaftslehre* (Dessau: C. Dünnhaupt, 1927); Robert Michels, *Introduzione alla storia delle dottrine economiche e politiche, con un saggio sulla economia classica italiana e la sua influenza sulla scienza economica* (Bologna: Zanichelli, 1932); the following work borders on the class of histories of economic thought but remains bibliographically superior to almost any of them: Horst Wagenführ, *Der Systemgedanke in der Nationalökonomie* (Jena: Gustav Fischer, 1933); and Giulio Capodaglio, *Sommario di storia delle dottrine economiche* (Bologna: Zanichelli, 1937).

26. The histories of Gide and Rist and of Haney were revised, with material added to interpret more recent developments in economics. The publishers simply reprinted the histories of Ferguson, Mitchell, Roll, and Spann after the war.

27. The short or incidental histories include the following: Louis Baudin, *Précis d'histoire des doctrines économiques* (Paris: F. Loviton, 1941); Paul Hugon, *História das doutrinas econômicas* (São Paulo: Editora Atlas, 1942); John W. McConnell, *The Basic Teachings of the Great Economists* (New York: The New Home Library, [1943]); Bertrand Nogoro, *Le Développement de la pensée économique* (Paris: Librairie générale de droit et de jurisprudence, 1944); Werner Stark, *The History of Economics in Relation to Economic Development* (London: Kegan Paul, Trench, Trubner, 1944); Raymond Roca, *Résumé d'histoire des doctrines économiques* (Paris: Domat-Montchrestien, 1946); Daniel Villey, *Petite histoire des grandes doctrines économiques* (Paris: Presses Universitaires de France, 1946); Giuseppe Prato, *Lezioni di storia delle dottrine economiche* (Torino: G. Giappichelli, 1948); Alfred Kruse, *Geschichte der volkswirtschaftlichen Theorien* (Munich: Richard Pflaum, 1948); Giuseppe Mira, *Lezioni di storia delle dottrine e dei fatti economici* (Roma: Soc. Poligrafica Commerciale, 1949); Heinz Gutsche, *Die Entwicklung der Volkswirtschaftslehre* ("Schriftenreihe Geist und Bildung, Bd. II"; Berlin: Colloquium Verlag [1949]); Augusto Graziani, *Storia delle dottrine economiche* (Napoli: A. Morano, [1949]); J. Lajugie, *Les Doctrines économiques* ("Que sais-je?"; Paris: Presses Universitaires de France, 1949); Anton Tautscher, *Geschichte der Volkswirtschaftslehre* ("Grundrisse der Sozialwissenschaften," Bd. I; Vienna: A. Sexl, 1950); Alberto Bertolino, *Esplorazioni nella storia del pensiero economico* (Firenze: Nuova Italia, 1950); and Maurice Bouvier-Ajam, *Traité d'économie politique et d'histoire des doctrines économiques,* Vol. I, *Notions fondamentales de l'économie politique et histoire des doctrines économiques* (Paris: Plon, 1952).

28. The following histories give at least half their total length to events in the history of economic thought that come after 1870; L. J. Zimmerman, *Geschiedenis van het Economisch Denken* (The Hague: Albani, 1947); Émile James, *Histoire des théories économiques* (Paris: Flammarion, 1950); Gerhard Stavenhagen, *Geschichte der Wirtschaftstheorie* ("Grundriss der Sozialwissenschaft. Bd. II"; Göttingen: Vandenhoeck & Ruprecht, 1951); and Philip Charles Newman, *The Development of Economic Thought* (New York: Prentice-Hall, 1952). One new history of economic thought, T. W.

Hutchison, *A Review of Economic Doctrine, 1870-1929* (New York: Oxford University Press, 1953) concentrates on the last section of the history of economic doctrine.

29. The recent histories of economic thought listed below, while they do not give as much as half their total space to a consideration of the modern period, do give a larger proportion of their space to the years after 1870 than usually found in histories of economic thought written earlier: Jenny Griziotti Kretschmann, *Storia delle dottrine economiche* (Torino: Unione Tipografico Editrice Torinese, 1949); Frank Amandus Neff, *Economic Doctrines* (Wichita, Kansas: McGuin Publishing Company, 1946); Henry William Spiegel, *The Development of Economic Thought: Great Economists in Perspective* (New York: John Wiley & Sons, 1952); John Fred Bell, *A History of Economic Thought* (New York: The Ronald Press, 1953). Joseph A. Schumpeter's *A History of Economic Analysis* (New York: Oxford University Press, 1954) falls into this class in this respect, but in most ways it occupies a class by itself, and will remain alone in that class for a long time to come.

30. First in this period came Charles Turgeon's *La Valeur d'après les économistes anglais depuis Adam Smith jusqu'à nos jours* (Rennes: Oberthur, 1913). Turgeon's account limps, since it restricts its survey to England. The expanded version of this treatise published in 1921 gives no more satisfactory an account, although it does include the French economists.

The next of these histories of the theory of value and the best of all of them came from Eugène Ruffy, *La Notion de la valeur, son évolution depuis Adam Smith jusqu'à nos jours* (Lausanne: Imprimerie Vaudoise, 1923).

Other histories of value written after 1910 include Georges B. Saridakis, *L'Évolution de la théorie de la valeur en Angleterre* (Paris: M. Giard, 1924); and Robert van Genechten, *De Ontwikkeling der Waardeleer sinds 1870* (Amsterdam: Elsevier, 1927).

31. P. N. Rosenstein-Rodan prepared a new account on the history of marginal utility for the *Handwörterbuch der Staatswissenschaften* which included a long bibliography (4ᵉ Aufl., IV, 1190-1223). Frank H. Knight wrote the article on marginal utility for the *Encyclopaedia of the Social Sciences* (V, 357-63).

32. Siegmund Feilbogen wrote on "L'École Autrichienne d'économie politique" for the *Journal des économistes* (6ᵉ Sér., XXXI [1911], 50-57, 214-30, 375-88, and XXXIII [1912], 57-61). Jacob Viner examined the journal literature that had criticized marginal utility in a two-part article, "The Utility Concept in Value Theory and Its Critics," *Journal of Political Economy*, XXXIII (1925), 369-87, 638-59. Henry Simon Bloch's *La Théorie des besoins de Carl Menger* (Paris: R. Pichon et R. Durand-Auzias, 1937), while not primarily historical, provided some interpretation of the history of marginal utility.

33. Karl Robert Blum, *Die subjektivistisch-psychologischen Wertlehren von ihren Anfängen bis auf Gossen* (Giessen, 1934). The title here misleads somewhat in that Blum considers a very limited number of predecessors.

34. *Die Wirtschaftstheorie der Gegenwart*, Vol. I, *Gesamtbild der Forschung in den einzelnen Ländern* (Vienna: Julius Springer, 1927).

35. Halberstadt: H. Meyer's Buchdruckerei, 1926.

36. *Jahrbücher für Nationalökonomie und Statistik*, 3ᵉ Folge, LXXI (1927), 460-62.

37. Gaëton Pirou, *L'Utilité marginale* (Paris: Domat-Montchrestien, 1932), and *Les Théories de l'équilibre économique: L. Walras et V. Pareto* (Paris: Domat-Montchrestien, 1934).

38. Nymegen: Centrale Drukkery, 1947.

INDEX

Académie des Sciences Morales et Politiques, 194-96
Adams, Henry C., 115
Adamson, Robert, 141
Antonelli, Giovanni Battista, 182, 203, 206, 207, 257
Armitage-Smith, George, 124, 129
Auspitz, Rudolf: and Dietzel, 140; career, 161-63; on marginal utility, 168-72; and Walras, 171; influence on Pareto and Fisher, 171; mentioned, 165, 207, 249, 251
Austrian School: Edgeworth on, 109; and J. B. Clark, 110; and American School, 114; coherence of, 142; members of, 161-72, 248; inappropriateness of name, 177-78; mentioned, 207
Austrian universities, 177, 253
Average utility. *See* Utility

Bailey, Samuel, 220
Bain, Alexander, 228
Barratt, Alfred, 93-94, 95, 107
Bastiat, Frédéric, 26, 64, 187, 189, 192
Baudin, Louis, 262
Baudrillart, Henri Joseph Léon, 202
Beaujon, Anthony, 204-05
Beaurin-Gressier, L., 254
Beckerath, Erwin von, 251
Bedford Chapel Debating Society, 118-19, 242
Beeton, Henry Ramié: and Bedford Chapel Debating Society, 119; in Economic Circle, 119; and Wicksteed, 119; and Junior Economic Club, 130; and Foxwell, 242; mentioned, 123, 124, 129, 131
Bell, John Fred, 263
Bentham, Jeremy: influence of, 10-11, 83, 84; on measurability, 48; on addition of utility, 62; mentioned, 94, 95
Bernoulli, Daniel: on marginal utility of income, 55; on value, 56; and law of diminishing marginal utility, 95; mentioned, 98, 219, 226
Bertolino, Alberto, 262
Besant, Annie, 126
Black, R. D., 225
Blaise, Ad., 189-90
Blanqui, Adolphe, 28
Bloch, Henry Simon, 263
Block, Maurice, 20, 202, 219
Blodig, Hermann, 248
Blum, Karl Robert, 263
Boccardo, Gerolamo, 179, 203, 205-06
Bodio, Luigi, 205
Böhm-Bawerk, Eugen von: early years, 111, 155; and Wicksteed, 137; controversy on marginal utility, 140; on interest, 150; early publications, 155-56; on marginal utility, 156; marginal pairs,

157; on divisibility, 157-58; on measurability, 158-59; on interpersonal comparisons, 159; on relation of cost and utility to value, 159-60; influence on Philippovich, 166; subjects taught at Vienna, 174; Ott on, 197; mentioned, 109, 117, 141, 161, 164, 165, 168, 169, 176, 181, 182, 207, 212, 249, 251, 253
Bonar, James, 119, 215
Boninsegni, Pascal, 179
Boucke, Oswald Fred, 221, 261
Bourouill, Johan d'Aulnis de: correspondence, 71, 72-73, 181; on marginal utility, 203-04; mentioned, 73, 182, 206, 207, 214
Bousquet, G. H., 261
Bouvier-Ajam, Maurice, 262
Bowley, A. L., 240
Bowley, Marian, 225
Brentano, Lujo, 173-75, 220, 248
British Economic Association. *See* Royal Economic Society
Brooke, Stopford Augustus, 118-19, 124
Brown, E. H. P., 232
Brown, Thomas, 14
Buffon, Georges Louis Leclerc, 100
Bunge, Nikolai Khristïanovich, 260
Butt, Isaac, 220

Cairnes, John Elliot, 12, 64-65, 121, 141, 226
Cambridge, University of, 73
Cannan, Edwin, 236
Cardinal utility. *See* Measurement of utility
Cauwès, Paul, 202
Chadwick, David, 17
Chadwick, Edwin, 16
Clark, John Bates: and Marshall, 85-86; and Society of Economic Sciences of Vienna, 110; independent discovery of marginal utility, 110-17; early life and writings, 111-13; on measurement, 116; differences from Jevons, Menger, and Walras, 116; review of Marshall's *Principles*, 117; mentioned, 118, 165, 207, 212
Clark, John Maurice, 110
Cohen Stuart, A. J., 205, 207
Cohn, Gustav, 218
Collège de France, 28
Colson, Léon Clément, 86
Complementarity, 53, 105, 233
Condillac, Étienne Bonnot de, 26, 36, 148
Conservatoire National des Arts et Métiers, 28
Consumer's rent, 76-78, 84, 236
Consumption: divisibility of, 31, 34, 35; order of, 41; circumstances surrounding, 54

265

268

59; Gide on, 188-89; Levasseur on, 194-95; Thurstone on, 239
Mees, W. C., 203
Menger, Carl: career, 24, 139-40, 141, 166, 229; source of views, 24-27, 230; and Cournot, 26-27, 230; avoidance of term "marginal utility," 39-40, 142; explanation of marginal utility, 40-42, 44, 45, 53; general equilibrium approach, 42; on utility and exchange, 43; on measurement, 46-47; on average utility, 52; on form of utility function, 53; on marginal utility of income, 55; on maximizing utility, 57-58; on labor theory of value, 58, 154; on demand functions, 59; acceptance of, 61, 131, 139-40, 156, 201, 214-15; later publications, 141-42; and Wieser, 143, 144, 145; teaching at Vienna, 173-74; controversy with Schmoller, 176; and books, 176, 230; on money, 181; independence in discovery of marginal utility, 215-16; on complementary and substitute goods, 233; on the household, 233; on history of marginal utility theory, 258-59; mentioned, 39, 89, 94, 109, 110, 112, 113, 134, 160-69 *passim*, 178, 182, 191, 200-20 *passim*, 249
Menger, Karl (son of Carl Menger), 225
Merchants' stocks, 67
Merivale, Herman, 17
Meyer, Moritz, 218
Meyer, Robert, 164-65, 174-75, 249
Miaskowski, August von, 248
Michaelis, Otto, 25
Michels, Robert, 262
Midwest Inter-Library Center, 230
Mill, James, 14
Mill, John Stuart: and Marshall, 76, 87, 88; and Jevons, 83; mentioned, 8, 15, 62-66 *passim*, 91, 121
Mira, Giuseppe, 262
Mitchell, Wesley C., 221, 261, 262
Miyajima, T., 116
Molinari, Gustave de, 256
Mombert, Paul, 261
Money, 181. *See also* Income, marginal utility of
Mongin, Marcel, 190
Montanari, Augusto, 260-61
Morgenstern, Oskar, 143, 213, 259

Needs, 40, 42
Neff, Frank Amandus, 263
Neumann, John von, 213
Newcomb, Simon, 67-68
Newman, Philip Charles, 91, 262
Nicholson, J. S., 108
Nogoro, Bertrand, 262

Oman, Charles, 225
Ordinal utility, 18, 49. *See also* Measurement of utility
Ott, Auguste, 197-99
Oulès, Firmin, 179

Owens College, Manchester, 13
Oxford, University of, 225-26

Pantaleoni, Maffeo, 81, 207-09, 216, 257, 259
Pareto, Vilfredo: and Auspitz and Lieben, 171, 172; and Lausanne School, 179; mentioned, 211, 212, 223, 257
Parsons, Talcott, 82
Patten, Simon Nelson, 164
Peck, Harvey W., 221, 261
Périn, Charles, 218
Petit, Eugène, 220
Philippovich von Philippsberg, Eugen: career, 161-62; influence on marginal utility, 166; subjects taught at Vienna, 174; mentioned, 164, 207, 249, 251
Pierson, N. G., 182, 203, 204, 214
Pirou, Gaëtan, 223, 257
Prague, University of, 24, 144, 166
Prato, Giuseppe, 262
Precursors, 39, 213
Price, 30, 34, 78, 94. *See also* Value
Price, L. L., 89-90, 219
Pringsheim, Alfred, 219
Probability, 107-08
Production, 74, 136
Professors of economics, English, 5-6
Property, 29-30, 34
Proudhon, Pierre Joseph, 33, 125, 151
Psychology, 14-15
Psychophysics, 95-100, 101, 102-03

Quack, H. P. G., 203

Rambaud, Joseph, 260
Rareté, 29-32, 41. *See also* Marginal utility
Rees, R. L., 127
Revue d'économie politique, 256
Ricardo, David: and Drummond and Whately Professors, 5-6; and Marshall, 87, 88, 258; mentioned, 62, 63, 64, 78, 89, 91, 110, 121, 143, 192
Ricca Salerno, Giuseppe, 261
Ricci, Umberto, 257
Rist, Charles, 220, 222, 262
Robbins, Lionel, 118
Robertson, Ross M., 225
Roca, Raymond, 262
Roesler, Hermann, 25
Rogers, Edward, 220
Rogers, J. E. T., 225
Roll, Eric, 90, 221, 261, 262
Roscoe, Mary Anne. *See* Jevons, Mrs. Thomas
Roscoe, William, 9
Rosenstein-Rodan, P. N., 263
Rossi, P. L. E., 28
Rost, Bernhard, 220
Royal Economic Society, 124, 125-26, 129
Rudolf, Crown Prince, 166
Ruffy, Eugène, 263
Ruppin, Arthur, 219

Saint-Marc, Henri, 175-76
Salin, Edgar, 262
Saridakis, Georges B., 263
Saturday Review, 65-66
Sax, Emil: influence on Wieser, 148; career, 161-62; on marginal utility, 166-68; mentioned, 207, 214, 248, 249
Say, J. B., 26, 29, 36
Schäffle, A. E. F., 25, 163
Scharling, William, 261
Schams, Ewald, 259
Schmoller, Gustav, 176-77, 251
Schröder, Edward Francis, 223
Schumpeter, Joseph A.: on Marshall, 87; on Auspitz and Lieben, 172; on Böhm-Bawerk, 247; mentioned, 221, 261, 263
Scott, William A., 221, 261
Seager, H. R., 175-76
Seligman, E. R. A., 86, 220
Senior, William Nassau: and Jevons, 2-6, 83; and Whately, 4; on value, 4-6, 56; on law of diminishing marginal utility, 5; Menger on, 26; Walras on, 36; mentioned, 148
Shadwell, J. L., 70
Shaw, Bernard: and the Bedford Chapel Debating Society, 119; on mathematics, 121, 126; and Wicksteed, 121-23; and Economic Circle, 123; and Fabian Society, 125-29; review of *Das Kapital*, 126; meeting with Sidgwick, 127-28; mentioned, 129
Shove, G. F., 88-91
Sidgwick, Henry: and marginal utility, 95; and Shaw, 127-28; mentioned, 93, 95, 100, 108, 182
Siegfried, Bernard, 262
Slutsky, Eugen, 213
Smart, William, 166
Smith, Adam: Marshall on, 91, 238; mentioned, 62, 70, 114, 121, 143, 192
Socialism, 120-23
Sombart, Werner, 147
Spann, Othmar, 165, 220, 221, 222, 262
Spencer, Herbert, 228
Spiegel, Henry William, 263
Stark, Werner, 262
Stavenhagen, Gerhard, 262
Stein, Lorenz von: and Wieser, 143; and Philippovich, 166; retirement, 173; subjects taught at Vienna, 173-74; mentioned, 178, 248
Stigler, George J., 95, 223, 229, 247
Substitutes, 53, 105, 233
Sully, James, 98-100
Surányi-Unger, Theo, 262
Suret, Louis, 172

Tangorra, Vincenzo, 219
Tasman, H. J., 205
Taussig, F. W., 79
Tautscher, Anton, 262
Taxation, 35, 148, 167, 205
Terminal utility, 85
Thompson, William, 100

Thornton, W. T., 17
Thünen, Johann Heinrich von: Marshall and, 84, 85, 88; mentioned, 169, 219-20
Thurstone, L. L., 239
Totomiants, Vakhan Fomich, 261
Toyer, Frances Aurelia, 241
Trading body, 52
Treub, M. W. F., 205
Turgeon, Charles, 263
Turgot, A. R. J., 26

Utility: character of, 18, 41, 42, 43, 51, 53-54, 55-58, 62, 64, 77, 98; Jevons' coefficient of, 19; and Fleeming Jenkin, 22-23, 86; early writers on, 36; Menger on, 40; curves, 44, 48-50; averages of, 52, 135-36, 184, 186; criticisms of, 61-69, 194-95, 198-99; Edgeworth on, 100, 105, 107-08; and indifference curves, 106; abstract final, 127; and demand curves, 136, 171; as a guide to conduct, 151; in relation to cost, 152-53; pseudo-marginal, 157; Auspitz and Lieben on, 169; collective curves of, 170; and economic policy, 182; stability of, 195; and primary wants, 208; irreversible curves, 208-09. *See also* Diminishing marginal utility; Empirical utility functions; Income, marginal utility of; Interpersonal comparisons of utility; Marginal utility; Measurement of utility; Ordinal utility

Valette, Auguste, 194, 195
Value: Auguste Walras on, 29, 30; connection of marginal utility with, 56-58, 125, 127, 148, 160; labor theory of, 5, 13, 29, 58-59, 120, 126-27, 136, 163, 195, 199; Marshall on, 78-79; surplus, 120; relation of cost to, 122; Wieser on, 145, 148, 150-51, 152-53; natural, 148, 151-52; antinomy of, 151; E. Martineau on, 190; Hippolyte Dabos on, 190-91; French dispute on theory of, 191; Levasseur on, 195-96. *See also* English Classical School; Exchange; Utility
Vienna, University of: Menger at, 24, 141; Wieser and, 143, 144; Böhm-Bawerk and, 144; faculty in economics 1871-89, 162; Auspitz and Lieben unconnected with, 169; curriculum in, 173-75; teaching at, 175; mentioned, 164, 165, 169. *See also* Austrian School
Villey, Daniel, 262
Villey, Edmond, 256
Viner, Jacob, 263

Wagenfuhr, Horst, 262
Wagner, A. H. G., 176
Waley, Jacob, 7
Walker, Francis A., 108, 182
Wallas, Graham, 125
Walras, Auguste: unhappiness of, 28; classmate of Cournot, 28; influence on Léon Walras, 28-32; and economics, 29; on value, 29, 30; and marginal utility, 30-

270